The Life

D0893162

Jeanne Cordelier and
Martine Laroche

The Life

translated from the French by
Harry Mathews

Pan Books
in association with Secker & Warburg

Originally published in French under the title *La dérobade*
First published in Great Britain 1978 by Martin Secker & Warburg Ltd
This edition published 1980 by Pan Books Ltd,
Cavaye Place, London SW10 9PG
in association with Martin Secker & Warburg Ltd
2nd printing 1980
© Librairie Hachette 1976
English translation © Viking Penguin Inc 1978
ISBN 0 330 26090 1
Printed and bound in Great Britain by
Richard Clay (The Chaucer Press) Ltd, Bungay, Suffolk

And, like Medea in the midst of so many dangers,
I would remember that I still have one thing: myself.

Stendhal

part one

chapter one

When the cop asked me why, I could simply have answered that I was sick of sharing a toothbrush with five other people after having rubbed it against a soggy piece of kitchen soap sitting on the edge of the sink. I could have said that hunting bedbugs had lost its charm for me.

He would have turned red in the face. His fist would have come crashing down on the desk, scattering several pounds of dust. And he would have roared, 'What do you take me for, a total jerk?'

As it was, I said nothing of the kind but only replied, 'I was waiting for someone. He'd told me to meet him there.'

An inquisitorial look flickered out from his reptilian eyes as he snapped, 'What about the other eighteen girls – did they have dates, too?'

I looked down, rummaged in my purse, and lit a filter-tip cigarette. He went on typing his report, asking me questions that I answered as evasively as I could. Actually what was bothering me most was that he was making no distinction between me and the others. That would have given me a glimmer of hope.

'You know, Officer, this is my first time. My *very* first.'

He couldn't have cared less – absolutely didn't give a damn. I wasn't even sure he'd heard me. I suddenly felt as if he'd kicked me in the belly, though, when he said, 'If that's true, we'd better get some mug shots of you.'

Things suddenly seemed to be reaching a point of no return. It was all I could do not to get down on my knees and start blubbering, 'Please, Officer, give me a break! I won't do it again, I promise.'

That would have been really great! My popularity with the other girls down the drain. A whole reputation to rebuild – all for one moment's weakness. Fortunately I got hold of myself and casually declared, 'You're wrong, you know. Can't you see I'm not dressed like the others?'

The raid had taken place early in the evening. I'd had a

customer waiting, so that I hadn't had time to change. The others were already dressed for work; I was still in street clothes.

My cop couldn't be bothered with these sartorial niceties. Clackety-clack: a small, final period at the bottom of a well-filled page – too well filled for my taste! I waited for the 'Okay, that's all. You can go. Next!'

The magic formula was slow in coming. My cop was re-reading what he'd written. I took the opportunity to glance over at the other girls, who were sitting in front of the other desks. Kim was answering mechanically and blowing the smoke of her king-size Marlboro into the face of the cop interrogating her.

Pascale, though, was in a state of panic. It was her first raid – mine, too, for that matter, with the difference that I already had a year of close calls behind me. But last night was Pascale's first on the job. There are such things as emotional shocks, you know. No sooner had we got to police headquarters than she started pissing in her pants; right while we were walking through the hallway – a regular deluge. There she was, crying and pissing; the others were laughing. I laughed, too, but only to keep from doing the same thing.

Later, while we were sitting on benches in a dirty-yellow corridor and waiting to be interrogated, Pascale began crying even harder. She never should have done it, she said, turning a tear-stained face towards Brigitte. That was when the others started to panic.

'Jesus, will you look at that bitch! She'll never make it. Just as sure as Christ made little green apples, she's going to end up putting us all in the clink.'

They all started talking at once, paying no attention to the two blue angels standing motionless in the corner by the door.

'What's got into you anyway? You want us all to end up pounding the pavement again on account of your shenanigans – is that it? Snap out of it, for Christ's sake! The cops are going to eat you alive. This is no time to start acting dumb, so whatever you do, don't forget: you were there by accident. You had a date with a guy you met at a café. His name was George, or John, or anything you like. Aside from him, you don't know anyone – not *anyone*. Got it? You don't know about having to pay for the room. You never laid eyes on any of us. The madam doesn't exist. You never even heard the word "steerer". Okay?'

Pascale just kept nodding her head and letting the snot dribble on to her clenched hands. Boondocks took a handkerchief out of her purse.

'That's enough. Now wipe your nose.' She lit two filter tips and handed me one.

'You'd better pray she doesn't blow it.'

Our Father, who art in heaven ... stay there! We'll stick to earth, where it's so pretty, sometimes. (As usual, I've mixed everything up: Sunday-school prayers and Jacques Prévert poems, the sanatorium and the whorehouse.) I asked France – I never could manage to call her Boondocks – if she was afraid. She replied that she didn't care for birds, and that Saint-Lazare was chirping full of them.

They started calling us in alphabetical order and we kept our faces anxiously turned towards the drowsy voice of the cop on duty.

'France, what's your real name?'

'Derain. Martine Derain.'

'Funny we never thought of telling one another. I'm – I'm Marie Mage.'

'What difference would it have made if we had thought of it?'

I was about to add something, but that voice made it impossible. Decked out in the dress I'd given her a year ago, her heels banging resolutely on the tile floor, Boondocks was already walking away. She vanished behind a door. Pascale went on crying, her head between her knees.

I'm watching her now out of the corner of my eye, getting jumpy about what she'll say. At the farthest desk, Valerie has just burst out laughing: she's half-draped across the typewriter, swearing she hasn't got a pimp.

'Look, you've known me long enough – why don't you stop asking me questions like that? I work for my own sweet self. I do it for kicks. I've lost track of the times you've picked me up, but it's always the same old song: what's your pimp's name? I haven't got one, period. You ought to change your tune.'

She runs a hand through her peroxide-blonde hair.

'I'm nobody's wife. I'm all alone. The francs I make are for me. The pleasure is all mine.'

Irritated, the lieutenant dismisses her. She swings her purse under his nose. 'Like it or not, I'm my own boss.'

She and I leave the office together while Pascale nervously retrieves the contents of her handbag, which had been scattered over the table.

In the monkey cage we've been assigned to, there are benches – nothing but benches. Sixteen women are waiting for the dawn. Pascale has stopped crying, and we're all trying to cheer her up. She didn't blow it, after all. Now she's worthy of our highest esteem. 'We've all been through it, and we know it's no picnic. Look at little Sophie here – it's her first time, too.'

I puff with pride. It's taken them long enough to accept me. (Have they really?) Boondocks nudges me with her elbow.

'It only hurts the first time!' Lowering her voice, she adds, 'You know I'm up shit creek, don't you? They'll book me. Will you bring me some smokes?'

'Book you?'

'I'm a minor. They'll lock me up at Saint-Lazare.'

'Lock you up? What do you mean, lock you up?'

'Just what I said, lock me up!'

'I won't let them! Listen, I'll slip you my ID card – use it to get out. I'll say I lost it. They'll buy that.'

'You're nice, but you're a little nuts.'

'Uh uh. Franzie, I don't want you staying here. We'll work it out. For me it doesn't matter. It's no problem.'

I light two cigarettes and hand her one. Cynthia takes out her knitting; others follow suit. Needles click softly in the night. I have a funny lump in my throat. Josiane, Kim, Muriel, and Sylviane take turns shuffling a deck of cards. A game starts up. Pascale is apparently asleep. Her head is resting on Brigitte's lap. (All we know about her is that she's her old man's number two.) We gaze sympathetically at the pair. The plump one is smoking contentedly, her thick black hair pulled back on her head. Her corpulence and eleven years spent turning tricks have given her an air of extraordinary assurance. Her little sister has stuck it out: she looks as if she didn't have a care left in the world. And will her man be proud!

Back at the card game, an argument's broken out. Josiane bolts up and sends her hand flying towards the ceiling. Kim and Muriel do the same.

'Let's have a little talk with Ducretin. The poor guy must get

12

so bored.'

His arms hanging limp, his feet swallowed up in the shadows, he leans motionless against the bars. He looks as though he's just been hit by lightning!

Josiane begins the routine.

'Hey there, Mr Moustache!'

The guard's round red eyes rove over her low-cut dress.

'What's your wife do while you jerk off around here?'

'She sleeps. And that's what you should be doing.'

Mumu takes it from there.

'What kind of balls do you need for a job like this? Or don't you need any?'

'Take a good feel, little lady, and see for yourself,' Ducretin replies, flattening himself up against the bars. He pushes his kepi back on his head.

'Girls, he's got a pair of big ones – just like the horse back home.'

'Hey, keep it down! I'm on duty, damn it! Go on, sit down. You want me to write out a report? I know things get antsy when they lock you up, but all the same ... Hey you, the little tramp – yeah, you, blondie. Stand back, you almost ripped my fly apart. No kidding, they ought to give you girls downers instead of beer. Jesus! What a horny bunch.'

'It's a good thing those bars are between us, right, Ducretin? Otherwise you'd have to protect the family jewels. I suspect you're not exactly wearing them out, and they don't get a chance to shoot off too often!'

'Oh, that Muriel! What a mouth on her!'

'Drop it, Mumu,' France orders. 'No brawl tonight. We're ankle-deep in shit as it is.'

As if a cold drizzle started falling, things suddenly turn gloomy. Of course I'd heard them talk any number of times about being busted. I'd heard about the endless hours spent at the police station sitting or lying on a bench (that depended on how much space was available – on how many girls had been run in). Of course I knew that one night, sooner or later, it would be my turn. I had hoped against hope that night would never come. Well, here I am! I still haven't fully realized what kind of contract it is that I've just signed. I now have a police record that will follow me through life till the day I die. I'm now an avowed prostitute. I press my eyes into the hollows of my palms and try to black out the memory of the blazing flashbulbs. Front, side, front, side. Sounds dumb, but I couldn't keep from smiling into the camera. How many mug shots did that cop with the little birdie make? How big a circulation will I get? And where, and for how long? Will I ever find a way to destroy those photographs with their black board backgrounds?

Last name, first name, date, and place of birth. As if my face weren't enough. They wanted details, wanted everything done according to the book. Nevertheless, it was still sloppy: anything better would have required more time, more tact, and higher pay.

No way to blot out those lights. They're flashing everywhere. Only tears will douse them, and this isn't the time or the place for that.

Anyway, the monkey cage is stirring again. Josiane and Muriel have decided to set up a stage by pulling all the benches together. The knitters groan. To shut them up, the others promise an unforgettable performance.

Muriel murmurs a few inaudible words in Boondocks's ear, then says out loud, 'Okay, do it your way.'

I ask what it's all about. France doesn't reply. Pressing herself against the bars, she calls to Ducretin.

'Hey! René-Louis!'

The guard stares at her impassively.

'Did anyone ever tell you you look like Georges Brassens?'

'Never heard of him.'

'Sure you have. The singer. It's wild, you're real look-alikes. Funny nobody ever told you. My girl friends noticed it first thing. Especially the moustache – it's *identical*. That's what we were whispering about.'

Ducretin smiles and pushes his kepi back a little farther. Red and yellow embers are shifting in his eyes, smouldering mutely, even giving off a little heat. His fat paw grasps one of the bars just above France's hands. (France looks tiny enough to slip through the bars and escape.)

'Listen, René-Louis: you know it's good luck to touch a cop's moustache when he's on duty, don't you?'

His mouth opening in an ecstatic grin, Ducretin waggles his head as he leans forward. The rest of the monkey cage is all eyes and ears, aside from a few devotees of the plain stitch.

14

'Okay? You'll let me touch it? I promise not to yank – I've got such soft hands, real soft ...'

'Real soft, real soft,' the chorus chimes in.

Ducretin leans his face against the bars. They make dents in his cheeks and wrinkle his puffy skin, which no one has stroked in a long, long time – not the way France is stroking now.

'You're all hot, big boy,' she murmurs. Her fingers graze his brownish mouth. 'You're dripping. What a crazy idea to get all gussied up like that. I bet you're real glad when you get to take your clothes off.'

'Real glad, real glad,' the chorus echoes.

'Come on now, let's have your prick. A hand-job never hurt anyone, and anyway, watching will make my girl friends happy. They can hardly wait.'

'She's right, Ducretin. We can't stand it any longer. We'll even jerk ourselves off,' says Muriel, lifting her skirt up to her belly button.

'We'll pop our cookies!' Josiane adds, with one hand in the crotch of her pantyhose.

'We'll all come together – okay, René-Louis? It's not going to stop you from being promoted, it'll do you a world of good, and it's all free, courtesy of the house! Just a little closer, that's it. Yeah, big boy, just say the word and it'll be Bastille Day for you.'

Boondocks shoves her hand through the bars. Her entire body is shaking in time with her arm. The knitters have dropped their yarn and put down their needles. It's hot and nobody makes a sound. Ducretin's hands grip the bars. He doesn't lift a finger when his kepi falls to the ground. His eyes are closed. In one burst he climbs to the top of the police department, and as his reddened face sinks against the bars, he's just been made chief.

'It's your little rake-off!'

A brief silence, and a long sigh...

'Nice going, Boondocks. You win.'

France requests a handkerchief. Pascale laughingly hands her the one she'd cried into so much a few hours before. We sing some more, and we laugh a lot. Knit one, purl two. Sunk in in-different sleep on the far side of the bars, Ducretin no longer hears us. That's what *we* should be doing – sleep, or at least snooze a little as we wait for the night to end. But nothing doing. I lean my forehead on France's warm shoulder, and with my eyes wide open, I start thinking of Gerard. In a little while he'll realize that I've been busted (unless, as often happens, he comes home at seven or eight in the morning with the scotch running out of his ears). I try to convince myself that he'll feel sorry, at least at little ... I can't manage it. Fundamentally, he doesn't give a fuck what happens to me tonight. His interest in me ends as soon as I stop being his meal ticket. In fact, as I see it, my having a police record may appeal to him. He may even give me a smile and a wink saying, 'Well, how about that, baby! You're a real woman now. You've made the grade.'

Made the grade! I'd just as soon make it knocking my head against the bars. Take it easy, Sophie. Let's not get carried away. You can do your number later, someplace else. You'd disappoint a lot of people – starting with yourself. So keep calm, give those fancy ideas of yours a kick in the ass, and cry if you feel like it: but keep it to yourself. At least keep your dignity.

You're the woman of a petty hood who's starting to be known on the Paris scene, thanks to your cash and the big tips he tosses the barmaids in his buddies' nightclubs and bars. This is no time to weaken! You have a reputation to keep up, and don't forget it.

But what about the others? How come they're asleep? What happened to their big ideas? Hey, girls, wake up! Sing, fart, tell dirty jokes, but do something. I'm all alone. You bunch of bums, don't let me down!

'France ... Franzie, are you asleep?'

'Hunh. What do you want?'

'Have we got any weeds left?'

'One. I was saving it for later. Want it?'

'Yeah. Let's share it, if that's okay ... What's the man at home say when you get busted?'

'Mostly he goes on snoring and doesn't notice a thing. It all depends what he's up to. Anyway, it's been a long time, you know. Why? You worried about your old man?'

'A little.'

'Forget it. They get over it a lot quicker than we do.'

'Quick, take it, it's burning my fingers.'

The final toke, best and gone.

'Franzie, did you ever try sniffing?'

'You nuts or something?'

'Well – my grandmother used to.'

'Forget your grandmother and try and get some sleep.'

'I can't. You think there's a chance they'll take us to Saint-Lazare tonight?'

'Listen, stop dreaming in technicolour. If everything goes as it should, we'll still be here tomorrow at noon. Now just let me get my forty winks. *I'm* in no hurry to get to Saint-Lazare.'

She closes her eyes, the bitch, clasping her purse against her scrawny chest. I take a gander around the monkey cage. Everyone is sacked out; some are thrashing around in their dreams. No dreams for me. I don't even want to think.

'Officer, Officer!'

At the fourth call, Ducretin comes grumblingly to life. The girls groan softly.

'Officer, please, I have to pee.'

A clank of metal; sighs; the bars swing open; a clank of metal. Dragging my feet, I follow Ducretin down the dirty corridors. I can tell by the smell when we're approaching the end of our promenade: it stinks of ammonia from fifty feet away. Ducretin yawns as he shoves a door open. It's 'Turkish' style, a hole you have to squat over – just like the ones in my housing project. I push the sticky door shut. Ducretin pushes it back open. I guess that means that the door is supposed to stay open. I crouch, psss, psss, nothing. Maybe if I pulled the chain? But then my bottom would be bathed in cold water. The idea turns me off.

My guard is getting impatient – as I can see from the way he rocks back and forth on his crêpe soles. You rip-off, sold-out punk, I'll have to go back to my bench with my bladder brimming. And that lump's still there, shuttling between my solar plexus and my throat.

Sure, now's the time to cry. It's so dark here that he can't see. I dig my fists into my eyeballs, deep, deep into their sockets. It's not true that tears will make the colour of your eyes fade! I don't believe that any more. It's a fairy tale for little girls. A clank of metal; I re-enter the cage among sprawled, sleeping girls. In a corner, two girls are whispering as they huddle together on the floor. I've lost my seat. I put my purse on the ground, rest my head on it, and stretch out my legs on the concrete. It's cold. I hitch up my big ideas for the journey to the forlorn land of dreams.

*

The paddy wagon is inching its way through traffic on Boulevard Sébastopol. On the sidewalks, thousands of antlike creatures are scurrying this way and that. A reek of rancid oil wafts over from stands selling french fries; and from the front of the van, the garlicky smell of the sausage sandwiches that the cops have just taken out of their little blue bags reminds me that my stomach has had nothing in it since yesterday evening. Just watch them put it away! Our mouths water in time to their shameless bites. A while back, as we rode past Rue Rambuteau, it was 1.00 p.m. on the clock there. How long can you keep going without food or sleep?

The window's open and there's a draught on my neck. In the course of the morning we were questioned by a new team of cops, and our handbags were searched once again. The lieutenant who was in charge of me confiscated my nail file and a tube of Darvon. He carefully put them in an envelope on which he wrote my first and last names and the place where I'd been picked up. I'll probably never get the things back, but I don't care. Oh yes, he also went to a lot of trouble trying to find out my *nom de guerre*. I pretended not to understand. He asked me what kind of a jerk I took him for. (It must be some kind of obsession with them. Last night the other cop asked the same question after I'd told him I never did it for money.)

In any case, the girls all agree: we're in for it.

Two interrogations can only spell trouble. Josiane says it's obvious: they want to close the house down, no matter what. That's tough on her because it's her first place and she's been there eleven years. Boondocks and some of the others say it's the men the cops are after. We'd better be on our toes if we want our daddy-os to stay out of the can. (France, naturally, is mostly worried about the men: she's married to a Corsican.) Some say it's a matter of shaking things up a little, a way of reminding Pedro, our madam, that her police connection is worth only so much and that she'd better start thinking about laying off personnel. According to oldtimers, nineteen girls at the Saint-Louis is something unheard of. The old lady's eyes are bigger than her stomach. Everyone may have to pay for it. Others, who are more optimistic, think that the whole business is just an act: a way of making the other madams think that Pedro has no more protection than anyone else.

According to Kim, a raid was long overdue. Last year,

18

number 3 and number 16 on Rue de Douai were shut down for six months. There were many streets you couldn't set foot in: Pigalle, Victor-Massé, Douai, Fontaine, and Frochot. The girls were busted four or five times a week and finally emigrated in disgust to Les Halles. Meanwhile, the girls at the Saint-Louis were working around the clock.

That was when Pedro got the reputation of being a stoolie – a distinction frowned on in the trade. The madam's fame finally rubbed off on her inmates. When other girls asked, 'Where are you working?' it was safer not to mention the Saint-Louis unless you had the build of a wrestler – or a strong death wish.

We're riding down Boulevard Poissonière. Our blue angels are busy digesting. I start daydreaming. Through the grid of the window grating I watch the sky and its punched-out, pallid sun. I watch it spilling ever so gently over the grey rooftops. This is the way I like Paris. Suddenly the van no longer has a precise destination. The angels have tossed their dusty capes out the open door. Their kepis follow, as do their guns – the holsters skid along the sidewalk under the startled gaze of by-standers. My girl friends' black dresses are dotted with flowers of all colours, their high-heeled shoes have turned into espa-drilles, and their handbags have shrunk into little plaited baskets. The gratings disappear from the windows, which open wider and wider. False eyelashes fly away on a gust of warm air. The sun breaks through at last. Makeup fades, com-plexions glow with natural radiance. We're on the expressway to the west. Our hair streams in the wind. Next stop the country, the dunes, the sea ...

chapter two

How about a little bit farther to the right? No dice. A shade left? That's no better. Then what about shoving it in deeper? Still no results. Well, you sadist, you bespectacled turd, why don't you put more effort into your probing and twisting and butchering? Maybe then you'll find it.

I'm digging my thumbs into the palms of my hands; my finger-tips have turned purple; I'm holding my arm stretched out as stiff as I can – and I go on watching the vicious moves of the square needle in pursuit of my good vein. She's grinding her teeth, the bitch! I'll bet that in her entire career of butchery no one has ever put up a fight like this. Blood is what the lady is after. And as she furiously pursues her goal, a black veil starts shrouding my sight – oh, Christ, I'm going to pass out!

Say, that's not such a bad idea. Rescue me, walls – the ground's slipping away!

At Saint-Lazare they don't bring you around with cognac, smelling salts, or vinegar but with a few slaps in the face. Where am I? Cabourg, the dunes, the sea . . .

'Go on, climb up. And take off your panties.'

Panties? Yes, panties. *No* panties! I don't wear any when I work. The girls think it's unsanitary, and I think it's practical. Anyway, no crime. All right. I'm ready.

'That's it. Bend your legs a little more. Open wide. Come on. Wider than that.'

Brandishing her unlubricated speculum, she makes sure to graze the insides of my thighs. It's cold. It hurts. The little glint behind her frames tells me that she's waiting for me to whine: then she can tell me that I've been through things as bad as this, if not worse, before. So I grit my teeth and open my innards, into which she inserts a kind of long, flat needle. You old snoop!

Now she's contentedly letting the needle wander over a little glass slide. I relax. Too soon: she wants more.

'Open wide.'

I begin wondering if she isn't a closet dyke and curse the moment I swallowed the results of my smear test. (It was fatal evidence for anyone trying to pass as a beginner.) Once again she parades the needle over the slide. I no longer dare move.

'That's all, kid. You can get down.'

I jump off the examination table. Where are the others?

They're in the corridor, sitting on benches – the same benches. (Everything that belongs to the state is the same: ugly, sad, and impersonal.) My pals look beat. I probably do, too.

'Hey, Sophie, is it true you passed out? That's what Valerie told us.'

I show them my riddled right arm. It's impressive: there are streaks of dried blood all the way down to my wrist. In spite of my exhaustion, I suddenly feel okay.

Sylviane says, 'I managed to smuggle in some cologne. It's stashed in my girdle. Come on, let's go to the john.'

I'm about to follow her when a little bell goes dingdong in my head. My eyes sweep the benches. Someone essential is missing.

'Where's France? Where is she?'

Well. what's so strange? Did I scream? Am I bleeding to death? Why are they staring at me like that?

'They've stuck Boondocks in the minors' section. Things may get rough – children's court, the whole fucking show. Especially since it's a second offence. She requested that you be allowed to visit her. She doesn't want anybody else. She also said you'd be able to contact you-know-who, and asked that you take care of it as soon as you're out. And make sure you're not being tailed!'

Poor France! I'd forgotten about her. I'd wanted to give her my ID card, I might even have got her to take it. Instead, I fell asleep listening to the others bullshit.

'Come on now, you've got to get that cleaned up. And quit moping. It doesn't help.'

I meekly follow Sylviane through the colourless corridor, towards the john. Abruptly, overwhelmingly, the hours of fatigue come crashing down on my shoulders. It's as if some enormous animal were hanging there. A huge striped cat or a grinning chimera has nested on the very spot where I'd felt that draught on my neck as we drove down to the sea ... Later, I must try taming it; but for the moment I just let my arm hang loose under the cool water and avoid the mirror over the wash-basin. My mascara has formed little grey puddles under my eyes, and my makeup base has kissed my cheeks goodbye. I'm not looking my best.

'Don't budge. It may sting a little, but – doctor's orders.'

Sylviane conscientiously dabs the bruised spot. I wouldn't have thought her capable of such care and attention.

'You know, it'll probably leave a scar. Myself, I'd have belted her one.'

As I listen to her, I feel that she's perfectly capable of doing something like that. Sylviane is thirty. Easily two heads taller than I am; she has a commanding figure. Her face looks peaceful and, above all, fresher than mine, even though I'm nine years younger. (Last night in the cage, she painstakingly removed her makeup.)

There are thirteen undetectable years in the trade behind her. I'd been dazzled by her presence. She has, to coin a phrase, real class, a high-born young lady from well-to-do Neapolitan society.

At nineteen, she met Gilbert on the beach at Amalfi. She took him for a blue-blooded swell. Unfortunately, the only thing blue about him was his eyes. He was a pig and a thorough-going pimp; where other people saw feeling, he saw ten-dollar bills: easier to transport and a lot more profitable.

Gilbert runs a number of 'businesses', and he has good connections. As hooker, mother, and business associate, Sylviane takes the bad times with the good and never complains. It's a waste of time asking her why she doesn't think about retiring. Brimming with satisfaction, she replies that she has absolutely no desire to become a stodgy housewife cooped up in her apartment in some posh district of Paris.

The others lost no time cuing me in. After a few days I was fully informed about the lives of all of them, Sylviane included. Behind all that fine nonchalance there looms the figure of a tyrannical fifty-year-old, a former john who apparently has some claim on her, and to whom this Italian woman grants generous access to the marital couch. As a result, Gilbert frequently finds himself obliged to spend hours meditating in the closet among his better half's finery. Normally, the thought of such a situation would make me smile. Now, as I look at this big, motherly woman bending over me, I feel like burying my head against her and blurting out my despair. Most of all I feel like asking her why she *really* doesn't want to quit. But once again I've missed my moment. She tosses back her red hair. Her gaze becomes distant.

'There, you're all cleaned up. Let's go.'

And off we go. Our absence, brief as it was, has given our pals a chance to put on their thinking caps. Beneath those wigs, the grey matter is positively churning. There even seems to be a whiff of rebellion in the air. Muriel is striding up and down, bouncing two bright little keys in the palm of one hand. There is a serious, decisive look about her that the others mimic.

'What we've got to do now is get our act together. They were chumps enough to leave the keys in the lock. Now it's up to us.'

'But they'll have duplicates.'

'So what? We'll plug the locks. Who's got some chewing gum?'

Mumu manages to collect two pieces. She pouts.

'How about chewing some paper?'

Surprise, surprise! Our steely molars do the work of ten pulping machines. The holes are plugged. We even stuff the cracks around and under the doors – we almost wish there were *more* doors. (After it's all over, Claudie, always ten steps behind everyone else, holds out a perfectly smooth round pellet. Mumu looks at her with contempt.)

'Michele, you've got the highest heels. Let me have one of your shoes. Jojo, pass me your scarf.'

It's Kim, the Eurasian, who's speaking. She's decided to hightail it. She sets to work with all the patience of her race. She meticulously wraps the silk around the shoe. Out of her half-moon eyes, she studies the window, selecting the exact spot she's going to hit, and then keeps hitting it while we sing, clap our hands, and stamp our feet – not too loud, just enough to cover her. The shattering pane makes a lovely sound: the sound of freedom.

'Sylviane – quick!'

Our Italian friend has a broad back. She crouches on the bench on all fours and assumes her burden without a murmur.

Kim goes flying out like some crazy bird. Her purse and shoes follow her. (I've volunteered to throw their stuff after them. I find it exciting. I'll be the last to jump.)

'Your turn, Jojo. Pull up your dress, otherwise you'll fall on your face.'

'Step on it! Oh, shit – you're a real pain!'

'Uh uh. I'm not going, not dolled up like this. I won't get ten feet away from here before they haul me back in.'

'Don't be an ass! Jump! Jump, for Christ's sake!'

Josiane jumps awkwardly. A high scream pierces our ears. I can't see her face, but it must be contorted with pain. All I can see is her blonde head bobbing back and forth in time with her sobs. She doesn't look up at us and doesn't call for help. She's already regretting that scream, stuffing it back down her throat while waiting for the others to jump and make their escape. Getting out of there no longer concerns her. It had been a pleasant idea that would have allowed her to go home, soak in a hot bath, then go right to bed, without even bothering about food. To be able to sleep – just sleep. She'd been talking about it since the night before: to be back in her own bed, between cool sheets, stretching out her arms and legs, with cold cream all over her face ... For her, such things are possible, because she sleeps alone. Her husband's doing ten years in Melun prison. And here she is lying barefoot on the concrete yard at Saint-Lazare with her ID and other papers gone ...

I've lost the courage to jump, either to help her or to run away myself. I've lost the courage to do anything but climb off Sylviane's back.

'She must be hurt.'

'Now what?'

'We've got to let them know. We can't leave her like that. She may have broken a leg.'

'Shit. I really wanted to get out of here.'

'What about me? What about her? What about Boondocks – don't you think she'd have liked to get out of here?'

This is no time to rest our laurels. If Jo has a broken leg, that's all the more reason to get moving! Whores have a sense of team spirit, let me tell you! We work fast in an emergency. Recriminations can come later. (And they usually do.) Here we are, going at it like maniacs, using our bobby pins to unplug the door, feeling guilty as hell. After all, we did encourage her to do it: 'Don't be an ass, jump! *Jump!*' If she hadn't, we'd have pushed her. We *did* push her.

Sylviane volunteers to announce our defeat to the guards. As we watch her go out the door, we breathe easier. It's not that we're incapable of such bravery – no, it's just that we prefer having a friend do it for us. She'll draw the first fire, while we quietly wipe our noses and wait for the storm to pass. She's gone a long time. It's already been a quarter of an hour since she left, and poor Josiane's still down there! And France is in the minors' section! And Gerard! And me – still unable to choose between the corridor and the yard below.

I could quickly step out through the broken window and jump, being careful not to slash my legs on the shattered windowpane, making sure I didn't break my neck. Jump, again – but this time into a taxi, gasping out the address, repeating it to make sure the driver understands; then smile at the butcher and the florist, climb my two flights four steps at a time (not forgetting to say hello to my touchy concierge), turn the familiar key in the lock, and find Gerard waiting for me between blue sheets, smoking a cigarette. Maybe for once his suit won't be lying on the floor – he'll have carefully hung it up. His socks will be in his shoes. His cigarettes and lighter will be on the bedside table next to my photograph. And the toilet bowl, instead of overflowing with puke, will be filled with red roses.

By patiently grilling the nurse who was taking us to our dormitory, we were able to learn that Josiane had been admitted to the hospital with a fractured kneecap. Poor thing. Poor Josiane. It means a few weeks without the visitors' room, a few days in the dumps. Her trips to the Melun prison were what kept her going. When she needed comforting, she went to the county jail. The day after a visit she looked radiant – her batteries recharged for a month. She keeps talking endlessly about the little farm in Provence she plans to buy when Henri gets out. Sure, it'll be too late to have a kid; but his sister will come south to visit them during summer vacations, with her little nephews who love her so. She'll be forty-two, Henri forty-six. The chance to live the good life will finally have arrived. The shade of olive trees and the crickets singing in the scrub will erase the memory of bad times.

Before she met Henri, Josiane's pimp was Jean, a black-belt judoka. She loved him the way one loves only at seventeen: unquestioningly. Since he was already married and his wife was a proficient cordon bleu, Jean figured Josiane would be better off in a whorehouse than in a kitchen. After a brief honeymoon, Josiane took her first faltering steps on the Croisette in Cannes. It was a poor start, and not very profitable. Lacking experience, she would usually end her nights dancing in discos instead of lying in bed with a customer at the Carlton. Jean had commerce in his blood, and he quickly sensed that even though his capital was being depleted, it was capable, under the right management, of earning a profit. So the two of them left Cannes for Paris. Pedro balked a little at first. The girl, underage, was an unnecessary risk. Nevertheless, Jo's round breasts, long legs, and green eyes quickly overcame the madam's reluctance. And after all, Jean was a pal. It wasn't the first time he'd recruited for the Saint-Louis. When they closed the deal, glasses of Dom Pérignon were raised to a glorious future. As she went up the stairs, Josiane forgot all about the sunny south. If she felt a twinge of regret, she consoled herself with the thought of the money she'd make. Hadn't Jean promised that she'd be flying home once a month to see her family?

Time went by willynilly. Postage stamps took the place of airline tickets, and kisses turned to slaps. On the day Jean landed in Fresnes prison, convicted of fencing stolen household appliances, Josiane almost went through the roof of the Saint-Louis. Swearing she'd never set foot in the goddamn place again she took off for the sunshine; and Jean, in his seclusion, went on addressing his love letters to a recipient of whom the post office had no trace.

Josiane spent six months at her mother's. She became engaged to a man from Cannes, broke the engagement, and then went off to Juan-les-Pins to work as a barmaid. It was there that she met Henri. Lying in the bottom of a rowboat, they came to a quick understanding. At the end of the summer season they left for Paris. Henri didn't know Pedro personally, but he had friends who were willing to intervene on his behalf. When, one evening in October, Josiane appeared in the doorway of number 59 Rue Fontaine, nobody asked any questions. Not the madam; not Arlette, the supervisor; not Louisette and Inna, the two cleaning women; not even the girls – and Lord knows they must have been itching to. Jo returned to her spot by the wardrobe, where her dress was still hanging faithfully, hoping for her return.

Josiane had simply taken a vacation. A long vacation.

Saint-Lazare is said to be the hospital where any girl who makes a living selling her charms in Paris or its suburbs is bound to put in an appearance sooner or later. But in other hospitals, no matter how gruesome they may be, the sheets are clean. In other hospitals, whatever the state of your body or soul, you're not usually repelled by the notion of laying your cheek against the rough cloth pillowcase. At Saint-Lazare, they don't even think of you as being sick. At most, you have gonorrhoea, syphilis, or a two-star chancre – maybe worse if you're the lucky type; or maybe just an acute attack of longing; in other words, nothing serious. Saint-Lazare is nothing more or less than a way station between the police and the sidewalk. It's a method of checking out prostitutes, not of curing them. In fact, if you've been spared these diseases, you're liable to contract them simply by brushing against the old rags they give you for sheets.

Having kept a healthy distance from penicillin so far, I've just used my toes to push away the putrid linen allotted me. In the bed next to mine, Brigitte is settling down for the night like an old trouper.

'What about you, kid – why aren't you tucking in? Not sleepy or what?'

I shake my head.

'When I was your age, I was made out of steel, too. They'd bust me at nine p.m., and after spending a night in the clink I'd be back at work in the morning.'

I don't feel like talking. She slides down between the sheets. Her purse and wig disappear with her.

'Watch out, Sophie. They steal the eyes right out of your head here.'

I nod my thanks. I'm carrying around about two hundred francs, my ID, some snapshots of my brothers, and a tube of antiseptic cream. How can I escape from all this filth? How can I fight off my exhaustion? The crapper – that's it! I feel my way towards it in the dark. Muriel and Sylviane are squatting ankle-deep in water, dealing cards. Their green baize table is a page from *France-Soir*.

'Want to play?'

Why not?

'Normally, there should be a shipment in from Pigalle or Les Halles. The girls will have cigarettes and beer. It'd be dumb not to cut ourselves in.'

'It'd be a crying shame!'

'There's no getting away from it, street hookers are better off than we are.'

'In a way,' Sylviane replies, leading a club. 'Except they get busted a little too often for my taste.'

'Yeah – but they're prepared for it,' Mumu rejoins. 'You'll never see one of them show up here without her toothbrush and her supper.'

'Quit griping. When was the last time they hauled you in?'

'Eight months ago. Actually, I was on my way to a girl

friend's on Rue Quincampoix, but those bastards didn't want to hear about it. They just said, "Cut the crap, we know all about you." I could have bitten their nuts off – especially since it was my day off. And to top it off, my old man was expecting me. I'd promised to make him roast lamb and beans – that's his favourite dish. When I got home after ten hours at the station, I found him standing in the kitchen with his hands shoved deep into the pockets of his dressing gown. I can see it like it was yesterday. "Fix me some chow," he said, "and tell me about it later." I took a steak out of the fridge – I was wetting my pants! He wanted french fries. While I was peeling the spuds I tried to straighten him out about the trouble I'd had. He told me to shut my mouth and watch out for my ass. I set the table with a smile. He looked at me. "I need a little exercise before eating," he said, and I backed off towards the bedroom. The bruise machine went into action. He laid into me good and hard, saying I was a tramp fit only for Krauts. Let me tell you, these days when I want to talk to my friend on Rue Quincampoix, I use the phone!'

Muriel's mind is elsewhere. I slap down my ace of hearts for a trick.

'Whew! Never thought I'd make that one.'

'So, if I read you right,' Sylviane asks, 'he still works you over the way he did when you started? That's something I'd never put up with.'

'Oh, you know, it's not that he's mean, but he's so jealous. He can't even stand my having a girl friend. Lately he hasn't been able to show up regularly because one of his kids is sick. So he calls me from his wife's place three or four times a day to see if there's anything I need. You see, he does have his good side.'

'Sure.'

'Hey! Sounds as though things are happening downstairs. What time do you have?'

'Nine-thirty. You think this is it?'

'Could be a shipment coming in.'

Leaving the cards on the edge of the washbasin, Mumu and Sylviane head for the stairs. I follow right behind them. Laughter and shouts reach us from far below. I'll be able to smoke! The stairway fills with a wild horde of women elbowing, pinching, and playfully tripping each other. Here come the new arrivals, our comrades in misfortune. We don't know them; but at a single word, smile, or wink, they're ready to share their food, their booze, their beds, and their life stories with us. I step back to let them go by – I don't want to seem too eager ...

The first to arrive are from Pigalle. The second contingent comes from the Madeleine. All have been rounded up by the pussy patrol.

'Those faggots have got their heads down tonight. Did the same bunch haul you in, too?'

We nod, our eyes devour the sandwiches piling up on the bedside tables. With their false eyelashes fluttering, the sleepers emerge from their clouds. There's an exuberant racket as the free beds are taken by storm. As old friends are reunited, they hug and slap one another on the back, then start bringing each other up to date. Cavorting on the bunks, they tell about their last big meal, their last VD checkup, and the last night they spent together right here, not so long ago.

'How's your old man? He and mine saw each other three weeks ago in Sologne. Did he tell you?'

'Sure. He's still crazy about hunting. It's his biggest weakness – after me!'

'How about the other one – did that deal of his work out? Did you get to talk to the lawyer? Is there any chance they'll let him off?'

'What about his woman – are they still holding her?'

'Which one?'

'Little Michou. I heard she'll get a rap for receiving. That's no joke.'

'How's business? What's the turnover like out on the street? It's been quiet with us. But the automobile show is coming up, so we ought to be raking it in.'

'The heat's more or less off, and the cops are not giving us such a hard time right now. We have to stick to the bars, though. No shoving it under their noses.'

'Things are a lot rougher around the Madeleine. Those bastards have a round-the-clock paddy wagon parked in front of the hotel on Rue Godot, the only one where they always let everybody in. These days, to find a place to lie down, you have to walk miles, with the john trailing behind. When you finally get there, you're lucky if he's still with you – sometimes they've shot their wad on the way. If they split you're in trouble. You have to pay for the wheels to get home. You can imagine how the expenses mount up. And then some of our men just don't go for this routine – take my old man, for example. He's got a jealous streak. What's going to become of us if things go on like this?'

Stone by stone, the wailing wall is assembled. I watch it take shape as I share a Camembert sandwich with Pat.

Like Boondocks, Pat is a minor. The difference is that she's working with an ID that does the trick. I sink my teeth into the long loaf of bread while she spins her tale. Instead of re-assuring me, her story leaves me worried. She absolutely insists that I take a look at her papers.

'How about that? Nice work for fakes, don't you think? My old man made them. He's got talent, huh?'

I start on the heel of the loaf and glance at her papers so as not to irritate her. Tarts are so touchy!

'He's pretty good. Got anything to drink?' I ask.

'Some rosé. Two bottles.'

I lick the plastic rim. I can hardly wait to taste it. Sweet Pat. Crazy Pat!

'You're underage too, aren't you? It shows. Only shitheads like them could miss it.'

Please. Let's get things straight from the start. I take a swallow.

'As of one month ago, I'm twenty-two.'

'Who are you trying to bullshit? The others, maybe, but not me. Why don't you own up? Don't you trust me? Look, I showed you my ID, so? ... You know, I may be young, but I'm not short on brains.'

It takes at least half an hour to convince her I'm not lying. Shit! I'd like to ditch her and turn in. Sensing as much, she shifts her ground. Evidently she needs to unwind. The rosé has hit me something awful. I start stroking that big striped alley cat crouching between my shoulders.

'You're beat, huh?'

'This'll be my second straight night with no sleep.'

'You can sleep some other time. Let's check the place out.'

We check it out. (I'm feeling grateful for that sandwich.) The lights have dimmed. The cubicles are aglow with candles, flashlights, and cigarette lighters. Some of the girls are playing cards. Some are asleep, or pretending to be. Some are talking in low voices, two to a bunk. Some are having a feast – cold chicken, mayonnaise, and tomatoes spread out on the sheets.

'My friends – Florence, Penelope, Christine, Tolo.'

I nod hello.

'Feel like oiling your works? It's great stuff.'

I suck avidly on the new beaujolais. One slug. Two. Three!

'How about a contest? Let's see who can piss farthest. Line up! You in, Sophie?'

'Sure I am!'

I had never imagined what a powerful diuretic wine could be. I go on and on. It's unbelievable.

'Damn it, you've got the Yangtze River there!' Penelope screams. 'How long since you went to the can?'

My legs spread, I watch the flood in amazement. That's *me*? If I wasn't so drunk I'd feel ashamed. But I'm smashed – *very* smashed. Pat is, too. She's on all fours, playing doggie.

'Hey, in there, knock that shit off,' an anonymous voice calls through the partition. 'If you don't feel like sleeping, show some consideration for people who do!'

'Up yours, bitch – and you can be Al Capone's wife for all I care!'

Silence. Huddled together, we wait. It won't be long before the girl who's been razzed takes up the challenge. We're ready. Our fists are clenched, and there's a vicious retort ready on our lips ... We switch off our flashlights.

'Well? Are we all scared shitless? I'd like to know which of you dumb broads mentioned Al Capone's wife. So? I'm listening.'

Even in the darkness, a quick gander at her in her birthday suit reveals the fact that she's three times my size. She's a Niagara of a woman – every part of her body is a cascade! Pat moves to my side.

'Doesn't look as if this one's got a sense of humour. There's going to be a rumble. You can count on me.'

'Okay, who is it?' Niagara roars.

By the light of the dancing Everreadies that are being switched back on, I can see that significant glances are being cast in my direction.

'Pat, pass the lubricant.'

I squeeze the almost empty plastic bottle between my fingers and milk it for the courage I need. No good. I'm dying of fright. France, France, why aren't you here?

'Do I have to kick you out of your sacks one at a time?'

'Save your strength, fatso. I said it and I'll say it again: Up yours!'

What's this she's been hiding behind her back? It's just split my lip open.

'A belt? So you fight with a belt, you bitch!'

'Let her have it, Sophie! Knock the shit out of her! Kick her face in! Rip her guts out!'

'Okay! ... Come on! ... Get a little closer, you fat cow! I haven't got a belt, but I'm going to give it to you right in the teeth.'

'Olé, olé!'

Niagara has just slipped in the piss. Pat grabs the belt and starts lashing her flab with it.

'That's what you need, you big piece of blubber! Now you won't have to take a shower.'

In the tangle that follows, I catch a glimpse of Brigitte's face, Sylviane's sturdy legs, Muriel's American-style uppercut, Claudine's wig, and I recognize the voices of Pat, Tolo, and Penelope ...

'Everyone knows that the girls at the Madeleine are all bitches!'

Lights! And in come the matrons, scratching their bellies underneath their white smocks.

'Ladies, the riot squad will be here in five minutes!'

I stagger off holding my split lip and try to find a bed – my bed.

chapter three

Gerard is about to leave for his tailor's. Standing erect in front of the mirror with his feet spread apart, he whistles as he straightens the knot of his tie, glances at his watch, and gives himself a generous sprinkling of Pour un Homme. The scent of lavender caresses my nostrils and fills the room. Before he met me, Gerard used Mennen's shaving lotion, and the smell was enough to make you puke. Pour un Homme was my doing, and I paid for it out of my first earnings. 'It's a gift,' I'd haughtily told the woman in the perfume shop, 'wrap it up nicely.'

'You're sure you don't want to come with me, baby?'

He's feeling great.

'No, really. I'm bushed. Just look at my mouth.'

'I guess you're right. I'll call you this afternoon. The cop who did that to you is a real faggot. You think the swelling will go down by tonight?'

He's worried to death. He himself is always careful never to mess up the display window.

'I hope so. I'm going to put salt compresses on it. They say that helps. In any case, it'll be a long time before I forget that guy. The girls said I landed the biggest bastard of the lot. Can you imagine – he wanted to know everything: enough to put *you* in the clink for five. A real shit. I told him to fuck off. That's when he hit me. Back of his hand. You know how stubborn I can be. After that, he couldn't get a word out of me. Still, I sure was frightened. Light me a cigarette, please?'

'I'm proud of you baby. I knew you were a winner when I picked you. As a matter of fact, I was talking last night with a friend – you know, Claude, the fat guy? His wife has just run out on him She's a real bitch. As I listened to him, I said to myself, That's something you don't have to worry about. What do you think about that?'

While I happily splash in the suds, he smooths his moustache with a contented air. He's a real pimp, old Gerry is. After all, why not lie? You cover your tracks, you gain time, and you win the enemy's confidence. Keep squawking, little ducky, I haven't forgotten about you. Some day it'll be your turn. Just you wait.

'You know I'd never leave you. What would I do? Pass me the ashtray.'

'By the way, I almost forgot. I got a call from the automobile dealer, and he says the new car will be in next week. How about that? If the weather's still nice and business is good, we'll go up to Deauville. I'll ask Pedro to give you a couple of days off – maybe Sunday and Monday.'

'The middle of the week would be better. Things are quieter then.'

'Whatever you say, baby. Well, got to get moving. The Arm-

33

enian is expecting me. I'll call you. Are we having dinner together?'

'Listen, I can't say for sure. I've got to take care of France. She's still on the inside. Maybe I'll grab a bite on Rue Bernoulli with her old man. You'd better phone me there.'

'Okay, baby. You know I love you?'

'I know.'

I keep my eyes glued to the rear window on the way over, even though I'm not really worried about being tailed. As an added precaution, I ask the driver to let me out two blocks away. When I get close to the bar, I feel the medals sprouting on my chest. It's the third time I've come here, but Gerard was with me on the first two occasions. This evening is different. I'm alone, and I'm bearing an important message.

As I go into the place – it's been rebaptized Pour les Oiseaux, which sounds a lot less Corsican than Catenatcho did – I start wondering if I shouldn't have phoned beforehand, even if talking on the telephone is frowned on. For a brief moment, thick red velvet hangings separate me from the rooms beyond, where a TV set is crackling away. I push my way through them and advance with little steps towards the bar, where a bored barmaid is playing solitaire.

'Is Monsieur Jean-Jean here, please?'

She looks me over suspiciously, then nods towards a group of men who are sitting riveted to the TV. I immediately make out Jean-Jean's shiny bald head and hatchet face, and once again I ask myself how France, so young and beautiful! ... To top it all off, he's the kind of man who has to remind himself to laugh.

'I have news of your wife, monsieur.' I bend over and whisper the words in his ear.

'Will you look at those bums? Just look at them! Ajaccio's let them score.'

Startled, I step back.

'Excuse me, madame. You were saying?'

'I have news of your wife.'

'Oh, yes. Wait just a minute. Would you like a drink? They're not worth a damn tonight. What's happening to them? I can't believe it.'

'I tell you, the referee's sold his ass. Did you see him? A free kick! There's no such thing as a free kick, and never has been.

What's that jerk trying to pull off? Huh? Can you tell me what he's up to?'

'Listen, if I knew—'

'Would you like a drink?'

'Thanks. A glass of port.'

'Josée – Josée! A glass of port for the lady. There, in the dining room. That's right.'

In the dining room, the silver has been set out on little red tablecloths that seem to flutter in the candlelight. There are, as usual, no customers. I find it increasingly hard to believe that the Berbardini brothers make their living from serving food and drink – in spite of what France says, and the conviction with which she says it.

The final whistle has just blown. Ajaccio has lost the game, 2–0. Jean-Jean settles down opposite me, looking discouraged. He seems to be in pain.

'So, madame, tell me. What has happened?'

'Your wife is being held at Saint-Lazare.'

I avoid mentioning France and, especially, Josiane by name. The proprieties must be observed. I stammer out my words, pretending to be more upset than I really am. That's also part of the script.

'So?'

'I went to visit her this afternoon. I wanted to bring her some cigarettes and try to get some news.'

'So?'

'So they refused to let me see her. But I'll go back tomorrow, you can be sure of that. She asked me to let you know. That's all.'

'Do you know if she has any money on her?'

'No, I don't.'

'If you see her tomorrow, try and give her this. Thank you for taking the trouble to come over. I'll have someone call you a taxi.'

As I drive to work in the taxi, I uncrumple the hundred-franc bill that Jean-Jean had slipped me and wonder what exactly goes on in men's minds.

'Hello, Claudie? It's me, Sophie. Any idea of what's happening?'

'Well, I went up there. How about you?'

'You're damn right I went up there. It's not out of bounds, as far as I know.'

'You too? Was it Inna who let you in?'

'No, Louisette. I wish you could have seen her face – you'd think I was the devil himself. "You mustn't come here, you mustn't," she stammered at me through the half-open door. "Get out of here! Go on!" You should have seen me take off. I figured the cops must still be on the premises. Was I ever scared!'

'I tried calling Pedro. Inna answered. "Madame Pedro is out," and bang! she hung up on me.'

'What are we going to do?'

'Me? I'm taking a sleeping pill and going to bed. No point letting a day off go to waste, even if it wasn't planned. We'll see tomorrow.'

'Listen, Claudie, do you think our old men are together to-night?'

'Could be.'

'You have any idea where I could reach him now?'

'Try Le Baudet – Carlos's place. Do you have the number? If he isn't there, try later at the Club 65 on Rue du Four. It's a disco for young chicks. But don't let on I tipped you off. Don't screw things up, Sophie – you promise?'

'Don't worry. Thanks. *Ciao.*'

What do you do on a night off when you've lost the habit – when there's no one you can call and simply say, 'How about dinner together?' or 'Want to go out, there's a movie playing that I'd like to see?' When it's too late to show up at your mother's with a freshly baked cake, when you've disdainfully torn up a customer's card (even though he was young and simpatico), what else can you do but try and find the one person who won't be overly astounded to see you suddenly emerge from nowhere? What can you do but try and find your man and hope that you find him alone? It's either that or a bunch of sleeping pills. As I have no particular desire to die and have very bad memories of the stomach pump, I phone Carlos's place. Thunderbird Gerry has not been seen this evening. Where can the bastard have gone? Where's he hiding? I pace around my two-room apartment, getting more and more depressed, postponing the decisive moment when I won't be able to stand it any longer and call a cab.

Club 65. 'For young chicks' – that's what Claudie said. It's the fashionable place where these gentlemen go for rejuvenation. They guzzle champagne and ogle the twisters' pink thighs, while ... No. Don't start thinking that way. You're full of shit. No, I'm not full of shit! It all takes place while I have johns crawling over me in the broken-down beds of Saint-Louis, while their sour sweat is dissolving my makeup, while I'm scrubbing myself with kitchen soap to keep from getting knocked up. And for what? For Mr Pimp to toss little chippies my bread and make them think he's a producer or businessman in need of some loving. I've had it up to here. I've just spent two nights under lock and key, the first on a concrete floor, the second on a cot swarming with vermin. I've got crabs, and my mouth looks like a bouquet of violets. Not a single friend I can talk to. France is waiting to be shipped back home to La Roquette; Josiane's in the hospital; Claudie is stuffed with tranquillizers; Muriel's probably getting the shit beat out of her; Michele is writing her kids, whom she hasn't seen in months because the woman who takes care of them is being watched – their loving father is on the lam, and he's worried about his precious freedom.

It's not fair. What about us? What about our freedom? Does it ever cross their minds? Can we ever claim it? You should have let me be, Gerard. You shouldn't have taken me out of my crummy housing project. I told you my shoulders were too frail to sustain the weight of all this muck. You got stubborn about it. You played the big scene from Act Two and held the nose of your .45 to my temple. You wanted to make a 'real' woman out of me. Well, you succeeded; and you're going to regret it.

I'm striding along the pavement in a rage. Half a bottle of port has a wicked way of warming you up and making you nasty. I've got more agression in me than I know what to do with. Buy a sprig, ladies and gentlemen, only one franc apiece ... It's like the time when I was fifteen and sold lilies of the valley at the Gare Montparnasse. Just one franc, with the leaves and the newspaper wrapping thrown in. 'Come on, don't be so shy – it'll make the missus happy. I can sell you a pot, if you

37

like. Step up! Take a sniff of that – it was picked at Chaville last night by candlelight. I'll wrap it up for you. The wrapping's important, so hold it a minute. And don't forget, it'll bring you good luck!'

Club 65. Blinking lights. An old pansy who talks with a nasal twang. Sticks his beak through the peephole.

'Good evening. May I see your membership card?'

My membership card? I feel like sticking my ID under his beak – he's right out of the pussy patrol. I smile as I rummage through my purse pretending to look for a membership card. If you want to catch your guy with his pants down, it's best to make a quiet entrance.

'I'm terribly sorry, I must have forgotten it. It doesn't matter. My husband's waiting for me inside.'

'*I'm* terribly sorry, mademoiselle,' yaps the Pekingese. 'I can't let you in without a card. It's a private club.'

You know what you can do with your 'mademoiselle' and your 'private club' – I fan myself with Jean-Jean's hundred-franc note. The bill tickles his nostrils, and I can't believe that on top of everything else the faggot is blind.

'Terribly sorry. If you haven't got a card and you don't care to give me your name—'

'I know, it's *private*! Good *night*. Taxi! Hey, taxi! Drive me some place for ninety francs. Just drive.'

I have to leave part of the contents of my purse at the door: nail files, matches, a ballpoint pen, tweezers, two Bufferins, a pocketknife, a comb with a pointed handle, a silk scarf, and the plastic bag filled with presents for France. I would have liked to give them to her myself.

I'm waiting in a cubicle whose walls have been daubed a sickly green. Its only furnishings are an iron table painted the same colour and two benches – the one I've just sat down on and another that, like me, is waiting for France to arrive. She wasn't joking when she said there were birds at Saint-Lazare. This is the fifth that's landed on the windowsill. They're hungry, the poor little things, hungry and cold. I've got nothing to give you. Not a thing. But why do they frighten her? What harm can a sparrow do?

Judging from what the social worker said to me, France must have told her that I worked with her at the beauty parlour.

It's lucky I know all about her training period at Oréal; lucky, too, that the lady didn't insist on seeing my salary vouchers. It's a world full of bastards.

There she is – I recognize her footsteps.

Sure enough, it's her.

'France – Franzie! How are you?'

We clutch each other.

'Why didn't you come yesterday? I was waiting.'

'No whispering, ladies, or we'll have to cut the visit short. Speak so that you can be heard, please.'

France shoots her a baleful look.

'There's a case of frustration for you. Doesn't look like she gets her chimney reamed clean very often.'

'Shh! Please, we haven't all that much time.'

'Don't worry, she's got to keep an eye on the others, too. Did you bring me some goodies? Some smokes?'

'Even a sewing kit. And books, toilet articles, cologne, a nightgown, a change of undies, and something else you really wanted.'

'What's that?'

'A rabbit's foot. I asked my butcher to save me one. I've got it right here in my pocket.'

'You're a good girl.'

Without her wig and false eyelashes, without the three layers of makeup that barely manage to make her look healthy, floating inside a smock that's much too big for her (but which, coquettish to the end, she has tied at the waist with a piece of string), France looks all of fifteen. Her wide eyes radiate a kind of candour that would be unimaginable to anyone who has seen her at the Saint-Louis.

'What happened the other day? Did they let you out early?'

'No, we were the last to go, because we'd raise hell. Kim took off – she jumped out of the window.'

'They'll put a lousy report in her file.'

'She doesn't care. She says that's better than spending a night here.'

'She's right.'

'Jojo busted her leg when she jumped. She's in the hospital.'

'Terrible luck! What about you – you stayed put?'

'I didn't have the nerve to jump.'

'It's probably just as well. And Pedro – what did she say

about it all? She must hate my guts. If they close the place, it's partly on account of me.'

'Speak a little lower, Big Mama is listening to you on the sly. When I went there yesterday, the door was shut. That's all I know.'

The matron shuffles off.

'Did you see my old man?'

'Last night. You can't imagine how happy he looked when he saw me come into the bar. We sat in a corner together.'

'What'd he say?'

'There, here's the hundred francs he told me to give you – and your rabbit's foot.'

Everything disappears then and there into the privacy of her panties.

'He said not to worry. He'll get his connections moving, and they'll spring you fast.'

'What else?'

'He said to keep smiling.'

Faced with those hungry eyes, I lower my own. The piece of string dangling from her waist has been reduced to a tangle of tight little knots. Cracking her knuckles, she asks in a choked voice:

'That's all? He didn't say anything else?'

'You know how bashful men get when they have to talk about their feelings. All I can say is, he looked very sad. He's worried to death.'

'Okay. Great. And your old man – what does he think about all this?'

'We hardly had time to talk. When I got home, he was on the way to his tailor's. He was supposed to call me at your place – at the bar. He must have forgotten.'

France has been swinging her legs back and forth underneath the table. Our feet touch. Her eyes blink. I feel like bawling. I sense that there's something she's about to tell me and that it's not easy getting it out. She's making a real effort.

'Listen.'

She glances hastily at the door before going on. She speaks quickly; her voice is muffled.

'If I've got to go back to La Roquette, I'd rather call it quits. My father and brothers wouldn't put up with it again, especially now that they know Jean-Jean. You understand, I introduced him as my husband. Sophie, there's one thing I've got to be sure of: if I ask you for a gun, will you bring me one? Answer me honestly.'

'You mustn't talk like that, Franzie. You'll be out soon. Please, you're getting me all upset.'

'Sophie, would you bring me one?'

'Yes.'

Our legs are linked under the table. I'm no longer able to hold back my tears. She grasps my hand tight in hers. She's biting her fingers – and my fingers. I take her free hand and press it against my mouth so as not to scream. We blubber together in rhythm – choking, dribbling, slobbering, blowing bubbles: we're sadder than wet cats.

'Sophie, remember what I told you when you started out? How there's no point looking for friendship from girls in this racket, because you won't find it? I think I was wrong. I know I was.'

Big Mama has just resurfaced. She has a little bag of candies in one hand; with the other she's picking her teeth.

'Look at that scumbag. I'd rather be in my shoes than hers.'

'So would I.'

'And what nice things are my little girls telling one another? Not feeling sad, are you?'

'No, ma'am, we're on top of the world – right, Sophie?'

'On top of the world! If my girl friend says so, then it must be true.'

Reassured, the matron moves on.

'Sophie, I thought about you last night – about the time you first came to work. Remember?'

'I'll say. How could I forget!'

'You should have seen yourself. You looked like a sausage in that tight black dress. And perched on those stilts you told everybody you were from London! You came on like a real prewar hooker. You didn't dare sit down.'

'You were settled on the bidet doing a crossword puzzle. I noticed you because you were the only one who didn't give me the once-over. You were the best of the crew.'

'Remember how the others asked you to stand on the bed and take all your duds off? The bitches! You fell on your face climbing on to the sack. Claudie was about to bust a gut when she helped you up, and you asked if you really had to go on and you began your striptease. What a disaster! Your bra was half falling off, the stitching was coming apart, and you had a safety pin holding the strap in place. Also your garter belt was turning tattletale grey ...'

'It was my mother's old one. I remember it all like it was yesterday. I started to cry. I was so ashamed! That's when you chimed in. You told them off: "So,,what of it? The rest of you were never beginners? Always had enough dough to wrap your ass in panties from Dior, didn't you? Get off her back, for Christ's sake!" And then when Muriel asked you what was wrong with having a little fun, and besides what the hell did it matter to you if they had a few laughs – you got up.'

'I got up – and wham, right in her kisser. She wasn't expecting that one. And while you pulled your clothes back on you kept yelling, "Stop, don't fight over me, I'm not worth it." One more time and I would have hit you, too! I was so uptight that night – I'd just had a screaming contest with my old man. Right after that there was a lineup, and the john chose you. Remember?'

'Do I remember! A guy from Bordeaux, and ex-soldier with a crew cut and clodhoppers. He slipped a two-hundred-franc tip under the ashtray. I almost didn't dare touch it. I couldn't believe it. He was a house regular besides, so there was no steerer to pay off. What a break! And so gentle too. He wouldn't let me wash him up. He put on a rubber, so I didn't have to put in my diaphragm. And the guy didn't even fuck me. He came by rubbing himself against my belly. You know, I get him every time he comes to Paris. If it's my night off, he goes away. Arlette told me. Guys really are funny.'

'Yeah. I've got two or three like that myself. Old faithfuls.'

'When I came back, you were on the bidet again. Nobody was talking. You winked at me and held out a pack of weeds. My first cigarette. You moved over and made room for me. I didn't say anything, but it was damned uncomfortable. You taught me how to play poker – and I lost everything the guy had given me! What a laugh.'

'You didn't find it all that funny at the time.'

'That's true. Speaking of bread – you remember your stash, those five hundred francs you'd stuck in your compact? Whatever made you decide to powder your nose during dessert?'

'It was shiny – and so were my old man's eyes when he saw

that five hundred francs floating in the baked Alaska. I had to confess to a little afternoon moonlighting.'

'Everybody has a stash. The thing is, it always goes up in smoke.'

'Like Claudie's. You've got to be pretty crazy to stash your jack in the oven! But you know, she's so tight, she found a way of mending those scorched bills? It seems her old man was in tears. He told her she was breaking his heart, that with the price of sea bass what it was it would take her fifteen years to pay off that dinner.'

'Franzie, what's that bell?'

'Visit's over.'

'Already?'

'Let's go, ladies. It's closing time. Hurry it up.'

'France, I hope they give you everything.'

'Don't lose any sleep over it – I've got this.'

She touches the crotch of her panties as Big Mama pushes me towards the exit.

Fortunately for her and for us, Pedro not only runs the Saint-Louis but also owns several bars: La Hacienda on Rue Victor-Massé, La Fiesta on Rue Frochot, and La Bohème, on the same street. La Bohème faces the Macao, an up-and-coming hotel where she's gone partners with her lover, Monsieur Dahl. He's a dirty little runt, five foot three, with a few hairs gummed down on his head. Like his mistress, he perfumes himself with Vol de Nuit. His one passion – aside from money – is his three poodles. We call him Baby Dahl.

Two days after the raid, since we've received no instructions and our pimps are starting to beef, we all show up at the Saint-Louis at half past ten. Pedro is waiting for us in room number 3, the practical jokes room – actually, the salon.

There she is, our boss-lady, in her printed silk dress, comfortably settled in the easy chair where the customers sit to make their choice. As always, we gather around her in a circle. We stand there decked out in our tight black dresses, our sprayed hair, our false eyelashes that almost wink by themselves. Behind our backs we clutch our handbags in our hot mitts. We rehearse our sweetest come-hither smiles, while she licks smooth the vermilion polish on her parrot-like nails. But we aren't thinking about money. No, this lineup is a more serious one.

When Madame Pedro makes her choice tonight, it will mean much more than ten minutes in one of the bedrooms with a ten-tonner on top of you. It will mean not a hundred francs, or two hundred, or a thousand: it may mean starting work at a new job, with other customers, other hours, other girls, other places – and champagne pouring out of every hole in your body.

And if tonight nineteen of us are curling up our toes inside our pumps, it's because we have made a choice. We want to stay out of the bars. We want not to drink. Of course, at the Saint-Louis we sometimes order a half-bottle, or even a full one. It may happen with a house regular, or with a rube who's out on the town. We get our kickback: twenty francs on the half, forty on the full. But it happens so rarely. And it's so easy to tip your glasses on to the carpeting or down the drain. Louis-ette and Inna have proved very accommodating; sometimes they even share a glass with us.

We dread bars as much as the sidewalk.

At the Saint-Louis we're in clover. We start work at ten-thirty in the evening and finish at five-thirty the next morning. The customers are almost all house regulars – that is, steady patrons – and the least-favoured girl has her own little follow-ing. The price is a hundred francs a shot for a 'house' customer –in other words, a man who hasn't been steered there. That's split sixty for us and forty for the madam, and we're allowed to ask for a little something extra, as long as we don't press the point. For a 'steered' or a 'taxi' customer, we pull in forty, forty goes to the house, and there are twenty left for the steerer or the cab driver.

Sometimes we put on a show as well. This is almost invariably a steered affair. Each performance nets us eighty francs even, and rarely a centime more: there is always at least one person in each group who won't reach into his pocket for the 'supple-ment', so that even those who are more kindly disposed scratch their cheeks with one hand while they put away their cash with the other.

Pedro is still smoothing her nails with little licks of her tongue. We've been standing here so long we're beginning to take root.

'May I shift to my other foot?' asks Muriel.

'No irony, madame, please! This is hardly the proper moment.'

When she's angry, Pedro forgets our first names and addresses us formally. She straightens up a little, shakes her blonde head, clears her throat, smooths the pleats of her dress, and adopts an expression of calculated fury.

'Louisette!' she screams in a hysterical voice.

The chambermaid appears at the door. Her mouth is open, her arms are hanging limply; she looks as though she had just lost something, or someone.

'You're sure the front door is locked?'

'I shut it myself, Madame Pedro.'

'Don't just stand there. Go down and tell Arlette to come upstairs. And tell Inna to turn out the lights. If somebody rings the bell, say we're shut, say we're closed for repairs, but don't let anyone in.'

We shift from one foot to the other. We've criticized the madam, we've despised her, we've even hated her – and yet right now we're so repentant that we're ready to get down on our knees, beg forgiveness, crawl on our bellies to her. That bitch knows it, too. In fact she's so sure of it that she greedily drags her pleasure out, making our agony increase with every passing second. Muriel farts in protest.

'You are disgusting, madame. You'll end on a street corner.'

'That's okay by me as long as I'm pulling in the bread,' Muriel responds, wiggling her rump.

'Out! I'm not keeping you – not here or anywhere else. When you get "home", say I expect a call. I should never have taken you on again.'

'You old buzzard! You'd better look out before one of your dives is blown sky high! So long, girls. Keep your noses clean.'

Out goes Muriel; and we can hear the wind raging across the tundra. Our friend has really brought off her exit. She spat out her mind, and now we'll get the spray.

I've just raised my hand, to ask if I may go to the bathroom, when in comes Arlette. Armed with her unfailing smile, she slips her hands beneath her white apron as she waddles into our circle. Her soft, pear-shaped countenance betrays not the slightest concern. From the depths of their sockets, her dark-rimmed eyes look from one to the other as if to say, 'Don't let it get to you, girls. It's only for a while. Good times will soon be back.'

Arlette, our ally, our sister. She watches over our failings, our blunders, and our late arrivals. She shares our joys and sorrows. She really knows how to sweet-talk our men – she can convince them that we're upstairs when actually we've just phoned in to say that we'll be an hour late, because there's a good movie showing, or we've been dawdling in a restaurant, or (but she never tries to find out) we have a date: and the men hang up reassured. Arlette knows how to coddle our pimps on the other end of the line. And she wishes she were pretty enough to take a turn in one of the rooms with the rest of us. Not that it stops her from taking care of herself, and very nicely, thank you. Arlette's an expert at juggling figures – a real CPA! At five-thirty in the morning she quietly takes us aside and says, 'All right, Sophie, you turned twelve tricks, but officially it'll be eight,' and I get to pocket the difference. She pampers the big earners: with us, she can cheat. It means that we lose some prestige in the madam's eyes. But what counts is pulling in the change and making the house a success. When all is said and done, nobody's the loser.

So why doesn't the old biddy spit it out and get it over with? I've got red ants running up and down my pins, my pals' false eyelashes are starting to flutter – and all this for not even a single *sou*! It's just a rotten way of firing us. There are no unions in this business. Seems that one day a man mentioned the subject. They didn't let him finish his sentence – the dreamer died of a bad case of lead poisoning. Union shops are all right for big businesses, but turning tricks is a craft. We're artists, after all! Can you imagine the disaster if hookers ever decided to register for social security, or started picking up their wel-fare cheques and old-age pensions? Our men's daily bread would be threatened!

The old lady's not very talkative this evening. As she thinks about our ingratitude, she snorts like an old mare. I'm thinking about Gerry, who's terrified I may be out of work for a few days. He's been shedding tears of purest J & B over the twelve instalments on the white Mustang convertible with the red-leather upholstery that's supposed to be delivered this week. It's amazing how sensitive and concerned my old man can be! If I have one evening off, he's totally destroyed. Yes, but wait a minute. Don't get the idea that all he has to do is *rely* on me: he has to *deal* with me, too. I've been putting up less and less with the way he grabs my take when I come home at six-thirty in the morning – *if* I'm lucky enough to find him there. He spreads the bills out on the bed; and, if he isn't too drunk, he plugs in the iron, sets it on low, and presses them flat. Not long ago I told him that seeing him do that made me want to puke. He slapped my face and said that if I wasn't happy I could go sit in the john until he'd finished with his book-keeping. There's a true businessman for you. An entrepreneur with ambition.

One Sunday, soon after my debut at Pedro's, we went to an inn on the banks of the Marne, a place that belonged to some friends of his. I was struggling with my lobster (it was the first one I'd ever had) and idly watching the barges drift by. Between mouthfuls he quietly told me, 'You know, doll, when you've cheated on me with as many men as there are boats going past, we'll be in the clear.' A real poet, Gerry, but a poet with his feet on the ground. He's calling me around midnight to see how I made out in the beauty contest at the Saint-Louis.

Pedro keeps shifting around in her chair.

'Arlette – come sit next to me. And stop smiling! What I am about to say to you, ladies' – she underlines the word 'ladies' – 'is very serious.'

Personally, I couldn't agree more but when all's said and done, it means no more to me than last year's horoscope. The closing of the Saint-Louis won't cause me any more pain than having a wooden leg cauterized. The place was getting over-crowded. I was turning soft, like the oldtimers. *Olé*, Pedro! let's hear it. I'll go where I'm told. I've got what it takes for the big trip to the local version of the Iberian peninsula – to La Fiesta, or La Hacienda, or, best of all, La Bohème. I'm not worried about earning my keep. I've got visible resources, not to mention those I keep under wraps. So go on, Isabella of Castile, go on and let us have it. From now on I'm on your side, and I'm carry-ing some heavy artillery under my skirt. But be merciful, and say whatever it is you have to say : I also have a full bladder.

'What just happened to your friend Muriel should be as plain as the nose on your face.'

We look at each other's noses. They're no plainer than usual. I'm not the only one who's itching for some fun, although there are a few ass-lickers with tears in their eyes. A moist eye means a brown nose, and *those* girls will never fart in anyone's face.

People have been farting on them for at least ten years; they're so impregnated with the smell of shit that they no longer even dream of climbing out of it.

'Any of you with big ideas about working somewhere else can leave right now. I must warn you that we'll no longer have room here for all of you.'

The brown noses chorus:

'Oh, no, Madame Pedro, we wouldn't *think* of leaving!'

'I'll have to find a spot for you in the bars, and I'm not looking forward to it. Neither are my girls. There are too many of them as it is.'

'That's all right. We're used to a tight squeeze.'

'Shut up, Sophie, or you'll be on your way out, too.'

Arlette glances in my direction and raises two fingers to her lips. I pipe down and shift my weight on to the other foot.

'As you can see for yourselves, we've come to a sorry pass,' the boss-lady goes on, fanning herself with her Calais lace handkerchief, which reeks of Vol de Nuit. 'I've been all too easygoing. First of all I took on Madame France. I was not informed she was a minor.'

Sylviane clears her throat.

'Even your men have lied to me. Yes, Madame Sylviane, they have – even though they eat from my table! And I've no objection to your telling them that when you go home.'

'Well, it's been a long time since I was underage, so save your comments for someone else. As for the girls my husband recruited, I don't think you have anything to complain about. They were all over twenty-one.'

Sylviane doesn't have to worry about having rank pulled on her. She's known Pedro for twelve years, and Pedro is well acquainted with the Neapolitan woman's fiery temper: recently they had an argument and Sylviane crowned her with a pot of begonias. So Pedro goes on to another subject.

'That's not my only reason for concern.' She stops to catch her breath and starts turning purple. 'Some of you have been stealing from the customers!'

Oh! Shocked, vexed, and insulted, we look around at one another. *Thieves* among us? The brown noses stare at their toes.

'Yes, ladies. Some of you steal, and you know it. Isn't that so, Madame Sophie? And I'm not forgetting your friend France, either.'

This time the old lady's going a little too far. I throw caution overboard, and I sail right in.

'Are you referring to the Jap who bitched about losing a thousand francs in number five? You know as well as I do I didn't steal them. You and Inna pulled the bed apart with your own hands. Before you stripped me, I even helped you turn the mattress over and move the box springs. Or is my memory playing tricks on me? Okay, so I wouldn't let you poke around inside me. I refused to let you take out my diaphragm, because I'd been with eight johns and I was a mess. We all know an abortion costs a hell of a lot more than a thousand francs – not to mention the bellyache, the probe, the hospital, and all the rest of it.'

'Madame, I'm not referring to anything or anyone in particular. If the shoe fits, wear it. And if you're not satisfied, get out. As for the thefts, I know what I'm talking about.'

There are times in life when you'd like to be someone else – someone a little less cowardly, a little more sure of yourself. I feel like crying, biting, fighting, letting her have it right in the gut: and I just stand there, rooted to the spot, helpless, weak, pathetic. There's no point in turning to the others for help. They're scared shitless. Arlette keeps waving at me with increasing anxiety. I remember what I used to tell myself when I started here and found out how old the oldtimers were: thirty. Me, still be here at thirty? I'd rather shoot myself. The thought consoles me now. I still have the same ideas – those big ideas. Only a year has passed – one year already! I can always shoot myself ...

Pedro goes on talking to the others. Her voice reaches me only faintly, if at all. It sounds muffled, soft, almost sweet through the snowy cumulus layers. I go drifting through the clouds and break through into the stratosphere. My heart is light. The muzzle of my .22 automatic is levelled at my jugular. Boondocks is with me, and she squeezes my hand. We're feeling great. Sunlight is splashing over us, purifying us. We're starting out fresh, and off we go down the highways of salvation. Meteors streak before our dazzled eyes. We forget everything. We forget brothels, johns, girls, bars, madams, hustlers, cops, Mustangs, barges, diaphragms, Vaseline, abortions, the Saint-Louis, Saint-Lazare, crabs, the clap, whips, dildos, wigs, false eyelashes, and our pimps. We no longer have what our pimps call 'strength of character'. But who gives a shit? Where we're going, it's superfluous. It doesn't exist. We never heard of it. It's something invented by pimps – and where we're going, there are no pimps, no men, and no women. There's us, just us and the clouds.

Pedro is still at it. She's keeping Jeanine, the maid; Michele, who's been there thirteen years and has a family to look after; Sylviane and her friend, Josiane; Cynthia, since she's the only black girl; Nathalie, because her lungs are shot; Brigitte, because she's a pneumatic mound of blubber; and Claudine, because she's an oldtimer. She'd like to keep Kim – guys go wild over the Eurasians – but since she's Muriel's friend, she'll have to fend for herself. Fabienne will take a vacation. Ever since her old man got his in a showdown two years ago, she's had no problems – just money in the bank. She finds the world is a nice place to live in. Martine will give Les Halles a try – she has a girl friend there on Rue du Cygne. She isn't exactly enchanted by the prospects but her girl friend has been flashing a big roll every time they run into each other, so things can't be all bad. Mona's ripe for one of the bars. She's spent two years at La Fiesta, and the idea even appeals to her, since she's something of a lush. Valerie and Pascale are heading for La Fiesta. Until La Bohème opens, Sandra and I will go to La Hacienda.

That's it. The house can hardly be said to exist any more. As Pedro leaves, she asks us to get moving. We drag up to room 19, neither talking nor laughing, almost like mourners. Fortunately, Arlette joins us: and as we peer into the closet and scream at one another trying to retrieve our worn out shoes and our old 'pro special' bras, she reminds us of lovely summer evenings when we used to tie water-filled condoms to strings and lower them on to the heads of the tourists below. We had a lot of fun. And now it's all over.

With our gear under one arm, we say so long to room 19, kiss Arlette goodbye, and walk up Rue Fontaine to Place Blanche; there we finally embrace and wish one another luck – even the ass-lickers join in. (Especially the ass-lickers!) Around us, Pigalle glitters festively. It's like a gigantic merry-go-round moved by some invisible force, it's like the soul of this group of pals who are scattering into the night, evaporating in the wind.

I walk on and find myself across the street from the Folies Bergère. The theatre is bathed in streams of multicoloured light.

'Feel like going upstairs, baby? What's the tab?'

There's no performance tonight, mister. Keep your money. I'm not the sort you think I am. Tonight I'm a free woman – and I'm going to Charlot Premier to eat my fill of oysters.

'What time is it? A new day steals into my room ...' That's from a song I used to sing in the sanatorium. It's eleven. I stretch out the full width of the bed. I guess Gerry forgot his address again. So what – I'm not going to let that spoil my good humour. Something tells me that outdoors the sun is shining. I feel good. My head is as big as a hill in Alsace – no doubt from to much Gewurztraminer last night. I ate as expensively as I could: seventy francs' worth. Belon oysters are great, but not when they come back up an hour later. That's enough to make you sick of them for ever. I like taking Alka-Seltzers. I hold the glass close to my face. It sends out a fine spray that prickles my lips, just like champagne. Oh, how I love champagne when I'm not getting a rake-off on it!

The sun *is* shining. How about fixing myself a nice cup of tea? What in the world can Gerry be doing? How can he still be out at this hour? Let's hope he hasn't been lured out of the country by another poker game. He pulled that on me once. Around four o'clock in the morning Arlette handed me the phone. A crackling sound on the other end.

'Hello, doll. It's me. Hop on the first plane to Brussels, and bring some dough with you. You'll be met at the airport. There's a flight from Le Bourget at eight.'

I didn't score again that night. After the place closed, I went home and emptied my cookie jar – miraculously intact, twenty-two hundred francs were nesting under the mattress. That made twenty-two hundred plus seven hundred and fifty: enough for a good-sized investment. I had spurred the cabbie on with promises of a fabulous tip. 'Step on it, driver. My old man may be in danger – or he may be locked into the biggest deal of the century.' At twenty to eight I was at Le Bourget; at ten to nine, still out of breath, I landed in Brussels.

I had no trouble finding my guardian angel. Impossible to

mistake him for a customs inspector. Everything about him screamed pimp from a mile away: his Prince of Wales suit, his spit-polished shoes, and the solid-gold watch in full view on his hairy wrist. Tossing his jade lighter from one hand to the other in a gesture of obvious impatience, he asked me, in his thick Marseilles accent, if I was Madame Gerard. 'Yes,' I said, and we tore through the Belgian capital.

I kept mum, as is proper for a woman in the life. He parked his wheels in front of a bar that looked shut. I followed him across a large dark hall, where chairs were resting legs up on wooden tables. We entered a smaller low-ceilinged room that was ill-lighted and smoky. There, gathered around a table, several other men were indulging in the pleasures of gambling with my darling Gerard. It was a comforting sight, the kind that gives you great confidence in the future.

I think that was the day that he really began to revolt me. Until then, I'd managed to find all kinds of excuses for him, and for myself as well. But that morning I saw him in an enlarging mirror. Not one of those small jobs, but a fine big one – shining and clear. It was hardly a pretty sight. He had a large nose overrun with little blue veins down to its round tip; tiny, rapacious eyes sunk deep in the hollows of his empty head; a full mouth spoiled by rotten teeth and capped by a sinister moustache; cheeks that managed to be simultaneously hollow and flabby; a complexion as lustreless as our life together. Of course, there were also his hands, those beautiful long white hands that were now deftly shuffling and dealing the cards, hands that had seduced me, and that I'd so lovingly kissed, hands that had made me come on the back seat of his Thunderbird as we sat parked in the suburb where I used to live, hands my father had been unable to put me on my guard against when he called them the hands of a loafer. They were all Gerard had left. It wasn't much it was hardly anything at all as far as I was concerned. Since those days, I'd become a lot harder to please.

He'd beckoned to me to come over. His breath was thick with tobacco and scotch. With consummate indifference I put the two thousand nine hundred and fifty francs down on the table. I settled into a chair and went on sitting there until noon. My head was empty, my legs weak, my eyes burning, and there was a bitter taste in my mouth. When we left the bar, we just wan-

dered around. On the corner of Rue des Petits-Bouchers, he
bought some sprats and some lukewarm potatoes. He hardly
had enough left to buy gas for the trip back to Paris. I remember
that on the way I felt like telling him that I wanted to leave
him, that it would be better that way, that together the two of
us would never get anywhere. Then, what with the fatigue, the
habit of just sitting there and pushing in the cigarette lighter
whenever I wanted to smoke, I said nothing. I turned on the
radio, watched the poplars fly past, and settled my head against
the warm leather. I slept. But to this day the cobblestone streets
of northern France have a special meaning for me.

This time, who knows? Beirut? Acapulco? Zanzibar? Someplace exotic, I hope. Whatever happens, I mustn't forget that
tonight is opening night for me. A new job. Tonight, it'll be the
Costa del Sol, the Costa Brava, and the world of flamenco. Tonight, at La Hacienda, I start all over again. I'd better be up to
it. What about going to the hairdresser's? Not a bad idea. I'll
walk as far as the taxi stand at Porte de Versailles.

It's nice out: grey and white, mild and cool at the same time.
I love going for a walk far away from Pigalle and becoming
just anybody. Marie doesn't attract whistles, but smiles. People
don't slap her on the ass, they gaze at her. They don't force her
to do anything; they ask her politely. And now she's become
quite overwhelmed by her joy, lowering her eyes, smiling back.
She's touched. Her heart is brimming with tenderness for the
tots that are being bounced along in their carriages. She says a
word or two to the contented mothers. She sniffs the talc, and
cologne, the milk. She checks an impulse to stroke a clean, un-
blemished cheek – she steps back, dreaming of some day knowing this bliss. But not with him. Never.

In the taxi I think about Evelyne. She's promised that if she
sees my customers, my regulars, she'll send them on to La Hacienda. I don't really believe her, knowing perfectly well that
she'll do everything she can to keep them for herself. Those are
the rules of the game. In her shoes, I wouldn't behave any dif-
ferently. Anyway I kind of like Evelyne.

She's remained a servant at heart. She's only a halfway
hooker, a dumb little working girl who's become street-smart,
and that's all. What bugs the other girls most is that in spite
of all their tricks and schemes, they've never succeeded in

making her take a pimp. Outings at Deauville, hunting week-ends in the Sologne, skiing at Megève, *la dolce vita* of Saint-Tropez and the luxurious inns of Saint-Germain-en-Laye don't impress her at all. And this fresh, forthright kid from Normandy has never hesitated to tell them as much to their faces. Those whoremongers, those man-obsessed women, weren't able to swallow that. Once five of them even jumped her with the firm intention of shaving every last hair of her head. We fought like tigers – France and I along with Evelyne, who was determined not to get scalped. When she emerged, she was minus a few fistsful of hair, and her dress was fit for the garbage can. It's hard to make your own place in the sun when you've decided to remain independent. All of which makes me like Evelyne. She says that when she has her own inn up north, I'll always be welcome in case I'm up shit creek, or if I need a job, or a place to hole up. I hope things never get that bad, but that's nice to hear. Right now, she's shacked up with a waiter from the Balto – someone who actually works for a living. His name's Loulou; seems he's nice to her and has no designs on her savings. His only weakness is the bottle, but she's working on the problem. When she leaves for work at ten, she locks him in. I think she'll make it. At any rate, whenever she confides in me, I bombard her with advice. She listens and then tells me it wouldn't hurt if I thought about myself a little bit.

So I'll think about myself, focus on little Sophie, breeze into the beauty parlour, and gaily tell my Figaro: 'Turn me into a raving beauty!'

chapter four

It's the same nearly everyplace. There's a curtain separating the entrance from the main room, and a record of second-rate jazz is spinning somewhere. Can Sandrine already have arrived? I drank four Cinzanos at La Cloche d'Or before coming. My head is hot and my temples are throbbing. Come on now, Sophie, your stage fright can't be that bad. Nobody's going to eat you alive. Hookers are the same everywhere. They may give you a dirty look and not respond to your greeting – so what? Go in. Go on in. What are you waiting for? If only I'd seen Gerard, we could at least have talked a little. He's never there when I need him. Starting out at a new place and not knowing where my old man is – it's a big help. Just what I need.

'Pardon me – going in or out?'

'In.'

'Well, move it. You're not allowed to stand in the doorway.'

Sounds great! A promising start.

'Hi, everybody. Look what I found behind the curtain.'

What she found is me.

'I'm from the Saint-Louis.'

'You're Sophie?'

'Yes, madame.'

'Well, Sophie, I hope you like it here with us. It'll be a change for you. Working at a bar's different. Did Madame Pedro tell you anything at all about it?'

'No, madame.'

'My girls will fill you in. Patricia – or you, Janou, look after our little Sophie.'

Madame Jacqueline, I love you. You look like the wife of the butcher on the street where I grew up. I can see you're not nasty, that you never will be to me, that you probably never are to the others.

'Like something to drink? You're entitled to three drinks a night on the house. Consuelo will take care of it.'

Consuelo is a rolypoly little woman, pretty and smiling, who seems to have come straight from the suburbs of Madrid. We exchange smiles. I perch my butt on a stool and start unwinding. Three girls are rolling dice at the far end of the bar. Others in the red plush shadows are combing their hair, stroking their cheeks with tiny silk brushes, and speaking in hushed voices. Where's the gusto of the Saint-Louis, the laughter, the gags, the shouts, the tears – where's my opening night? In their outmoded dresses, the girls here look like ghosts, or like languid declawed cats. My fears evaporate. There's no aggressivity here. What makes them like this, and why? Only Madame Jacqueline and Consuelo seem alive.

Patricia talks in gentle, muted tones, with a faint, singsong Provençal accent. She's pretty: she wears her blonde hair in a chignon on the nape of her neck, and her green eyes need almost no makeup. A smile lights up her perfect oval face: her old man is getting out. She'll be retiring in July.

'I'm thirty-three. It's about time! You'll see, Madame Jacqueline is really nice, and the customers are okay, too. It's two hundred a trick – a hundred and ten for you when it's a house client, and ninety when he's been steered here. You can ask a little extra in the room. You make forty francs on a bottle of champagne. You can take out a half-bottle, too – that's twenty for you – but full bottles are preferred. On an all-night job, you owe the house three hundred. For a group scene, you ask for three hundred and leave the house one-fifty. We do a few circuses, but not often. There's a rotation system for days off. In general, Sundays are slack. But some girls like Sundays – it's not a problem. Talk to Jacqueline about it.'

'What about Pedro – does she show up often?'

'She drops in.'

'Where's "upstairs"?'

'The girls who've been around the longest get to go next door four times a night. It cuts down on the chances of a raid. The rooms are clean. Otherwise, you have to go to the Macao on Rue Frochot.'

'How much can a girl average if she's willing to work?'

'It depends. First of all, there are no big winners here. We all make four or five hundred francs, except for Janou and Doris, the two blacks from Martinique. There's always a big demand for them. But you're young – why don't you try working the street? It's not bad, you know. Some of my girl friends—'

'Oh, no. Not me! Say, I'm going to have another Cinzano.'

'Sophie, sweetheart, tell me – haven't you got anything a little dressier?'

'I get a lot of action in a skirt and sweater, Madame Jacqueline.'

'Well, we'll see.'

Hey, all you customers! The Cinzano's throbbing away inside my skull. Let's not be shy now! I'm not used to waiting around like this and I'm getting calluses on my ass. Full speed ahead, Charlie, cruise right in here before I get rusty. Normally I'd have scored three times by now. There would have been a house regular, a guy from Toulouse or some place like that, and I'd be starting on my first tourist. I'd already have stashed away at least three hundred francs. Get going, Charlie, let's hear it from you. Sock it to me, buster.

'Consuelo, do you have that record of Brel's, "When All You Have Is Love"?'

Yes, I know, it's not on the Spanish hit parade, but I'm starting to feel high, and I get sentimental on such occasions. The little lady from Madrid cheerfully complies and squats down behind the bar. It'll be great if she's always like this. But am I hallucinating? No, it's the real McCoy – *olé!* He enters with lowered head, oblivious of the danger. The crowd cheers as he circles the arena and then charges the cape. Let the sangría flow, Sophie! I prepare the banderillis. His black eyes gaze at me. He's getting mistrustful now. He backs away, pawing the ground, then comes back for more. It's my turn to gaze at him. He's no bull calf, for all his restiveness: he's well into his forties. Give me my *traje de luces*, and stick a rose between my teeth. A pass with my muleta, and I've got him! But he's a brawler – he's charging again. Now, the veronica across the heart ... The crowd falls silent. He bows his head in defeat.

'Sophie's the name.'

'Delighted to meet you.'

He kisses my hand. I'll proceed to the kill later. Later – but right now, come closer. Let me stroke your horns. Let me tame you. That's it, Maurice. Be nice.

'Monsieur Maurice is Minouche's friend. He's a writer. The usual, Maurice? Do you want it served in the back?'

Curtain. (Jacqueline has pulled it shut.) So here we are, Maurice and I, sealed off from the world. I imagine this is where you get a good grope before you go upstairs. If he *is* going upstairs ... O Saint Sophia, my patron and only saint, pray for me! Let me score!

'You're new here? I have the feeling you haven't been in this line of work very long? Am I right or not?'

'You're not far off.'

'That schoolgirl's outfit really turns me on, but suppose you stop playing the duchess. Look, I'm getting long in the tooth, and I know you girls inside out. For the last two years I've been trying to pry one of you out of this place. Minouche. I'm planning to marry her and send her old man back to his misery. But I like you. Tonight I'm going to treat myself to a little change of pace.'

'I know you like me.'

'Listen, you – if I ask you to wait for me, you won't go running off with some john, will you?'

'As long as you don't catch the Orient Express and it isn't the Emir of Kuwait who invites me out on the town.'

'Wait for me, baby. I'll be right back.'

Just my luck to pick some nut who specializes in pipe dreams.

'Sophie dear, what's happening? Monsieur Maurice just went rushing out. I hope you weren't disagreeable to him?'

'On the contrary ... What exactly does he write?'

'Thrillers. You know he's got it bad for Minouche. It's a long story ...'

At the table facing mine, Janou has just sat down opposite a fat man. She calls him 'my beloved'. He's kissing her fingers and reciting poetry:

Thy mouth makes beat my blood in feverish rhymes,
Therefore so many as there roses be
Kiss me so many times ...

She laughs, the idiot, and he looks at her as though he loves her. Jacqueline has disappeared behind the red curtain. It's midnight. I haven't one penny in my purse, and Gerard hasn't called. (Gerard hasn't called in a long time.) It's been a strange night.

A new couple has just appeared at one of the tables. The girl laughs a nervous little laugh and pulls down her dress.

'Wait a sec, sweetie, not here in front of everybody. Take it easy.'

The people here aren't interested in watching them, and the man knows it. He isn't the patient kind. He wants to feel, now, right away. Feel and be felt. Between two glasses of champagne he quickly writes out a cheque. The girl takes it and bends down. Her head disappears beneath the dark tablecloth.

The poet continues:

Pleasure, and the pulse that stuns the ears,
And the heart's gladness of the goodly game –
Let me think yet a little; I do know
These things were sweet, but sweet such years ago,
Their savour is all turned now into tears ...

'Here you are, Sophie. I wish there'd been more. I went all the way round the square looking . . .'

'You're crazy! I'll never find enough vases to put them in.'

'Then we'll buy some. There'll be roses for you every morning when you wake up. Come on, let's get out of here. I feel like looking at you someplace else – someplace in the light. I'll pay for your staying out. It won't be the first time. *Vamos*, little one.'

'What about the roses?'

'Jacqueline will take care of them. Let's go.'

It's been a strange night indeed.

'I'm cold. Where are we going?'

'Anyplace where we can make love. You're not cut out for this kind of work. What the hell do your pimps do to all of you? That's all right, don't worry – you'll be able to show him a nice take for this night's work.'

He *is* a strange guy. 'Anyplace' doesn't turn out to be quite what I'd imagined. The luxurious apartment gradually fades away as I climb the stairs of a grimy hotel that smells of bed lice, brown soap, and cum. A hotel 'for transients', Hôtel Pigalle.

Disappointed, I silently undress. Maurice, on his knees, is looking at me. Get up, Maurice – you may be wide open, but I won't insist on finishing you off. I'm tired. And you might show a little mercy yourself. No, you won't. The bright glitter that flares in your black eyes tells me that I won't be spared. Poor me!

Go ahead, Maurice, help yourself – but do it fast. This place is giving me the creeps. The bedspread is sticky. Don't keep going after my lips. They belong to me – they're about the only thing I've kept intact! Turn your face away, you're dripping sweat. And don't jiggle around so much. What's the point of making the springs squeak? Oh, stop looking at me like that. It's not my fault if you can't get it up. No, in spite of the roses, the champagne, and the fabulous cheque, I'm not going to make a special effort. You're really out of luck. On some other evening, when I was in the mood, I could do all kinds of stunts for you – cartwheels, headstands, backflips, anything. I'm really sorry. You seem like a nice guy, the kind of nut I go for. There's nothing repulsive about you. Your body's almost like an adolescent's. Your mouth is fresh. Your shorts are clean.

Your armpits are beginning to perspire, but I can't really blame you for that. You're doing everything you can to make me feel good, aren't you, Maurice? You're trying to make me happy. You're going at it with a will – the only thing is, you can't get it halfway up. Your cock's like a damp rag, and this isn't my night for playing the Good Samaritan. Tough luck for both of us. We're going to have to find our separate stairways to paradise, that's all there is to it. It's every man for himself – but that's no reason to get hot and bothered.

'Sophie, you've got me so worked up, I can't get a hard-on. I've been drinking, but it isn't that. Let's have a smoke, then you can go.'

'I'll go.'

'You won't say anything to Miriam?'

'I don't even know her. Can't you call your own shots when you pay the freight?'

'She almost got herself done in on my account.'

'There's a good subject for one of your books. The repentant hooker who chucks it all for the love of a customer. It'll make 'em weep.'

'Don't be cynical. It's not your style.'

'How do you know? Listen, Maurice, I don't give a damn about your romance with Miriam. It leaves me cold. And since you pretend to be so much in the know, let me tell you something else. All that matters to me is the bread. That's *it*. We could have had fun together. You're making a tragedy out of it. Well, that's your problem. Anyhow, you're forgetting to mention that so far you've coughed up a hundred thousand to bail out your Juliet. That's a lot of money, a hundred thou. I don't know of many men who'd have done it. Just between us, Maurice, are you sure her old man wanted to knock her off? Let me finish. She's thirty-five years old, and I gather she's spent fourteen of them turning tricks. She's a kid on crutches. Sorry to sound so sceptical, but I don't see where the fuck sentiments come into it.'

'You're cruel.'

'Not exactly. Light me another, will you? I see things clearly – realistically, if you prefer. My own bag happens to be making mental movies – I run short subjects all night long! Tonight I'm tired, so I'm talking. I'm saying whatever comes into my mind. I've had it up to here – no, up to *here*: but I'd never be capable of playing Miriam's game. *Never*. And why not quit pretending you're somebody else? What would happen if you stopped dreaming about packing a gun and started digging the fact that you pack a fountain pen? Don't you think it might make life a little simpler? You're generous in the same way hoods are. You fuck their women. You talk their language. What more do you need? Danger? A few years in the clink? Being on the run year after year? Tell me about it – I'm dying to understand.'

'Sophie, you're turning me on more and more. I want to make you come.'

'Wouldn't you just as soon tell me about yourself?'

'I don't know any more.'

'Have you got a wife? Kids?'

'She was put away. She's been in the asylum for eleven months now. I've got three daughters. Minouche adores them.'

'So why aren't you living together?'

'She's paying off the fine her pimp laid on her. I've already thrown in the hundred thou.'

'That ought to help.'

'It's only the down payment – half the full amount.'

'That *is* bad news.'

'Soph, I don't know if I'll still feel the same way about it then, but right now I'd like it if three months from now you came south with me and my three kids. I have a house in Saint-Raphael. Five thousand for two weeks – that ought to keep your old man quiet.'

'An awful lot can happen in three months. I don't like making promises.'

'Why don't I give you my phone number and address. I'll be expecting a call from you – or a visit. You can clear out now, if you want.'

Extravagant, generous Maurice! I wouldn't mind spending some time with you – but I've got to think about tomorrow. And does this fly crawling across my forehead mean that there's a storm brewing?

'Since when have you been telling johns your real name? Is this some bright new idea of yours? And answer me when I talk to you!'

'Would you rather he'd made it out of my ass? Or to you?'

'You're way out of line. You're forgetting how to talk to me, and I'm going to have to straighten you out.'

'You're the one who makes me that way. You and your insinuations and dumb questions. I suppose I should have told the guy, just make it out to plain Sophie?'

'Of course not. What's wrong with "Cash"?'

'So the first guy I meet can snatch my purse and pocket the thousand I sweated for? Boy, when you want to sound like an asshole, it really comes easy.'

'Belting you one is going to come even easier if you don't cool it.'

'Listen, we haven't seen each other for two days. You're not going to start all over again.'

'No. I'm just going to keep going. So now you're spending your nights with just one guy. At that price, he must have really socked it to you.'

'He didn't even fuck me, if you care to know. He couldn't get it up. Feeling better? Anyway, out of the thousand, I owe three hundred for staying out, plus two bottles at seventy-five each. Go on, you're so good at figures : how much profit does that leave you?'

'If you don't stop riding me, you're going to get it.'

'I'm not riding anybody. I'm just putting two and two together.'

'You're digging your own grave. And wipe that look off your face before I do! Who is this guy?'

'How the hell do I know? You think I ask them for a résumé? And why don't you quit trying to make me think you're jealous? It won't work, no matter what you do.'

'How stupid do you think I am? A guy who shacks up with a whore for a whole night has plenty of time to talk about himself. Did he give you his phone number at least? Or his address? Where'd you go – his place or a hotel? What's his name?'

'Gus. We went to the Pigalle, across the street. The place where your ex-wife is working.'

'Knock it off – don't start on that again. Gus who?'

'Gus Horseshit!'

'You're going too far, Sophie. You really *want* to get belted?'

'You're the one who's going too far. You'd rather see me knock off ten guys for the same price. That's what you want, right? Ten in a row – that would guarantee that I didn't have time to get off. Admit it. Well, don't worry, I haven't gotten off in a long time – not with you or anybody else. The possibility has somehow slipped my mind. Vanished without a trace. I have this great void between my thighs. A hole, a slit, a piggy bank, a jackpot. A void!'

'Shut up, you tramp, or you'll have the cops on our neck. That's what you'd like – getting me picked up. Then you'd be sitting pretty.'

'Real pretty. That's it, hit me. Go on and hit me if you've still got the balls. Hit me harder, you creep, you're not even hurting me. Bust me open, you faggot. Go on, bust me open, bust me wide open. Not there, Gerard! Gerard, not my breasts. Gerard, you're hurting me, stop, please, please. Look, I'm bleeding. There's blood on me. No more, Gerard, no more. Not my head, not my head ... My hand – you're crushing my fingers.'

'On your knees!'

'On my knees, but take your foot off – please!'

'You're shit.'

'If you say so.'

'Not "if I say so". You're shit.'

'Okay, I'm shit. Now get your foot off.'

'You're going to be fucking Arabs in Clignancourt. That'll teach you what life is all about.'

'And you're going to be taking it up the ass. The day I start fucking Arabs, ducks will start dressing for dinner.'

'You're going to get the works, bitch.'

'Go ahead, you bastard, give me the works. That way you can add a new trophy to all the crabs and lice you've killed.'

You can keep right on hitting me. I don't feel a thing any more. Just don't forget that the concierge is balling the chief of the Fifteenth Arrondissement; and the butcher, the florist, the people in the neighbourhood, they all know you – you and your big cars, you and your pimp's face.

And when I'm finally laid to rest, you'll be rotting in jail, like a grub. Like a turd. Then one morning, at dawn, they'll come for you.

'You little shit! Put down those scissors. Put them down!'

That morning a fine, icy rain will be falling. Your lawyer and a few other men will be standing in the deserted prison yard, where the guillotine's been set up. It'll be barely dawn and they'll be anxious to get back to their warm beds.

'If you don't want to get cut, stay away. Get back.'

Since you'll be half dead with fright, they'll have to hold you up by the arms and drag you all the way to the guillotine. You'll sob and shit in your pants. Your pants and your shoes will be loaded, full of stinking shit. The lawyer and the others will hold their noses in disgust. As you climb the wooden steps, you'll squirm like some enormous fish on the end of a line. You'll start shedding your scales. Your gills will be going in and out spasmodically and you'll be a pathetic sight. In spite of the rain, you'll feel like a fish out of water, Gerry! You'll be ready for the frying pan.

'If you're interested in prolonging your career as a pimp, let me through. Get your ass out of that doorway. I need air.'

'You're crazy! What are you trying to prove? Think what you're doing!'

'I am. Now step aside. And move it!'

'But baby—'

' "Baby" is dead and buried. Let me out. I'm hurting. There's nothing here that'll make me feel any better. Nothing, and no one. Move!'

'You're nuts. They'll arrest you. Take a look at yourself in the mirror. The cops'll make a beeline here. Have you thought about *me*?'

'That's all I ever do. Call me a taxi.'

'You're going to your mother's?'

'Sure I am. She'll be really delighted to see me like this.'

'Don't go!'

'Drop dead!'

'Rue Boursault, please. Number fifty-one.'

'Hey, what happened to you, lady? You sure you don't want me to take you to a hospital?'

'My pressure cooker exploded. Pow! Got me right in the head. Rue Boursault. Fast.'

Mister, I'll go to the hospital right afterwards. Yes, of course I will. Cross my heart. Honest.

So here I am reduced to explaining myself to cabdrivers. I would laugh, if my lips weren't so swollen. Oh, that scumbag! He's probably packed his things by now – that is, if he hasn't gone back to bed. The dumb jerk. The impotent son of a bitch. What did I ever do to deserve a creep like him. In the future – if there is a future – I'm going to have to be more careful. You see, mister, he might turn mean. Even dangerous.

Meanwhile, I wonder what kind of a face Maurice is going to make when he sees mine. I think I'll start of by speaking to him through the door. Is he in for a surprise! He was hardly expecting me so soon; but after all, he's responsible for what happened. If only he remembers me. With a man, you can never tell. One day he loves you, wants to reform you. You're the only woman in the world, the girl he's been waiting for. Next week, right under your nose, he's on his way upstairs with a girl who in no way resembles you – who's completely different. And that's when you have to be careful. You mustn't smile; above all, you mustn't get the bright idea of saying hello. When he sees you, he pulls a long face. He's forgotten you, old girl. Your insistence embarrasses him. You read a mixture of disgust and contempt in his eyes. How did he ever manage to fuck you? That's a tough question. Luckily, the other girl's rump is swaying in front of him, at just the right distance. He casts one last look at you, and then and there the mystery vanishes. All becomes clear, both to him and to you. He's found the woman who will restore his manhood, and you've lost a trick – a good one. And yet each week for three months you've been going upstairs with him. Guys are like that: as changeable as the weather. Not all of them, fortunately. You're left with the hope that Maurice belongs to the category of those who don't forget – and that he has enough change to pay for your cab.

chapter five

'Hi there, big girl. I'm writing you from a customer's apartment, where I've been convalescing for the last two days. Don't panic, everything's all right. Nobody tried to strangle me with a wet towel. I didn't get a shiv in my innards. I was just stomped on by Gerard, in a big way – just like in the movies, with blood and gnashing of teeth. Motive? None. Totally unfair. Something about a cheque – but it's too long to explain in a letter. My depression is thick enough to cut with a knife. I tried several times to reach you by phone, but they always told me you were busy. You're going to end up rich. If you do, I hope you'll cut me in some day. As for me, I got off to a bad start. With a guy like mine, I'm liable to spend my whole life up the creek – unless I decide to run out on him. And to tell the truth, I've been thinking about nothing else for the past two days. I'd like to go far away and put plenty of space between him and me.

'I'd come down to Toulon, but I'm flat broke. There's a hundred and fifty francs in my chequing account ... I paid Mama's rent, and the kids have been outfitted from head to toe. Every time I see them, they ask about you and send hugs and kisses. There's still no sign of Papa. But I heard his case didn't go too well. They handed down the sentence – maybe you heard about it already. He got three years *in absentia*. Poor guy. What a dumb thing at his age, getting involved in another scheme like that. With his record, he'll probably have to serve out his time. It really bugs me. You know, I really do like him. Every time the doorbell rings, I hope it's him. I can't understand why he hasn't shown up yet. If he thinks I bear him a grudge, he's wrong. He can hole up with me as long as he needs to. After all, he's my father.

'What about you, big girl? How's your love life? How's work? I can't wait to see you – I've so much to tell you about. Are you any happier? Has Yves broken off with that teenager? Did she finally get rid of the baby? What a stupid business – guys never seem to understand what they're doing. If I'd listened to you, I wouldn't be in this fix, but it's too late now ... Kismet!

'I've started working at La Hacienda – you know, on Rue Victor Massé. They shut down the Saint-Louis. Oh, it'll reopen, for sure. With Carmen's connections, there won't be any problem. Anyhow, I don't plan on going back. I was starting to suffocate in the place.

'Listen, Sis, La Bohème will be opening in a couple of weeks. I've got my job lined up. Old lady Pedro still needs girls, so why don't you make the trip? One look, and I'm sure she'd take you on. You and Yves could stay with me at the beginning. The two of us would be together, and that would be great. I really need you.

'I'm planning on going home tomorrow, or the day after at

the latest. Call me as soon as you get this letter. I'll mail it special delivery.

'I'm waiting!

- Baby

'PS Remember at the sanatorium how we used to start our letters with a cross to show we were bored?'

I was at La Bohème for opening night, and now I rule the roost there. I strut my stuff in a red silk kilt and give everybody free advice. People pretend to respect me – apparently, I scare them.

Most of the girls are new. There's Vicky, who counts the freckles on her hands and thinks about Renato. Four brief nights of love each month are all he gives her in exchange for her labours. Passive, she's got all the symptoms of the second-string wife.

Beyond the wrought-iron screen that separates the dance floor from the main room, Fabienne is waving her arms in time to a mambo. Fabienne from the sunny south, who'll gladly go stockingless in wintertime as long as it puts money in Carlo's pocket. He's a well-known pimp on the Paris scene – got a dozen girls working for him. She makes passes at my customers. She's the turn-the-other-cheek type. I don't buy it. As far as I'm concerned, Jesus is dead, long live his successor – and his successor has a fast right I've got to watch out for.

Seated at the bar, Sandrine and Nathalie are shooting craps while they wait for customers. Nathalie's known as the Shrimp, because of her smell. Both girls are so nearsighted they can't tell a trick from a dick a foot away. That's why the Shrimp gave up working the streets. She's Jewish. Her husband, who spoils her, is a Jew from Faubourg Saint-Antoine. Fabienne says she reeks. I haven't noticed anything so far.

One of the dice gets away from Sandrine, and she lets it roll. She's as flabby as a half-empty balloon, although she can look pretty when she sets her mind to it. She's been married and divorced. Now she's remarried to a guy by the name of Jeannot, a jealous Parisian who enjoys cutting little strips out of the fleshier parts of her person. She doesn't give a damn whether or not she's his second-string wife. I knew her at the Saint-Louis, where I was the one who christened her. Stumped for a *nom de guerre*, she'd said, 'How about Corinne, that's my daughter's name.' A true shit-head who mixes everything up, totally without imagination.

On the far side of the bar, Madame Rose is peering at the clock. Her emotion-etched face betrays her impatience. Ten o'clock, and not a paying customer in sight. She's working as madam to feed her two kids – they're doing fifteen at Clairveaux prison. We don't have much in common. The same can be said with regard to Josepha, the barmaid. She's a sad-eyed Corsican who swears by men and by men alone.

In less than an hour, Sancho and Miguel will put in an appearance. They're the house guitarists. Notes will burst from their fingertips, and they'll smile as they play my song, knowing that each time they come near my table I'll make it worth their while. (Everyone has a right to his share of the pie.) And I'll dance. I'll dance till I drop. That way I won't have to think about my sister (she's arriving in a week) or about Gerry. He's promised to stop breaking open the milk bottles in which I collect small change; he no longer takes money from my purse but only from the top of the chest of drawers; he now discreetly does his bookkeeping in the living room; and he's been shouting from the housetops that everything is terrific between us. We celebrated making up by going on a junket in his new car through the Berry region, where he was born. I don't feel like thinking about Maurice, either, as he shuttles back and forth between La Hacienda and La Bohème; or about the kisses we exchange in his pad on Rue Boursault while my girl friends are restoring their energy, while the cream-coloured day is dawning, and I'm dying for sleep.

I'd like to forget about the nights when business has been slow, the early mornings when my heart has been heavy. I'd like not to forget France. I haven't heard anything since Jean-Jean told me to stay away from her because I was causing trouble. When she gets out, she'll go to Corsica and stay there until she comes of age – a year of sun, swimming, and real life. I can hardly believe it. Seems she had no choice in the matter: it was the 'man's' word that settled things.

O Saint Simon – our steerer – please give me the high sign! Tell me that the giant you're bringing in is all for me. You won't lose by it I promise.

Simon hoists himself up to the level of this Atlas's ear and points a wobbly finger in my direction. The man assents. He's not the kind to bother with details. Beneath my colleagues' irate gaze, Rose seats us at one of the tables. She suggests a full bottle. Atlas rejoins that a half-bottle is quite sufficient. Obviously, he simply has a dry sense of humour ... Nothing to be offended about.

Josepha approaches, wiggling her backside. The cork pops. Let's drink a toast. That should warm up the atmosphere a little.

'Here's looking at you. Mm – nice and cold.'

'You do the drinking. I never touch the stuff.'

That certainly loosens things up.

'You're not from around here, are you? Your accent—'

'How much do I owe?'

'Hey, not so fast. We just sat down—'

'For the works?'

'A hundred and fifty, plus twenty for the room and forty-five for the champagne. We don't have to hurry. Some guys tip the barmaid, but you're not obliged to.'

To go from La Bohème to the Macao, you only have to cross Rue Frochot. Simon gives me a wink: there's sixty in the till for him.

Usually, as soon as we reach the stairs, the men lose control of their hands. This one must be an introvert. The door slams. I'll soon know what I'm in for.

'Don't bother undressing. Take off your stockings and panties.'

I don't like this type. I don't like it at all.

'Don't you want to make yourself comfortable—'

'How much to let me shave your pussy?'

'... A hundred.'

'I'll give you seventy.'

Sophie, what are you doing? Sophie, have you gone bonkers? You saw the razor. It's a real straight razor, with a bone handle; and there isn't any bell next to the bed. And that blade ... if he cuts my throat, I don't even get to scream. I'm a born loser, really off my nut. This isn't happening. It's not me who's doing this.

'Open up a little wider. Put your hands behind your head.'

'Without soap? What's the gilt paper for?'

'I'll keep them for a souvenir. Don't clam up!'

Jesus! If I come through this, I'll get down on my hands and knees. Never, never again! Scrape, scrape. If I budge, he'll slash my thighs, or my throat ... He'll cut up my breasts! Mustn't let him know I'm jittery. Got to smile and keep from being tense. Lord, if you still can see straight, look down on me! I don't want to die like this – punished in the very place of my sins. And what about my customers? I'll lose them all. A shaved crotch is so ugly. And what about Gerry? Am I ever going to get it! O sweet little Jesus, I've lost my way, please dream up a deluge, or send an angel knocking on my door. Make something happen – a fire, a raid, the end of the world ... Help!

'Don't watch. Keep your hands away – you can wrap it up now. It's not a pretty sight.'

He's too much – a weirdo, a genuine weirdo. I've made it by the skin of my teeth. Ouch! I want to cry. I want him to leave. I want him out of here fast. Shit! I'm such an ass. I make myself sick. How low can you sink, how far can you fall?

'Hi, girls. You're all looking radiant. Didn't think I was coming, did you? You were wrong! Hello, Madame Rose.'

'Hello, Sophie. There's someone waiting for you in the back.'

'A customer already? *Muy bien.*'

'No. A young woman.'

A woman?

'Good evening.'

'Are you Sophie?'

'That's right.'

'My husband met some people in jail who knew you. Not you personally – your husband. They said you were a good sort.'

'That's always good to hear.'

'I also met a girl in the visitors' room. She said she used to work with you – a big blonde, name of Josiane.'

'Her husband's in Melun?'

'That's the one. She said that if I ever needed work, I was to come and see her at the Saint-Louis, and if she wasn't there, all I had to do was ask for Sylviane or Sophie. I went up to Rue Fontaine. They told me I'd find you at La Bohème.'

'So you're looking for a job, right? You've already worked, I hope?'

'One month in a house in Grasse.'

'That's all? Why didn't you stay? What was wrong with the place?'

'It was a slaughter run. Nothing but Arabs. Twelve hundred of them in a month.'

'Stay right where you are. I'm going to get a couple of cognacs.'

'Oh, no, madame. I don't drink.'

'You're having a cognac. Afterwards we can have a quiet talk.'

This is turning into my night for good deeds. The truth is, I've rarely encountered such despair. The poor little thing is all shook up; and she hasn't got a centime's worth of know-how. She's a little housewife; and only necessity has forced her from the suburbs. I wouldn't be surprised if she had a kid or two on her hands.

'Now drink that down. You'll feel better afterwards, I promise you. Cheers! When do you want to start? The old lady needs girls. There shouldn't be any problem.'

'You think so?'

'If that's what you want. What's your name?'

'Claudia.'

'Is that the name you work under?'

'Down there it was Claudia.'

'Forget about down there – I had a girl friend once in the sanatorium who looked like you. A really sweet girl. Her name was Malou.'

'You're nice.'

'Skip it. How did your husband get himself into the fraternity house?'

'We'd been married four years. We were living quietly with our little daughter. I never asked questions when he went out. Sometimes he'd say he had business to look after out of town. and he'd go away for several days. When he'd come back, there'd always be champagne and presents for me and the kid. I used to complain that he was extravagant, but he'd say he only wanted to make me happy. We never changed apartments – I still live in the same two rooms on Rue d'Aboukir. I had no idea of what he was up to. Six months ago the police came knocking on my door. I had to leave Isabelle with the concierge. It was horrible. They held me for questioning for two whole weeks. I was handcuffed in a cell. They kept coming in and asking me questions. They called me a liar and a tramp. They beat me up. They threatened to send me to jail and have me deprived of my rights as a parent – they told me Isabelle would become a public ward if I didn't talk. But I had nothing to tell them. I didn't know anything. It was from them I learned that Bébert was a second-story man.'

'Don't cry. You're going to start pulling in some change, and that'll make a big difference in your life.'

'My life! Bébert's been sentenced to five years. You think you can start your life over just like that? The thought of money disgusts me. You don't know what I gave the lawyers to try to get him paroled. Ten thousand. Ten thousand! I never thought I'd see so much money all at once. That's why I went to Grasse. My husband's partners advised me to. They found me the job, and they didn't say anything to Bébert. I think if he knew about it he'd kill them when he got out. I'll never tell him what they did. I said his friends had chipped in for the lawyers. He'd never have agreed to anything like that on his own. But later, from one visit to the next I persuaded him to go along with the idea so I could send him money from time to time so he'd have enough to eat – and so the little girl could have everything she needed. But five years is a long time. You see, when he gets out, our daughter will be nine and I'll be twenty-six. And if I don't look out for myself, I'll never make it. Right now, there's a woman taking care of my girl at her place. But I want her near me – I want her with me. She's all I have, now. I want to be able to pay for a babysitter by the day or by the month. I want my little girl, and that's that.'

'You start tomorrow at nine-thirty. Do you have enough money to get your hair done?'

'Not a sou.'

'Here's a hundred francs. You can pay me back tomorrow night. Take it! One thing they forgot to tell you is that I like to laugh. So smile. When you've made a little money, you'll have to have your teeth fixed. Then you'll be absolutely terrific. Right? I have to go now. I'll be waiting for you tomorrow night at nine-thirty.'

'Till tomorrow, then. And thank you, madame.'

'Sophie. You can save "madame" for the two boss-ladies behind the bar. So long.'

The door slams. The girls wince.

72

'That girl had a face a mile long. What'd she want?'

'"That girl" was looking for a job. She starts here tomorrow.'

'Oh, so you do the hiring now? Without consulting Madame Pedro?'

'And also the firing without consulting Madame Pedro. So, Miss Couscous, if you don't want to land on the sidewalk with my foot in your ass, I advise you to cool it.'

'My, that Sophie's getting touchier by the day! Don't you agree, girls?'

'I'm not being touchy. It's just that I've had my fill of listening to shit-heads like you. Get angry if it suits you, but keep out of my way or I'll paste you one.'

'Sophie! That's enough, do you hear? Who do you think you are, anyway? How much longer is this bullying going to last? You're here on the same terms as your colleagues. You have no right to raise your voice. If this goes on, I'll be obliged to tell Madame Pedro.'

'Do it right away, please. As a matter of fact, I have to speak to her.'

'You're being impertinent. In my day—'

'In your day, I was still an itch in my father's balls.'

'If you'd have been married to one of my boys—'

'I'd have asked for a divorce, and I'd have got one fast – and they'd probably have awarded me alimony. Now drop it. Leave me alone tonight, Rose. And as for you, Miss Algérie Française, unless it's to cut me in on some swag, don't speak to me. Josepha, bring me another cognac in the back room.'

Twelve hundred Arabs ... What a debut!

part two

chapter one

For me, too, there was a first time.

Being a prostitute is like living through an interminable winter. At first it seems impossible. Then, as time passes, you start thinking that 'sun' is nothing more than a word thought up by men.

Everybody has a debut in the working world. It may be in a beauty parlour, in a department store, on a stage, in a factory, or in an office. All of us have felt that funny little tightness on the left side of the chest, the sense of anxiety in the pit of the stomach, the fear of not being good enough or being stuck with an irritable foreman, a tyrannical supervisor, a boss who's too demanding, a hysterical stage director. We've all felt spied on, evaluated, picked to pieces. We've all had stage fright our first time out. The difference is that when you're turning tricks, there's no emergency exit once the bedroom door has slammed shut: you're up a blind alley, and there's no way out.

There you are, in a dump that's more or less clean, holding a towel in your hand, looking at somebody you've never seen before. The more you retreat, the more he advances; since the room is fairly cramped, you soon find yourself with your back against the wall. The guy's arms are around you, they're all over your body like slimy tentacles that grope you, strip you, and drag you down as he pulls you over to the bed. This octopus has smelled a beginner. His mouth is watering at the thought of the feast he's stumbled on. White froth appears at the corners of his lips, his eyes swivel upwards, his face turns purple. As for you, you've turned white, you've lost all your energy, and you just lie there on the sack as if you were nailed to it, waiting to be put out of your misery. You're so out of it that you forget to take the basic precautions of getting paid and making sure he's clean.

With a dull stare you watch the bulge in his fly growing bigger; and since nothing happens and he still goes on looking at you, with his mouth drooling, you become almost impatient. You look up at the cracked and cobwebbed ceiling and your eyes follow the patterns above you. For an instant you escape from the nightmare: you're back in the church playground, playing hopscotch. It seems like yesterday. You almost feel good, and you shut your eyes to make the dream last. When you reopen them, after a split second, reality blinds you. Reality has taken the form of a cock, a real family man's wiener, a little soft but still enterprising.

The man pounces on you. His features are drawn. He calls you his little girl, his baby doll, his cherry pie, his quim, his yoyo, his honeyfuck, his tramp, his darling whore. As he penetrates you, he gasps for breath, grinds his teeth, and kicks like a mustang. And as he shoots his load, flooding you with a month's abstinence, you lie there in the same position, unmoving, with your arms hanging limp, your legs spread, your eyes staring. You feel soiled, spoiled, destroyed. While he recovers, flopped comfortably on top of you and dripping sour sweat, funny ideas start going through your head. When he deigns to get up, indifferently dripping all over you, you mechanically walk over to the bidet and sit down on it in disgust. You wait before turning on the faucet. You need to recover, too. You run the water full force – hot, cold, mixed. You grab the soap and furiously .rub your crotch, your belly, your breasts, your armpits, your eyes. Tough luck if it stings. You feel a morbid need to scour yourself. You rub and rub like a lost soul. The cool water brings you to your senses, and you shout, 'Darling, don't forget my little present!'

You've almost accepted what you've become.

The man finishes dressing before you do. Now you're alone in the room. There's a stack of ten-franc bills on the table – fifteen of them, or ten, or five, it doesn't make any difference. You stuff them into your purse in your hurry to be outside. You leave the hotel like a thief, looking left and right out the front door. Fresh air! You need it. To keep up your courage, you fondle the bills without looking at them: fifteen, ten, or five, it's still money. You start making plans. Cars splash you as they drive by. Men are sweeping the gutters. You look down at your soiled stockings. Little black patches have stained your legs up to the knees, up to the heart, and you feel like getting it over with and jumping under the first set of wheels that whiz by indifferently. You're not yet completely a hooker. It's your first day, and in the old firm, first days are hard. Where you're concerned, they've turned out to be disastrous.

My first customer's name was Jacques. He looked like Bing Crosby. He took me to a little hotel on Rue Daunou, and that was where it happened – just as I've described. And while I fortunately have a gift for forgetting unpleasant memories, I've never completely managed to forget that one. Of course, it didn't happen out of the blue, simply by chance. It required a combination of circumstances, a chain of events – all of which I eagerly latched on to, late one afternoon, when I came home from work.

As usual, at six o'clock I head for Mado's, the local bistro where, while my mother nervously sips her Pernod, my father plays pinochle. The weather's marvellous – it's June, and I'm twenty years old. The empty wine bottles that I'm taking back for the deposit clink cheerfully against my calves through the netting of my shopping bag. I'm humming as I pass through the inner courtyard of the public housing development. From open windows, the familiar female voice of the TV announcer reaches my ears. A patch of blue sky, billowing from the television antennas, looms overhead. Life at 14 Rue Hoche is becoming very middle class.

It's a glorious day. In two months I'll be getting married. We already have a pressure cooker and two dozen kitchen towels. Best of all, we have an apartment at Porte de Vanves – two rooms and kitchen, with a john on the landing. We'll have to share it with my fiancé's grandmother, though if all goes well not for long: she's pushing eighty. Yes, it's a truly glorious day. Jean-Paul has a good job – he's on the production line at Renault. Twelve hundred a month: with my eight hundred, that's enough to keep us snug and sneaky, even if we don't count the government family allowance. (Jean-Paul wants to have children right away. I don't blame him. It's been four years now that he's had to leave the table before dessert.)

I'm in such a hurry to get away from home that I actually find Jean-Paul handsome. Nothing unpleasant is ever going to happen to me again, everything's peachy, everything's great. Kids are hanging by their knees from the railings surrounding the entrance to the project. Their mouths are sticky with candy.

They all look alike, and I have a hard time making out my brothers.

Full of confidence in the future, I walk on. One flight up, among the kitchen towels and geraniums, Madame Parme's canaries are fluttering in their cage. And then, wham! As I reach the street, it hits me like a burst of sunlight. Just look at it – all that shining, blazing chrome. It's an insult to poverty. It's a truly provocative, arrogant siren whose glamour wipes out the bikes and mopeds around it. You can't help feeling that next to it anything on two wheels becomes a shabby affair of rusting baggage racks, plastic canteens dangling from handlebars, and frames pasted over with little pennants from faraway lands. And those tyres, worn smooth by all the trips from factory to corner bistro, have lost all hope of getting into the Tour de France and are quietly, flabbily sinking into the warm June asphalt. (The cruddiest-looking bike of all is my father's. For a year now he's been talking about repainting it. Naturally, he'll never get around to buying a new one.)

The shock is brutal. I lean against the wall. Who can the the owner of this marvel be? The last time I saw a comparable car in Malakoff was six years ago. That one belonged to Louis the Corsican, my sister's second fiancé. I really have to take a closer look and see what this one's like. The seats are hot and redolent of sun. A pack of American cigarettes is lying on top of the dashboard. I dart a look into the sideview mirror, moisten my lips, smooth my eyebrows, and pull down my sweater. Lord, would I ever love to be sitting next to the driver, with the stereo roaring in my ears as I inhaled a Lucky. It must feel good to flop down on the front seat and leave the boondocks far behind you, with no memories and no regrets ... Stop imagining things! Even if he were King Petroleum himself, I wouldn't ask him to fill up the tank. I'd just say, 'Drive me once around the traffic circle, and then take me home. I'm getting married in August.' Or maybe I'd just slide on to the red leather seat and not say anything. Maybe he'll notice me when I go into Mado's. Maybe he's handsome. If he isn't in the café, couldn't I wait around awhile for him?

Seated on the sidewalk with the empties between my legs and my head bowed beneath the declining sun, I dream of escape. If only I could go away. Just go away. Across the street bursts of childish laughter rise skyward like soap bubbles. If only I could forget all of this: the kids clustered on the black railings, the windows where someone is always peeping through yellowing curtains ... You see, there's not much doing here by way of entertainment, so we spy on each other. We gossip about the slightest gesture, the slightest kiss. Everything gets to be repeated, drivelled over, exaggerated, and soiled. People here don't live – they watch. I'm sick of being watched. I'm sick of hearing about petitions drawn up by neighbours whose one dream is to have us evicted from our two-bedroom apartment in the housing development. I'm fed up with being insulted, and I'm fed up with our gimpy manager putting me on the carpet. (My brothers aren't the only ones who break windows.) I've had enough of reading graffiti informing me that my mother is a slut. I'm fed up with having to pay for my father's years in jail – he paid quite enough for them himself. I'm tired of hearing the weekly knock on the door that precedes the ugly mug of a social worker. It's never the same woman, and each time she uses a new excuse to come in.

'Hello, dear,' she benevolently drools, 'is your mummy here?'

No, madame, my mummy's down at the local bar, and my daddy too. You want to check if there are sheets on the bed? You're out of luck. It so happens that my sister is taking advantage of Mummy and Daddy's absence to tear off a piece. No, I won't let you in. Lulu's already been interrupted four times this week – you want to make her frigid or something? No, of course, you just want to find out about our youngest. Don't worry, he's still getting only the best. We still make up his formula with Préfontaines – you know, the 'velvet wine'? Ever since they operated on him for a narrowing of the pylorus, we've been taking supercare of him. Me? What do I do? Am I still working? Oh, yes, of course.

You see, Madame Busybody, I know all about you and your Sunday-school palaver. I've had to deal with you before. Remember? I was six months away from getting my junior high school diploma. Sis had just run away for the first time. You suddenly burst into my life at a time when I was spending all my Sundays doing homework, and you coolly announced that I had to be saved, that I needed rescuing from my family environment; and so I was taken out of school. You'll never know how much that exam meant to me. I would have been the first member of my family to tack a diploma up over the bed, and we would have gazed on it with pride, all eight of us; but that was something you couldn't understand, dear Welfare Counsellor, you half-ass psychologist. No, you had to settle me with a family far more degenerate than my own, where dishonesty and hypocrisy flourished in the depths of sofas on which I was never allowed to sit.

It was in eastern France, at Chavanne-sur-Surant, remember? No, your memory's spotty. All the same, it was me the gendarmes came looking for in that ritzy house one day. Oh, it was for peanuts. It was for nothing at all. It just so happened that two suspicious-looking youths – black-leather types, deliquents, you call them – were strolling up and down the streets of that peaceful village. They were frightening the villagers, so a motorcycle patrol ran them in to the station. The police persistently refused to believe that the boys had hitchhiked down from Paris. Since they were on the lookout for an old Citroën that had disappeared from Bourg-en-Bresse two days before, they conveniently accused them of stealing the car. Then they searched them. And that was too bad for me, because it turned out that one of the boys had a snapshot of me in his wallet. It was a little ID photo with a drawing on the back – a heart pierced with an arrow, and the words, 'I'll love you always. Marie.' Hard to deny evidence like that. Nevertheless, I did. I denied it and swore that I must have a look-alike. I fought hard. When the police dragged me up to my garret room and opened my wretched pasteboard suitcase, I threw myself at them. Not because of the things I'd stolen – they didn't amount to much, after all: a few T-shirts for my little brothers (and even so, they'd turned yellow when I ironed them, and I was afraid I'd catch hell). And it wasn't because of the slab of Gruyère cheese, something my mother was crazy about. No, madame, it was because of the used sanitary napkins that I'd hidden underneath my pathetic threads. It was simply because I was ashamed – because there was no one I could talk to about those things.

And so, hooted at by the respectable citizenry, off I went like a thief, between two gendarmes, who guided their bicycles with with one hand and with the other held me fast by the arm.

What's this – leaving already? Since you're here in the kitchen, don't you want to take a look in the cupboard? You won't be disturbing anyone. No? You're feeling a little dizzy –

a little nauseated? Oh, I understand, it is a little stuffy in here. Next time, don't bother climbing the six flights. Go straight to Mado's. You see that place on the corner?

If only I could forget all that! And go away. And when it comes to going away, I prefer the front seat of a Thunderbird to the baggage rack of a rusty bike. Up to now, Lady Luck has made herself scarce. I wonder if this couldn't be it, this big set of wheels and its owner. Every girl deserves her fair share of luck and dreams. With my heart pounding, I open the door of the café. Are my breasts big enough? Am I wearing enough makeup? My mother shoots me an angry glance. Oh, not to-night, Mama – don't chew my ass out in front of everybody. I know, I dawdled awhile and the grocery store's about to shut, but please, not tonight. Not in front of him. Because he's there. There's no mistaking him. He's sitting across from my old man at the pinochle table. It doesn't take genius to recognize him. He stands out among all those others in their factory blues. In his grey suit, white shirt, and tie, he glitters the way his car did among the bikes. 'Above all, dear Mother, don't raise your voice. I'm going straight to the grocer's. Just give me time to go over to Papa and say hello to him.'

'Hi, Papa.'

I lift up his cap and pop a kiss on to his bald spot.

'Hello, kid. Throw out a card, Gerard.'

His name is Gerard. His eyes unravel my sweater, rummage under the pleats of my skirt, and slide down my legs like a run in a stocking. And brazen hussy that I am, there I stand stark naked in the middle of the café!

'One of your daughters, Lucien?'

Smiling at me now, father plays a heart.

'The youngest. Got a lot going under her hat. Right, kid?'

Oh, yes, Papa, whatever you say. Don't stop talking. Just let me keep looking at him. He's not handsome. He has more than good looks – assurance, elegance; and he has beautiful, manicured hands, with a ring on each pinkie. A little old, per-haps – not all that old, though. And he never stops smiling. It's getting to be almost embarrassing. There's a disturbing look in his eyes, an indefinable quality that impresses me. No wed-ding ring.

'Hey, kid, get a move on. Madame Berto's going to close up.'

I've forgotten the empties, forgotten my errands. I cross the room – I've even forgotten how to walk! I feel his eyes on me, and in me. Will I see you again, Gerard? In the doorway, I work up enough nerve to turn around. His look answers yes.

I see him again later that evening. After I've fed the kids and shut off the gas, I go back down to Mado's. He's still there. He's sitting at a table with my parents and Paul, a friend of theirs. I approach on tiptoe. My eyes are darker, my lips are shinier, and I've changed my clothes. He smiles the same smile and runs his tongue over his lips. Bending close to my father's ear, I ask if I can stay with them for a while. Gerard pulls a chair and politely invites me to sit down. Since they're finishing a meal that has been washed down with cascades of Côtes du Rhône, and since my mother has just launched into 'Autumn Leaves', no one besides him is paying any attention to me. I bless the dead soldiers lined up on the table. Let the 'Autumn Leaves' all blow away! In response to the general demand, my mother follows with a saltier number, casting fiery glances at Paul. Wreathed in pipe smoke, my father seems happy enough. Beneath the table, Gerard's knee brushes my thigh. The sudden contact gives me goose pimples all the way up to my armpits. To celebrate the event, Gerard orders a bottle of champagne from Blandine, who's slumped in a doze over her dishcloth.

Everyone would be perfectly happy spending the rest of the night right here. Mado, however, is starting to show evident signs of fatigue. Therefore, after the last drop of bubbly has been downed, Gerard suggests ending the evening at Big Suzie's place on Impasse de la Gaïté. His knee gives my leg a nudge, meaning, 'Are you coming?' Silly question! And as I somehow find myself sitting next to him, we drive thigh to thigh through the deserted streets of Malakoff. In the back seat, Paul and my father are replaying the afternoon's pinochle games. My mother hums. The air is mild.

When we get to Impasse de la Gaïté, Big Suzie gives us a ceremonious welcome. We have no sooner crossed the threshold than a bottle appears on the bar. She spreads her arms wide and flashes a neon smile. She has a kind word for each one of us. On seeing me, she exclaims, 'Say, Lucien, your kid's turning into a looker.' As my father's chest swells, she favours me with a greasy kiss. Elvira, the barmaid, clears a huge bouquet of red carnations off one of the tables. We take our seats. Gerard is now sitting opposite me. One cork pops, then a second, and a third. Black butterflies start fluttering behind my eyelids. At the bar, the girls are rolling dice or playing solitaire. A mulatto woman slips into the seat beside Gerard. As he strokes her rear, he presses my foot with his, and his eyes seem to say, 'Don't worry – from now on, you're my baby.' It's getting late, but this doesn't stop Suzie – who's definitely zonked – from taking a flying leap into the past. Sandra, the mulatto, is now reclining against Gerard. He seems completely at ease; he even relinquishes my foot. Paul is gazing longingly at my mother. My father's eyes plumb Jacqueline's cleavage. She's a tall brunette who seems to prefer our company to that of the stragglers at the bar. Suzie talks on and on.

'I was sweet sixteen when I met the Bike. He pulled out a prick that was covered with tattoos. And the bigger it got, the better I got to know his women. There were twelve names inscribed on it, and no room left for me, number thirteen, the newcomer. He said, "Don't worry, doll, there's still room on my nuts." He was a real man, the Bike was, and he didn't wait for my twenty-first birthday to turn me out. At seventeen I was holding my own at the Sphinx – ah, they don't make places like that any more (and that's too bad). At the end of my first month, he gave me a diamond as big as my fist. I dug that. Next month I got the syph. A real downer. I honestly thought I'd lose my guy, because, ladies, let me tell you, in those days a chancre didn't mean one night at Saint-Lazare but it meant staying at the awful hospital Falguière for as long as it took to get rid of it. And until then, they kept you inside. In my day, they didn't kid around when it came to hygiene – we were still on the register then. But the Bike wasn't nasty about it. He saw how low I was, so to make ends meet, he fenced the ring. At first it left a big hole in my life. I felt like I was walking around bare-ass. But I didn't say anything. I loved him, and I think he really cared for me, too. Jesus, being an old bag really leaves a shitty taste in your mouth. Hey Lucien, fill me up a mug so I can swab my throat clean.'

Gerard had just wrapped his leg around mine. I'm sleepy. Tomorrow, up at seven and back to the assembly line. I curl my legs under the seat and rest my head against my father's shoulder. Gerard offers to drive us home. When he lets us off at Avenue Marie-Louise, he casually tells my father that he'll drop by tomorrow around eight. Message received.

That night, in spite of my weariness and all I've drunk, I have a hard time falling asleep. I've got a man on my mind. I'm waiting for him to unlock the doorway to chaos. My little brother's warm body and the scent of his fresh breath help calm me down – until eight o'clock the next evening.

Because of my longing for escape and my mother's need to conceal her frolics with Paul, I quietly and imperceptibly become a part of their triangle. I start frequenting suburban hangouts. I sing songs for drunks till the wee hours, now that I no longer get up early. I'm on sick leave. Through a doctor friend, my mother has obtained a certificate that exempts me from work. Between Gerard and me, things haven't gone beyond brushing thighs, pats on the ass, and friendly kidding – 'When you're my wife, we'll have a real ball!' I smile, knowing that he's already married, that his wife is working Pigalle, and that he also has a stake in Suzie's place: Sandra. I listen and flirt mildly. I don't take him seriously any more; in a month Jean-Paul will be discharged from the army, and two weeks after that I'll be married. I play hide-and-seek. I play with fire. I'm sure of myself, sure of my youth and my possibilities, and I don't think about the pitfalls.

Then one day, after a well-laced lunch, the four of us end up in the woods at Meudon. Paul asks Gerard if he still keeps the blankets in the trunk. He wanders off, steadying my mother as she teeters along on her high heels, slightly drunk. Together they plunge into the bushes and the remembrance of things past.

They'd met at the Petit Drapeau twenty-two years earlier. Paul was with a buddy. She danced all night long with the two of them, and at daybreak, since they had to split up and she didn't know which one to choose, the buddy asked the manager for a set of poker dice, and they'd rolled for her. Let the best man win ... They played two out of three. She was well-stacked and cuddlesome. My father won her. Paul put a good face on it, but apparently he never completely gave up hope. Today's the return match – a belated one, but they both seem to be enjoying it; and one of the participants is missing.

Paul has never married. He's shacked up with Rose, a former

hooker who still turns an occasional trick on Place Sainte-Opportune, in Les Halles – oh, nothing to get excited about, far from it. She pulls in the daily bread, that's all; and that's enough for Paul. He's just about able to put on a clean shirt three times a week and pay for his round of drinks, but my mother seems satisfied. For his sake, she's painted herself a new mouth, darkened her eyes, lightened her hair – she's getting younger by the minute! I watch them disappear into the bushes. I don't want to think about it.

A kind of uneasiness abruptly springs up between Gerard and me. I don't feel like teasing or laughing any more. I'm afraid. I'm afraid of what he's going to say. Between two drags, he speaks. I glance sideways at his angular profile. I find him ugly.

'It's too nice a day to spend the afternoon in the car. How about us going for a stroll, too?'

Us, too – like Paul and my mother. There's undoubtedly another blanket in the trunk; but that's not what I want, Gerard. You've got it wrong. It was only a game. I don't feel like making love with you. I've never cheated on my fiancé, and I'm not going to start so close to my wedding day. The mere idea of your having me is repulsive. I feel that with you it'll be dirty, feel the way I did when I saw them in the restaurant sucking each other's tongues. It did no good to look the other way, I could see nothing but those wide-screen mouths full of bad teeth. It's all very well for my mother to say that my presence doesn't embarrass her because I understand her; I still find it revolting. It would be revolting with you, too, because you're old, and you have rotten teeth. It's different with Jean-Paul. Our mouths are healthy, and our tongues are fresh. With him, even if it doesn't make me feel great, making love is nice because we're the same age, and I love him.

Do you understand, Gerard? If I say no, you won't be sore, will you? You won't get angry with me, or force me, or call me a cock-teaser? Maybe I was, a little; but it was all in fun. You took me on long rides in your convertible. I learned what *pastis* tastes like. I saw some nice inns. And I helped my mother out. Now it's all over: now I'm saying, 'Time out!' Take a walk in the woods without me. I'll go back to spending my Sunday afternoons at the movies with my brothers. But I'm afraid you don't understand.

'Come on, let's go – you don't want to stay here. Give me your hand, and let's walk a ways.'

Right. Let's walk. Let's go find Paul and my mother. They shouldn't be too far off. Mama, where are you hiding? Mama, now *you're* letting me down. There's a bog here, and I'm scared of getting stuck in it. Mama, don't be mean. Answer! There'll be other Sundays for you to palpitate among the reeds. Hey! Mother dear, this is an SOS, and it may be my last. Answer me! The mud's already up to my ankles.

'Why don't we sit there for a while?'

'There' looks pretty damp, but since he insists ... The ground around us is bursting with flowers. I start picking them feverishly. It's a diversionary measure, a way of postponing the fatal moment. Perhaps, with a little luck, Paul and my mother will—

'Leave some for the others. Come over here. Next to me. You look so different. What's up? It isn't your first time, is it? Look at me, sweetheart. Don't be frightened. I only want to make you happy. Lean back. You're beautiful. I've been waiting for this so long – ever since I saw you walk into Mado's, remember? Don't be frightened. Your mother isn't going to show up. She's got other fish to fry. Oh! Those tits, those thighs! That pussy! You're a gift from heaven. Now move around, sweetheart. Grind it – grind it, you little slut. I'll never let you go. I like you too damn much.'

Gerard, you're getting it all wrong. I don't feel a thing, except for the mosquito bites. Hurry up, get out of me. Just keep on kissing me, that feels nice, and you do it well. As for the rest – it's too soon. A little bit too soon. Maybe, in time ...

I meet Gerard every night now when I come home from work. We drive up to the Clamart woods and he parks his car on an out-of-the-way bridle path. My head sinks back against the seat and he uses his fingers to make me come. He says he loves me, but it doesn't make me feel happy.

I've broken off my engagement. I stomped on my ring in a fit of rage. I tore off the lovebirds I wore as a pendant around my neck. Jean-Paul leaned out over the stairwell sobbing and shouting. I wouldn't go back upstairs. My eyes blinded by tears, I kept going right on down those steps.

chapter two

I was happy to go back to the grindstone. It was while I was strolling along the river one day during my lunch hour that I met Braco. He's a Yugoslav student who translates French poets into his native tongue. We kissed on the very first day. After that we met in Square du Vert-Galant, the little park underneath the Pont Neuf. We let our feet dangle in the Seine as we ate our Camembert and bread. When I said, 'I'm washing my feet clean,' he said, 'You're washing your soul clean, too.' I thought that was beautiful – and *he's* beautiful. In a week, he's going back to his own country. I feel sad ... He also said, 'I'll be waiting for you at the station in Zagreb on August tenth.' And I answered, 'I don't know how I'll get there, but somehow I will!'

Today is the ninth. Gerard is acting funny this evening. I don't know how to announce my departure.

'What's the matter – trouble with your wife? A headache? Business?'

'You might have told me you were going away.'

'Going away?'

'Oh, cut out the act. Your mother tipped me off. I know you're joining your intellectual friend in that land of rocks.'

She sold me out, the bitch.

'Listen, Marie, I'm ready to consider this as no more than an escapade – your first and your last. You'll find out soon enough that it's the kind of dumb thing kids your age do. But just get this: your real place is with me, not with some pencil-pusher. You can't live on fresh air and dreams. As a matter of fact, your parents feel the same way. I had a talk with them. And when you've gone through your fifty bills, you'll come running back to the barn and beg me to take you back. I'm not sure I'll still want to. Listen, you have the whole night to think it over. If you change your mind, let me know. I'll be at Mado's at noon. Now give me a kiss. I'm in a hurry tonight because I've got a lot I have to see to, understand? Just the same, I wouldn't want to spoil our last evening – after all, I don't know if in a month from now I'll still feel like taking you back.

'Do you follow me? Your place is right here, with a real man. Baby, it'll take you a week, it'll take you less than a week to understand that you weren't born to be poor. You weren't meant to wear the same sandals all summer and the same clogs all winter, to spend your vacations leaning out of some top-floor window. You're not meant for that! You're listening to me, aren't you, doll? Those hands aren't meant to do laundry. Do you get what I'm saying? You've got the makings of class. You were meant to live the good life, not to wipe the asses of a bunch of brats. For Christ's sake, wake up! You've got an example right under your nose: your mother. You call what she does living? Having to get laid on the sly while your father's out playing boccie? Let me tell you something. Your mother's so hungry for life she'd let anybody lay her. Why, I could if I wanted to. Sure, she's still not a bad-looking doll. But what's she got? Paul! – and even he admits he doesn't come up to my knees.'

Paul – that shit-eating creep! The two of you'd make a lovely couple. Why don't you set up house together? In any case, I don't give a damn. At twelve-thirty tomorrow my train's pulling out. Maybe I'll stop off in Venice, maybe I'll never even set foot in Malakoff again. So, Gerry, if it appeals to you, make love to me one last time. It'll be my going away present.

Gerry put me on the train the next day. On the platform my mother blubbered and waved her handkerchief. Their downcast faces and woebegone looks somehow conveyed the impression that they were watching their capital disappear down the drain. Could they have been devising machiavellian schemes behind my back? Who cares! I'm through with their triangle.

At Zagreb, Braco is there waiting. On the way to the exit, he takes my suitcase and tells me that even though he's no longer in love with me, that needn't spoil my vacation. I'd almost forgotten that he was no diplomat but a poet. We spend our first few days in his parents' luxurious villa outside the city. A maid serves me my breakfast on a silver tray: ewe cheese and raki. I'm feeling on top of the world. We head for Travnik, a little mountain village in Bosnia, where Braco has relatives. As we ride on our third-class wooden benches, his poetic soul comes back to life. He falls in love again. At Travnik a sheep is slaughtered in my honour. That night, Braco mounts me nine times. I begin to think his view of poetry and mine are poles apart.

We set out for the Dalmatian coast. In Split, Braco asks for my hand. I refuse, and in front of a troop of beet-red Germans, I get *his* hand across my face.

'I'm not giving you back your passport,' he shouts, 'you're not getting out of the country!'

After an hour's negotiations, conducted under a sun that would have made a donkey swoon, I recover my passport, with a little help from the local authorities. The cops lead my poet off to the station house. It's a love story with a lousy ending. I cry quietly. My cheeks are ablaze, my shoulders are suffering from third-degree sunburn, and I'm totally strapped.

I travel by third-class carriage as far as the Italian frontier and spend the night on a bench near the Trieste railroad station, next to a fountain spraying multicoloured jets. Tomorrow I'll be in France, in Toulon, and my sister will underwrite the final stage of my journey. Dear God, may Lulu be there! Let the Sixth Fleet be anchored in the roads – and don't let *her* get any ideas about running off after romance!

Sitting across from me in the train that's taking me to France, an Italian couple on their honeymoon never stop kissing. Their mouths are full of pizza, and my eyes are as big as saucers. They probably think I'm some kind of voyeur. After several hours of gastronomic delirium, the train comes to a stop in Toulon, and in a flash I'm on the platform. *Vive la France!* Tossed by friendly hands through the window of the departing train, my suitcase bounces on the asphalt. Thank you, thank you, whoever you are. Arriving home bare-ass would have been all I needed.

From the station I hitch to the Medina, the Arab district, and, Lord be praised, I see Lulu through the display window. She's wearing two daisies at the ends of her braids.

Poor Lulu! This isn't how I imagined you. Why do you insist on hanging on to this lousy job? Why don't you come to Paris and work with me? We'd rent a room together. We wouldn't be rich – but we'd go dancing on Saturday nights. We'd go back to the street fair at La Nation, ride the roller coaster, and you'd hold on to me, shrieking that this was the last time you'd ever be suckered into it. We'd find ourselves lying groggy on the floor of the barrel-of-laughs, with our skirts over our heads; and then we'd go wandering out among the noise and the merry-go-rounds, eating cotton candy. Guys would follow us and whistle. We'd each have three boy friends at a time so as not to become attached and to stay single as long as we could. There's still time, you know. There's only six years' difference between us; and six years is nothing. Let me tell you, certain people would go out of their minds with joy to see you come back home.

At the moment, the problem is getting your attention. Hey, Lulu! Look at me, instead of arguing with that Arab. Take a step, a step ... step on a crack break your mother's back! Take a little walk. Look at the little Arab kids playing in the gutter, look at the sky, imagine the sea out there, a lovely clean blue sea full of flying fish and transparent pearly shells and unknown, inaccessible flowers. A calm, warm sea that is indolently swaying just beyond the Medina's grime ...

I rap on the pane. The sound hits her between the eyes. She comes out. We embrace as the other girls watch with cowlike eyes. In spite of my affection for her, in spite of the fact that I haven't seen her for several months, I can't manage to share her passionate enthusiasm. It actually embarrasses me. She starts asking question after question, and I feel sorry I came. Now she's raising her voice and introducing me to the madam and to the other girls.

Lulu, I'm hungry. I haven't eaten anything since yesterday morning. My head's spinning – your lair has a potent smell, Lulu. Forgive me, sweet sis, it's on account of the smell, and because I'm exhausted and hungry. Lucette, don't be sad if I leave tonight. I don't want you to think that you revolt me. I just hurt, that's all. I hurt the way I did when I opened your purse and found your girl friend's letter asking if you were coming down to take on the fleet. I didn't know what that expression meant, and when I found out, I cried.

Goodbye, sweet sis. And thanks for the ticket home ...

Seeing them in exactly the same spot, with their sunken eyes and mottled complexions, I could have sworn they'd been standing there for three weeks. No doubt about it. They haven't been to bed yet! Mama! Gerry! You shouldn't have, you really shouldn't. You ought to have gone home. Three weeks on a station platform with all the heat and dust is brutal punishment. You should have taken some rest. You should have had some fun. To think that I was standing on the threshold of the east at Sarajevo, camping on the Isle of Love off the coast of Vele-Luka, swaying to the sound of violins on the ramparts of Dubrovnik, eating every meal with Tito (his eyes caressed me from his framed picture): and you just stood there? Oh, I'll never forgive myself! Let me give you a hug and a kiss. You were worried. You were afraid you'd never see me again. There, there, it's all over. I'm back. Gerard, of course I haven't changed. Sure, we'll go back into the woods at Chaville, or Meudon, or Clamart, wherever you like. Of course you can still ball me. I'll even share my sunshine with you. My suitcase and skin are chock full of it.

A month has passed since I came back. The sunshine is fading from my cheeks. From the kitchen window I look out at new high rises: they ooze monotony.

Mother is desperately peering into the garbage pail.

'You slut, what do you do with your dirty Kotex these days?'

Don't be alarmed, Mother. Above all, don't shout. It's just that I've got a bun in the oven. I know, you're going to start tearing your hair again and screaming that this is another one of those forbidden things. You've forbidden me so many things – don't play with the oysters grandma spits up, don't kiss boys on the mouth, don't stick pins into lice, don't ever sleep with a man or he won't love you any more. 'He won't love me any more.' That's the only explanation you gave me. But if you accept my little baby, nothing else will matter.

No more lonely nights. I'll have someone to talk to, someone to whom I can say: 'Hey, wake up, sleepyhead, and hold out your chubby hands. Bliss is staring you in the face. Happiness is right there, as plain as can be. Look – Mama's unbuttoning and taking it out. Mama's giving it to you. And the crowd hasn't noticed a thing! Mama'll hold it for you. Mama wants you to have it. Look up with your beautiful gentian-violet eyes, and see how tenderly Mama's letting you take it. Take it, little mite, squeeze, my little prince, it's all yours.'

In other words, Mother, it could be so simple. All you'd have to do is stroke my forehead and say a kind word; and I, that instigator of gentle debauchery, that guilty lover, will sink into your arms and open up my heart. But you scold and insult me, and every evening I have a hard time swallowing my food. My baby is tearing at me, making me swollen and feverish. He makes me not only want to die but throw up. I can't put it off any longer. Tomorrow, I'll have to pass the word along to the careless father.

By an irony of fate, the next day is a school holiday, a day meant for children. The father of my future child drives like a maniac up to Rue Chaptal, where dwells a great wizard, the possessor of miraculous injections. I wait in the car. Our minutes are numbered – at 14 Rue Hoche, curfew starts at eight o'clock. It's an immutable tradition dating back to my childhood.

Mr Careless at last returns, a smile on his lips.

'It's okay. I've got the shots. Now, up to the woods at Clamart, and presto! You don't hate me for not being a family man, do you, doll? What's wrong, cat got your tongue?'

Farewell, little bundle of love – I don't have the time to get it all sorted out. With my butt glowing in the light of the dashboard and my heart about to spill out of my eyes, I take the flush-the-works injection like a good girl. It's a mixture of norlestrin and benzogynestryl 5.

Three days go by. There are no new developments, aside from the awful bellyache I take to work. Gerard counsels patience.

At the end of ten days we go back to Rue Chaptal. This time, in addition to the injections, I take a dose of quinine orally, spiked with rope-skipping, getting hit in the keester, getting hit in the gut, and lots of other barbarous calisthenics. This shock treatment lasts into December.

Gerard is growing visibly impatient.

'The kid's hanging on. There's only one other solution – an abortion. And the sooner the better. You're starting to develop a gut.'

I say yes to everything. All we need is an excuse for me to spend a night away from home. That's a whole other problem. Luckily, on 12 December I have to go to Le Havre for the day: a supermarket is opening, and I'm supposed to set up one of the booths. To my parents, I announce that I'll be spending forty-eight hours there, since the following day I have lunch with the buyers. My father declares that in no time

I'll become a successful businesswoman. Dear Father – ready to believe anything!

On the evening of the twelfth, I'm half an hour early in front of Chez Dupont, where Gerard has told me to meet him. As tyres hiss by, I strain my ears for the ones that will reassure me and end my anxiety. I only have half a night at my disposal.

Behind me, sidewalk stands display mounds of oysters. People pass by, couples are going in and out. A lively tumult reaches me, along with the smell of onion soup. It's almost Christmas, and you can feel Paris vibrating beneath the snow. I'm cold and starting to feel frantic. But I mustn't. I've gone to too much trouble setting this night up. It's a night that I've conjured with and run to earth. Gerard, I'm cold, and water is seeping into my Capezios.

It's eleven by the station clock. The Thunderbird splashes me as it pulls up to the kerb with all its horsepower rearing.

'Say hello to my friend. This is George, the doctor. We'll be doing it at Micheline's place – she's his wife.'

Hello, Mr Big Wizard. You're the man with the phony cures, and if you're a doctor, then my sister's a nun. Hello, George. Why shouldn't I say hello to you? After all, in a few minutes you're going to learn all there is to know about me. Good evening, Mr Abortionist. I hope in spite of all those scotches you can still see straight and won't miss the right hole. I hope it won't hurt too much. I hope I can go home tomorrow morning. And thanks, Micheline – thanks for doing this for someone you don't know. Even if they never gave you the chance to refuse, thanks for running the risk of taking into your home a minor who's pregnant up to her eyeballs.

Gerard parks the car in an unfamilar neighbourhood. Thick snow blankets everything. An elevator plucks us from the ground and comes to a lurching stop. A door opens.

Gerard shoves me on to a bed. It looks like an operating table, covered as it is with a surgical sheet on which are disposed rolls of cotton, kitchen towels, a blue plastic basin, a thermometer, and a flashlight.

'How many months?' the woman asks.

'Three,' answers Gerard, 'and into her fourth. We tried

everything,' he adds. 'When I plant them I plant them. It's really hanging on.'

What are they talking about? What's the meaning of this pitiless exchange? Why am I shaking like this? Why am I so cold, breaking out in goose pimples? Why are the three of them staring at me like that? Why are the men taking off their jackets and rolling up their sleeves? Why are they asking Micheline to fix them a scotch? What am I doing here tonight? And why am I so scared?

'Come on. No need to be so modest. We all know what an ass looks like.'

An ass, maybe, but this isn't just any ass – it's mine. I'm not used to showing it in public just like that.

'Here, baby doll, swallow this. Bottoms up! Go on.'

Thanks, Gerard, for taking such good care of me. I feel better now. My ears are getting warmer. But the sheet under my butt is cold, and that gismo between my legs is like ice.

'Relax. Open wider. We'll never get any place if you clam up like that. Micheline, hold her head down.'

'The bitch is really tight. I've used the Vaseline. Come on, now, make an effort and help us out. You think we enjoy doing this?'

Gerard, I don't think anything, I have no faith left in anything, but please, don't shout. Don't get mad. I'll relax – there, how's that? Can you see better? Can you find the hole?

'I've never seen anything like it. She's got a cervix the size of a pinhead. We're not out of the woods yet.'

'You're sure the probe isn't too big?'

'It's the only one I could find. It'll go in, or I'll know the reason why. We can't spend all night on this.'

'Bring the bedlamp nearer, and fix us a couple of more scotches. I'm getting cramps in my mitts.'

Once every second bells start ringing inside my head. They make a colossal racket. A pendulum is banging against my temples. I have ten or maybe a hundred hearts in my belly, all beating at an incredible pace. What if I die? Seems there's a fragile something called the peritoneum; if it bursts, you're done for. But I don't want to die. I'll settle for staying alive. I'm only twenty. I won't take up a lot of room on the planet. All I need is a little sunshine and a chance to go dancing outdoors Bastille Day. So don't let go of me. Listen to me. Look at me. Wake up! Can't you see I'm croaking – that I'm actually croaking? You're not going to let me die, are you? Look at my legs – I'm spreading them wide. I can't do better than that. Look how I'm pushing out my arms and keeping my head down and stretching my fingers ... So give me your hand. It hurts, it really hurts. Your hand, Micheline – you promised you'd hold my hand!

'By God, I think we're in business. Three-quarters of an hour to set a fucking probe! Well, by tomorrow it should be all cleaned out. Put her to bed right away, and keep checking her temperature. I'll leave a shot in case her fever goes up. The two of us are going to take off. Everything okay, young lady? You can't say we didn't knock ourselves out for you.'

Slowly, interminably, the night crept by. Lying next to this unfamiliar woman, I swallowed my moans and tried to tame the little red garden snake they'd inserted in my belly. It never gave me a moment's respite. I turned from side to side trying to quiet the gurglings that kept hurting me. Then it was dawn.

I watch it come. It's rather pallid and sad as it slips through the folds of the orange curtains. Micheline is sleeping with the sheet drawn halfway over her face. It's already tomorrow; and the throbbing pain that racks my lower back has by now made it clear that I won't be going home today. But I'm not scared of being punished. I've lost my fear of blame and blows. I hurt too much to think of anything else. It's almost a relief. I no longer dread the thought of being hospitalized. To tell the truth, I never thought I'd avoid it. In a while, Micheline is going to get up and leave for several hours: that's the only thing I'm worried about – that and finding myself alone and not knowing what to do with the thing that's about to emerge from inside me.

If I come through this without too much damage, I'm going away. In three weeks I'll be twenty-one. I know of an agency that organizes trips out of the country. I'll go spend a year in London working in a family. I'll go away, and nobody will be able to talk me out of it or stop me. I'll be of age.

No one will understand. They'll say, 'Little Marie's gone away! And she seemed so nice.' The children won't understand either. They're going to feel awfully lonely. There'll be no one to pay for their popcorn at the movies, no one to sneak

them bread-and-sugar snacks when they've been sent to bed
without their supper, no one to ward off my mother's blows or
soothe her fits of anger. No more getting them out of a jam
by sewing back the buttons they lost, no more removing ink
spots from school smocks, no more paying the grocer on the
sly for the candy they've charged. No more pillow fights and
no more chocolate-flavoured breakfast cereal. No more hugging on the mattress, no more kisses on little Patrick's Cupid's-
bow mouth. That'll be over. All over.

But if I stay here, I'll be courting disaster. I feel it; I know
it; Gerard has told me as much.

'You're almost of age. You're going to have to choose:
either you go on wallowing in your housing project, or you live
my way.'

His way means turning tricks. And turning tricks – very bad
for little me.

I can see Lulu's face behind the dirty display window in
Toulon. She bobs back and forth, the plastic daisies dangling
from the ends of her braids. Lulu talking with her hands,
making her breasts pop out of her bodice, wiggling her hips
in her black skirt. The Arab nodding his head in approval.
Two people who'd never laid eyes on each other climbing a
dingy stairway. Lulu swinging her purse as she comes back
down, Lulu catching sight of me, Lulu always talking too loud,
as though she felt obliged to shout. Lulu turning to speak to
me, and smiling tenderly ... But there are two lines at the
corners of her mouth, two lines that I've never noticed before.
They've taken the warmth out of her smile.

Oh, Lulu, oh, Lucette, if only it were you here lying next
to me instead of this woman! How relieved I'd feel. You've
always known how to take care of me. Once, I had to take
care of you. You'd wanted to kill yourself by swallowing an
overdose of Darvon. Your head was a mass of blood and
bruises because Mama had kept going with the broom handle
a little too long, and because – not wanting to vex her – Papa
had finished you off by sending you spinning against the
radiator, where you'd split your lip. All that because Jeannot
had whistled to you from the courtyard below. You'd wanted
to go out dancing two nights in a row, and you'd forgotten to
lay out the boys' school clothes for the next morning. You
dragged yourself into Mama and Papa's bedroom, and I fol-

lowed you. I saw you swallow the pills. I told them, and they said if we didn't cut out the playacting, if I didn't stop the crap, I'd catch it, too.

Then they left and went down to Mado's. You got into bed. I sat down at the kitchen table and started doing my homework. The boys came in and said you were crying. I squatted down by your side on the mattress, but you weren't crying. You were groaning, begging for blankets. Yet the room was stifling. You kept asking, 'Why? Why?' and your head would roll from one end of the bolster to the other. You had a pain in your belly, and you begged me to make you vomit, and the boys kept sobbing and saying, 'Lucette isn't going to die, is she, Marie? She isn't going to die?'

So I went down in my nightgown and ran barefooted all the way to Mado's. Mama and Papa had left. I ran to the doctor's as fast as I could. When I came back home with him, you were lying on the mattress perfectly still. There was a pot filled with water on the floor, and the kids were taking turns dipping towels into it and applying them to your forehead. The doc knelt down and picked you up in his arms. We watched your progress down the stairwell. He paused on each landing. I thought you'd never make it. You'd never reach the hospital on time. The kids and I ran into the kitchen and hiked ourselves up over the windowsill. We saw you rounding the corner of the second courtyard. We followed the sound of the doctor's car until it had completely died away in the night. If I'd known that I wasn't going to see you again for two and a half years ... I didn't know there was a way out of the hell we lived in.

Mama and Papa refused to let us ever mention your name. You no longer existed. We were supposed to forget you; I couldn't resign myself to that. As time went by, I began thinking it must be *you* who wanted to forget *us*. Then one day a buddy of yours from the Etoile d'Or told me that you'd be expecting me at Gare Montparnasse on the two-thirty train the following Saturday. You came hopping down the station platform on your outsized heels. You gathered me into your arms and lifted me up without a word. You smelled good, Lulu; that day I would have followed you to the ends of the earth.

Your place looked like an actress's dressing room with all

those photographs pasted up on the walls. You explained them to me one by one. I followed your pearly fingernail across the glossy paper. You'd come a long way since you'd left home ... We drank sweet white wine from a little low table cluttered with panties, bras, stockings, and garter belts, a real jumble – the entire paraphernalia of a dancer, in fact. How credulous I must have been, Lulu, not to grasp that the revue you were playing in was as old as the world. My head was spinning: you kept refilling my glass while you told me how, after the hospital (where you almost died), a social worker got you a job with a doctor. It wasn't unadulterated bliss – he used to spend the time between patients chasing you around the desk, and she used to show up regularly for the latest bulletins. So you split. You went back to the dance hall where you'd hung out before; and there you ran into a girl friend who was making her living by taking off her clothes ... You followed in her footsteps. You quickly got used to stripping in public, and you found champagne less bitter than beer. And even the boldest welfare counsellor would never dare poke her nose into Le Narcisse. That's where you met Louis the Corsican, your first pimp. And there I was listening to you, dazzled, while you recounted your successes. Me, who even now can't erase from my mind what I saw in Toulon, in the Medina, where you're now living, and where you're dying – a lot faster than you ever did in Malakoff.

Lucette ... I can't bear this pain any more. I'll have to wake the lady up. My pelvis is about to split in two, and I've got the shakes. If only it were you here, I wouldn't be ashamed of feeling weak. I can see her leaning over me, with her rumpled hair and puffy mouth. She'll talk about infection, and she'll offer me a cup of java – and you know I never touch it. Mama says that considering those weak lungs of mine, it's foolish of me to go off in the morning on an empty stomach. Today, everything's weak – weak, brittle, and breakable. And now this other woman has started to stretch, rambling on about how she'd dreamed that George was balling somebody my age. She's getting everything mixed up – injections, the hospital, and life with her man. She stumbles over to the curtains and opens them. The sky tumbles into the room. My head reels.

Micheline has inserted a needle in my right buttock. For a

moment this new pain has made me forget the original one. I lie there face down, listening to her wash up and thinking about the warning she's just given me. It was my third – there had already been Lulu's and my father's: 'You be careful, girl, and keep your nose clean, because once you start, that's it. There's nobody who can stop you from being sucked all the way in. I'm getting old. I'm not going to do for you what I did for your sister. Once I took my revolver and went up to Pigalle to bring her home. No sooner was my back turned than she was off again. All I'd managed to do was make myself look stupid. Once is enough, Marie. You're lucky – you're brighter than she is, so take advantage of it. Don't end up the way your sister did.' I won't let you down – I'll let Gerard down instead. I'll go away, I promise. I'll really go away.

Before leaving, Micheline felt my forehead, and her cool, perfumed hand made me feel better. She took my pulse and said, 'I'll be back at noon, one o'clock at the latest.' Then she went off, fully confident that I'd sooner drag myself through the streets than cause her trouble.

Got to move around, that's what they said. How about dancing? Or doing a little housework? Come on, little feet, down you go. Hold me up, little legs. Heart, poor heavy heart, don't beat so hard. Little head, don't ditch me now. Tummy, stop jerking like that. Hips ... now listen, hips, you'll have to loosen up. If we all pull together, we may just manage to stay vertical. That's it – give it another try! It hurts, I know, and it's a mean, sneaky, and stubborn pain. You feel like a lost puppy. Lost! Hurts! Doggie! Hey there, old head, you fathead – don't play dumb. Don't let me down. It'll be all right. I know what, I'll turn on some music, you always liked music, you still like it, huh? Take it easy. Don't go spinning around like that or I'll never make it to the radio. For God's sake, help me – what's the use of looking at the world upside down? The world's still the world we live in, right? And we have no plan to give it up. It's a lovely world. It's so big. And we haven't seen it yet, or hardly ... Tell me, little head, you remember how we always used to have a good cry in front of the mirror after a big night? That was so fabulous. I'd talk to you while I lapped up my tears with little licks of my tongue. We felt good, didn't we? It's better getting a few knocks from me than from my mother. I know – I was supposed to put up *and* shut up. But I had the right to cut loose, too, didn't I? Did I have the right or didn't I? If I hadn't cut loose, I would have gone crazy. Don't be narrow-minded, and just forget about all that. It's you I'm talking to today, because all the rest of my body has left me in the lurch.

Music! Music, damn it – I'm still alive! Whistle while you work, and we'll turn everything inside out for a thorough housecleaning! We'll get rid of all these spots, inside and out. We'll make everything nice and shiny. Oops – it's coming. It's on it's way. It's running down my thighs, and it hurts, but it's certainly something that's worth suffering for! And maybe afterwards the fever will go down, and we'll sleep at home tonight, I'll squirrel down on to the bolster next to little Patrick and start forgetting. It'll all have been nothing more than a nasty dream, a nasty, nasty, bad dream! ... *All you people turning grey, remember the day when you were young like us*, sings Aznavour. The bathroom. The bathroom, quick! *Eager like us to live, and eager to give your heart the freedom it craved.* Jesus, it's coming out of everyhole. I'm going to die right here and now. Just hang on, Marie. Go on, puke and shit, you can clean it up later. *Why can't you let us be free? Or just let us be? And time will take care of the rest. Halleluja! Halleluja! Youth has its one brief day.* Push, push, it's coming. Don't look. *Let it have its way (Halleluja! Halleluja!), give us time to say our say ...*

Now, slowly, take your hands from the basin. Relax. And don't bend down too fast. Take it easy. It's all over. There he is. Rinse him off the way Gerard told you to. You have to do that – they need to know if everything's come out that's supposed to. There's more? Oh, no – Mama, I broke the bank! I have twins. There must be a curse on me ...

Get up, for God's sake! You're not going to keep lying there in your own shit. So they're boys, what the fuck do you care? Even if I'd wanted to ... And you didn't want to. I didn't. So what's the point of staring at the thing? It's dirty. Clean up and get back to bed.

Bed. I can't get into bed. I can't get up. My back! Halleluja, halleluja! Come on, give it another try. The bed's getting nearer. Beddiebye. Down, little head. Leave me be. Let it bleed. You've done your share – sleep now, and rest.

*

Gerard drove to the Salpêtrière Hospital like a madman. I got out, dropped the blanket on the back seat, and went off without even turning around. Once again I saw the world upside down. It was hard to make progress walking through the clouds. They were thick, like dirty-grey cotton, and they came up to my waist. I saw the roots of trees stretching down towards the dark earth. I saw ambulances driving over rooftops, their sirens muffled by the cloudy mud. I saw nurses walking on their hands with their cloaks tucked up around their waists. I saw rain rising towards sidewalks in the sky. I spoke with a batlike woman who hung head over heels from her desk. I squatted down to tell her that I was hurting and that I'd lost a lot of blood; and she took me under her white hood, and we set off together on a winged trolley, down long white corridors peopled with diaphanous shapes.

After that they made me feel better. One of the shapes leaned over me and pricked my right arm. I felt so good that I glimpsed heaven. I even heard the angels speaking – oh, not for long: angels are very discreet, very soft-spoken. They're not like us.

At present it feels as though I were coming back down; but I'm in no hurry. No hurry at all. A while back I was glad to be going up – I didn't know what it was like up there. I know all too well what it's like down here. That's why I'm keeping my eyes shut. Shh! In order to re-enter the world of the living, I'll play dead. I can hear them already. Their voices are thick with hatred, reproach, and insult. These are the living, with their mouths full of snarls and rotten teeth; with their scabs, their fractures, their dirty sores, their abdomens full of pee – living skeletons more dead than alive. Why have they put me in a ward with old women – with only old women? Why am I tied to my bed? Why don't they let me move around? Why? I want to speak to a nurse right away. I want to be untied.

'Untie me!'

'Why don't you shut up, you little slut? You didn't call for your mother when you were whoring around, did you? I have a daughter your age. Thank God she's not a tramp like you. In my day, when they scraped you out they didn't bother with anaesthetics. Too bad that things have changed.'

I remained tied up until the evening rounds. The doctor patted me on the cheek and told me I'd need written permission from my parents before I could be discharged. I cried. Every visiting hour I tremble at the thought of seeing my mother arrive. I'm like my old man: I don't like shouting. When she throws one of her hysterical fits and opens the windows so that the entire yard can hear her, he says, 'Listen – talk, don't scream! Can't you see the kids and me are getting woozy from listening to you?' I don't want to have to face her and her neurotic temper.

It'll be Christmas in a few days. I don't want to spend Christmas in here. I dream of going over the wall, but how could I manage it? I don't even have a pair of slippers. I could pinch the ones belonging to the old woman next to me. She's been wheezing for the last two days and nights; I don't think she'll be using them any more. But then what?

It was Lulu who rescued me from that hole. Gerard had managed to reach her in Toulon, and she took a plane back there that very night, after making me promise to behave myself.

When I went into Mado's at apéritif time, my mother and I caught sight of each other simultaneously. You'd have thought she'd been expecting me. I felt like throwing myself into her arms, burying my head in her bosom, and asking her to forgive me. After all, she'd had my oldest brother when she was sixteen: she could understand. She and I were both of us women now. Who knows – this accident might bring our misunderstandings to an end. I started towards her, fearful but not mistrustful. Nothing, after all, had changed. I hadn't been away so very long. She was still there drinking her Pernod; and in the back room the cardplayers were still exchanging the same affectionate gibes. My father was in his usual seat, across from Gerard. Paul was there, too, as well as Schmol the Alsatian with his protruding chin, old man Picard nursing his Kir, chubby Dédée, and all the others – the regulars. Blandine was wiping the counter with the same cruddy dishcloth. Mado was rolling poker dice with Coco the Algerian. The boccie trophies were displayed in their usual place on the shelves that ran the length of the room. The old coffee machine that Mado stingily refused to replace was grunting away familiarly. The curtains still hadn't been washed. The stovepipe still forced its way into the cracked ceiling. Louis and two other boys from 14 Rue Hoche were still playing the pinball machine with unrelenting frenzy. At the same old table next to the jukebox, Mariette the Wino was smooching passionately with her bricklayer friend without a thought for the elven kids rotting away in welfare institutions, and with her belly swollen with the twelfth on the way.

Nothing had changed. Absolutely nothing. In the mirror, Gerard's eyes met mine the way they had the first time. As a welcoming gesture, my mother gave me the speciality of the house – a masterly back-and-forth swipe across the face. I could almost hear the applause. Black butterflies fluttered before my eyes, followed by tiny bubbles, furrows, and zigzags. Somewhere inside my head, I heard her voice resounding and rebounding from all the other mouths and forming a choral refrain: 'Still weeping tears of gratitude. Go home, you slut. We'll settle things there.'

The slut didn't go home right away. She went walking along the railroad tracks. For a time she stood leaning out from the footbridge and watching the trains pass, spitting on them.

Very early one morning soon afterwards, with nothing in her pocket except fifteen francs and an address in Surrey, she boarded a long grey train. Her parents were still asleep, but on the platform the boys were waving their hands – they grew smaller and smaller and at last disappeared from view.

The McOils, an Irish family settled in Godalming, received me with great warmth and enthusiasm. I made the acquaintance of Katie and Terry, a pair of blond children aged two and three. While their parents went off to see Shakespeare, I took them into my bed and sang them French lullabies. I stole some pudding from the fridge and blamed them for it afterwards. On Sunday I ate pork and boiled potatoes with them, and I discovered Sherlock Holmes and several new television channels. I learned how to build fires in a fireplace, I listened to French radio programmes while I did the dishes, and I went to see *La Ronde* in a French movie theatre near Victoria Station. I wandered through the streets of London unable to speak ten words of English, utterly at a loss. At the end of two weeks of good and faithful service, however, I managed to save enough for a pair of black patent-leather shoes with very high heels – and to steal a dress from a shop.

In the evening, when I shut my bedroom door, and the children and grownups have withdrawn into their dreams, I act out my own. In my tight-fitting dress, on my high heels, with my nose in the air, a smile on my ass, smiling breasts, a moist mouth, and brimming eyes, I take French leave. I have fantasies of black stockings and necklaces that hang down to my waist. I play at being a woman of the twilight ... And I think of Gerard: Gerard, from whom I ran away. But was it really from him that I ran away? Wasn't it more from that inner courtyard and gloomy project apartment, where the drooping flowers despair of ever seeing the sun? Wasn't it from the parlour that greets my eyes every time I go to the window? Wasn't it from the beatings, the shouting, the scenes, the hard times towards the end of the month with the dinners of fried rice or lung stew? Isn't it the world of 14 Rue Hoche that I'm running away from? So why torture myself? Why go on wiping the asses of other people's brats? Haven't I wiped my own brothers' asses often enough?

If I hadn't met Gerard, it would have been somebody else. Sure, before I knew him, my ambition in life wasn't sashaying down breezy streets winking at the men passing by. The idea of being a hooker hadn't crossed my mind. In fact, it was quite foreign to me. But what if he's right? What if it's the way out of poverty and the start of a scintillating existence? What if I tried it on my own? It may not be such a bad idea after all. I know streets in Paris where girls do it – Rue de la Verrerie, for instance, near the place where I used to work. Those girls look anything but unhappy – they're always laughing. And they're beautiful to boot. If I do that, I won't necessarily end up in the Medina the way Lulu did. Arabs aren't the only men who frequent whores. I've seen distinguished-looking men go off with the girls on Rue de la Verrerie. So to hell with the straight and narrow. The place to get started is Paris.

Gerard actually managed to sound almost touching on the phone. He couldn't hear me clearly, and he kept shouting, 'Come home, baby, I love you and I'm waiting for you!'

Gerard kept his word. He met the one-fifty-five p.m. train at the Gare du Nord. He was wearing a kidskin overcoat. He was rubbing his hands so as to find something to do with them, and his nose was red with cold. He looked ugly, already somewhat aged, but for the next two months I nonetheless followed him from one Montparnasse hotel to another, hotels with wall-mirrored bedrooms that made me blush. We lived off what his wife and Sandra earned. It was the grand life, or almost – bars, nightclubs, champagne. His friends continually addressed me as Madame Gerard. Of course I didn't have a wardrobe to go with this kind of life, but one was on its way: Gerard was giving the matter serious consideration. That's why one evening, having finished one oyster and started on another, he announced that he'd found me a job. I'd be selling cigarettes at a bar run by a woman he knew. The place was located in the neighbourhood of the Opéra. Things were really looking up!

chapter three

And that, girls, is how you get sucked in. That's all there is to it. Even if you've come from a tough part of town and think you know it all, you let yourself be taken like a babe in the wood. There are no more honeys, dolls, or sweetie pies: there's just a girl. She's eighteen or twenty, she's been bobbled and screwed up, and she's sobbing her guts out as she leans her head against the door of the john in some bar. You see, the kid's sobbing her guts out because she really thought she'd come here to sell cigarettes. She believed it right down to the bitter end – even when the madam was pounding on the door of the can to announce that there was a customer at the bar.

His name is Jacques. He's drunk a cognac with the little lady, and now he wants to fuck her, no matter what it costs. He's ready to shell out fifteen bills – five more than is customary – but he insists on her. He wants her because she still has smooth cheeks, because there are no circles under her eyes, and because she 'doesn't look like one'. Because she isn't wearing sexy underwear, and with a little luck her panties will still have that down-home odour that excites him: where she comes from, there aren't any bidets – you wash your ass in the dishpan when it isn't stacked with greasy plates. He wants her right away because his nose tells him she's a beginner, and he wants to be the first man aboard. The lady who runs the place has told him that he'll indeed be the first. He'll finally be first at something in life! So quick, before the others come and ruin her. He wants to be the first to rub off her shine – *il primo*, get it?

That's how you find yourself stuck in a particular kind of hotel room on Rue Daunou. That's why, on a glorious spring day, you just want to lie down in front of a passing car.

After Jacques came Raimondo, an Argentine dying to tango. He taught me a funny step where the feet don't have much to do, but where the mouth writhes in disgust. 'Swallow,' my Argentine kept saying, 'swallow!' I closed my eyes, clenched my fist, and wiped my mouth on the edge of the tablecloth. Tangoing lost its charm when Raimondo complacently slipped me fifty francs. All the same, it still wasn't time for me to fold up my dance card, and I ended the night with Bata, on a bed too narrow to contain his fat. Bata was a grub whose belly was as wrinkled as a caterpillar's. Bata was a senile man who, after he'd watered me with his rank sweat, left me standing on the sidewalk of Rue de Montpensier with a ticket to *Holiday on Ice* for my pains.

When I got home, I woke Gerard up, screaming, 'I want to be free again. Give me a chance!' I was hurting inside. Another haemorrhage had started – my fifth since the abortion. I craved sweetness, I craved all the sweetness there was in the world. And as he irritably emerged from his deep sleep and fixed me with his hawklike gaze, I knew very well that he wouldn't give me a single crumb of the sweetness I yearned for. I felt fear welling up inside me.

He spoke in a voice I didn't recognize.

'You want to leave? So leave. But you've got to realize one thing: I love you. Make no mistake about it. If I put up with your doing this kind of work, it's only so that we can get someplace fast. I want us to live high on the hog. When I took you on, it was a contract for life. You understand, baby, I'm thirty-three, and I know damn well I've been a failure at everything. As far as society is concerned, I'm less than dirt under its feet. The only thing left for me to do is to call it quits and put a bullet through my skull.'

As I listened to him, he seemed pathetic. I'd imagined all kinds of reactions, but not that one. It was real melodrama, the sort that makes little girls cry, and this little girl was crying. She was shaking with long drawn-out sobs: because she knew very well that if she didn't leave him now, she was through. It was a rough contract she was signing. It might not be for life, but it would last long enough to destroy her body and soul. Poor little girl, nice little girl – always ready to pick up a stray dog!

And so the little girl watched stray-dog Gerry reach under the mattress for his .45. She felt as though she were watching the screening of a black-and-white movie. This was *cinéma vérité* all right. Between sobs she asked him not to do anything foolish, and to put his rod back under the mattress. He told her to go back to her dopy fiancé. Only a sucker would put up with the way she was carrying on – but not him, not stray-dog Gerard. He needed a woman, a real woman you could count on. So it was just as well she split. But when she went over to the closet to get the few things of hers that were hanging there, he cocked his gun. It made a sharp click. She whirled around panic-stricken, saying, 'Listen, Gerard, maybe we ought to try and get things straightened out. You know, I'm not a bad girl, basically. I really want to do the right thing. You've got to understand. I'll try again – but not that way. Not that way.'

He asked her to come and sit down next to him. He held her very tight in his arms. She cried a little more – it was a bad habit, she could never manage to shake it. So he said to her, 'We'll take a trip to Capri – how about that, baby?' And she sighed yes and sank against his bare chest.

Gerard had flair. He'd sensed how much I needed a change of scenery right then – without waiting for vacation-time. Seeing new surroundings was a matter of urgency for me. I would not go back to Le Sportsman. What would suit me best was going to work in a whorehouse: a real one, with women of some style in it. For a beginner like me, what could be better than a little nourishing contact with others? What could be better for an amateur than working as part of a team? I would learn from my exposure to the others and, who knows? I might even become a big winner.

After ringing up an 'impresario' and chatting a few minutes with a knowledgeable madam, Gerry chortled, 'It's in the bag. There's a spot open at the Saint-Louis on Rue Fontaine. My buddy Antoine says they pull in the change there by the bucketful!'

That very evening Gerry parks his pram in front of the bar

Le Fifty. The doorman rushes over to the car.

'Forget it, buddy. We're not customers.'

True enough – my new life was to start across the street, at the Saint-Louis. I follow Gerard into the place on tiptoe.

The lady who receives us speaks in hushed tones.

'Please come into the side parlour. Monsieur Antoine is expecting you.'

The side parlour consists of two tiny rooms. On the walls of the first room, pictures of Spanish dancers have been nailed up amid a display of shiny black-and-gold fans, banderillas, castanets, and red plastic roses. In front of a miniature bar, laden with gladioli, high stools of carved wood await the weary traveller.

The lady draws back a thick garnet-red hanging. A cigar clamped between his teeth, 'Monsieur Antoine' stretches out his arms towards his friend. I'm introduced. The lady withdraws.

The ceiling lamp sheds a yellow light. I sit down on an ugly upholstered bench set against the wall. Monsieur Antoine, whom his friend addresses as 'Toine', smiles a great deal without ever removing his cigar. The lady now comes back with a bottle of champagne protruding from her kangaroo-front apron.

'Madame Pedro is on her way down.'

A bell rings. The lady hurries off. From behind the red curtain comes a sound of footsteps and men's voices. A second, more strident ring. This is followed by a cavalcade of high-button shoes overhead, laughter, a slamming door, and women's voices. Holy Mary! In no time at all, I'm going to be one of them. I empty my glass. My guardian at once refills it. Mother of God! Have they actually brought me to an old-time brothel? Is it true that only distinguished gentlemen frequent such places? Do the men still smooth down their whiskers with a leer in their eyes and one thumb tucked into their waistcoat? When they visit the ladies do they still wear frock coats afoam with shirt lace, carry knob-headed canes in the crook of their left arms, and have watches tucked into little pockets over their hearts?

Mary, Mother of the Seven Sorrows, tell me: is this truly a place where girls who have bloomed like the flowers of your garden offer up their pink-marble shoulders to the perusal of sinners? Tell me truly: is it their heavy, honey-coloured locks that cast these shadows on their pale cheeks as they look one another over? Or might it be boredom? Tell me, Mary – and forgive me, Virgin Mother! I've been brainwashed. I've been innoculated with the serum of perseverance; and so here I am, ready to put myself up for sale, ready to rent myself out without a fuss, down and dirty, the proverbial cooked goose – *money, money, money!*

The velvet frames a graceless face: Madame La Boss, no doubt. Holy Mary-and-Joseph, I can tell you one thing right now: she's not one to water her lodgers' geraniums after working hours.

The chief geisha has a raspy voice.

'Antoine!' she exclaims, raising her hands heavenwards.

'Pedro – as snappy-looking as ever! My friend, Gerard. The kid—'

'She's of age?'

Ciao, Mary of Bethlehem! End of dreamtime. Back to hardcore reality.

'She's been a consenting adult since last month. Right, baby?'

'We'll let Antoine's wife handle her. She should do well here.'

'Claudie will fill you in, madame. She's been part of the establishment for five years. You'll see, everything here's on the up and up. Go ahead, Pedro. Have her come down.'

I'd rather she was called Petunia. I'd rather be elsewhere while they're planning my future. Too late. Here comes my mentor. She's out of breath, and apparently surprised to see her pimp. She looks as though she'd just walked out of some fashionable cocktail party: a chic lady out on the town. She stares at me out of wide, expressionless eyes. As for me, perched on my four-inch stilts, trussed like a roasting chicken in the black dress I'd snaffled in London, I feel about as comfortable as a minnow on a slag heap.

'She ought to be christened before going up to nineteen.'

Pedro casts a sidelong glance at me.

'Got any ideas?'

No – I'd thought of everything but that! How about Victoria? Matilda? Conception? Iphigenia?

'Madame Pedro, the Lebanese girl won't be coming back. We should call her Sophie.'

'Good idea. Sophie – it's a name customers remember easily.'

*

And that was that. I'd just been rechristened in a whorehouse in Pigalle. A-men!

Gerard patted my rump. Good Sophie. Good little filly.

Heady scents floated past my nose – a mixture of plain soap, mouthwash, lily-of-the-valley deodorant, hydrogen peroxide, and warm sweat. My palm slid along the rickety banister. The garnet-red carpet that ended at the third floor was threadbare; here and there I could make out the dark wood of the steps. The blood had rushed to my cheeks. Opening a door, Claudie turned around and said:

'Here's number nineteen.'

I stood there speechless in the middle of the bedroom. Around me, girls were quietly seated, doing their knitting or reading or crocheting. Claudie introduced me.

'Sophie. She's married to a friend of my old man's.'

There was a deathlike silence. I was the newcomer – the nineteenth girl. I felt utterly out of place. She asked them to make room for me on the sofa. Nobody budged. They were studying me, groping me with their eyes, taking me apart. All but one: a slip of a brunette, oozing beauty, with a bottle of beer between her feet, completely absorbed in the crossword puzzle she held on her knees. This was France – France who came so wonderfully to my rescue that night! Like me, she was a fugitive from the boondocks around the outskirts of Paris. She had been lucky enough to learn her way around her local hobo jungle, its Gypsy trailers and guitars, its empty-lot carnivals, and its unmown grass: an escapee from the world of reinforced concrete.

A slow-moving, deep-voiced beauty from Martinique, whose woolly hair was imprisoned beneath an auburn wig, moved over so that I could sit next to her. Not another word was said until the moment when Muriel asked me to do a striptease.

The Saint-Louis was my vocational school. I met and got to know some famous men, some unknown men, and some nice guys. I rode bareback on a prince who thought he was a thoroughbred, and while I dug my heels into his sagging flanks, France whipped his rump, and he pranced over the threadbare carpet, whinnying with satisfaction and licking the dust. I made a Canadian sing 'My Way', and while I kept telling him that his voice was exactly like Sinatra's, France filched his dollars. I taught a thirty-five-year-old virgin how to use a rubber and explained that if he insisted on putting it on all the way, the chances were that he'd have a premature ejaculation or no ejaculation at all. I held a nymphomaniac's hands behind her back and her head between my thighs while France buggered her and her husband sat in a chair calmly enjoying his Havana. My first visit to the Claridge took place in the company of Josiane and an American who loathed hooker hotels and preferred paying whatever it took as long as he was shat on in an elegant room off the Champs-Elysées. I was foolish enough to let a wild-eyed man from Luxemburg tie me to the radiator, and as he disembowelled the mattress with his penknife, I heard the sound of the last trumpet ringing in my ears.

I met the Marquis de Ṣade resuscitated as a thirty-year-old Dutch tycoon. Herbert's invariable custom was to make a first, provisional selection. His blue eyes would quickly sweep around our circle, he'd pick out three potential victims and order them to strip; then he would eliminate two of them, paying them off handsomely.

The door slams. I'm face to face with my torturer. Nothing's missing. There's the bottle, planted upright in the ice; and between the champagne glasses, a worn towel from which emerge the thongs of the cat-o'-nine-tails.

I rub the nape of my neck. He walks around the bed and chairs to look me over, starting with my feet, hesitating at my thighs, proceeding up to my breasts, ignoring my face. I'd like to say something, but what? He isn't the small-talk type. I smile. He doesn't smile back. Yet he likes me – sadists have always liked me, ever since I was a very little girl. And now Herbert, who does indeed like me, is filling our two glasses. I relax and reach towards the tray.

'No. Whatever you get, you earn.'

I remain silent. It's part of the game. He picks up the bottle and disappears into the bathroom. What sort of game are we playing? I start: Dom Pérignon poured down the bidet? What a waste! This guy ought to be locked up. Oh, no, sorry, it isn't so: he's carefully plugged the fanny-bath.

'Lap it up. On your knees.'

Well, if you feel strongly about it, I'll give it a try. But honestly, it's only to make you happy. Especially as I find this 'glass' a trifle revolting and inadequately rinsed. You see that ring of grey scum? The help in this establishment seems to be extraordinarily careless. I even suspect the barmaid of scratching her crotch as she washes the glasses. No telltale signs in your glass? You're lucky. Perhaps I was unfortunate and she cleaned the receptacle I'm lapping out of on a day when the little beasties had got to her.

'Don't pretend. Swallow it.'

Swallow – and think about the two thousand francs on the edge of the table. Swallow, and imagine what you'll be able to stash away from a job like this. Think of the cute pair of Christian Dior shoes that you saw in the window at Jourdan's, and the matching bag, and the silk print you're going to give Dédée on Mother's Day – she wants it so bad she dreams out loud about it every time she sees you. Remember the boots your kid brother showed you on display at the local shoe store. He's fed up with stuffing pieces of cardboard in his clod-hoppers. Think about them. Think about Gerry. Think about yourself – well not too much. Don't think about anything. Have a slurp – it'll sober you up ...

'That's enough. Crawl over to the mirror, on your knees. Each time you lower your hands from your head, I'll let you have it across the breasts.'

Not the breasts – that wasn't part of the agreement. That hurts too much!

There isn't any agreement, he points out. I'm not here to make you feel good. That's it, clench your teeth, clench your fists. That's it, watch yourself moan, you wicked, disobedient, bad little girl! Wipe your eyes again so I can get a better shot at you – there, where the flesh is tender, smooth, marble, silky, where it's taut as the whip cracks against it. Let your mascara run. Let your nose run. Hold back your screams. Mingle your tears with my joy. Come here: I want to flow into you, I want to pour myself out. I want to stroke you and lick your wounds. Come here, and forgive me!

That was Herbert for you. After torturing me for over an hour, he threw himself at my feet, begging for forgiveness, and ran out as I stammered my very first word.

I went upstairs, broken, short of breath, without my panties, without my stockings or bra, carrying my dress on one arm. I couldn't bear anything touching my skin. The girls made room for me on the bed, and France and Cynthia took turns applying cold wet towels to my breasts, my buttocks, my back, and my thighs. They kept chattering away, drivelling envy and foaming with jealous rage at the thought of the two hundred bills stacked flat in my purse. If they'd dared – if I hadn't been the wife of a friend of Antoine from Nice, if the right man had happened to be in the clink at the time, or if France hadn't been around – I really think they would have polished me off with their fangs, their heels, their claws, and their gibes; and they would have certainly picked me clean. I let them talk. I dozed till morning – that left them a clear field, didn't it?

Time passed. The swellings subsided. I forgot. And so did the others. And then one evening a breathless Arlette opened the door of number 19. Herbert was back. He was waiting for me in number 2.

My girl friends turned purple. I went prancing upstairs. On the table the bucket of champagne was in its proper place; but there was no towel.

- He said, 'Don't be afraid. I won't hurt you – much less than last time.'

He asked me to take off all my clothes and lie down. He sat on the edge of the bed offering me glass after glass of champagne. We got to know each other.

'Why are you doing this? Who made you do it? Why can't it be at your place instead of here? How old are you? How long have you been at it?'

'And you – what's your age? What kind of work do you do? You're married? Why do you enjoy hurting people? Why did you ask for me again? Where do you live? No, I've never been to Amsterdam. They say it's beautiful – the canals, the tulip fields. Sure, I'll come some day.'

'You'll come as my guest. You'll sleep in my house. You'll get to know my wife and my two sons. I'll tell them you're a college student I met in Paris. At night the two of us will go out together. She'll understand. It'll be nice. It's a big house. You'll like all of them.'

'What do you mean?'

'I mean the house, my wife, my children, the town ... I have some snapshots – would you like to see them?'

'Show me. Is that her?'

'Yes. But you'll see, she's better looking in the flesh. The glasses make her look stern.'

'Do you beat her up?'

'Never. Sophie, I have a surprise for you. Close your eyes and lie back.'

'But you're hurting me! You're nuts. What are you doing with that fine-toothed comb?'

'I'm combing your pussy, Sophie. Your pussy!'

After that he ran off without saying another word, just like the first time. I collected the money on the edge of the table. That night my buddies back in number 19 turned bright green.

I'd talked too much that evening. What was the use of advising him to see a psychiatrist? Why didn't I just do what I was there for? Why tell him that it seemed a shame for a man like him, with a brilliant career and a lovely family, to take refuge in whorehouses? I'd acted against my best interests. Now I won't turn him on any more. I'd have done better to shut up, or simply say, 'It's nice being with you.' I thought I'd never see my Marquis de Sade again.

I was wrong. He came back, and without any violence we made love for two wonderful hours, during which I forgot that I was working. He gave me a long goodbye kiss at the foot of the stairs. On reopening my eyes, I saw Claudie's dress disappearing with a flutter at the top of the lookout station. When I went back up, she said, 'Some girls just don't know how to behave ...'

I couldn't have cared less. I'd earned my keep for the next three days; and I was in love. Whenever Herbert came to Paris, he would call me at the Saint-Louis the night before, and I would cancel my next day's engagements. Gerard had no objections to my spending my night off with Herbert, since it was so greatly to his advantage. I'd slip Gerard a thousand, and it was in the bag – a thousand in his bag, the same amount in mine. I never asked Herbert for anything, but he went right on paying me as much as he had the first night. It's true I was in love – I wasn't going to irritate him with vulgar questions of money!

We'd meet for an apéritif at the Café de Paris on Avenue Matignon. We'd switched brands of champagne and exchanged Dom Pérignon (it brought back unpleasant memories) for

Cristal Roederer. Afterwards we would dine at Drouant's, the Petit Bedon, Prunier's, or Lasserre's. We'd end the night in his room at the Crillon. Sometimes, when he had a hard time reaching an orgasm and he was grinding his teeth and kneading my shoulders, I'd hold out a belt to him; he'd grab at it like a lunatic and flail the walls until he collapsed exhausted on the bed; he'd weep, spread his hands out palm upwards, and ask me to forgive him.

I think I loved him. We met three times a month, every month, for two years. He followed me everywhere. He always had my latest phone number; always, that is, until the time came when I left Pigalle and went to work elsewhere. I didn't leave any address, perhaps because I was afraid I'd disappoint him. They said he'd looked for me from one end of Montmartre to the other; that he spent a fortune just talking with former girl friends of mine who could tell him about me; that he'd even paid some Pigalle steerers to try to find me. People told me so many things about him that I didn't know what to believe. Hookers are such liars. Herbert, my dear, sick lover, my wild-eyed demigod, isn't it more likely that you threw your poor self into some canal?

The Saint-Louis was the opposite of no-man's-land. Any kind of bird could settle there and not risk losing a feather.

The ones who settled there that night came out of the Highlands of Scotland. They were big-beaked birds and they spoke with a strange accent. One of the males perched on the chest of drawers, the other two on the foot of the bed. The females, with their wings chastely folded over their full, warm curves, made their nests in armchairs they'd pushed back against the window. The last warning bell had stopped ringing, the curtain was going up. Josiane let her dress slip to the ground; mine fell like a stone. It was my first *exhibition*. The females pecked about in their starched-lace bodices, the males waved their flippers as they cheeped that, by Saint Andrew, we were real bits of fluff, lovely flossies, and that even in Glasgow the likes of us weren't to be found.

Jo decided the time was ripe to ask for our little present, and one of the females puffed up like a pouter pigeon.

'We've gane deep into our pockets lang since, and if there's mair to pay, there'll be nocht left in them!'

This knocked me for a loop, but supercool Josiane settled down on the treasurer's knees.

'Go on, ducks, come across with a little swag, and you won't have made the trip for nothing. Just you wait. I have Saint Peter himself in this bag here.'

'Listen, my Romeo,' said the lady from Inverness, 'we canna stay here till mornin', so give these lassies what they ask and let's start hamewith. This is a quair business we've traipsed into!'

Romeo drew a ten-pound note from his tailfeathers and stroked Jo's curves with it. With my champagne glass at my lips, I watched her pick up the little suitcase. Its contents were as great a mystery to me as to the spectators. From it sprang forth an elephant's trunk, which she waved in circles above her head, shouting, 'Ladies, take a look at a real deewee!'

I put my hand between my legs and decided that all things considered I'd rather someone else took my place. I anxiously watched Jo accoutre herself with this sadistic implement, carefully fastening its straps around her buttocks and thighs. The goose pimples spread to my ears as she mischievously and perversely extended her gigantic phallus in the direction of the females. Was there magical power in the sight of this herald's trump? In any event Grouchy Joan, whom we had to thank for our 'little present', lunged behind the drapes screaming, 'Let me awa! By the door or by the window, let me awa!'

Romeo took her under his wing, and they clicked beaks. He took her hand in his and forced her to caress the 'lassie's bonny fat cock'. The magic became more ambiguous: was she crying or laughing? What was certain was that she was fondling the rubber 'ballocks' as if weighing them, and stammering how they were no joke, and she'd never imagined there could be 'thingummies like that'.

Jo had artfully disengaged her trunk. Meanwhile, spread-eagled on the mat, I was dreaming of Loch Ness, of gentle forests of Scotch pine, of the calling of the clans, of Mary Stuart, of the palm trees at Inverness, not to mention my gas and electric bill. It was essential to think about anything besides the rubber tusk that Josiane was aiming between my thighs. She reassuringly murmured, 'Cool it, it's just an act. All

118

you have to do is squeeze your cheeks ...' I blew a kiss to all the elephants in Africa while her glass clinked against the champagne bottle and she called for silence.

Good Lord in heaven, they must have been from hunger, with plenty of coin to play with, those jocks, to sit there fluttering around while we were playing them for chumps! Jo was twirling the thing, her mouth a study in irony. 'Turn yourself on, Sophie!' The stiffening trunk banged against the ceiling, wrapped around my leg, disappeared in the confusion of sheets, and plunged into the bolster. I panted away and the bedsprings performed a concert of fabulous chamber music. We fell into each other's arms with a joyous burst of laughter, unaware that around us everyone was masturbating in unison. Even Joan. Especially Joan. The curtain fell on a scene of wild debauchery and of somewhat revolting absurdity. Herself excited by the group masturbation, Jo had decided to condense matters and pass straight to the final act. Lowering the lights, she had like a good girl impaled herself on her Romeo's prong, while the others, haggard and unkempt, had settled down at the foot of the bed. The champagne was no less warm than Jo's tongue, and I let myself be explored to my most intimate depths without daring to tell her that the show was over.

That had been my first *exhibition*; there had been many more since then. No longer did I dread that showy instrument of torture; no longer did I let my pals indulge their desires – when their tongues wandered out of bounds, I kneed them smartly in the ribs to remind them that this was work and not play.

I thought myself inured: pure delusion. The odd birds at the Saint-Louis never failed to surprise me. For instance, at about four o'clock one warm summer night, our dear Arlette cornered me in the corridor and pressed her fingers to my lips.

'The "colander" is here.'

She seemed pretty excited, and her tongue hung out. I wondered what all the mystery was about.

'He's a government minister who flits in and out of here like a ghost. Come rain or shine, he shows up wearing a hat pulled down over his eyes, leather gloves, dark glasses, and a white silk scarf that hides the lower part of his face. He always asks for the newcomer. With him, it's fifteen hundred in the bank for sure. Go up to nineteen and put on a pair of rompers. I'll call you when he's ready.'

My pals were biting their lips and nudging each other in the ribs while France adjusted the shoulder straps of my rompers. I was beaming. Is it my fault if I'm attractive and don't have tits like a cocker spaniel's ears? Is it my fault if my belly isn't all tucks and pleats, and the hair God gave me is prettier than a Helen-of-Troy wig? Is it my fault that sashaying comes easy to me, or that instead of having calves like a fullback I've got classy legs, or if my ass doesn't drag along the ground? Is it my fault, for Christ's sake, if I'm only twenty-one and you're all past thirty?

Franzie took a hairpin out of her chignon.

'Here – you'll need it.'

The plot was thickening ... When Arlette rang, I went down, leaving the others to chew their bitter cud. Arlette was waiting for me on the third floor, with a colander in her hands.

'Hurry up. He doesn't like to be kept waiting. Go into five and sit down in front of the mirror. Then put this on your head – fix it however you like, but remember that every time it falls off you get three hundred francs less. You won't see him – but he'll see you.'

That part was simple enough: it was a two-way mirror.

'Speak in a very loud voice. Tell him stories about your johns. Do a little pantomime. Address him as *Monsieur le Ministre*, he likes that. But I warn you, getting him off isn't easy. When it's over, he slides an envelope under the door. Okay, go to it.'

Sophie, they're calling for you on the sound stage. Step on it, girl, the cameras are rolling. Props: colander, hairpin. I'm on my way, *Monsieur le Ministre*, don't get impatient. I just need time to string a few locks through the holes to attach the damn thing ... This is my first starring role – did you know that? Here I come. Fasten your seat belt! Lights! On my head, please. Full blaze on the colander, pick out the details, the legs, baby, the legs – no, not *my* legs, the colander legs! Don't change a thing. You've hit the right angle – it'll look great in close-up. Here I go:

My name is Yum-Yum. I come from a place that everybody's been to, yet you don't know the first thing about it. It's a place you've explored hundreds of times – you've gone deep into it! It's a warm, cosy kind of place. Even if it's a bit damp, it makes you feel at home. It's the kind of place you'd like to settle down in. It's a country where you don't talk about politics but about pleasure. It's a place where leaders get to be led, where tough guys turn soft, and the misunderstood find understanding. It's a place where unhappy people rejoice, pleasure-seekers are satisfied, unknown people come into the limelight, and intellectuals turn stupid. My existence takes place in the very depths of Woman.

My name is Yum-Yum, and my imagination is running out through the holes of the colander ... Say, old Minister, I could tell you dirty stories and do all kinds of things with my hands and mouth. I could simulate the kind of orgasm that wipes you out, the kind that would make your eyes roll every which way, like some machine gone out of whack, the kind that cracks your joints and burrows into your cerebellum, the kind that makes you want to live backwards ... Hey there, Mopy Dick – stick your ear against the mirror for a while. Have you ever had that kind of pleasure? Come nearer, don't be afraid, I'm a benign microbe. You and all your kind can go on masturbating in peace. Germs don't pass through partitions, yet. The Minister of Public Health is working on the question. Soon venereal disease will flourish only *outside* of brothels. You'll be able to visit them without risk. It'll be the street you'll have to avoid – the street will be swarming with giant staphylococci, and they'll attack you on every corner. You'll have to stay on your guard, because the little bastards will be as strong as hell and thrive on just about everything : a BLT down may do you in. You're trembling – cold, maybe? Hey! Don't run away! I want my fee. Wait – I'm going to tell you about Buttermilk. Buttermilk was an old necrophiliac, used to fart when he came and ...

I went on like that for a whole hour, with the colander poised on my head and my eyes glued to the crack under the door, through which an obliging hand finally slipped the envelope. I clutched it the way poverty clutches the working classes! It was a lovely white envelope, so neat and carefully sealed. Just from fingering it I could tell there was plenty of jack inside. I didn't open it right away. I tossed it from one hand to the other as I hummed to myself. I stretched out on the bed, laid the envelope on my belly, and spoke to it softly : 'I earned you, you know. I really earned you.'

People console themselves as best they can. You need excuses so badly when you look at yourself in the mirror and, in a low voice meant only for your own ears, keep repeating: it's not you, Marie, it's someone else, it's someone you've never laid eyes on. It's someone like the girl Madame Jeséquel insisted on teaching algebra and who didn't understand the first thing about it. Sophie, it'll end up being as abstract as algebra. You're going to forget it the way you forgot those equations, you're going to burn your dresses and shoes the way you burned your school notebooks. One day, you're going to become yourself; and your childhood will come back to you in every detail. Then you'll begin to understand. There will be fewer and fewer blank spots in your memory. At last you will have forced open the gateway to happiness. A kind of happiness that isn't anyone's for the asking: a fierce kind of happiness that wards off attack, that has to be earned with your teeth, your fists, and your grief. Whatever you do, don't despair. That happiness is your due.

Enough crying for tonight. I know you've been hurt. You've just been ridiculed and humiliated, worse than on the night of the striptease. You look down into the street. Your heart is heavy. If you weren't so high up, you'd jump – it would just be a way of flashing prettily, ruffling the atmosphere a bit, making a splash of gaiety, that's all. A nice red puddle in the midst of all the blackness ... Back on Rue Hoche, you used to lean so far out you'd get dizzy, and your feet would no longer feel the reassuring comfort of the pots on the cupboard just below the kitchen window. In those days you already had good reasons to take a flying leap – but at least you didn't get everything backwards. What difference does it make what the girls did tonight? You won't always be the newcomer, the last girl on the scene. Someone else will come along. And then you'll join your pals on the other side of the mirror. You'll be laughing at the newcomer's dismay. This time she'll be the one who finds the toilet paper in the envelope, with a different message attached. You'll laugh even harder than the others, because you like to laugh, and because you too like to play practical jokes.

Now get dressed. Soon it'll be time to go home. The night's coming to an end. Don't be mad at France because she didn't warn you – she's one of the oldtimers. France: not particularly generous, not particularly beautiful, but pretty, so pretty: incapable of dishonesty and as thieving as a magpie; anything but gentle, but gentle nevertheless; not really tough, just insanely violent ... That night when I'd struck oil with this guy who'd made me sniff some snow, France was out of her mind. She was like some raving maniac. He'd turned her girl friend on, the bastard, he'd had the nerve to make her blow coke. That was Franzie: emptying his pockets and his wallet and then brutally kicking him out on the landing, bare-ass. That was France: hitting me hard again and again, while I covered my face with my hands, screaming insults as I tried to tell her it wasn't my fault – it was the first time I'd even heard the word cocaine, I had no idea what it was; she had to forgive me if I was laughing for no reason at all or if I felt like singing and scrambling up the curtains ... That was France. My buddy, accomplice, teammate, shield, muscles, sister.

France, my very own Boondocks. Today, at dawn, like every other day, I walk with her silently up Rue Fontaine. Taxis are crawling along, cruising for customers who have lost their way among the gaudy fauna of Pigalle. It's the hour when the doors of bars open wide like great puffy mouths, exhaling their fumes of alcohol and stale tobacco. It's the hour when tired girls climb down from their perches, when the most cunning makeup becomes a harsh mask, when blue-ringed eyes turn sleepily sad, when with windmilling gestures the pimps add up their accounts ... A man staggers by trying to find his way home to bed ... A noisy bunch lurches past: sailors with their hats pushed back on their heads, drifting about in search of some outbound ship ... A few obstinate women are trying to postpone the dawn, hoping they'll pick up the Oil King. Multicoloured signs wink and blink out. A whole world is sliding out of sight. It's an illusory world, like the world of those legendary vampires who live and die with the enchantment of the night.

The Saint-Louis was all of that. Who knows how much longer I might have stayed on there if, one night, just after performing my first good deed of the evening, I hadn't run into this man on the landing. I said to him, 'What're you looking for, big boy? Lost your way? Don't you know you're not supposed to prowl around up here?'

I bawled him out because I'd already been at the Saint-Louis for a year – I'd acquired what they call professional experience – and the man looked to me like a Peeping Tom. He replied to my arrogance with one simple statement:

'Police. You lead the way.'

I hesitated. He hadn't shoved his badge under my nose, and I thought he was an impostor. So I aggravated my case by saying, 'Police, my ass!'

It was only then – still keeping his cool – that he produced a calling card from the inside pocket of his raincoat. He was an old cop and the approach of retirement had made him patient. He also happened to be Lieutenant X of the Vice Squad, and the right arm of Monsieur Z, who was chief of the division. I learned that the latter was in the kitchen keeping Arlette busy.

Poor Arlette! She'd been caught by surprise and hadn't had time to give three rings that would have sent us scattering from attic to cellar. Poor France: she didn't have time to hide in the special doubled-backed closet for minors and girls on parole. Poor me, I had to go into number 19 in the company of a guardian angel who needed no introduction. A kind of uneasiness settled over the little room. Knitting, crocheting, fashion magazines, playing cards, all fell to the floor amid a dismal silence. I started to feel so out of place that I almost asked for police protection! Fortunately Monsieur Z didn't take long in joining his colleague, bringing a whole bunch of his pals along with him, and as if by magic things immediately became more relaxed. Greetings were even exchanged. 'Hello there.' 'So we meet again.' 'Thought you'd retired – didn't you take your name off the list six months ago?' On both sides there were silences, laughs, and oaths.

When their luck runs out, hookers are sure to do two things: lend a helping hand and kick each other in the shins. We walked out of the Saint-Louis singing our marching song. The ladies' limo had pulled up to the door. Our beloved Arlette had a hard time keeping her hands in the pockets of her white apron as we started on our way – destination police headquarters.

part three

chapter one

When I was a little girl, I didn't play the piano, and I didn't play with hoops and dolls. I played with kitchen knives, broken bottles, and stiletto heels. I wanted to be a master of dark deeds, performed at night in the depths of the forest. I'd had it drilled into my head that this was the only thing that paid off. If you wanted to get someplace, there weren't umteen ways of going about it.

What if I actually liked filth? What if I'm craftily nourishing my disease? I refer to Gerard as my husband without believing it. Thanks to me, he's turning into a big shot. To others, I pretend he's a tough guy: I myself know he's only a coward, a bully who's terrified I might leave him. And now, day by day, the trap is closing in on me. Gerry believes in his new personality. He works on it, fashions it, polishes it up. He's beginning to feel as comfortable in his he-man role as he does in his silk dressing gowns. And while I wither away, he feeds on me and robs me of my rights and powers, night after night. And yet there are certain evenings, certain tender evenings, when I still try to believe in him; and I keep straining to boost him up, give him a stature I know very well he doesn't deserve.

When I was a child, I vainly kept trying to soften the look in my mother's eyes. I used to kiss her underwear; I used to drink her perfume until it made me sick. I loved her passionately, the way one is supposed to love. And yet whenever she lay down at my side after she'd been away, the mere touch of her skin was enough to propel me out of bed. When the slugging season came around, was I the one who provoked the onslaught in the hopes that it would be followed by a time of caresses? I thought life would turn out to be beautiful, but that's life for you. I still have a lot to learn.

Lulu was impetuous; Marie was too docile. How many times did I hold out my own wrists to be tied – if I'd been able to, I would have bound them myself. Anything not to displease Mama, to charm her, to win her love at last. The time of hugs and kisses never came. I started dreaming funny dreams. I would grasp a handful of poisonous sand in the palm of my right hand, and at supper every evening I'd slip a few grains into my mother's glass. She didn't die. My poison was ineffectual. She went right on laughing and, as soon as night fell, she'd go running out of the house. So I chucked my sand into the sink. My sleepless nights began. I kept my eyes glued to the hands of the alarm clock. How many times did I dream of swerving cars, flames, and crumpling metal? Every intersection between Meudon and Malakoff became mortally dangerous. From Chaville to Versailles, all the traffic lights were green: going down the grade at Petit-Clamart the brakes would fail, and I'd put my hands over my ears to shut out the tremendous crash ... But the click of her heels in the courtyard below would restore me to my senses, and I'd have to start all over again.

Then one evening, when I'd just begun my fantasy – at the very moment when, with the car out of control, the driver had laughingly started to take the curve near the traffic circle – she came in. I watched her stepping over the mattresses in the darkness. Holding her shoes in her hands, she murmured, 'Marie, are you asleep?'

'No, Mama.'

'Then come rub my belly for me.'

That night I straddled her uncomplainingly, until my wrists gave out. I learned with horror that her belly wasn't the imagined smooth-surfaced egg out of which I'd emerged, but a pit swarming with things known by barbarous names. Under my fingers, her colon, her duodenum, and her pancreas produced spasms and throbs. It was a whole world of fetid ooze. She knew her belly by heart and spoke of it tenderly. As I listened to her, I abandoned my dream fantasies. By the time I removed my thighs from her flanks, she would be snoring, open-mouthed, and I would gently pull the sheet up over her shoulders. Sometimes, half asleep, she would keep my hand in hers and murmur, 'At least you're not selfish. You're not like the others.'

Mother, Mother, how wrong you were! I was more selfish than they were. I wanted everything, absolutely everything from you; and you'd shown me the way I could win you. So to make those meetings occur I lived by your schedule and let my homework suffer. I lay in wait for you in every corner of our small apartment. I massaged you standing up and sitting down. I massaged every part of you. I succeeded in making you laugh, and when that happened, nothing else in the world mattered to me. When I sat perched on the ridge of your belly, listening to you purring, I'd forget how tired I was. You used to say 'Ouch! More gently.' You used to say, 'You take after me. Later, you'll have pains in *your* belly.'

I thought I'd brought it off. I thought that you wouldn't be able to do without me, and that I'd succeeded where Jacques and Lulu had failed. Then one day there was a newcomer at Mado's. I don't know what you saw in him; but I do know that your escapades started again and my hands irritated you. Banished from your belly, I went back to my fantasizing. You had amputated my heart; and so I began dreaming of marrying a blind man or someone as screwed up as I was – someone who would never run out on me.

Was Gerard the amorphous creature I was looking for? Do the two of you exert the same power over me? Why do your two skins have the same feel? Mama, Mama, for years I gleaned all the harvests of your belly, knowing that it was no use. Eleven years is a long time. I'm tired, and my wrists have lost their strength.

I made money my ally. I have Gerard eating out of my hand. Despite appearances, he's the one who's under my thumb. He lives at my beck and call. I picked someone just crummy enough to be incapable of getting away from me. Someday I'll indulge myself and ditch him the way I was ditched.

When I now try to sum up my life, everything is a muddle. My eyes are two opaque windows looking out on the world.

A man came into my life, and because he paid me without laying a finger on me, because he told me, 'You're fine and healthy,' because we spent evenings kissing each other's hands as we listened to Miles Davis, I thought that my blindness was at an end. I fell head over heels in love with him. I entrusted my heart to him – he was a cardiologist.

One anguished evening, I dialled his number with trembling fingers. I said to him, 'I feel awful.' He replied, 'Keep yourself busy. Buy yourself a donkey – the upkeep is minimal. Take a trip round the world. Learn Hebrew. Have children.' I almost answered, That takes two. I hung up thinking of the horrible glossy postcards he'd sent me from Nepal, with tender scrawls on the back promising to tell me about his trip.

When Gerry came home, I fell into his limp arms, sodden with tears and drink. When it's not in Gerard's arms, it's on Lulu's bosom that I collapse. I've saturated it with caresses. It's a generous, understanding bosom, ready at all times to mop up all the hurt and sadness in this wide world. I slide down its gentle slopes into the depths of its warm, silky dale, and there I roll and slither, I let myself go, I soothe myself, I settle down for as long as it takes me to shuck off my anguish, bury it in the proffered breast – preferable the left one. It's the fuller of the two, the more romantic, the more vulnerable. Oh, Marie, don't you worry about that for one second – Lulu's breast can take it. It just quivers ever so slightly underneath the nylon. A few tears roll down on either side of the stiffened globe, and Lulu laps them up with quick licks of her tongue; and then, with her erect knockers pointed at the ceiling, she searches for inspiration, tries to burst the bubble of anguish that has enveloped her little sister. Straining to their absolute limit, and still unable to attain the mists where Marie is trapped, her breasts collapse, crestfallen; but if they're weary, they're still unvanquished, and they're still capable of providing tenderness, even if nothing more. But I need something more. So I wade, splash, and skip stones. I keep hoping.

Things are changing at La Bohème. Lulu, Malou, and I are working as a team. The madam's authority is teetering. When she hires, we fire – first making sure that the newcomer isn't married to some young nephew of Al Capone. If she is, then we use stealth. What matters is denying her access to the bar and cutting her out of the action. Each of us has her own method. Malou will buy her a drink and propose a hand of rummy, and at the same time take an extended interest in her new friend's beautiful watch. If the girl has no watch, Malou takes an interest in her shoes or her purse: that keeps her out of the way. Sophie receives the new arrivals, shows them the cloakroom, and even helps them hang up their things. The girl doesn't find it at all surprising that in the course of the evening Sophie, looking concerned, takes her off to the powder room, explaining that she wants to put her in the know: and that keeps her out of the way. Lulu uses the direct approach. 'Did I hear a nasty comment, and was it meant for me?' The girl hasn't time to reply before Lulu ruffles her snout with the back of her hand, indicating to Rose that the newcomer is displaying manifest ill will.

We tie matters up by having a few with the new recruit, whose one desire is to be on our side. We've promised Pedro, who on certain stormy nights has threatened to kick us out, that we would show tact. We would no longer reject unsatisfactorily married broads out of hand: we'd remarry them. At that point, Lulu and I started wondering if such commercial flair wouldn't allow us, if we took the trouble, to trace our family tree back to the commercial magnificence of Sidon and Tyre rather than to humble roots in Auvergne.

One morning in June, a tall brunette in a leather dress enters La Bohème. She has one brown eye and one green one. I gaze in astonishment into those beautiful, unmatched eyes. She seems to move in a realm outside time. We're so bewitched we forget our sneaky ways. Not Lulu, though.

'You're sure you haven't come to the wrong fuckery?'

'Positive. My name's Odette, and this round's on me.'

Lulu is getting her back up. Two-Eyes fends off her attack.

'Scotch all around?'

Lulu gives in.

No need for us to lay out our bread in order to get her talking: our friend is eloquence itself. She talks, and talks; and she takes us into a world of pure science fiction. Hanging on to our seats in the spaceship, we listen to her in fascination. Unaware? Suicidal? Clearheaded? I can't tell. What's certain is that if she ever managed to convince us of the truth of the unbelievable things she's saying, we'd go home, wake up our men (assuming they're there), and send them out to do the hustling. We rub our eyes and pinch ourselves. No, it's still the same year. So what? Back in gear, she continues with her ravings. Our mouths are watering as we imagine the privileged life that hookers will be leading in the year 2000!

But when you think about it, do men deserve such cruelty? Is it possible that an entire dynasty will be overthrown by her words? We can't help but shed a tear or two over the fate of our guys. Hoarse sounds rumble in our bosoms and hinder our breathing. Two-Eyes inspects us loftily, her hands on her hips. We shiver and shake and hide our heads together, pouting at the thought that our colleagues of tomorrow will have bitches from the Women's House of Detention pimping for them.

Two-Eyes is beating her breast to underscore her points.

'I've never had a pimp! You've got to be an idiot to turn over your bread to some guy. I repeat – I got into the old firm on my own, and the guy who cops and locks me is going to have to have one this long.'

A lewd shimmer troubles Odette's beautiful eyes. Behind these futuristic declarations, can there be a woman who goes for men? Though I won't admit it, I admire Odette. She says out loud what I secretly believe. I could go on listening all night. And not for an instant does she suspect that while she's baring her soul in the limelight, in the shadows we're stringing bows with arrows ready to pierce her eyes, womb, and heart.

While the others turn back to their routine, a machiavellian plan is hatching in my little redhead. I want to beat the shit out of this beast until she can no longer move – after which I'll stretch out a repentant hand to her, and ply her with food and drink . . . I have a long night ahead of me : a night during which I can let my undertaking slowly come to a head.

At dawn, when La Bohème closes up, and it's already tomorrow, and the girls are heading back to their empty rooms, Lulu, Malou, and I set out on our punitive expedition. Two-Eyes is going up Rue Frochot towards Place Pigalle. We follow at a distance. No point in alarming the prey.

At Boulevard de Clichy, aware of the pack on its trail, aware of the danger it's in, the beast turns around in its tracks.

'What do you want?'

'Nothing at all. We're just walking around. Just out for a stroll.'

The animal trots off, tripping slightly as it goes. I start to soften. Is it because I know she's pregnant? A creamy early-morning light sweeps across the housefronts on the boulevard. I glance at Malou, who is gazing down at the asphalt. Is she thinking the same things I am? Her black mane thrown back, fiery Lulu leads the way. It's been a rotten night for her – ninety francs from one steered customer on whom a cabbie got a kickback. She has the bit between her teeth.

Odette has apparently forgotten her address. The four of us find ourselves lined up together at the same red light. The Barbès clock reads ten past six. Panting, the animal gets away from us. It's almost upended by a taxi as it crosses against the light. We hurry after her. She swerves to one side. She turns right, then left, then backtracks. We finally corner her on Rue du Delta.

She's at bay – back to the wall, purse clutched flat against her chest, hands empty. Her wide eyes send out a continuous SOS. Lulu aims for the belly. Purse and arms drop. Lulu punches like Yves, precisely and methodically. After the belly, the breasts. The animal totters as it tries to protect itself. Her contorted face seems to defy us. Not for long. We finish her off with our fists, feet, and heels. The blows fall thick and fast. She falls moaning on her side, with her skirt over her head and her wig on the sidewalk. Before hopping into a cab, my sister gives Odette's purse a kick. Its contents scatter in the gutter.

'How about a bite at La Cloche d'Or to get our strength back? How's that sound to you, Sophie?'

'My treat – if you promise that we do not talk about this any more.'

When Lulu and Yves first moved in with Gerry and me, I was happy to have my sister around. Thanks to her, I learned about the Gambay tomboy who used to break chestnuts on her brother's head with a hammer, and who accused her sister of sticking a pin in her abdomen when she was stung by a wasp. It astonished me to discover that I'd tied pots and pans to the tails of cats, who would then tear around the village miaowing like lost souls. Lulu stirred deeply buried memories which no one had ever told me about. That made me happy. I was Marie once again. I used to listen to her while she was washing up or laundering the men's shirts. I also learned about my cruelty and tenderness, about my joys and my wants. I gazed at her in amazement: when she spoke to me like that, the other woman, the one I had such a hard time understanding, disappeared, and the big sister I had always wanted to preserve emerged once again.

Unfortunately, things went downhill fast. At La Bohème, Lulu doesn't get many customers. I get a lot. This makes her aggressive, jealous, bitter. She takes pleasure in demolishing the values I still believe in. She doesn't like Malou, she can't stand hearing France's name, and all my efforts to steer customers her way and to adapt myself to her prove fruitless.

At home, though money's in short supply, there's no lack of slaps and blows. Our superpimps, who work hand in glove, like thieves at a carnival, refine their sadism to the point of making us shine their shoes before kicking us in the gut with them. Yves, who doesn't give a damn about anything, punches Lulu in the face, with the result that four days out of six she goes to work with a shiner. That's no good for business. So I split my take with her. That means I get my portion of blows. My stomach isn't particularly sensitive, but I do find punches hard to digest ...

Suddenly I start longing for a different atmosphere. I sit with my head between my hands and dream of a lovely apartment where Malou and I could work by phone. Unfortunately, little Lulu and her Toulonese pimp won't move out. I keep my thinking cap on day and night. Eureka! On to the bare boards of my imagination rolls the little seed that I'd tucked away to ripen two weeks earlier. It's become a surprisingly smooth, round, red bean; and it bears an astonishing resemblance to Odette. Wasn't the purpose of our recent escapade to get Two-Eyes to marry my old man?

And so one morning I invite the statuesque Odette to lunch at L'Alsace.

She takes the bait unhesitatingly. She's glad to know that she's finally been accepted and that she even has a friend. She doesn't ask herself why I invited her. It seems perfectly normal to her for us to be sitting there in front of a vast platter of seafood and a bottle of Alsatian wine. She's delivered herself postpaid, and she shows no signs of resentment. She almost apologizes when she mentions the scabs on her head, which still bother her whenever she combs her hair. Without any malice, she admits to liking me better than my sister; she wants to know if I can put her on to someone for her abortion; and she asks me for help in finding a studio apartment not too far from work. Don't give it a thought, Odette. Today you're lunching with your fairy godmother.

I keep my eye on the door. We've started on our second bottle when Gerard just happens to walk in ... A psychedelic smile lights up my face. He's smiling, too, as he approaches us. It's a most expressive smile that says, 'You sure you know what you're doing? You're sure you won't make a scene if I sit down with your friend?' My eyes answer, 'No, go ahead. I'm sure.'

Come on, Gerry. Show a little nerve. I know you didn't

expect this of me. You've always taken me for an idiot. You thought I was jealous. You've been wrong right down the line. I was jealous, but not of anyone else: I was jealous of my dough, which you keep openhandedly pouring down the drain. You're a fool. As you approach, I pray that you'll find her attractive, that she'll give you a big hard-on, and that you won't make her feel like throwing up. I pray that it'll be her and not me who pays the instalments on your lousy wheels, who pays for your booze and your duds. I'm saying a prayer to Little Jesus for her to make you forget I exist. I pray that you'll get into her, and that you'll get her to take you on – broke as you are. I'm working for me, Gerry – just me. How can you be jerk enough to think even for one split second that I'm doing all this on your account?

The more I look at you, the more easily I imagine you as a somewhat quaint but handsome couple associated under the Ass-Holes Incorporated. Get to know each other. Love each other. Do whatever you like. As for me, I'm through. Goodbye and good luck. Now that I've introduced you to her, and you revolt me more than ever, I'd like to withdraw. As a parting gift, I'll let you pick up the check and the cost of her abortion as well. I'll leave you alone over coffee. Oh, she's ripe as a melon in July! *Qué será, será* . . .

Afterwards she'll be doing the hooking instead of me. I'll gradually stop going to La Bohème. I won't make scenes when he comes home. I'll suggest his taking her to Deauville for the weekend. I'll suggest their going to Monte Carlo together. I'll tell him he should spoil her a little. His friends will gradually start addressing her as Madame Gerard. He'll grow fonder of her, and less fond of me, and I'll quietly tiptoe off. The future belongs to those who hoist their sails! Don't thank me, Odette, and don't say I'm a godsend – I don't want to be accountable to anyone, and certainly not to the Good Lord!

I hadn't imagined how easy it was to recruit a wife-in-law for one's husband. And I didn't feel a thing – no sadness, and no regret. Without realizing it, I'd walked all the way down to the Pont au Change, trying to tote up the days of happiness I'd spent with Gerard. A violet light was spreading over the far side of the river, engulfing the towers of Notre Dame. I went in and lit a candle.

In no time I become Odette's bosom companion. She complains about her husband's spending time away from home, about his lack of ardour. I'm not to blame: our husband simply prefers scotch and barmaids. On those nights at La Bohème when business is slack, little sister slowly spills the story of her life under the mocking gaze of the other girls. Youth had come and gone with the speed of a tornado: and from orphanage to solitude, from tears to squalls, that wind had carried her all the way to Paris . . .

When she got off the train from Rouen, Odette headed straight for a newsstand. Being in Paris was all very well, but she wanted to stay, she had to find a job pronto. The thought of going back empty-handed and becoming a farm girl brought tears to her eyes. To her, there was nothing drearier than the Perche countryside with its rain-sodden hills. She had turned twenty-six the previous month. It was high time she did something.

Settled on the terrace of the Café Mollard, with her little cardboard suitcase squeezed between her legs, she carefully made her way through the classified ads for household employees. She longed to have a second croissant, but every time her little chubby red fingers approached the basket, her Norman good sense held her back. Paris wore its glum, early-March face. Hailstones the size of peas were rebounding from the asphalt. Buses were spewing forth a crowd that hurried half-asleep to its daily grind. The big station clock read eight.

Odette had almost reached the bottom of the page. Her heart was growing heavy as she licked up her last drops of café au lait. There were not even a dozen ads remaining. Suddenly her arm relaxed, her plump little hand reached out for another croissant, and her legs loosened their grip: she'd found it. (Even if she didn't know how to write and still signed her name with an awkward cross, she'd at least learned how to read; and what was inscribed beneath her clipped fingernail was the very thing for her.) 'Hotel seeks cleaning woman, nice appearance, references not essential, good remuneration, accommodation. Call 874— . . .' Good remuneration? She'd got stuck on the word, but the voice on the other end of the line had reassured her: it meant she'd be well paid.

The farm outside Rouen began sinking into the mists of oblivion. 'Get out at Place Blanche,' she repeated aloud as the waiter promptly turned over the saucer in which she'd left the change of ten francs. She had nineteen left.

Her heart swelling with hope, she made her way through the hail and rushed down into the Métro. March weather has its unpredictable whims. When she emerged from the subway again, a pale sun was sweeping across the rooftops of Place Pigalle. (It was one stop too far – but she hadn't dared ask people to move out of her way, and her suitcase had been a handicap.) She lifted up her face for a whiff of spring. No doubt about it, life was great.

By day, Pigalle was like a hooker without her makeup: it offered nothing in particular to catch the eye. After asking directions from a cabdriver, Odette walked partway down Rue Pigalle and partway up Rue Fontaine. She stopped in front of number 59, and with beating heart she rang the bell embedded in the wall. Clutching the flaps of her green nylon negligee, Madame Pedro came down to let her in. They sat down together in the kitchen. Matters were settled rapidly. After stammeringly accepting a cup of coffee, Odette went up to the fourth floor behind Madame Pedro, who was explaining to her what a day's work at the Saint-Louis involved.

When Odette was shown her room, she could hardly believe it. She set her cardboard suitcase down on the little bed covered in flowered cretonne. The door slammed shut. The landlady had asked her whether later, once she got used to the hotel, she'd agree to work nights. She had enthusiastically answered yes – she was going to start living a topsyturvy life! Exhausted as she was by all these emotions, she wanted to laugh and cry at the same time. As she sat on the edge of the bed, she wept softly. Tears as warm as a spring shower fell on her rough hands.

During her first day at work, Odette was amazed that none of the hotel guests was in his room when she went in. Nor was there anything lying around – no clothes, no shoes, no towels, no toothbrushes. The beds were barely mussed. It was enough to make you think that the hotel was inhabited entirely by ghosts. They were ghosts who smoked a lot, and used astronomical quantities of Kleenex and condoms. Odette decided she must have happened on to a traveller's hotel, a place for transients; and perhaps in Paris it was the custom to make your own bed before checking out. There seemed no point in asking questions. In any case, the other maid, an old woman from Guadalupe, hardly encouraged conversation. Having pointed to the broom closet, she had described the routine of work in a farrago of incomprehensible words. Well trained in household chores, Odette managed to give an excellent account of herself without further details.

At the end of her day, feeling light at heart, she went out to the *café-tabac* at the corner for a sandwich and beer, then came back to room 21, on the fourth floor, ready for a good night's sleep. She slipped between the sheets made soft by countless launderings and burrowed her head into the pillow. She couldn't remember ever having been so happy. Sleep had started to numb her limbs and drown her thoughts when bursts of laughter and talk reached her ears. She shook herself, got up on her elbows, and cocked an ear. Latecoming travellers, no doubt, or a busload of tourists – she had seen several that morning on Place Pigalle. In any event, her day was over. Her head sank back on to the pillow as she drew the topsheet up to her chin. She felt sleepy.

Nonetheless, the voices kept rising from below, and the laughter grew shriller. It slipped past the door between the sheets – brief, nervous laughs filled with women's names: Valerie, Brigitte, Josiane, Kim, Muriel, France ... It was an insistent laughter. She turned towards the door and heard the strident ringing of a bell, followed by a clatter of footsteps that sounded like a cavalry charge racing downstairs. Then silence returned.

Sitting on the edge of her bed, Odette tried to make something of all this. Since the silence continued, she went back to bed. Once again the laughter welled up, shaking the walls of her room. It seemed reasonable enough at this point to ask these travellers to be a little more moderate. She put on her flannelette bathrobe, and, her feet bare and her hair rumpled, left her room.

On the landing below, the door from which the laughter was pouring forth stood ajar. Odette knocked hesitantly.

'What is it?' the voices responded.

Odette swallowed hard. If she was going to get any sleep that night, she'd have to risk it.

'It's the cleaning woman, I'm in twenty-one, and—'

She did not complete the sentence.

'And what?'

The door of number 19 opened abruptly. Odette blinked and wondered if she wasn't dreaming.

'Well, come in, kid, don't be scared! Are we by any chance disturbing you?' the voices went on.

Oh, how she would have liked to run away! She wanted to fade into the walls and disappear for ever. How naked she felt, how alone and ill at ease under those mocking eyes!

'Sit down, baby. If you're part of the help here, we might as well get acquainted. We're on the staff, too. Come on, girls, make some room for her.'

As if in a dream, Odette sat down on the bed, took the cigarette that was offered her, and even though she wasn't thirsty, started swigging beer from a bottle. Her eyes weren't big enough. Her ears were too tiny. Her mouth was too inarticulate.

'So you're the day girl? Too bad. With your legs, you should ask the old lady to let you work nights. You'd pick up some crazy tips. The animals are all horny weirdos. You'd give them a hard-on just handing them a towel. It'd make life easier for us and you'd get a fancy increase in take-home pay. By the way, what's your name?'

Her voice choking, Odette described how she had arrived that very morning. In the grip of some strange compulsion, she started talking about herself – about everything: the farm in Normandy, the owner who was always after her, always shoving his hand up her skirt every time his nasty-tongued better half looked the other way. She told them about the jealousy of the women who worked in the kitchen, her exhausting chores, the bread and milk after fifteen hours' work, and the garret she shared with spiders and mice. She told them of her unsuccessful marriage with a shopkeeper in the town, and her train ride from Rouen to Paris, her breakfast at the Café Mollard, the ad in the paper, the Métro ride, and how she'd missed her station. No doubt she would have gone on talking for hours if the bell hadn't interrupted her.

The girls went stampeding down the stairs. Sitting in the middle of the bed, Odette followed the laughter and the clicking heels. She finished a beer that someone had left behind. Something more urgent than her fatigue and her longing to get back to bed made her stay in the room. She wanted to hear those laughing voices again. She settled down with her back against the wall and waited. The girls came back up, making comments on the selection, which had been no selection at all: a bunch of Americans who'd slunk off with their tails between their legs. Business was bad. The cash flow was drying up. Three hundred francs a night, maybe five hundred – doodly shit. Odette's ears grew bigger and bigger. She couldn't get over it. At 3.00 a.m., when she went back to number 21 with a good ten beers inside her, her eight hundred francs a month seemed so ludicrous to her that she cried; and this time the tears that splashed over her hands were hot and bitter.

Odette is crying now, silently, just the way she did that first night at the Saint-Louis. She hung on for four years, there and at the Oklahoma, playing tough and smart; and now, at thirty, she's been had. She's had plenty of guys in her past, and good-looking ones at that. But it's Gerry, with his screwed-up face, who's been her downfall. It's no good my joshing her and telling her, 'You're only crying out of one eye!' She doesn't smile; she glares at me through her tears. Her brown eye says, 'It's not true what they say, you're not my husband's wife.' The green eye, dry and cold, is denunciatory: 'Tramp! Creep!' History repeats itself. I'm tripping up Odette just the way Judas did Jesus on the Mount of Olives.

Now Two-Eyes has gone away. I wash my hands of it. I'm not responsible – I'm as much a victim as she is. He's the guilty party. He's the one who's raking it in on both sides, and who's started finding the proximity of his wives-in-law dangerous. He knows me. He knows that I'm perfectly capable, just on impulse, of wising this little sister up. So he's sent her off to the Arabs at Barbès. You see? I had nothing to do with it.

There's a sadness in the air at La Bohème, in spite of the summer, which has appeared on the scene with great bursts of sunlight. Lulu is the next to leave; she goes back to the Medina. Malou keeps talking about going on a vacation with her daughter. A newcomer has replaced Odette, but I couldn't care less. I'm tired of fighting. What I need is to float on the tide for a while ...

My salvation takes the form of Maurice. I'm sure that if I

dangle the right bait under Gerard's nose, if I confront him with words that are closely followed by figures, he'll sign my leave papers. I'm so eager to be myself once again and go back to the Mediterranean that I arrange a veritable candlelight supper, at which, with no regret, I unstash a chunk of my savings and slip them under my guardian's napkin. He licks his fingers and directs a tearful look at me.

'You're a princess, baby – a real woman. Not like that other bitch. I even think she's been popping her cookies with those North Africans.'

It would make me so happy if he'd just shut up and give me his permission. The only thing is, when Gerry's been drinking, he has to let it all out. He even becomes affectionate; and that's the hardest part for a little woman like me to take. Sweet Jesus, that man can make things so difficult!

'She seems to dig black meat, your friend does. Mark my words, baby, that slut won't last out the winter. She's a bitch. I have to get high just to slam her a little, and I don't even enjoy it. You with me, baby?'

I'm with you, Gerry. You're stirring my bowels ... You're not big enough to keep two wives on your string. You're just a two-bit pimp. But the day you're down and out, don't count on me to spoon feed you. Now come on, let's have your blessing. I want to take off for the sunshine and see if I can still function like a normal woman. Amèn!

On a warm July morning two days later, I hit the road with Maurice and his two daughters in an old supercharged Peugeot. Gangway for the blue sea, the olive groves, and the crickets! Maurie's in heaven. He's started talking about an autumn wedding.

It may be hot, but there's nothing new under the sun. Maurice is still spinning fairy tales: his dream villa actually belongs to his publisher. In spite of everything, I knock myself out trying to make him feel good. I get out of breath playing hide-and-seek and tag with him and his kids. Then all of a sudden monsieur stumbles: down he goes, and out pop his false teeth. Thick clouds suddenly fill the sky. Lightning abruptly strikes me. I'm put to shame and publicly stigmatized. Is it my fault that monsieur wears false teeth? Is it my fault that it's been raining for two days, if the water's cold, or if he's been losing at the casino? Is it my fault he's half impotent, if I'm the one who's here instead of Minouche, or if men turn around in the street to look at me?

Oh, Maurice, Maurice! You forget that you're the one who bought me these miniskirts. You forget that you're the one who made me walk on ahead with your daughters. Poor you – with or without false teeth, it's all in your head. No kidding, I could ditch you right now – but the sun is sublimely hot and the sky is as glorious as ever, in spite of your insults. And don't forget, Mr Hotshot, we have a business agreement. I'll wait till we're home before saying goodbye.

To prepare my homecoming, I write to Malou: 'Keep your eyes open, kitten, take good care of my customers, and give some thought to my suggestion that we share an apartment.' Lord, will I ever hit some smooth sailing that will allow me to recycle myself in some provincial convent? Whether by veil or by sail, I'm ready to weigh anchor for brighter horizons.

I drive back with Maurice, who has threatened to stop payment on his cheque if I don't travel with him. Hanging on to my seat, I watch with weary eyes as plane trees, zones of light and shadow, hollows, valleys, copses, and vast forests go flashing by. Maurice doesn't look at anything. He's just moving. There's a grim look on his face, his hands are glued to the wheel, his foot to the floor. The old Peugeot starts eating up the asphalt. The children are asleep on the back seat. I get bug-eyed at every turn. 'Scared?' Maurice asks as he pushes the machinery to the limit. I rest my cheek against the pane and close my eyes. After ten hours of terror we reach Porte de Versailles.

'Get out. Go back to your hood. That's what you really deserve.'

Fine, Maurie. No need to repeat yourself, my head isn't that thick. When you wham it with a hammer, I get a bump. So long, buddy.

My neighbourhood actually looks good to me. Will Gerard be home? The concierge catches me on my way in. There's a leer in her eyes when she invites me into her lodge. I imagine the worst.

'Let me make you a cup of coffee,' the supersnoop whispers as she moves towards the hot plate.

Here we go. She's going to spill the beans. She drops the

mail, grasps me by the shoulders, clucks her tongue, lets out a deep sigh – and do I ever learn things from the lips of Madame Boisramé! She even manages to surprise me.

It seems that Gerard has been leading *la dolce vita* during my absence. His girls have been putting quite a dent in my mattress. They've rummaged through my things, used my perfume, and God knows what else. As I climb my two flights, I feel pathetic, jealous, and rejected. I'd been ready to marry Maurice in October, but now I start looking forward to having Gerard around. Curled up on the doormat, the neighbour's cat stares at me out of its beautiful yellow eyes. Hello, puss, you gutter phoenix. Yes, you've got my tongue. All these riddles are too much for me.

Two hours later Gerard arrives. As a welcoming gesture he belts me twice. It's a way of bringing the colour back to my cheeks. The pretext is that I forgot to send him a postcard.

He's sleeping now. His eyes are shut, and he's drooling as he dreams of the milky bosom of some passing *dushka*. Once again, Gerard has broken my heart.

I return to my post at La Bohème on a Sunday evening. From the other girls I learn that Malou left on vacation the day before. I'm furious with myself for not having phoned her. Aside from her absence and the emptiness it's left, nothing has changed. Fabienne wastes no time in telling me that she's handled all my customers. She reports exactly what each one gave her, and this reassures me: they've remained faithful to me. A woman has phoned for me several days in a row but refused to leave her name. France! Who else would wrap herself in such mystery? With a song in my heart, I phone the bar Pour les Oiseaux – 'There is no one by the name of France at this number. There is no one—' I hang up in a fit of doomsday depression.

Work has lost all interest for me. My period is two days late. My friends are off having a ball under starry skies. The girls who've stayed behind are down in the dumps. My gloom is so vast I don't know where to start working on it. It sticks to my skin, my hair, my fingers. I try drowning it, but it seems to thrive on scotch. Come on, Sophie. Snap out of it. Make yourself some money, make yourself a winner, make yourself a star – it's either win or die! You're here to earn your nightly bread. Get those feet moving. Pounce on that little bird-faced man who just came through the door. Look how down-and-out he seems in that grey suit that's miles too big for him. Give him a hand – play him your barrel organ, shove your sun-ripened breasts under his roving eyes, spread your skirt on to his knees.

'My name's Sophie.'

'I'm Paul.'

Oh, Paul, you're so clumsy-looking. Your neck is so skinny I'd like to strangle it. But I won't. You look very sweet, and very generous. Am I right in thinking that you're not from around here? Oh! You spend nine months of every year in Africa? Lucky little fellow, you must have seen a lot. You must have gazed up at rainbows, and stroked brown backs, and tamed gazelles!

'What are you doing so far from home?'

I took Paul's moist hand. We spent half the night at the Macao. He was a funny guy, riddled with inhibitions. It was fun shocking him. He kept saying, 'Sophie, I won't be able to live without you. Come with me to Africa next year.' He went on talking, with his cheek resting on my belly, while I caressed his close-cropped hair and dreamed of the bluebird and vast forgotten sunscapes. When we left the hotel, he insisted on paying for another bottle. Since I'd made more than enough for one night, I accepted. He'd taken a fancy to slow foxtrots. After three dances, we went back up to the same room. The bed was warm. Between two clinches, Paul apologized for his bursts of passion. It was a beautiful night. I had twelve hundred francs in my purse, and I'd just made the acquaintance of a nice guy whom I had every chance of seeing again.

My homecoming, which started off so badly, is turning out rather well. Summer is at its peak, and La Bohème's doors stay open all night long. Lightly clad girls purvey their charms to the passersby ... In his shirtsleeves, Simon hustles the crowd in every known language. Josepha talks enthusiastically about her native land, and its coves, its wild hinterland, and her house on the hill. As she listens, Madame Rose moans over the fate of her two sons, condemned to remain under lock and key. Life could be beautiful. No one has to grab men by the collar and drag them into our hostel, nor am I one to hide from them. The only trouble is, I feel so listless all the time. My red silk skirt no longer twirls in the light ...

I'm pregnant.

Gerard, who refuses to deal with this chore (he describes it as revolting), has made an appointment for me with an abortionist: a kind of hairy-hammed giant whom I follow into his cavern with my stomach in knots. The lumberjack quickly relieves me of my seven hundred francs. I lurch out into the night, knowing once again that I'm about to spend some time in the hospital. The prospect doesn't frighten me. It's one of the risks of the trade. It's one of the minor dirty tricks that everyday life plays on you, or at least on me. I'll bet Gerard won't come home tonight or tomorrow. He may not even telephone. He says my suffering upsets him. He can't bear the sound of my groans.

When I had my last abortion, six months ago, he used urgent business out of town as a pretext for getting away. When he came back, I was bedridden with a fever that would have felled a horse. I told him that I'd called a doctor, who had diagnosed a retained placenta. I had to go to the hospital immediately. It would cost at least two thousand francs

He laughed in my face, and said, 'I really took a bath at Deauville. So if you want to get that shit cleaned out of you, you better ask your buddies at La Bohème for the jack.'

My pride took quite a beating. Sophie, the big winner, forced to ask for handouts to pay for a curettage. Cynthia had given me five hundred (her take for the night) and France twice that much. She'd had a run of luck.

She insisted on taking me home. Outside my door I plucked up my courage and told her I'd lied: Gerard wasn't on the run. We stood there next to one another for a long while, leaning our heads against the wall, not saying a word. It was the second time I'd heard her cry ... Where is she now? Has she managed to have a baby with Jean-Jean? Was she the one who called me at La Bohème? Will things be the same if we ever get back together? Won't she have met a Malou of her own? Franzie ... She's so much like me. Between us, a gesture or a look is enough. We belong to the same race, to the same vintage batch. France, I miss you. How fabulous it would be to live with you! If only our men could grasp the fact that it would mean fewer risks for them – and for us, it would already be a big step forward, a breakthrough towards independence. Furthermore, I wouldn't be here now, mashing my belly against the bathroom tiles, hungry for coolness the way I'm hungry for you, biting on a bath towel so as not to scream.

You'd put a hot-water bottle filled with ice cubes on my tummy. You'd make me a cup of cambric tea. You'd take my temperature. Like a trusting child, I'd let you coddle me. When the cramps became too strong, you'd gently push the probe into my womb, taking care not to make the pain any worse: you'd deftly insert it just far enough to speed up the expulsion. Tomorrow, at the first drop of blood, you'd withdraw it gently, and we'd go together to the gynaecologist's – to that hooker's gynaecologist who, like his patients, makes a living by spreading their legs.

At four hundred a go, the nice doctor doesn't have to worry about where his next meal is coming from. But you have to admit that he's conscientious, polite, even charming. There are backbiters who say he's a rotten doctor because he treats a sore throat as if it were a dose of clap. So what? Everyone has his speciality. They ought to consult a nose-and-throat man.

They also complain that he isn't the obliging kind. Who needs to be obliging when he has it made? It wouldn't do much for his reputation if one fine morning the police said to him, 'All right, Doc, we're shutting down your office and sending you off to the clink to join your clients' husbands.' Frankly, he'd have to be the biggest jerk alive; but don't worry – there's no chance of Dr Profit getting involved. He has too much to lose. Who can blame him? Anyway, if he started getting softhearted, can you imagine what his office would look like? A washhouse, a lake, an ocean, Versailles with all its fountains playing! The poor man would end up drowning.

Everything is simple with old Doc Profit. His motto seems to be 'order and method'. Tomorrow, or the day after at the latest, I'll go into his consulting room. He'll be standing there with his hands lying flat inside the pockets of his immaculate white smock, and I'll hear the inevitable 'Hello, Mamzelle Sophie. Everything okay?' A forced smile will accompany his words. I'll answer, 'No, Doctor. Everything's a mess.' He'll keep right on smiling, and I'll feel the cold rubber sheet under my buttocks. He'll take a quick look inside and ask me what I'm complaining about – after all, I'm bleeding. He'll shrug his shoulders and fill out the paper that will allow me to be cleaned out without any trouble. 'Supplementary curettage' is what the medics call it. You see? It's as simple as pop goes the weasel.

With this permit, plus ninety bills up front when you sign in, you breeze into the Bluebell Clinic easy as pie. They even settle you in a double room, with a coin-operated TV set, if you please. And no one would ever think of asking indiscreet questions. The place is nice. It's terrific. My name for the procedure is well-organized hypocrisy. Everyone knows that before coming here you got your womb butchered by some bum or other: one slip, one clumsy move, one insufficiently disinfected probe, and zap! You'd have quietly cashed in your chips. But who cares about that? Appearances are safe. The docs wash their hands of the matter. Their consciences are crystal-clear.

And how dare you think of complaining? Listen, you little rebel, just you shut up! You play with your body, so you pay with it. That's logical. All's well that ends well in the best of all possible worlds. At least that's what you try and tell yourself next day when you wake up half zapped, with your nostrils swathed in chloroform and a couple of pounds of cotton (in addition to two Kotex pads) between your thighs. You walk out feeling as though you've travelled crosscountry in a tanker truck. You wonder what the fuck you're doing on Avenue de la République at five in the afternoon with greasy hair, pale cheeks, and haggard eyes. You feel like a turd that somebody's just stepped in.

That night you go to work. It's true that you promised the head doc to take it easy for at least two weeks. He patted you on the cheek reprovingly, and for a moment there you were sucked in. You timidly raised your eyes and looked up at the Grand Panjandrum, and your pale lips spread in a wonderful smile of gratitude. A sucker. He played you for a sucker. That man in white is totally blind. As he was mechanically patting your cheek, his mind was wandering off to his Thursday-evening bridge game, or to his evenings at the Traveller's Club, where with others of his tribe he'll rinse his gums with bourbon and babble about all the misery in the world.

And he was right: because in a few hours, you'll be back on your beat. *Noblesse oblige!* Just the same, plan on spending a quiet night. Leave the acrobatics to the others, since they seem to get such a kick out of them. Tonight, cheat a little, use those mitts of yours, give a few recitals on the one-holed flute. That'll make everybody happy (including yourself), especially the pimps: you won't have wasted a night, and you'll have taken good care of your health, which is not only priceless but worth its weight in gold.

If I behave this way, it's not out of greed but out of defiance. It's a defiance that involves not only the doctors but the other girls as well. They'd be all too happy if I stayed away more than one night. And I mustn't forget Gerard, to whom, unfortunately, I still feel obliged to vindicate myself. But mainly the defiance concerns me and my relations to established laws and systems. I'm as stubborn as a thousand mules rolled into one. I have to have my nose rubbed in shit before I'll admit it stinks. It's my only hope of someday getting out of this life. I have to use every available means to disgust and revolt myself. I need to make myself die, the better to be reborn – all by myself, with no help from anyone. That's how I make my way through the labyrinth of hookerdom: head first, and eyes wide open. I'm never easy on myself for a second. I never say no to a customer, whether he be lame or hunchback, one-armed or one-legged, sadist or masochist, or just plain repulsive. A washed crotch means a clean crotch, and condoms weren't invented to hang on walls.

I want to learn how far I can go, and then go there, collapsing so that I can rediscover myself. It's becoming a real obsession. I seem to be living in a nightmare that from time to time is streaked with brilliant lightning flashes of reality. Day after day I suffer as I stretch myself to the limit, trying to resolve the mystery that has estranged me from my own self. I look in the mirror and don't recognize what I see; I make faces that no longer mean anything to the person that perceives them. When I sink into one of the fits of depression that are becoming more and more frequent, I get the feeling that one day I'm going to end up committed to an asylum from which I'll never emerge. Who can I share my anxieties with? Who'd understand? To whom could I confess that I'm afraid to go home to my mother? One look from her, and I become transparent. I no longer dare kiss my little brothers for fear of soiling them. I wear placards on my back, brow, and breast: little slate signs on which has been lettered in white chalk the word WHORE.

*

I'm not the only one who's bothered by my obsessions. Gerard, that sucker for the obvious, wants me to play hooker by day as well as by night – with him.

'Come on, baby,' he drools, 'be nice. Tell me about one of your tricks.'

Baby has nothing to tell. She only left the Bluebell Clinic this morning. She can't keep her eyes open, and her tummy's on edge. She quietly draws the curtains, sets Zola's *The Human Beast* down on the pillow, and stretches out on the rumpled bed.

'You lazy slut. All you ever think about is sleeping. And then you're surprised when I do my balling elsewhere!'

'Don't try and find excuses. Just let me rest.'

'I don't need excuses. Here's something for you – take that in your little puss ... You give me a pain in the ass wasting your bread on shoes like these. Or does the lady want to be a little girl again and play cutie-pie?'

My chin copped that one. I'm too beat to talk. If I do, I'll get to bite on the other moccasin. Let's calm the savage beast.

'When are you going to start acting like a woman – like a real woman? I'm ashamed to walk down the street with you in shoes like that. I don't know why I don't bust you wide open when you pull stunts like this. At least the other one looks like a woman. She knows how to dress.'

'You mean she looks like a hooker. Like a tart. Boy, if you hadn't turned into a pimp, you'd sure have made a great john. You're a pain. Fuck off. Go live your life with Odette. Just get off my back. Can't you see I don't give a damn any more?'

'How about *that*? Feel anything?'

'Not much. Beat it. You're so repulsive you make me want to puke. You're totally zonked again. As for my taste in clothes, it's mine, and I'm not about to change it.'

'You're going to change it right now. Take a good look at what I'm doing with your crappy shoes, and your skins, and your swishy cocksucking skirts – out the window! Gone with the wind! On their way to the garbage bin!'

'You're out of your skull. Take it easy – do you want them coming after us?'

'Stay where you are or out you go too.'

Poor little me. When he had defenestrated half my wardrobe

and ten pairs of shoes, he lay down mumbling, 'Baby, let's make up. Tell me about one of your tricks ...'

I opened the bathroom window part way. Below stood the butcher and his wife, her hands turned outward on her hips; the hairdresser, with her mouth open and a curler between her teeth; one of her customers, who had just emerged beet-red from under the drier; the concierge, raising her crooked fingers to heaven; and the florist, who was leaning against the lamp-post. A delivery van had come to a stop right in the middle of the street, blocking traffic all the way down to Rue du Hameau. The driver had got out and was shouting how Jesus Christ there were a lot of crazy people who hadn't been locked up, not by a long shot, and the goddamn cops were never around when you needed them.

Naturally, this scene didn't exactly encourage me to leave then and there. I curled up on a corner of the bed, wondering, once again, if I'd ever find a way out.

chapter two

We've gone to La Venta to celebrate Malou's return. The paella and the wine make us nostalgic. Our eyes are shining, and our fingers intertwine ...

Malou stifles a laugh.

'I think I wet my pants a little.'

You can't take that Malou anyplace. She's just a kid!

'You're impossible. All it takes is a draft or a badly rolled joint and you're back in the gutter. You're just an animal.'

Her little grey eyes grow wide.

'An animal?'

'What I mean is, you lose control so easily. We've got to get going. We're running behind schedule.'

'I say to hell with Mama Pedro and Poppa Dahl. To hell with the pimps and Rose and Josepha and the girls!'

'Let's have another bottle, and to hell with everybody! We're going to take off one of these days, you, and me, and the lamp-post. We're going to have a fantastic time. We're going to take it real easy, in a lovely apartment building in some nice part of town. And on the nights we feel sad, we'll stuff our cheeks full of caviar and tell our life stories.'

'We'll have a stereo.'

'And lots of blues to listen to. We'll snap our fingers, and guys will go down like flies. We'll entertain Jack Daniel, Mr Lever and all his brothers, John Lennon, Mr Pepsi and his cola cousins ...'

'Picasso ...'

'And Manolides. Down with our pimps! Send 'em all to the shithouse! Up with freedom! You know that poem of Paul Eluard's? You don't know it, so listen: "On my classroom notebooks, on my school desk, on the trees ... on pages that I read, on pages that are blank ... on my bed that empty shell I write your name. I was born to know you, and to name you: Freedom! ..." I don't remember any more, it's something I learned in school ... Better get moving ... Come on, driver, step on it. On to Pigalle-by-night. On to the infernal region ...'

'Hi there, girls, hello, Rose, hello, Josepha! Sure we're late, but people don't seem to be exactly waiting in line.'

'You didn't miss a thing. Sandrine's the only one who's busy.'

No complaints. They're good, loyal girls, these doxies. I could whirl around right this second and be sure I'd catch them looking at me with affection. But if you're a bunch of fucked-over dopes, that's tough tittie! You'll all die on some street corner. What's taking that gasbag Sandrine so long? What can she be yakking about to that guy? Every time she opens her trap, something dopey comes out. She's one I can see at forty, leaning on a lamppost with a butt dangling from her mouth. A real caricature. The incurable hooker. She's twenty-three and has already been through two pimps. It'll take at least fifteen toughs to make her understand that men have been using her as a piggy bank. And don't start imagining that you can make a broad like that see the light. You'll only make her get her back up and start gnashing her teeth. They've seen it all, they know it all, and nobody in the world is going to tell them anything. Nothing exists for them except the life. They won't even listen to you. Anyone who tries to open their eyes simply has no 'strength of character'. Ask any pimp, he'll tell you how important 'strength of character' is – for women.

Good old 'strength of character'. They're so right. When you're forty years old standing on a street corner, you feel a lot less lonely if you've got strength of character for company. You can chew the fat with strength of character and bring back memories of your salad days. You can give it a slap on the back and offer it a smoke. But, ladies, strength of character isn't going to fill your belly. If at least they understood that much. I'm not asking them to send their men off to the pen. God forbid! I like men myself. But where strength of character is concerned, they rave on about it without ever having had to prove whether or not they had any. I wouldn't put a high price on their strength of character after the cops had given them the third degree. With them, John Law has no need to unsheathe his savagery. Their prodigious stupidity and their eagerness to impress people are enough to bring about their downfall. The only thing, ladies, is that it's not strength of character I want to grow old with but a guy who has gentle hands. And it's not the cops I want to impress, it's my customers.

Sandrine's john reminds me of a supervisor I had in school. Hey, specs! Look at me! Move those eyes of yours. It's me, little Sophie. Don't you think my dancing's cute? Don't be scared, look at me. You're not married to that broad you're sitting next to. I know it bothers her, my dancing like this, right in front of her table, but I can't help it – as soon as I hear music, there's nothing I can do about it, I just have to shake and move my ass and legs. Now watch. Keep your eyes peeled. I'm going to give it the big twirl, and with a little luck you'll see Pike's Peak ... You like that, you dirty old man! Just as I thought. Wow – look at the sparks behind those blinkers!

So if it's getting hard, what are you waiting for? Ditch that pile of nothing next to you. Ask me to sit down at your table. Say, Mr Jello, just what are you up to? If you haven't got the nerve to kick her out, take the two of us upstairs. I won't be angry if I can't have you all to myself. I'm not the jealous type. Still not sure? Hold on. I'll do a split for you. Or maybe a cartwheel and two entrechats ... Okay, seen enough? Make up your mind, because I'm starting to run out of breath And I sure don't want you to shoot off in your pants because of me. That wouldn't be playing fair with my fellow worker. Make up your mind, slowpoke ... One spin to the left, one to the right. One grind, speciality of La Bohème. A smile full of promise, a velvet look ...

Two minutes later I'm sitting at their table.

'Sophie, come and sit down.'

Come on, Sandrine, smile. Guys don't come here to be frowned at but to forget the frowns of their wives. They want us to be gay, silly, and funny. So let them think that's how we are. Let me take the wheel, and we'll see if we can't shake a fistful out of him.

'Sophie, you're a wonderful dancer.'

'I like dancing. What about you? What do you like?'

'Who knows what he likes! He's been sitting here on his ass for half an hour telling me about the Impressionists. I never heard of them. All I know is that his name is Ernest and he's an ambassador.'

'You like painting?'

'I like watching you dance. Dance for me. Let me see your thighs. Your friend needn't stay.'

Sandrine, I warned you. A sad whore is a very sad thing indeed.

I did my act all by myself, like a big girl. Ernest was drooling into his champagne glass as he watched me. At the bar, my girl friends were desperately hanging on to the lapels of their reluctant customers, trying to make them forget I was there. It must be said that a broad without panties has her charm. Two tables down from mine, Malou had her arms draped around the neck of an Italian patron. She was tanked to the gills; no need to have her blow into a balloon to find that out. I danced by her and said, 'Easy, Malou. Don't drink too fast, sip it slowly. Don't forget, wops can be a handful.'

'I don't give a damn,' she shot back, 'this guy's promised to take me to Rome.'

She was starting to slobber on her blouse. A trip to Rome – what luck! The Colosseum, the Fountain of Trevi, the Baths of Caracalla. Go to it, Malou! Getting smashed one more time won't hurt you. But don't forget to have him cough up the ticket first.

I went back to my table. Ernest got me to dance a languorous slow number with him. Trembling we melted into one another, and I stretched against Ernest like a drowsy kitten. Nothing. Zero. Not getting it up, His Excellency isn't. Cold as a cadaver. What if he's a permanently disabled veteran who lost his nuts in a trench? *Merde!* It's enough to make you cry. A strapping man like him, and no balls! What lousy luck!

Smile at me, Ernest. Reassure me. Tell me you've still got your bollocks and that they're heavy and full of lust for me. Tell me they're about to burst, Ernest. Tell me that I'm not wasting my evening for ten bills, or nothing at all. Look at me, Ernest. Focus your specs on my eyes. Don't be afraid to hurt me. There, that's better. Like that. You're taking my hand – you're reacting. You're putting it between your lips. Between your teeth. You're biting. Bite hard, you bastard. You jerk, you're hurting me. But it doesn't matter. I can take it. Now that I understand where your head is at, you can go to it. Cut loose, sharpen those choppers of yours. I'm your mummy's big titty, so nibble away, you spoiled little puppy. Hurting someone is what gets it up for you. Biting's what gives you a big cock, huh, baby? You like the taste of blood? You know, this little lark's going to cost you a pretty penny. I don't like being hurt. I don't like it at all.

Ernest gobbled away till dawn, never going upstairs, never saying a word, just sitting or dancing. All he did was bite my hand. I could have ditched him ten times over during the evening, but I patiently stayed with him, nursing his obsession, and I did right. When he left, he slipped two five-hundred-franc bills into my sore mitt, from which the skin was beginning to peel.

I held my swollen hand under the cold-water tap in the ladies' room while in one of the booths Malou was chucking up her ticket on the Rome Express.

What looks more like a Jap than another Jap?

Two rice-heads have just emerged out of the smoke of filter-tip cigarettes.

'Hey look, Chinks!'

'They're Japs, for Christ's sake: eyes like new moons, tri-focal lenses, cheeks shined with Johnson's wax, black um-brellas, and whisky flasks in their hip pockets. Malou, some days you're plain stupid. You think the Chinese can afford to carry whisky around to use as a disinfectant?'

'That's how you recognize them?'

'I'll explain.'

Bounce those cocker-spaniel tits of yours, and give them your ultramarine gaze. (My own is mood indigo.) Twist your shoulder while I bend my neck. Smooth back those ears, and I'll flash my legs.

'I'm not their type.'

'You're plastered. Take a gander. He's tearing your blouse off with those shifty eyes of his.'

'It's you he's looking at.'

'You're nuttier than Silly Putty. Listen, you have to speak English to them – *what is your name, darling?*'

'What are you saying to him?'

'Pipe down. Champagne, yes, you are drinking the champagne? It's in the bag. Malou, ring for Josepha while I make conversation.'

'Watch out. I think mine understands French.'

'So, Mr Shotguzzler, dost thou deceive? *Parlez-vous français*? Oh, I see. You're the guide.'

Well, fine – between a gentleman and a lady, a word is sufficient. We can always come to an understanding. If Malou pitches in, if she stops rocking like an unmoored motorboat and makes it back to shore, there's a good chance that each of us will finger a minimum of five hundred francs. For what it's worth, without realizing it, just by wanting to, I've hooked the kingfisher himself. O Asinawata, in your smooth coppery arms, beneath your lustreless gaze, between your slimy thighs, I'm about to explore Tokyo and environs. Come on, you yellow son of a bitch, respond. I don't like passivity. When I'm zonked, my reactions tend to become violent. I have a perverse desire to make you take a bite out of your glass. That way you could eat and drink at the same time. Say something, you gook. Give me a clue. Light up those peepholes of yours. It's me, Sophie, little Sophie, and I'm feeling bored tonight.

It's too bad you're so hard on the eyes. If you were handsome, we could really swing together. I'd strip Pigalle bare for you, demystify the Champs-Elysées, plunder Saint-Denis, upend the Opéra and the Madeleine, and rekindle the lights of the City of Lights! Oh, if only you had been handsome, I'd have opened not only my legs but my heart to you. Dripping, cowed, devoted, I'd follow in your footsteps, urging you to glue the pieces back together. The two of us would spit and drool on the remains, and fly high on our kites to heaven. The

155

cumulus clouds are beneath us, we're in love! You and me advancing towards old Japan, the Japan that's older than we are, older than all the others that I've ever known – the Japan that even you've never known. We throw back our heads, bury our eyes in our palms, stretch out our fingers, unburden our brows, unbind our legs – and you subdue me beneath the branches of a scarlet apple tree. Under the amber caresses of your fingers, my loins spatter you in a burst of fireworks: Bastille Day in Tokyo!

Why do you have to be so ugly? Actually, you're not really ugly. You're insignificant-looking, fogged up, anonymous, insipid – just like the others. You're only you, and I can't blame you for that. Poor you. Poor me.

After an hour of palaver, Malou and I start moving. Our mouths feel puffy, and our legs are soggy with Dom Pérignon. Full of arrogance, we unravel ourselves and yawn so hard we almost dislocate our jaws. We take our rice-heads in tow as though they were two sailors on shore leave – we're almost pulling them along by their flies. Passing between the cars of the crumbums who don't even know how to drive, we cross Rue Frochot on the run. As we clamber up the grimy stairs of the Macao, we catch sight of Michou, looking like a truck-driver in drag. She's the chambermaid with whom my Jap settles for the rooms, reluctantly, with his trifocals glued to the bills. Not the trusting sort, these foreigners.

Once these crassly material problems have been settled, Malou and I give each other a look fraught with significance. Proposing a foursome to Japs is casting pearls before swine – and we're not wastrels. Despite the shit all around us, we have kept our taste for what is elegant, fine, and beautiful. We do not enjoy dulling the implements of pleasure. Face to face on the rickety landing, Malou and I regretfully bat our eyelashes together.

'Pal, my deepest sympathy.'

'Happy fucking, buddy.'

The door slams ... Words of love, followed by the crinkling of bills ... A striptease in the minor mode ... Gurgles in the plumbing ... groaning springs ... mendacious sighs. Between Jimmu Tennô's thighs appear halo'd spasms, dark circles, luminous globes ... a parallelepiped, a rectangle, an isosceles triangle ... The square of the circle ... an explosion of earth and sky. Climax, sweet climax, once you're on your way, why do you insist on holding back?

'*Good for you, my darling?*' I ask him.
'*Good, very good.*'

I've made him feel so good that he deposits a chaste kiss on my shoulder. It makes me shiver. I find his way of showing gratitude very sweet and unusual. In general, after making love (virtually before they've finished ejaculating), Japs dash off to the bathroom and douse their penis with Johnnie Walker. Since they never take off their shoes, it's always a funny sight to see them rushing to the bidet with their black-ringed muscular little yellow calves and their bandage-swathed tummies. Jimmu Tennô's tummy is swathed, but at least he's taken the trouble to remove his shoes.

He's dawdling over my breast. I encourage him. I scratch the smooth skin of his overly soft back. I bring my lips close to his pug nose. Without his glasses he looks younger. How old can he be? Between thirty and forty-five? There's no way of assigning a date to that brow of his.

Malou's laugh pierces the partition. We've agreed that the four of us will meet at La Bohème. I'm holding Malou's money. There was no need to fix a price: Jimmu handed me two hundred dollars. Now he draws away from me and fumblingly recovers his specs. I don't feel like moving. I feel just fine.

The ceiling overhead is full of cracks. From the street rises a sound of horns.

Jimmu, if you wanted to, we could start all over again. All you'd have to do is give me a little something extra in exchange, say a green bill like the one you parted with a while ago. I'd take you up to heaven again, and you'd keep me from having to go back down to hell. Jimmu, you're clean and you're uncomplicated. Let me stay with you tonight. We don't have to speak the same language to understand one another. Let me stay with you, Jimmu – tonight I'm full of strange longings.

Jimmu does not rush off towards the bidet. Jimmu rolls over crossways on the grimy bed. His hand grips my hip and brushes my pubes, and he whispers things I don't understand.

Vicky has just come upstairs. Through the closed door, I hear her and the chambermaid asking for twenty francs for the room, and I hear the grumbling voice of the customer. The door of number 1 slams. Malou goes downstairs singing.

Jimmu takes hold of my fingers and moves them across his groin. We start over.

Vicky, simulating ecstacy, is making the walls shake. On the landing, Fabienne and the Shrimp are haggling with two Lebanese over the price of a lesbian extravaganza. Their voices mingle together. 'Downstairs, it was all set. You expect us to believe that in Beirut people fuck for free? It's a good thing Frenchmen don't put up such a fuss. So are you going to make up your minds? I'm telling you, there's nothing fake about it. We're both real dykes.'

Fortunately, you can't understand, Jimmu Tennô, or you might start having your doubts. You might end up thinking that I'm something less than a real lady. Arch your ass, Jimmu, and don't let yourself be distracted by the noise outside. Just let yourself go between my legs. Afterwards, if you're still in shape and your pins aren't too wobbly, I'll take you to La Cloche d'Or, and we can sample their snails, poached crayfish, frog's legs *provençal*, smoked salmon, and Iranian caviar – all washed down with red, white, or blue, anything you like.

It's ten past five when Jimmu and I go back down to La Bohème. Simon is sipping a *pastis* at the bar. Rose is doing her accounts. Josepha is emptying the ashtrays. The girls are yawning and stretching. Malou and Snotguzzler are half asleep, their cheeks settled against the red leatherette wall seats. A bottle, three-quarters empty, is standing on the table.

'Let's go, blondie. The night is young. We're going to La Cloche d'Or for a bite to eat.'

Malou stretches and half opens her eyes. The guide comes to life. Stroking my hips, Jimmu Tennô leaves it all to me: I have been delegated full powers.

'There's five hundred coming to you. Let's go. I'm famished.'

Malou brushes back her blonde bangs and unwinds her legs.

'I've really tied one on.'

'So come and get it out of your system.'

Having tugged Jimmu's necktie knowingly, I once again find myself holding Malou's damp forehead over the toilet bowl.

'You've got to quit boozing.'

'My liver's had it, Sophie. I want to die.'

'You'll get over it. Look, here are your fifty bills. Now give me a nice smile and come and have something to eat.'

'Couldn't we commit suicide?'

'I'd like to see how it all turns out. I want to know what there really is underneath all this shit. Think of your kid. Think of Bébert rotting away in Melun. You're all they've got.'

'That's the trouble.'

'Do it for me, Malou. No kidding. The night is young.'

Malou shakes her head in the toilet bowl, mottling its sides. She hangs on to my arm. Her stomach is empty; her head is still full.

I take charge of things. Jimmu Tennô and Snotguzzler follow us to La Cloche d'Or. The four of us eat like kings: we may talk about faraway places, but our eyes never leave our plates. The guide translates for us. Jimmu nibbles my pearl-coated fingernails.

At nine-thirty, we take leave of one another in front of Cook's on Avenue de l'Opéra. Our eyes are falling out of their sockets, our tongues are thick, we can barely speak, and I've made a date to meet Jimmu at the Fiumicino airport six weeks from now.

Rome, 15 November. Jimmu's there, shoving against the barrier that separates the people who are waiting from the people who are arriving. I wave to him. I need to believe. Roma: the Eternal City, the city of the thousand fountains, the city that Malou would so love to see.

Malou, La Bohème, the girls – all so near and yet so far away. Gerard agreed on the spot. He wasn't one to turn down a hundred dollars a day, payable in advance in traveller's cheques. He made me promise to behave myself. Old Rose says that in her day no man would ever have permitted it. Her day's a long way off. It's buried somewhere under the folds of her malevolent eyebrows. In her day, men didn't allow anything. They enjoyed unlimited power.

Today it's different. Jimmu is waving his arms above his slicked-down hair. Today belongs to me. I'm flying away, out of reach of my daily life. Tonight I'll be stretching out my legs in a four-star bed. Tonight I'll be wallowing in gilded luxury. Tomorrow, when I throw a hundred-lira coin into the murky waters of the Fountain of Trevi, I'll make a wish : to come back to Rome with the man I love.

An Italian official undresses me with his eyes, not deigning to bother with the passport I hold out to him.

'*Prego, signorina, prego.*'

'*Grazie, tante grazie.*'

Jimmu is separated from me by only a few yards. How I wish I loved him! He knows nothing about me beyond the fact that I adore champagne. I know that he owns the biggest jewellry store in Tokyo, and that he finds me attractive. But we're incapable of having a conversation that lasts more than two minutes. It's not easy going back to someone you don't know.

He kisses my hair. He grips my suitcase between his legs, smiles at me, and, taking a little package out of his pocket, he encircles my wrist with three slender strands of pearls. '*Jimmu, darling, I love you!*' Everyone is watching us. Lenses are trained on my enthusiasm. We timorously turn away from the flashbulbs. Jimmu brushes against my hip. I rub my lips against his starched collar and stammer into his neck, 'Take care of me. When I'm so far away from La Bohème, I lose my footing. It's all so new. I'm having a ball, at your expense. But I'll never love you. So make me love you a little. Just enough to get through this trip.' Fortunately, he doesn't understand French.

Cheek against heart, we push through the crowd. I feel great. Around me, shouting voices reveal a new accent, one that's thick with sunshine. A chauffeured Lincoln Continental takes us to the Hilton on Monte Mario, far from the gaudy, noisy streets. With his hands lying flat on his knees, lulled by the soothing drone of the motor, Jimmu doesn't utter a sound. No strain! I open my eyes three-hundred-and-sixty-degrees wide. The air conditioning is giving me the shivers.

Thursday, 18 November. 'Hello, operator? Room one-seventeen. I'd like a number in Paris ... I'll hang on, thank you ... Madame Rose? It's Sophie ... From Rome. Is Malou around? ... Yes, I'm fine. No, I'll hang on ...' I almost like the old grouch tonight.

I hear a buzzing over the wire. La Bohème is buzzing. It's buzzing in a peculiar way – about my friendship with Malou. Tongues are buzzing with talk about a particular kind of intimacy. They're dyking it up together. They must be dyking it up. They're dyking it up together. They must be! — Me, dyke it up? Never. Not even when I was a little girl. Instead of all that you-feel-mine business under the blankets in the dormitory, I preferred cards, mumblety-peg, jacks, all the configurations you could make playing cat's cradle during naptime with a strand of yarn.

As for dyking it up — that almost happened to me, once, at the beginning, when I was with Gerry. Late one afternoon my friend Niquette happened to see us as we were saying goodbye on Rond-Point Yuri-Gagarine. In our part of town, people didn't leave each other with a wave of the hand. They squeezed each other's fingers and bit their lips as they discussed where they'd go for dinner that evening. She was starved, little Niquette, and she thought he was fab! I wasn't selfish, even if I didn't particularly feel like going shares. Gerry was no ordinary piece of cake — he was a fruitcake with a butter-cream filling: a slightly nauseating dish. I let her take a nibble. But when the three of us were bare-ass on the bed, I felt like throwing up. It just wasn't possible for me to do to Niquette what Gerry insisted I do. I could imagine the way she washed. Scouring odd corners was not for her; and I didn't feel in the mood for spring cleaning. At the time, my head was a little garden: my heart was a peony, my eyes were cornflowers, and I had snowdrops in my fingertips. When the going got rough, I used to hide among my flowers. But that night, no luck: they'd all cleared out. It was no use digging up the snow or rummaging in the moss or calling them by name. There was nothing, not even a faint echo. My nails had turned black. My peony was dropping its petals. My eyes had lost their blueness ...

That night, uncomfortably settled in a bargain-basement arm-chair, I pretended to read *Police Confessions* and finished off a bottle of wood alcohol while Gerry suckled Niquette, that greedy girl. Her feet interfered with my perusal of those lurid pages, and I wondered when for misery's sake the circus would come to an end.

Me and Malou? That's sacrilege. I liked men even as a child. Those little darling boys — what tortures they endured at my innocent hands when we played doctor. Matches shoved into their rectums, not to mention pebbles and straws. It was all done in order to diagnose a high fever — that wonderful fever that leaves you raving, that contagious fever that gives even doctors the shakes. And what a lousy doctor *I* was!

The little girls got a very different sort of treatment. Come on up, duckie-wuckies. It's your afternoon off. You can help me finish doing my two sets of laundry – fast colours and runny ones. Rub, rinse, and hang them out to dry. Then, my little blonde sweethearts, lie down on the fleabag and spread your hairless thighs wide so the doctor can examine you. It was really something the way my classmates from grade school opened up. Don't budge, you little hussies. Just relax. Nice doctor's going to get his instruments. Oh, how marvellous to have Dédée's sewing box for a little black bag, and to be able to shove the little flower-shaped buttons into that virgin flesh. They used to describe their symptoms to me with their legs in the air and their hands over their eyes, those sluts, those sweet little hookers in the bud. As treatment, I prescribed two Our Fathers and one Hail Mary. Then we'd gobble up the oranges or cherries they'd brought, depending on the season; and afterwards they'd go racing down the six flights of stairs with drained eyes and glistening thighs.

Malou, I miss you so, you can't imagine ... Yes, it's a glorious city. Italians have eyes in their fingertips, and that makes you feel funny. ... No, it's okay. There are twin beds, don't worry. What about you? The girls aren't giving you too much of a hassle?

What's the use of going back? Going back to what? Jimmu, keep me with you, and make me your wife. I'll work very hard at loving you. Find a way to make me stay. My friend's voice and those Spanish guitars are tearing my guts out. They're hurting me so I want to scream. No, I'm not crying. I've caught a slight cold. Listen, Malou, I've got to say goodbye for tonight. Yes, fine, give Maurice a kiss. Yes, I'll write. Don't worry about me. I'm fine. So long.

Why not love Jimmu? Everything would become crystal-clear. No more ruckus, no more hesitation or doubt, no more hateful words, no more booze. The daily struggle would be over – flushed away. Look at me, God: you know perfectly well that I have no competitive instinct and that I'm tired of lengthening my eyelashes, spreading my thighs, and offering up my soft underbelly ... Where are they keeping that man –

the one I've been in love with since childhood? In the midst of what tribe, in the depths of what dungeon is he waiting for me? Under what squalid skies is he advancing to meet me?

Swimming in November. Hobnobbing with the gods of Greece. Wandering through soukhs and distributing dollars to Arab children who stick to you like flies. Visiting the Great Mosque and contemplating the hairs of Mohammed's beard. Gazing on the Sphinx and its mutilations. Going sailing on an ancient Egyptian galley. Crossing yourself in front of Pharaoh in the middle of a troop of beet-red German tourists. Drinking the best champagne out of a silver goblet, morning, noon, and night. Hearing yourself addressed as Princess by the man at your side, who never demands anything of you ... Shouldn't I have been happy?

What am I complaining about? I'm not complaining. I'm merely observing that his generosity is taking me further and further from the desired goal. I'm ready to drop everything and leave it all to my buddies – the Maurices, ambassadors, plumbers, unchartered tours, pearl bracelets, pyramids, camel rides, Gerards, and all their progeny. Look, I'm not the greedy sort. I'll even give up the five-carat diamond Jimmu has promised me if I go to Tokyo or New York with him. I'm dumping the whole works. Today I'm saying goodbye to Cairo and to Jimmu.

Jimmu's got the blues: two sad little eyes revolve behind his misty square lenses. Last night – and it was the last – his princess chucked him out of bed. And it was the first time he'd unswathed himself! Too bad she noticed too late. Don't cry, Jimmu. Don't be angry with me. A princess who's abruptly awakened is a very delicate thing!

At the airport bar the champagne tastes flat. I've had enough of him, and enough of his pallid devotions and abject submissiveness. And what if, without realizing it, I was letting happiness pass me by? Oh, let the hostess's voice burst from the loudspeakers! Let the roar of the engines numb me until I get back to Malou, and La Bohème, and Gerard – until everything is back to normal. Champagne à la kickback is a lot more intoxicating than the kind Jimmu buys.

'I'll send you some dolls from Bangkok.' He managed this sentence in French.

163

Jimmu, forgive me for not loving you.

'Passengers flying to Paris on Flight Six-eighteen are requested to proceed to Gate Number Seven.'

chapter three

Merry Christmas and Happy New Year! The holiday season's over. How did it go? I don't remember, and it doesn't matter: I don't like holidays, and it isn't Gerard who'll be the one to change my mind about that. I'm lugging his present around on my back – a beaverskin coat, ripped off somewhere out of town. Santa Claus's bill was paid with my foreign currency. Thanks, Gerry.

We launch into January as flat as pancakes. It's a withered, hostile month that makes it impossible for me to imagine that the sun ever existed. After a week off, it's been hard getting back into harness.

It's so cold at La Bohème tonight! The shivering girls are hugging their bare shoulders. Malou is coughing. The rum doesn't seem to be warming me up. Dubious shadows are passing back and forth beyond the coloured glass panes. The door abruptly opens; a gust of air chills me to the bone. Shadows loom threateningly in the half darkness, and somewhere between Pigalle and Place Blanche a siren wails. It's open season on hookers – but you won't catch me! ...

It's the twilight hour, when my heart goes to pieces and spills out of my breast, roving towards the dark mass of the trees outside, bruising itself in its pursuit of some cause worth fighting for. Little milksop heart, don't beat so fast. We're not lost in the woods. On the other side of the thin wooden door that's protecting the two of us, there's a cop on duty. He's a man with a heart, but he doesn't know it; so if you don't stop your drumming, if you don't stop playing the stag at bay, he's going to take us both away and lock us up. I don't want to sleep on some cold bench – and I don't want to slow you down, either. I like hearing you knock out that beat. You do understand me, don't you? I just don't want to wake up tomorrow in the clink, all scroungy. Please, little heart, shut up, or I'll make mincemeat out of you ...

'Playing hide-and-seek? Come out of there, on the double. There's still room in the wagon for you.'

Okay, pig. I'm right behind you. No need to shake me like an apple tree and yell in my face. You stink of death. You're scaring my poor heart.

For a raid, it's really a raid. Nobody's missing. Even the mudslingers from the scandal sheets are there. Forgive me if I conceal my smile, gentlemen of the press. Tonight I prefer to remain incognito. Due to circumstances beyond my control, I'm only granting interviews to the emissaries of John Law – you thugs! One day you're all going to stew in the same pot – and I'll be the one who strikes the match and lights the fire under you.

All Pigalle is surrounded. The johns must be chewing their toenails. Crammed brutally into the van, the girls are seething with indignation.

'How can they do this when the night's just begun?'

'Especially since there's nothing going on.'

'Hey, blueballs! Admit it's easier to run after a hooker than a hood. Hey, fuzzy-wuzzy answer me when I speak to you. Or is my umbrella making you nervous?'

Dear Jesus, work a miracle – blow on her umbrella and turn it into an olive branch. Otherwise, I guarantee you, the fur is going to fly. Too late. A rainbow stripe appears on fuzzy-wuzzy's forehead. The girl is lifted from the ground by a wicked, cowardly left to the gut. Her backside bounces right off the wooden bench. Without getting up off the floor, she shrieks her loathing for everything in a uniform. I'm ashamed of my silence.

Amid sighs and gnashing of teeth, the paddy wagon at last gets under way. A street hooker is singeing the end of her hair with a cigarette butt. Another keeps pricking her stockings with a needle. Every time the point grazes her leg she utters a little mouselike cry. Sitting on my lap, Malou is coughing her heart out. In this manner we bounce along as far as Avenue Trudaine.

'All right, cutiepies, you're getting special treatment tonight. We're changing cars. Try not to get any smart-ass ideas.'

A dozen large blue vans are parked beneath the trees. A crowd of bystanders, with their collars turned up around their ears and their hands snug in their pockets, smilingly watch the sheep being led off to the slaughter. Walk on in peace, honest folk. The sidewalks of Pigalle are yours till tomorrow morning.

Tonight, the flash freaks aren't satisfied with ambushing us as we emerge from our bars. They get to police headquarters before us and lie in wait for the herd as it starts up the great stone stairway inside the penal area. Then snap snap, they're at it again. Hanging out into space, they grind out their miles of filth. Some of the girls shriek and cluster together. Others, stunned by the flashbulbs, roll down the stairs with their skirts over their heads. But some march up the steps raising one clenched fist. A fearful hand-to-hand struggle begins. I'm caught in the tumult. I cover my face with my hands and press my back against the wall to keep from falling. Malou, crouching underneath my coat, is sobbing.

'Sophie, my mother couldn't take it if she saw me in the papers.'

The night passed drearily. They turned us loose at 8.00 a.m., without sending us to Saint-Lazare.

We walk across Quai de Conti. I slip my hand into Malou's pocket. She adjusts her stride to mine.

'Come sleep at my place, Sophie. I can't stand being alone any more.'

She'd talked about suicide all night long. I'd listened to her wearily; I had nothing left to give. And here she is squeezing my hand, and her little face is gazing up at me with a look of such pain that I'm ashamed. Malou, whenever you start to shake, I long to take you under my wing – but first I've got to get out from under Gerard's heel. Someone once wrote, 'No bird can sing in a cluster of doubts ...' And I'm a lark who's got off on the wrong wing. Even if I'd flown all the way to Japan, someone would have come and brought me back; and my entire bird's life wouldn't have been long enough to make up for that. Do you understand, Malou? I'm like you. I need a warm, cosy nest filled with blue eggs. I need a nest made of lace and rice paper and gossamer, a cradle between earth and heaven where I can hide my head under my wing and escape from the assaults of the dream-busters.

'Well – are you coming?'

'Natch.'

After the harshness of winter, spring arrives with all its flags flying. The January raid is only a bad memory. Nevertheless, since the evening began, Malou has talked about nothing else.

'Stop it! You'll bring us bad luck.'

'I tell you, I can sense them. I want to leave.'

'You're going to stay – and don't look at me like that!' Yoohoo, Malou: what was it that just vanished from your eyes? Talk. Say something. Your peepers are like two stones. What's up?

'First take care of your own problems, Sophie. Then we'll talk about mine.'

She dons her raincoat, I down my Haig, I've failed; and she knows it. Her arrogance is merely a confirmation of the fact. She tiptoes out, not slamming the door and not looking back.

Customers can line up all the way from La Bohème to Place Clichy; their pockets may be crammed with castles in Spain, and their kissers may be full of gold; but if any one of them can charm me off my barstool tonight, I'll pay the freight! Go on, girls, enjoy yourselves. I'm planning on getting totally zonked.

Nevertheless, when Alain, an oldtimer from the Saint-Louis, comes walking through the door, I cling to him like poverty to the lower clergy. Afterwards, in the bathroom, he turned my face towards the harsh fluorescent light, and said:

'Sophie, you're drinking yourself into the grave. You're all bloated.'

It was worse than if he'd told me I was getting old. I lean my head against the mirror and start to sob. On the misted glass, someone else's face appears. My God, have I changed all that much? Alain, looking sheepish, pays to see me smile.

As I'm leaving the Macao, Simon nabs me.

'Sophie, listen, baby. Listen to old Simon.'

'What is it you're selling now?'

'Don't talk stupid. I've got a solid-gold john for you. He has francs coming out of his ears. I told him about you. You're his type. He's going to give you four hundred. We split, and we don't tell a soul.'

'Where have you stashed your boy?'

'Upstairs in the Macao. I've arranged things with the chambermaid. He'll be waiting. Go to it, baby. Go on.'

I usually prefer examining my customers before the big bang, but after all I've drunk this evening, I feel nervy enough to take on a cyclops.

There's a door half open on the third-floor landing. No light. Not the tiniest sound. It's as weird as it is unusual.

'Ahoy there! It's Sophie. Where are you?'

'I'm in here.'

'Turn on the light. I'm no cat.'

'My name's Edgar. Come over here.'

'First turn on the lights.'

'I'll turn them on, but don't come in right away.'

Another loony!

'Where are you hiding now?'

'I'm here, behind the screen. Come over here. Don't scream. Promise you won't run away.'

Straight ahead, Sophie. It's only another kook who gets his high trying to scare little girls. Real freaks only exist in fairy tales. So take a look behind the screen. Scare the shit out of him. Catch him from behind.

What's sitting on the bidet is out of a nightmare: a stunted creature who's trying to hold the cake of soap in his stumps. The head, shrunk to coconut size, is pierced with four gaping holes. Thick tears fall from what once were eyes. You poor shapeless thing, is it God or the Devil who's keeping you alive? Stop shaking. I'll stay. Come here, lean against me. Hush, you don't have to tell me your story, I've heard about the war. Easy, don't hold me too hard – your orthopaedic corset's crushing me. Oh, no, please don't run your stumps through my hair – I'm hanging on to my sanity by just one of them! Oh Málou, why did you abandon me on this horrible night?

Edgar, goodbye. It's getting late. It's time for Simon to drink his *pastis*, for Josepha to do her housecleaning, and for Rose to do her accounts. The other girls are going home to their loneliness; and I'm going to have one last scotch before running off to join Malou.

In the taxi that's taking me to Rue d'Aboukir, I start feeling apprehensive. The red lights seem to be proliferating, and I find the traffic insanely heavy for this early hour. What a night! The distance separating me from Malou is interminable. The driver, an old Russian émigré, keeps apologizing profusely. He's lost. He's driven twice around Place de la Bourse, and now he's started down Rue Réaumur, which is one way. That's the last straw. I abandon him there.

I run from Rue Réaumur to Rue d'Aboukir. The key isn't under the doormat. You little bitch, if you've run out on me, I'll rip your guts out.

'Malou! Kitten, open up, for Christ's sake! It's Sophie. Open up, kitten. Just because I'm smashed is no reason to lock me out. Malou, open up or I'll break the door in! Louloù, you can't have hopped a train without telling me. You can't do that to me, you have no right to. Loulou, don't leave me standing out here. I'm too pissed to go home … Malou! Answer me. Say something. You're frightening me, Malou. Don't be difficult – open up. It's Sophie.'

'Hey, cut out the racket. You want to wake the whole building?'

'Okay, you win. Now the concierge is getting into the act. You're really making us look good. – I left my suitcase at Madame Langlois's. It would be a big help if you had another key. Stay where you are, I'll be right down for it.'

Lucky the old snoop is fond of the green stuff. One bill gets me the key. I climb the stairs, sobered up and so proud of my nerve that I've almost forgotten about you, Malou. My anxiety returns as I turn the key in the lock. I feel my way across the kitchen, groping for the light switch; I know just where to find it in the bedroom – I've often been the one to turn it off when I slept over. (You always drop off to sleep before I do, and you never complain about my reading late.) Lou, you've got to be there. I hurt so much inside.

Fortunately the light reveals her lying demure and snug in the middle of the bed, with the top sheet pulled up over her eyes. I feel like leaving the way I came. Tomorrow she'll find a scribbled note on the kitchen table: Thanks, Lou. Thanks just for being.

But I also feel like sleeping. I feel like kissing her and stretching out next to her warmth. Fatigue and booze have suddenly clobbered me. Her quiet sleep dispels my fears. Exhausted, I sink down beside her. Her hair hides her face, but I feel her breath against my cheek. Everything's fine.

Malou, just let me babble away in your ear. I won't disturb your sleep. You know, I was afraid you might do something silly tonight. I would have never forgiven myself. What difference does it make if you leave La Bohème? You know what's best. And if you can't manage, if you're ever short of change, I'll help you. Don't worry about that. Malou, we're going to have a lot of laughs when all this is over. Lou, I know I talk a lot: but you're the one who's plugged into the truth. Your man loves you; you've had a kid together; and he wasn't the one who turned you out. Bébert is coming back and you'll go live in a house in the suburbs. Sundays, you'll invite me out to drink cold wine in the shade of the wisteria. You'll be wearing a broad-brimmed hat with cherries on it; mine will be smaller, with a spray of lilac pinned to it. You'll do your weaving while I knit. Bébert and Isabelle will plant winter flowers. And people will say hello to us as they pass by the blue gate. We'll answer them with tranquil smiles. Our past will be wiped out.

Sleep, Malou. I'm going to sleep, too. What's this – why is everything all wet? Don't tell me you've wet the bed! Malou, wake up. Malou! Answer me, or I'll slug you. Oh, Malou! What have you done, Malou? What have you done?

I get out of bed and shed some light on the truth. It's not pretty to behold. Her left wrist is so deeply slashed that the foaming flesh reveals bone all the way down to her hand. The bleeding has almost stopped. Malou gazes up at me. Her bloodless lips draw back in a pathetic smile.

'Don't start crying. Don't budge. I'm taking you to the hospital.'

As I go down the stairs, I feel as though I've done something irreparable. I want to strangle the concierge, who is shouting and slapping her hands against her thighs. I want to strangle her three brats, who pop their heads through the open door, to murder anything that moves or breathes. Because, upstairs, my friend is dying.

The concierge finally agrees to call the emergency police patrol. She wants to go up. Not on your life. Get back into your cage, you old buzzard. Give yourself whatever sort of emotional high suits you, but keep an eye out for the cops.

I wrap Malou's arm in a clean bath towel. After opening the windows and shutters, I kneel down at the head of her bed.

'Why did you do it? We'd promised to do it together, if

things ever got really bad. Tell me, why are you trying to run out on me? And there I was talking to you like a jerk about hats and cherries. I was imagining blue gates, and wisteria, and a love story for you – you had a house in the suburbs and your feet up on the fireplace fender! Forgive me, my poor little meadow mouse. I didn't see how wretched you've been. You always say you feel dirty after you've turned a trick, but don't worry: their dirt hasn't gone deep. You're clean, Lou. In all that filth, you shine. You'll make it. You've got to make it. Lie back, don't look at me. I've got all this bilge water in my eyes.'

Malou's breath is a soft rattle; just the way Lulu's was one night when we were kids. If you make it, Malou, I swear I'll protect you from every evil thing.

The emergency patrol arrives, preceded by the concierge. They wrap Malou up in a grey blanket and load her on to a stretcher. In the street, shopkeepers rush to their doors. A strange sky moves overhead.

'You're a relative?'

'No. A friend.'

'Get in. We'll be needing you.'

In the van that takes us to the hospital, it's no longer Malou I'm crying over, but myself.

Jacques Prévert once said: 'There'll always be a chink in the winter's wall to give us a glimpse of summer ...' And I'll always be there, Malou. I'll watch over you until your wings are healed and you can fly far from the storm. You're a good little trouper. If there weren't all those needles stuck into your veins, I'd hug you.

'So what's resurrection like?'

'Tiring.'

'Running out on life isn't so easy. I saw your concierge and slipped her twenty bills. She didn't exactly turn up her nose at them, so there won't be any problem there. As far as the cops are concerned, you're not married. You're still Claudine Langlois.'

'What if they investigate?'

'Don't worry about it. Whenever you were busted, you always showed an ID card with your maiden name – so?'

'If they investigate and find out I'm married, Bébert's going to cop it. You know how much they give you for prostituting your lawful wife?'

'Stop wasting your time with such stupid thoughts. You prostituted yourself on your own, after he was already in the clink. That should be easy to prove, if things come to the worst. Anyway, it's most unlikely they'll push the investigation that far. All they've got is a case of unsuccessful suicide. After all, you're still with us, very much alive – and now in the process of sneaking a glass of port with your girl friend. So everything's going fine. Stop feeling so sorry for yourself. It's contagious, and if I start we'll never get out of this mess.

'Yesterday I wrote Bébert. I said you were in the sack with a bad case of intestinal flu – nothing serious, but you're not allowed to write letters or move around. Hold on, let me finish. I've sent him his weekly money order. No reason for him to go hungry just because his wife takes herself out of circulation.'

'Sophie—'

'Quiet! Stop thrashing your arms around, or you'll bust the machinery. I also caught the daily news bulletin – I spoke to the doctor. In a week you'll be up – provided you keep your head screwed on straight.

'I also wrote to Beauvais, and I got an answer this morning. Here's the letter. Your daughter's waiting for you. This way, you get a good six weeks' rest, till the end of July. After that, it all depends on how you feel and what you want to do.'

'I'm staying with you, Sophie.'

'What matters is for one of us to get in the clear – then the other one will have somewhere to go to. Hey, stop crying. It's not good for what ails you.'

'What about you?'

'Everything's coming up roses. Gerry has decided to show me Italy. Rome, Naples, Capri. A real honeymoon.'

'You're not happy.'

'Happy? Maybe we can glue the pieces back together. We'll see. In any case, I've decided to move into an apartment when I come back. He's agreed to a trial run. Once I've moved in, I'm never moving out, whether he likes it or not. It'll be hard getting started, but I don't give a shit. I'm fed up with fattening some madam's bank account. The only thing that bugs me is not knowing where Paul is.'

'Paul?'

'My agricultural expert – the one from Africa. That guy seemed so nice.'

'You ought to get married.'

'Who with? Anyway, Gerry and I are taking off in July. Think of it, Malou – the sun and that blue, blue sea ...'

I watch Malou awkwardly setting down her cards. Once again I feel like telling her: clumsy! Basically, that's why you never learn anything. I feel like telling her lots of things; I like being mean to her or simply saying, 'Instead of waiting for that fucking telephone to ring, why don't we go to the movies? This is our hundredth game of gin today, and I can't take it any more. I need some fresh air. If I can't hear the telephone ring, I want to go out. And in any case I want to end this dumb game ...'

I look at her chipped nail polish and greasy hair.

'Aren't you getting a little sloppy these days?'

She looks up at me in surprise and puts down her cards. She doesn't reply. Now she stretches and yawns. I look at her: she has skinny legs, skinny arms, full breasts, and a little meadowmouse face. I know her by heart; and tonight, more than ever, I feel that she isn't cut out for this life. Without me, no doubt, she would have given it up.

'Some days you look like a real slut. Yes, yes, I know, you don't give a shit as long as Bébert gets his money orders and you can pay your share of the rent. A little ambition never hurt, Malou, believe me. If it's just for peanuts, you might as well go back to reeling off lace in a department store. Am I right, or am I not? Come on, Malou. Get ready. Tonight we give the world a scare.'

'I don't feel like working tonight.'

'You never feel like it. Come on – we didn't rent this apartment to lounge around in. You think I actually enjoy turning my bed into a fuckery? No, don't answer – you don't know what you're talking about anyway. Just sit up and let me fix your eyes for you.'

We walk in silence down Rue de la Faisanderie. As we pass the police station, we politely say hello to the blue boys shivering in their capes. Dreams are on the house. We don't look back, but we can feel their gluttonous eyes caressing our buttocks all the way to Place du Paraguay.

Innocent as can be, and ready for anything, we stroll down the sidewalk of Avenue Foch, where, agleam with luxury and chrome, a number of class hot rods are cruising singly.

'Wouldn't you like to work out of a car?'

'No. See the guy in the Peugeot? I think you're on. Try to connect me, but go easy.'

She's off and away. Malou throws caution to the winds, sticks her big pink tits through the window, makes googoo eyes, and gesticulates, never noticing the man's hands slyly going into action in the area of his fly.

'Don't tell him your life story! Can't you see he's about to shoot off between your knockers?'

We call the guy a freak, a voyeur, and every other name we can think of. His lips adrool, he brings himself off without paying anybody anything.

'Satisfied? Poor, dumb Malou, can't you get it into your head that the less they see, the better? You've no flair at all.'

I feel her cheek on my shoulder ...

To hell with being practical! We almost run all the way to Rond-Point des Champs-Elysées, dancing rings around the trees that smell so wonderfully of summer. Life is terrific. Cars can pull up if they like, and propositions can rain down on us – we're deaf and blind. We've made up our minds. Tonight we're going to do whatever makes us really happy. As we run, Malou's chignon blows loose, the blue of her eyelids fades, and my mascara starts stinging my eyes. We couldn't care less. We've just arrived from Rouen or Tuba City, and we intend to make the most of it. We're two cousins from out of town, we're on vacation, and God how beautiful Paris looks, with the Arc de Triomphe rising skywards and its Texan tourists striding down the most beautiful avenue in the world.

We dawdle awhile in front of the *Figaro* building, reading the headlines on the newspapers posted outside. Men brush against us. We look at each other inquisitively. Don't feel guilty, Malou. I'm thinking the same thing you are. If one of them murmured in our ear, 'I'll take both of you – my townhouse is just around the corner,' we wouldn't say no. We'd accept because the guy would be right and we wouldn't have to argue about the price. He'd offer each of us five hundred with no beating around the bush, because we'd look unspoiled to him, because he'd be sick of B-girls who mask their eyes with false eyelashes and use so much perfume they have no smell of their own : because we don't look like hookers.

But gents, alas, are out of season. The place is full of meat-beaters, men with neither taste nor money. So what? We're on vacation. The terrace of Le Madrigal is nearby, and its chairs stretch out their arms to us. The people there are laughing in every possible language. After one glass of port, Malou's eyes light up. Start strumming your mandolins – she's got the hots for the wops at the next table. She gets so worked up her tits start spilling out of her bra.

'Sophie – what do you think?'

'Stop throwing your charms around. Why are you turning them on like that for free? Can't you see they're about to bust a blood vessel? Come on, let's change scenes.'

We go up the Champs towards Rue de Berri. Paris has lost its glamour. We're in front of the Val d'Isère when a metallic-grey Taunus pulls up next to us.

'How much if your friend comes along?'

'Three hundred.'

'Get in.'

I sit next to the driver. He seems thirtyish : candid face, sporty looks. The requirements of work reassert themselves, and I forget I'm hungry. Malou is humming in the back. The guy turns on the radio.

'What are your names?'

'Malou, and Sophie. How about you?'

'André. I'm from Bagneux.'

You don't say. Somehow, big boy, I don't get the impression you were raised by the Holy Fathers. So drive, man, and cool it, because we don't live in some fleabag but in a townhouse!

The embers are glowing in the fireplace. It's so cosy here. How pretty Malou looks after she's had a couple of drinks! How I'd love to play a hand of gin rummy, listen to a good record, or just dream ...

'Say, girls, your pad's terrific. It's respectable, quiet, everything. You're sure not busting your asses.'

'Everybody's got his thing. Hotels are so depressing – not to mention the risks. Also, we like to have things clean. We have two bathrooms here. No shabby sharing.'

'You know, we usually work only by phone. We're making an exception for you.'

'Give us our little present now, and then we'll be all set.'

All set, my foot. I watch him take three one-hundred-franc notes from his plastic wallet. Malou is pouring herself a glass of port while I get an attack of nausea.

'You don't understand. It's three hundred each.'

'Don't give me the runaround. One-fifty for each of you, and not a penny more.'

Holy Mary, Mother of God, pray for us sinners! We've struck a nasty type. Look down from the back of your donkey on his blanching lips, his narrowing nostrils, and his broad clenched fists. Cross my heart, he'll never set foot in our digs again. I'll give him a fake phone number once we've polished him off.

'Don't get sore. There's been a misunderstanding. Never mind, we'll take real good care of you just the same – won't we, Malou?'

'Sure. We're going to spoil the little baby. Come and see our bedroom.'

'Hey, whoa! Not so fast, chickens. I've got all the time in the world. So, pretty Sophie, how about pouring me another scotch?'

There's one last little blue flame shimmering around the embers in his eyes. After that the fire will go out. His fists are still clenched ...

'It's rather warm, don't you think? Shall we make ourselves comfortable?'

'You're nuts lighting a fire in August. Business been good? Your pimps must be happy.'

'Save that kind of talk for the girls at Les Halles. And while you're at it ask them if they've got a place of their own.'

Malou looks at me out of the corner of her eye. She's understood. I feel relieved.

The blue flame tilts the other way, and we tilt with it. We start being cuddly and affectionate. Our eyes sparkle wildly. We coo as we caress the thighs of this athlete. He resumes quite imperturbably:

'I suppose I don't have to worry about syphilis?'

Ye gods and little fishes! I expound an elaborate thesis concerning this dread disease, which makes the teeth and hair fall out, gnaws right through to the spinal marrow, and ravages the genitals and brain.

'Why do you want to talk about things like that? We're perfectly healthy. Do you want to see the results of our latest check-up?'

He makes a face and empties his glass.

'Okay, girls. Let's go.'

For an hour and a half we romp on the bed. You can't say old Andy is shortwinded. As for us, we invent, innovate, outdo ourselves, astound ourselves, lose track of each other, and generally knock ourselves out. Completely sobered up, Malou whispers in his ear that she likes the way he makes love. Uttering a shout that may well ruin our local reputation as decent young ladies, he collapses on top of her. An incredible sense of well-being overcomes me as I take my first hit on a cigarette, which I then pass to Malou, who is still trapped in that embrace. I breathe deeply.

After the game, I feel that a little hygiene is in order. We drag our football player to the bathroom; then singing his praises, we lead him into the living room. We slip on his jockey shorts and nylon socks, and when we finally have him dressed, we feel like bursting into 'La Marseillaise'. Anything, as long as he leaves, as long as he takes his football and his spiked shoes out of here fast.

Wiped out, we collapse on the living-room sofa, counting the seconds to the final whistle. Forlorn hope: it's only halftime. The sportsman looms in front of us, taller and stronger than ever. He thrusts his hands into his pockets. I suddenly feel frightened.

'You've gone through my pockets. Let's have it back.'

I look at Malou and see my own pallor reflected in her cheeks. I calmly stand up.

'Listen, André, we didn't take anything from you, and you know it.'

'You're both thieving sluts. Sophie, you've got more lip than your friend, but I'm not like the other assholes you spend your time conning. Now I want the stuff back, and fast.'

'We didn't take anything. You fucked us for an hour and a half for thirty lousy bills. Now get out of here. Out!'

'Watch it, girls. I'm not the patient type. Shall we start with the furnishings—'

A loud yell fills our ears. The television set shatters.

'Stop it!'

'Up yours, bitch.'

'André, stop it, don't be a jerk – we'll give you back your three hundred francs.'

Lamps, flowerpots, records, knickknacks, books: all go flying through the air.

'Stop it, please, please. Take your money and get out.'

One hand grasps; the other strikes. I've got a split lip.

'Why are you doing this?'

His clenched fists are huge. He seizes the whisky bottle and smashes it into the glass-panelled door. Lifting Malou up by the neck, he aims his left fist at her eyes. With a scream like an animal's, my little meadow mouse goes crashing to the floor.

'Had enough? Or shall we continue?'

Half-conscious, we crawl to the bedroom.

'I think I'm blind.'

'I think I've lost all my teeth.'

I laugh a nervous little laugh as I hand over our purses.

'Why all the rough stuff? You could have just ripped us off without hitting us. It's all there. Help yourself.'

'Shut your mouth.'

The bastard even takes the small change. He starts slapping Malou around.

'You're nothing but a hooker, and you're a lousy fuck. I'll be back.'

The door slams. We lean against it, trembling, not saying a word.

'What hit us! I think we'd better go on vacation again.'

'Don't make me laugh, it hurts too much.'

'Malou – his licence number! We're nuts. Let's get him.'

Too late: Rue Dufrénoy is dark and deserted, except for a solitary man talking to his dog. Strange noises come from the open windows. Inappropriately enough, the night is a pleasant one. Holding my hand on my mouth, or rather my mouth in my hand, I re-enter the building.

It's time to go to bed. Tomorrow is another day . . .

From the distance a bell resounds in my head. I get up and run to the phone.

'It's the door,' Malou murmurs.

I stagger to the hallway, woozy with Valium. Through the peephole I see the landlord. As I open the door, I cover my mouth – a vain gesture, since my hand isn't broad enough, and my lips protrude on either side of it in a vast grimace. He starts talking with overfed ease.

'Mademoiselle, after what happened here tonight, I cannot allow you to stay on. We'll take stock of the damage at the end of the month.'

He casts a contemptuous look over my shoulder. The place looks like a junkyard. Such hooligans, these tenants.

'Have the carpeting cleaned immediately. Bloodstains are hard to remove.'

So he'd heard the whole business! We could have died under his roof without his lifting a finger. What a lousy world!

We've hardly moved in, and already we have to get out. When I think how much I'd counted on this apartment! Peace and quiet, farewell. We're out in the cold again. All because some madman comes along, beats the shit out of us, breaks everything, leaves the place in a shambles, and walks away whistling. Oh, if only I had the guts to hang myself.

'I heard it all. What'll we do?'

'Sleep.'

'I've lost the urge. I hurt all over. Pass me the mirror. What about going back to La Bohème?'

'Never. I don't like backtracking. Anyway, champagne is even worse for you than getting punched in the face. You were in complete agreement when you joined me here: no more madams, no more bubbles, and no more girls – nothing but the two of us! You were jumping for joy when you left that place, you went out of your mind when I found this apartment. You said you'd never be able to work any other way again. So we're going to get ourselves organized.'

'I don't want to end up strangled to death.'

'You're not dead, you just have two black eyes.'

When Maria, our Portuguese cleaning woman, came in the next afternoon and entered the living room, she let out a loud scream.

'*Meu Deus, meu Deus*, what has happened to my young ladies? Whoever left the place in this state?'

'Come in, Maria – we're here in the bedroom. Leave the curtains drawn. I'll help you clear up the living room. But first, make us some nice strong tea.'

'Oh, no, first you need medicine and care. Ah! The young ladies were not wise to bring home people they do not know. You have such nice gentlemen who come to see you – Monsieur Maurice, for example, and Monsieur René. Not look in the street, Mademoiselle Sophie! Are other girls for that, but not you.'

'Okay, Maria, we won't do it again. The man wasn't a gent, that's all.'

'What about Monsieur de Lespinay? What is his opinion of this?'

'Monsieur de Lespinay has no opinion. He's just kicking us out. We won't be seeing each other any more, Maria.'

I had imagined all kinds of reactions, but not this one. Maria has fallen to her knees, sobbing. Malou does the same. Then Maria starts talking. She says she'll follow us wherever we go. She says that now, before we make up our little minds, we need to take a vacation. She tells us about a pretty little village near Lisbon, and about her mother and her son, José. She tells us about boats that sway in the moonlight, the warm sea, the fados ... She gives us the works. The three of us are bawling away in the midst of the wreckage. Maria is weeping over her son in Portugal, Malou over the daughter she's had to board out in Beauvais. As for me, I'm weeping over myself, thinking about the opportunity I've lost, thinking about my lip (it splits open at every word I say). I'm crying over myself because there's nobody else I can cry over – and that makes it worse.

The telephone starts to tinkle. Stifling my sobs, I pick it up. I hear Gerry's voice speaking thickly over the wire.

'What's happened to you?'

My own voice is deformed as I answer, 'Oh, nothing. My head's bashed in.'

Gerry's voice continues, 'Talk louder, I can't hear anything.'

My voice whispers, 'I can't. My lips are all swollen.'

Gerry's voice, insistent: 'What's the name of the guy who did it to you?'

My voice, shouting: 'Are you living in dreamland? You think I ask for their driver's licence before I make out with them?'

I remove the receiver from my ear.

'Baby, do you want me to come over?'

No, Gerry, old chump, it's too late now. You should have been hidden in the closet last night with a blackjack ready. Go ahead and get drunk in peace. I'm not all that beat up. In two or three days I'll be back at the grind.

Our vacation lasted a good week. In the shade of the window curtains, Malou and I kept dealing them out. Maria turned out to be more attentive and helpful than a mother. She did the shopping and the cooking. She answered the phone, explaining that the young ladies had gone away for a two weeks' rest and jotting down our appointments.

On the tenth day, we stuck our noses out of doors. At the first drugstore we came to, I picked out a pair of sunglasses for Malou, who still had circles under her eyes. Laughing, we pranced around in the early-afternoon sunshine. Each found the other pretty and told her so.

During our convalescence, we had never once stopped dreaming up wild schemes. I hailed the first taxi we saw and told the driver in a commanding tone of voice, 'To the Madeleine, please!'

chapter four

Just what is the Madeleine? A Napoleonic church; a hanging cloister; a flower market; and Rue Godot-de-Mauroy, where I made my honest-to-God debut. It happened before London, Le Sportsman, and the Saint-Louis, on a warm November evening ...

Mama Dédée was off in Nantes, having a ball. My father was away fishing. Gerry was playing cards at Mado's. I left the kids to their own devices, and on Dédée's stiletto heels I slipped away towards the Madeleine. When I arrived at Rue Godot, I wrapped my scruffy loden coat about my semivirginal breast.

Why Rue Godot? Only the Devil knows. It was cold that night. In front of the closed shops they had selected as their posts, the girls were rubbing their arms. Their jeering voices were bouncing off the stars, and, by the Holy Virgin, I no longer had any idea what I was doing. I staked out a claim at the far end of the street. It was far away from them, and near the church, where men wouldn't come looking for me. I waited in the shelter of an archway. I waited for the time to pass, and drew my purple nylon scarf tight around my neck.

A man came along, with his foibles and his folding money. I whispered, 'Two hundred,' pulling the loden tighter across my breasts. When he went away, my heart started beating again. Another man stopped. I murmured, 'I'm waiting for someone.' I clapped my hands together indignantly – no, I wasn't a whore! I went off with the third one. I got into his car. Oh, Mama, I called out your name as I collapsed on his shoulder. It was a good shoulder. It listened to me without interrupting, and everything came out all mixed up – you, Papa, my schoolteachers, getting kicked in the stomach, the lung stew, Gerry, my supermarkets, and the strange darkness inside of me. When I was through, he said he'd take me to a friend of his – a priest. I went off with him. I would have gone off with the Devil himself.

Later, while I ate the spaghetti Saint Paul had prepared for me, I told my life story all over again. As I listened to their homilies, I stared at a branch of pink apple blossoms that had been stuck in a glass bottle. I promised not to succumb; I promised to follow the straight and narrow; and I forgot their wonderful faces.

The best thing to do if you're not familiar with a neighbourhood is to settle down at a sidewalk café and take the pulse of the surroundings. The Madeleine-Tronchet seems like a promising spot.

After two tea-and-lemons, we realize that it's no place to make out. It's full of respectable people, sexy little salesgirls, grandmothers stuffing themselves with strawberry tarts, and hurried businessmen gulping down their coffee at the counter. We're about to weigh anchor when a man discreetly gives Malou the high sign.

'We'll meet back here. If I'm busy, wait for me.'

Malou's exit has gone unnoticed. I watch her skirt swaying amid the crowd and order another cup of tea. The waiter, a sympathetic, red-faced fellow, smiles at me in complicity. I lower my eyes. When I raise them again, I immediately see the person with whom I'm going to inaugurate this part of town.

He's waddling along in front of the terrace casting great goo-goo eyes at me, running his tongue over his lips and waving five big fingers in my direction. Christ, if only he had the discretion of Malou's customer. If I don't get up, he's liable to come over and fetch me ... Go on, Sophie. Where's your nerve? Nobody saw a thing.

I haven't gone two steps before he's wrapped a hairy arm around me.

'No. Walk behind me.'

'Don't be so uppity! I like walking down the street with a beautiful girl. Fifty *is* okay with you?'

'Plus the room.'

'I'm Marcel. And you?'

'Sophie. You know a hotel around here?'

'On Rue de Castellane. That's where I go when I'm doing TV repair work in the neighbourhood. It's quiet, you'll see. You know, you're cute. Say, where did you use to hang out?'

'Someplace else.'

'Someplace else! Someplace else doesn't mean anything! What's wrong – in a bad mood? Got the rag on?'

Take it easy, Sophie. You're in need of cash.

At the registration desk, a little grey man with a suspicious eye and a mottled complexion takes the twenty-five francs and hands me a cold key.

'Number twelve, three flights up.'

Marcel pinches my calves on every stair.

'You know, Sophie, in my business you get to meet funny people. There's no shortage of opportunities. Those house-wives just love it. Listen, there's one I know not far from here. She calls me every week. I even told her it would be cheaper if she got herself a new TV set. Well, forget it. The only thing she wants is her Marcel. Her husband's a brush salesman for the Paris area. If I wanted to be a bastard, I could make her leave him. I might point out that I'm pretty good in the sack. You'll see.'

And I saw. We even had a good laugh together afterwards, as we sat on the edge of the bed, smoking a cigarette.

'So now you understand, Sophie. I have my clientele, too. I make women happy. I'm the tender sort. No freaky habits, nothing. Just loving and cuddling – and they love that, the little devils. You see, even with the others, the ones like you, I've never missed. Not once. You liked it, right? I could tell. Here, there's fifty more for you.'

I stuffed the bills into my purse and deposited a kiss on his ill-shaven jowl.

'If you come by next week, I'll be around. Take a gander inside the café. So long. I'll lead the way.'

In the stairway, I pass Malou on her way up, followed by a guy with a protruding gut. As I brush past, I breathe in her ear:

'Stay on top!'

'What?'

'On top – you on him. Dig?'

Wheezing, the man has halted on the landing. We exploit the opportunity for a brief chat. As he passes in front of us, Marcel slaps me on the back.

'That guy's a real clown. I'll tell you about it later.'

'I worked my first one on Rue Vignon. And you?'

'Right here. The one going out.'

Gasping, the mammoth pushes Malou ahead of him. I hear the key turn in the lock.

As I go past the desk, the little grey man beckons to me. 'No more than four. Be sure to tell your girl friend.' Without knowing why, I answer, 'Thank you.'

To avoid going back to the Madeleine-Tronchet, I strolled down the street looking in the shopwindows. The sun was warm on my neck. I felt good, and anonymous. I saw a little outfit I liked, and the hundred francs came in handy as a down payment. As I was leaving the shop, a man stretched out his arms to me.

'Sophie!'

'Paul!'

'I've never stopped thinking about you. You haven't changed. What about finding a nice quiet spot – that *café-tabac*, for instance. Tell me about yourself. You've left La Bohème?'

'You know, I wasn't planning to spend my whole life there. The atmosphere got to be depressing. The girls were jealous, old Rose was always making cracks, you had to split with the steerers – it was no fun. I'd rather not talk about it – I thought about you too.'

'Tell me more, my little darling. No, don't. We'll talk later. Right now, take me home with you.'

The taxi drops us at the corner of Rue Dufrénoy and Rue de la Faisanderie. We walk into 119 like a married couple. Maria has put flowers everywhere. The apartment is quiet and soothing. As I show Paul in, I realize with a pang how attached I've become to the place. That maniac *would* have to barge in ...

So long, Paul. You'll have to pursue your dreams without me. I have other fish to fry – man-eaters with spikes in their fins. And besides, Malou is waiting for me.

The bells of the Madeleine count out their six peals. What difference does it make if I'm the only one listening? Let the bells of heaven ring, let the birds of heaven sing! Hi there, all you middle-class housewives. You're right to be buying flowers – they're pretty, they smell good, they brighten up the home, and when they wilt, you can throw them out. It's so convenient to chuck things out when they start getting in your way. Now that I've found Paul again, I'd like to chuck Gerry out. The trouble is, he's no daisy. He's a thistle. He's a carnivorous flower who clutches at my skirts every time I try to climb one step higher. And wow, whenever I take a look at the main stairway, I get this unbelievable dizzy feeling ... Fortunately, there's Malou. She's waiting for me at the Madeleine-Tronchet. Malou doesn't throw wilted flowers out. She puts them away in a lacquered box. Malou's not wasteful. She keeps everything, even secrets, and so I can tell her anything.

'Sophie! I was starting to worry. Like a glass of port? My treat.'

'If it's your treat, of course I will. Guess who I just left? Paul – my agricultural expert. Take a look at his cheque.'

'What kind of name is that?'

'Well, what kind do you think it is! Old French nobility. Not all my customers are plumbers. He's made it a profitable day. What about you? Satisfied? Come on, smile. There'll be good times again for both of us. There will be, honest.'

'You remember the first time you took me out to eat? We'd just come out of La Bohème. You said, "It's my treat – and I feel like chili con carne." Before we went into Birdland you buttoned my raincoat over my bosom.'

'You were so excited. You kept saying, "I love jazz. I love it here." I liked that. It made me feel as though I was giving you a present. You drank wine out of those huge snifters – you had to hold them in both hands. You laughed. Oh, Malou, how you laughed that morning, nodding your head in time to the beat. After the chili con carne you felt a little warm, and you un-buttoned your raincoat. I did the same. As I remember, it was quite a display. You couldn't see anything by then, and I couldn't see much – but I could still hear, and I didn't like the running commentaries on our tits. So we finished our drinks. Outside, you kept hanging on to my arm. I buttoned your coat back up. We wandered around the streets. We passed all those people who were going off to their daily grind – their eyes were still sticky with dreams ... "Don't stop talking, Sophie," you kept saying, "just talk." It was then I decided we'd go to Orly and have a cup of coffee on the observation deck. It would be something new for us, going to watch the planes take off.'

'Then – do you remember? – we took a taxi, and you told the driver to step on it because we didn't want to miss our flight. We made up some crazy story, and the guy gave us a funny look in the rearview mirror.'

'That's right – I even remember he was wearing a beret. And *then* I wonder what possessed us – it's really insane when you think back on it. We hopped like two jackrabbits on to the first plane for Nice. Why Nice? We didn't know a soul there. There was that little hotel we picked out at random for a three-night stay; and that restaurant on the port – grilled mullet, *vin rosé* ... And those respectable little dresses we bought during the afternoon. It was sheer madness!'

'And those two guys in the nightclub, and then at the *brasserie* the next morning. We all got the giggles over beer and hard-boiled eggs. I kept telling my guy I was in love, and yours re-cited "The Grasshopper and the Ant" in an Arab accent. You were laughing like crazy, and so was I. I was splitting my sides.'

'Later, though, it wasn't so funny. You kept dawdling in front of that hotel. You couldn't make up your mind. I had to shove you down the primrose path. And then for three days and nights, I had to curl up in the a corner of the room and listen to you make love. I can't tell you how embarrassed I was. I know we'd made out with guys together, but with him it was different. You were like another person. You really had a thing for him!'

'Don't let's talk about it.'

'Anyway, when we got back to Paris, I had to de-stash what I'd hidden in your flowerpot. It'll take me a long time to forget the smile Gerry had on his face when I plunked down those three five-hundred-franc notes.'

'You really think you'll leave him?'

'I'm waiting for something that will make it happen naturally. I have a patient disposition. Very, very patient. Got to be going, Lou. He's expecting me not far from here for chow. It's an affair for the menfolk.'

At Le Baudet, it's back to tribal rituals. Jean-Pierre, the fat barman, offers me a greasy hand and a phony smile. Perched on her high horse behind the cash register, her mouth full of gall, Pascale – the senior woman of the big man from Nice – is wrapping rolls of change. At the far end of the bar, Fabienne is playing solitaire and dreaming of taking the other's place.

Fabienne – what exactly is your position in the starting lineup? Certainly not first. You know it, and it bugs you. You're a stand-in – that's what you are. But how much will you take? Your man is Mr Pimp himself. He's the real thing, with an adaptable smile, and adaptable heart, and an adaptable prick. He's a purse-snatcher. And you crawl on your knees to him. You'd go stockingless in wintertime to provide him with an extra fifty. You bawl because you think he's in the clink and meanwhile he's living it up on the Riviera with some doll. Six months later, when he shows up again, you're amazed he's so tan, and you actually believe him when he says he got that way from his daily walks in the yard. And he, like a real pimp, gets his kicks every time he counts the bills that you deliver each week to his lousy barman. Keep playing solitaire, baby you've got a whole life to go on believing, and I hope you enjoy it. And the worse he treats you, the more you love it.

Listen, I'm not tearing you down. I understand the whole business. But what bothers me is your pretending not to notice me. When I think of the months that we spent side by side at La Bohème! Don't you understand I'm no better off? Look, there's my guy coming in on his wobbly shoes. You see what I mean? It's a nitpicking world!

To think that all I want is a smile, and you're all sitting there

with your teeth in your mouth. That's it, go on, Gerry, do your
big act. Kiss the ladies' hands and give Jean-Pierre's a firm
shake. It's sucking off Carlos by proxy. It's important to you
that he knows you've come to his place to toss your money
around. That's what makes a man look big.

In the back room, men – real men – are talking in confiden-
tial tones. Gerry tells me that I'm not behaving like a woman.

'I'm a nice guy, but there's a limit. I'd like you to show my
friends a little respect. If it's the roughing up you got the other
night that's making you so frisky, I can let you have a few myself.'

Just you wait. You're going to get a surprise package. And
what a surprise! And then you'll be able to tell your sad story
to anyone you like: anyone but me.

Gerry has laid his long fingers on my knee, and I caress the
shiny nails, lost in my thoughts.

'Knock off the droopy look.'

Like good girls, the other women have sat down on the side-
lines. If I'd brought my knitting we could have spent a pleasant
evening. Too bad! We'll have to settle for blini and caviar. No
point in pretending to be above it all. Let's go, sweethearts. Let's
dig our snouts into the trough. And since we're in such clever
company, let's keep our eardrums stretched. This is an important gathering. We are going to listen to our men talk. Let's
hear their opinions on the events of the day. And let's not be
small-minded. We can certainly sympathize with so-and-so,
who was caught with his hand in the till, or disapprove of that
fag whoosiz, who turned fink. We can feel gratitude for the
corrupt lawyer who keeps the dossiers circulating, and we can
spit on judges in general. Let's show our indignation, sisters,
and prove ourselves worthy of our menfolk.

Hush – now they've started talking about Valerie. Valerie,
that turd, is the shame of everyone in the life: after her man
was busted, she did a disappearing act and went off with her
Fancy Dan. Generous-hearted Valerie even gave her pimp's
wardrobe to her new lover. What a disaster for all his friends!
Gerry, who up till now has been content to nod his approval
with his mouth full, sums up the discussion:

'For me, a woman is sex on two legs.'

Wow! I should be flying. It can't be him that said it. It's

too subtle. Too romantic. I discreetly tug his sleeve and press my lips to his ear:

'And you, my love, you're an *ass*.'

Underneath the table, my ankle feels as though it were splintering. My smile doesn't falter as I dip a spoon into my *café liègeois*.

'You're smashed.'

'Right. You're so right.'

It's true that I'm drunk: drunk and clearheaded. Oh, my! How touching it is the way they're saying goodbye! And how they all seem to love one another! Deceit. Lies. You're sons of bitches in pinstripe suits. You are all potato beetles: destructive, ever present, devouring our leaves, sucking up our sap, withering our roots, until the time comes to ditch us some dark night, when we're all wrinkled and gone soft and alone under the shadow of middle age.

In the car, Gerry the potato beetle decides to stop off in the woods before going home.

'Which one?'

'What the hell do you care? A wood's a wood.'

The champagne is turning to vinegar. This means another field day at my expense – the second in a month. That's too much.

'I'm not stopping in any wood. If you're in a pastoral mood, go by yourself.'

A backhanded slap. A sob. A red light ... There's my chance: and so I find myself with my butt on the sidewalk looking up at the statue of Joan of Arc. If I could only get up quickly, grab a taxi, and get to Malou's ... She's probably waiting up for me.

What's that cop doing capering around in this windy place? He's coming this way. He's seen me by now, of course. Gerry, sobered up, jumps out of the car. I sit tight. I'm a woman – a drunken woman. Dear old Gerard starts talking. He can show considerable spunk on occasions like this.

'Good evening, Officer,' I hear him saying, 'my wife's been drinking a bit. Help me get her back on her feet, will you?'

I laugh. Only a short distance from the Comédie Française, and he's playing the role of his life. I docilely allow myself to be picked up. They settle me in the back seat. I've loused up my exit. I weep softly, with my face against the cold leather, while the cop says in a friendly tone of voice:

'She'll feel better after a nice nap.'

After stepping on the gas two or three times, Gerard administers his special variety of sleeping pill. It's a little rough, but effective. I doze all the way to Rue Auguste-Chabrière. When we reach our love nest, he rifles my purse with skillful fingers.

'You've been getting out of hand ever since I've allowed you a little more freedom. A little discipline is in order. What you need is a whorehouse – a real one, with real *women* in it.'

He mentions Rue de la Goutte-d'Or. A pretty name. I wearily ask him, 'Where's that?'

'At Barbès. Porte de la Chapelle.'

'Never heard of it.'

'You're going to start hearing of it. And after you've been humping fifty Ay-rubs a day, maybe you'll get back into line.'

During the night, I had a terrible nightmare. I woke up clutching my crotch. Gerard was sleeping on his back. I bent over his face.

'Gerard – are you awake?'

He looked at me out of eyes that were puffy with sleep.

'I don't want to take on Arabs.'

'Go to sleep. You give me a pain.'

So I give you a pain, you pasty-faced fruit! But what if when the new moon rises I took it into my head to cast loose and get out on my own a little? Then where would you be? Would you head for the Atlantic with a bottle in each hand – one for you, and the other to throw into the sea with the following SOS: 'My wife has disappeared. She's taken the shirt off my back. Anyone finding her should kick her ass all the way to the lost and found department ...'

You clown. You're a heavy sleeper, and you have no memory: you've forgotten that, so far, I'm the one who's been running the boat. The winds have been contrary at times, and I've had to row upstream. I've been shipwrecked without having left dry land. But I've bitten a notch for each miserable day on the mainmast of wasted time. Sleep, because I can already make out the shore on the horizon. There are the cassia trees! I start munching on their orange pods. It feels so nice on my island. Be nasty if you want to. I'm not going to Rue de la

Goutte-d'Or. Instead, I"m surrendering myself to the setting sun.

The ensuing days are calm and prosperous. Showing our usual prudence, Malou and I continue to explore the neighbourhood of the Madeleine with an eye to moving there in the near future. The owner of the Madeleine-Tronchet and his wife have definitely adopted us. The waiter joshes us good-naturedly. It's like life in a real family, and we even take our meals there. It must be said that the service is first-class, and that we tip generously.

It's mid-September. The Parisians have returned to their capital with sun-ripened cheeks and hangdog looks. We decide, Malou and I, to give them a good time, no matter what. They prove grateful, and our first week is a profitable one. I divide my nights between Rue Auguste-Chabrière and Rue de la Faisanderie – between Gerard and Malou. She's feeling on top of the world, and so is he. On the evenings that I spend with him, he carefully irons his bills at low heat before pinning them together and going off to his bars to spend them. Meanwhile, curled up in the depths of the bed, I return to my dreams. After several glasses of port, I begin thinking that this period in my life, devoted half to Malou and her mischievous complicity and half to Gerard and the relative peace he allows me, may never end.

Since Malou has a sluggish disposition, and I've still kept a highly developed sense of obligation, I take it upon myself to write the drafts of her letters to Bébert.

'You're out of your mind,' Malou screams, 'he's going to think I still love him.'

She copies them over docilely, nevertheless. I can hardly wait for Bébert's replies. I unseal the letters before she does and read them out loud to her. Propped between two pillows, Malou listens to me with astonishment – until the day when Bébert insists that she come to the visitor's room wearing neither panties nor a bra.

'Now see where your dumb ideas have landed me,' Malou shouts. 'From now on when I go to Melun I'll have to walk around the prison bare-ass.'

To calm her down, I propose a deal.

'We'll split every trick I turn while you're waiting in line at the jail.'

'Sophie, I don't care about that. It isn't the point. I just can't. Don't you understand? Sophie, I don't love him any more. I don't love him any more.'

I take her little meadow-mouse head between my hands and lick up the tears

'Listen, Malou, it isn't a question of loving. He's just served two years. He's got three more to put away. And he doesn't know what's happened to you, Malou, that's the main point. He's living in a dream – a dream of you, a memory. You and I have never been in a cell like his, but with a little heart we can imagine it. A cell is four dirty walls riddled with dampness. It's an open latrine, where you can't even take a shit in peace, because even your most basic, your most intimate activities are spied on. Malou! Wake up! Do it in memory of your daughter's first smile. Afterwards, there'll always be time to tell him that you're calling it quits, that you spit on this kind of life. And you know I'll be there – I'll bust myself helping you get straightened out. But not now. We're lucky enough to be able to tell, just by breathing the air, what season it is, whether it's winter or spring. We can get high on being sad. But all he has is those twenty minutes each week. And even for those twenty minutes, there's some shitty screw keeping his dopey eye on him. Understand?'

Our faces are almost touching. I look at her trembling lips and quivering nostrils. Her tears are a relief to me. Cry, have a good cry, little meadow mouse! She collapses against me, and I stroke the strands of her all-too-fine hair.

She murmurs, 'How about killing ourselves?'

'How about running away to some place at the ends of the earth, where nobody knows us or anything about us? We'd arrive unannounced in our print dresses in some warm, inviting village. We'd learn how to live – just plain live. There wouldn't be tears streaming out of your eyes but millions of droplets of sunshine ...'

'Millions of droplets of sunshine ... Oh, Sophie, why are we stuck in this life? Tell me why?'

'Malou, there's something I never told you. When I started out, I took a look at the girls I was working with, and I made a pact with myself. If I'm still at it when I'm thirty, I told myself, I'll just check out quietly. Since then, three years have passed. But I haven't forgotten. I don't want to die. I want to get out, and I know I will get out. You don't know Prévert, but listen to what he wrote: "There'll always be a chink in the winter's wall to give us a glimpse of summer." You see, Malou, we're just going through a long winter. That's all.'

I lay her head down on the pillow, dry her eyes on the edge of the sheet, and light two cigarettes. We smoke in silence. I feel good, and I think that she does, too. Her breathing has become steadier, and her fingers are unclenching. I turn out the light.

When I look back on that world of ours, I realize you were my only friend.

chapter five

On 30 November, Monsieur De Lespinay honours us with his presence. He checks the household objects item by item, right down to the teaspoons. The dear man tells us he may have the place fumigated after what has gone on in here. (It's a crazy world!) If he's going to that much trouble, I suggest, he should have the phone number changed. That way his new tenants won't be awakened at all hours of the night.

As for Gerry, after a few troubled nights, things have calmed down. The fiasco at Rue de la Faisanderie has given him a chance to reassert his control. He knows I'll resist going back to a bar, or to a house; and since he's always dreamed of seeing me pounding my own beat under the open sky, he raises no objection to my doing my number at the Madeleine – provided I can bring in a steady five hundred a day.

'Malou, we'll *always* find five hundred.'

'You're the doctor.'

As we cast one last look at the façade of number 119, we let our gaze linger a while on the second-floor windows. For us, the future's just moved to another part of town.

Another part of town; another way of seeing things. Clever Gerry decides that I need a breath of fresh air. Through the misted car window, I looked out on a dying countryside. Blue smoke is scattering above the juniper bushes. Lifted by the wind, tangled balls of bramble roll over stony fields. Wooden posts rise towards the soiled sky. Rust-coloured cows are digging up the frozen ground with their horns. A navy-blue immensity darkens the valley. The thistles are shivering in the blackness of a moonless night. '... Our summer day withers away ...' I don't love you any more, Gerry. I don't think I ever loved you. But I'll let myself follow my shabby love-life down to this country inn. We'll taste the food they lay out for us, and we'll sleep in the shelter of its exposed beams. Tomorrow is another day ...

November goes out, December comes in. We haven't been picked up once by the boys from the Ninth Arrondissement. By now, the manager of the hotel on Rue de Castellane knows us and lets us use the place whenever we want. Business is picking up. 'Everything's coming up roses,' as Gerard loves to say. I open another bank account without telling him and each day deposit in it everything over five hundred francs. I have my mail delivered to Malou's. The sly stunt I'm about to pull on my old man really keeps me on my toes. Sitting snug and warm on the terrace of the Madeleine-Tronchet, I start building castles in Spain ...

'You'll see, Malou. The first million's the hardest. After that, it's easy.'

She listens to me sceptically as she sips her glass of port.

'See you later. I have a trick waiting.'

I'm slow-stepping my way towards the hotel, with my customer in tow behind me, when – what a surprise! Gentlemen from the pussy patrol have beat me to it. I know several of them by sight, and I'm not exactly unfamiliar to them.

I slow down. The man draws level with me.

'What's going on?'

'Nothing. Take my arm and start talking to me. Say anything, just do it. Please do it. Otherwise they'll bust me, and I don't feel like spending the night at the station.'

'Just take Uncle Jacques's arm.'

'Thanks. My name's Sophie.'

As we pass in front of the hotel, I can see that they're giving it the works. I bury my face against the man's shoulder and think with regret of our quiet little bedrooms on Rue de Castellane. They're scratched for good. When I next look up, I see Malou emerging from Rue de l'Arcade with a pimply adolescent waddling along behind her.

'That's my pal. I've got to warn her.'

'Leave it to me. You go on ahead. Wait for me in the first café.'

'Okay. I'll be waiting at the Madeleine-Tronchet in the back room.'

A few minutes later, the three of us are sitting together over a glass of beer. Jacques is listening to every word we say.

'You always work as a team? Do you make it together?'

'You bet.'

'I have a little hideaway on Rue Jacob. Could you be tempted into coming there with me?'

'You're our Prince Charming. You rescued us from danger, and your wish is our command.'

'All right, my beauties, let's weigh anchor. The sails are snapping in the breeze ...'

The hideaway on Rue Jacob is a modest eight-room apartment, crammed with a harmonious hodgepodge of objets d'art and paintings by old masters. I want to touch and caress everything.

'Let's drink and be gay, my lovelies. There's nothing in this world quite so restorative as debauchery.'

What an interesting gentleman. As long as men keep talking like that, our pimps' daily bread is guaranteed. Come on, Malou – he's played fair, so let's really put our hearts into it.

Jacques opens a door. We gasp in admiration.

'It's a real art-nouveau bistro! What a snazzy place you have.'

'I get the feeling you don't worry too much when the bills come in.'

He smiles and pours three glasses of port. We drink to Maria, and are then treated to a genuine feat of magic. Stepping behind the bar, Jacques presses down a key on the cash register. A little drawer comes shooting out, and then a number of bills start sliding across the marble surface. They feel delicious to our fingers.

They add up to one thousand. They make up for the bad days. We mumble our thanks. It's not his generosity that intimidates me. That's nothing new. It's the way he performs the gesture. He's aroused my curiosity. As we proceed to the bedroom, I pop my question:

'What's your line?'

'I'm a psychiatrist, my dear Sophie.'

'That's great.'

An enormous round bed is the only piece of furniture in the bedroom. The room is entirely decorated in black.

Jacques produces a little sailor suit from under the pillow and hands it to me.

'You can change in the bathroom. Don't come out till I call.'

I do as he says. When I enter the room at his signal, Malou is sitting on the floor with her legs spread wide, playing dominoes. She's wearing a pleated navy-blue skirt, a white blouse, white socks, and little girl's cotton panties. Stretched out on his back in the middle of the bed, Jacques is smoking, apparently unaware of our existence.

'Hey, little girl, would you like to play dominoes with me?'

'Only if you promise not to cheat.'

'I promise.'

For over a quarter of an hour, we shift the black rectangles around without batting an eyelash. How many girls have spent time in the black bedroom? What did the others think about this man? He smokes one cigarette after another without paying the slightest attention to us – or so it seems. I feel like having another glass of port, or a cigarette, but I know that if I ask for one, I'll be breaking the spell.

Malou pulls up her socks. Jacques still doesn't budge. We'll have to start things moving a little – we'll have to create a situation in which his needs can be satisfied without his having to take the initiative. (It's a glorious world – and a depraved one!) What can we cook up?

'Go on enjoying yourselves. Don't go away. I'll be back.'

So now we're alone in the bedroom. The cigarettes, unfortunately, are in the bathroom. Anyway, little girls aren't allowed to smoke. Malou points her finger at her temple and gives it a twirl. All right, Malou, so our saviour has a few screws loose. That's his privilege. Shh! He'll be coming back any minute. Let's not rock the boat.

The door opens. We stifle our giggles and pretend to be absorbed in our game. Our governess doesn't seem to be in a joking mood. Her black gown, white apron, and cat-o'-nine-tails bear witness to her severity. Her voice has completely changed.

'So! I've caught you again. Go stand in the corner at once!'

'Will we have to go without dessert, ma'am?'

'Not a word out of you, Michael. Lower your trousers. And you, Miss Lisa, tuck up your skirts.'

The whip cracks smartly – a little too smartly, for my taste. With my buttocks ablaze, I beg our governess to desist. I promise I'll never do it again. She makes us kneel down in front of her. Raising her skirt, she orders us to hold out our hands, palms up, and not lower our eyes. She merrily masturbates herself, and each of us in turn receives her hot semen on our fingers.

Once again, the three of us are sitting at the bar over a glass of port. Jacques has resumed his man's role.

'Why did you have us do that, when you could have watched us make it together?'

'For the simple reason that all I would have seen is playacting. You enjoyed yourselves, didn't you? Am I wrong, Sophie?'

'You're right.'

'Here's my card. If the idea still appeals to you, give me a ring Wednesday between eight and twelve.'

Promising to call, we leave Jacques to his fantasies.

There can be no doubt about it: the Hotel Castellane has been blown. I sometimes have to go as far as that vast sump called Gare Saint-Lazare in my search for a room – which is then refused me. Often, when I turn around, I find that the john's slipped off. Even Malou is letting me down: she's started talking about working in a bar again. My bank account has levelled off. Gerry's bitching. It's a washout.

After Malou goes home, around six, I explore the reserved territories alone. I extend my forays as far as Rue de Provence and Rue de Mogador, hugging the walls under the fierce stares of the regulars. Department stores are spasmodically spewing forth their human contents. Geysers of flesh are pouring out on the sidewalks, absorbing and submerging me. As I drag along, I think with regret of the crackling fireplace on Rue de la Faisanderie. Rue de la Faisanderie: a dream that failed. A complete fiasco. For a moment I think of the Saint-Louis. I know that it's been reopened, and that everything is just the way it used to be, back in the days when tricks were treats. Uh uh. The thing to do is react – not backtrack.

I suggest to Malou that we canvass the area around the Etoile. We've been taking driving lessons. We're sure of getting our licences in three weeks: some friends of Gerry's have an inspector on their payroll. Malou has started smiling again. I pick up on that and get her to come to the Champs. Here, we've decided, is where we'll start over again.

'We'd better split up – we'll attract less attention that way. Assembly point: Le Deauville, at six-thirty.'

'Let's leave ourselves a half-hour's leeway. If I'm not there by seven, it means there's been trouble.'

I agree, and touch my forehead for luck. We separate in front of the Passage du Lido, into which Malou disappears. I watch her for a moment, then set out for Rue du Colisée without much enthusiasm.

I hate pounding the pavement. I hate the ambivalence it creates. There are guys who would much rather think that I was a salesgirl supplementing her pay, or a model dreaming of being a cover girl, or a respectable housewife out for thrills. Guys have a nose for the cruiser, for the easy lay, for the easy prey that it doesn't take much to lure to out-of-the-way bachelor digs, or to town houses in the Sixteenth Arrondissement, or even to a place in the country. Of course, some will settle for a blow-job on the back seat of a car parked among the shadows of a park, but in either case, you should see them start running when the time comes to reach into their pockets. They can be pitiless with a hooker who hasn't made it perfectly clear what she's doing.

For me this pounding the pavement means exposing myself to the stares of all those others to whom I have become transparent. I never dare pass in front of the same sidewalk café twice. I feel that what I'm doing has become all too obvious. The least practised eye is going to find me out and look at me as if I were trash. Yes, yes, I know all about the girls who flaunt their big breasts and snazzy legs – the ones who stand proudly on street corners come winter or summer, the ones who never flinch under the most scathing looks. Naturally, nothing will ever happen to them. Vipers can try their sweet-talk on them, but it won't work. Those girls aren't about to let themselves get trapped by false promises. On the contrary, they're the ones who do the trapping. They're the ones for whom each man will happily turn into a willing victim.

In any event, it's not by sticking to Malou that I'll get to be that good. 'That good? Sophie, are you trying to be funny? Nothing could be more degrading than that. That way you'll never shake loose – and don't count on me to keep you company! Anything *but* that. No kidding, there are times when I can't understand you at all any more.'

That's what Malou would say if I talked to her about the street. Then she'd burst out sobbing, and I'd console her by explaining that it was just for laughs. I just wanted to see how she'd react. Sooner or later, though, that's how it's going to have to be. Everything would be easy again if only I had France with me! Together, the two of us could take over a street – we could buy one! But what's the point in thinking about her? Trying to find her in a town like Paris seems a waste of effort. Actually, when I think about it, the street is insanity, degradation, and unconditional surrender.

Dear Lord in Heaven, I may not be able to see into my own life clearly, but as far as my eye can see there are men brandishing their own bit of insanity. There's such a long line of them I'll never get to the end of it. Their lunacy goads me on, harrying and attacking me. Lord, I'm dying on my feet in the murky light of dark alleys, and there's no one to hold out a hand to me. Can they possibly be condemning me to wander all my life through these forbidden streets where dawn rises out of the sewers? The meagre respite they allow me is barely enough for me to put out my breasts and thrust out my hips so they can grab them again. Do they want to see my body wither and go barren? Do they really enjoy turning me into a latrine (as one doctor did) so as to behold my cheeks bulging with urine? Or are they unaware of their insanity, like the grimy grease monkey who could only come when he sank his oily nails into my throat? Who are these faceless beings to whom life makes me submit? Like that slippery-fingered sneak who helped me climb on to the armoire and then took off with my dough and my duds while I was yodelling cock-a-doodle-doo? Or that shivering old man who got under the sheets fully dressed and begged me to sing him the 'International'? Or the young dodo who gave his genitals a thrashing because he'd expected something different? Or Mr Everybody,

the kind who leaves a brothel the way he would a restaurant –
his pants spotted, his conscience clean, and a ready reply on
his lips? Who are you? Who am I?

Hey there, you men of mine – instead of holding out your
cocks hold out your hands! Open your eyes! You're my mirror.
I'm ready to lick your wounds, supply your wants, and satisfy
your sordid desires. There's still no room for hatred in my
head; but my womb is stuffed with your contempt, and my
tiniest blood vessel is freighted with your insults. Please, hurry
up. There's no time to waste. Look at me: I'm an acrobat
perched on the high wire of scorn. Don't let me tumble into
indifference. Gather your hands together. They know what
gentleness is. Link them together in a net of love. Then, if I
fall, it won't have been for nothing.

'Got some time to spare?'

On your toes, Sophie. They haven't given up. They're back
on the attack. Watch out for booby traps: he could be a pig, or
a viper. Spread those nostrils of yours, and don't let your in-
stincts run wild. Get the feel of him, size him up, make him
talk. Flash him the possibilities with your eyes, but hold your
tongue. Okay, I know, he looks like a john, and if you don't say
anything you'll miss the opportunity to turn your first trick
this evening. But I'm telling you, it doesn't feel right. Come on,
here we go. Jump right in.

'It's one-fifty.'

All right, Sophie, you've taken the plunge. Don't start playing the stickler.

'Why the long face? You get to go twice.'

To hell with worthy resolutions, and to hell with the other
girls! So I'm cutting prices – go bite your nails, we'll all be
together in heaven. Let's just hope I haven't run into a cop.

We go upstairs in a respectable-looking hotel on Rue de
Colisée. The guy hands me my fifteen bills. And the joke goes
on for three-quarters of an hour. Monsieur is having problems
getting it up twice in a row. I'm doing my best. I'm suiting my
actions to my words, and my mouth to my fingers. Finally, he
grouchily comes all by himself.

'I can tell you're a beginner. I'd have done better going back
to Josie. She may be an old bag, but at least she knows what to

do. You ought to stick to your regular job. Why did you start doing this in the first place?'

'Listen, this is no confessional, so keep your sky-pilot ideas to yourself. Anyway, you're nothing but a dodo.'

'Hey, wait a minute. If you start insulting me, you're in for trouble. I don't go for that – especially from a tramp like you.'

'Take it easy! When you go home, open up your dictionary, and you'll see that a dodo is a bird that inhabits certain islands in the Indian Ocean. It belongs to the turkey family.'

What a nightmare it would be to wake up every morning and find a face like that on the pillow! To think that there's so much competition for this job. Getting assholes like that to have orgasms ought to be recognized as a public service, like bottling mineral water.

Before we get to the front desk, Lummox makes it a point of honour to give me his arm. Suddenly my hand clutches it. My heart starts beating feverishly.

'Those three guys in the lobby are cops. My name is Marie Mage, I'm your girl friend, and you didn't pay me. I'll more than make it up to you.'

'When?'

The creep! The cops are on their way over. Out come the badges. I'm separated from my lover. I hand my ID to the cop, who asks, 'So this gentleman just happens to be your boy friend?' I'm ashamed to have to answer yes. I try and catch Lummox's eye. It's a waste of time. He's staring obstinately at the toes of his unshined shoes. Just look at him go to pieces, the fink! I can imagine the tale he'd like to tell the fuzz. 'You know, Mr Policeman, it wasn't my fault. She's the one who solicited me on the sidewalk. I was just window-shopping, I wasn't thinking about that at all, and then she started fumbling at my fly. There was no point in struggling. She swore she'd give me a bargain rate and almost dragged me here. The flesh is weak ... You're a man. You can understand. Let me have my identification papers back. I'm married, Officer, and I'm just as much in favour of law and order as you are.'

What's the point of arguing? I go off without making a fuss. The black Peugeot is waiting. People have begun staring at me. I'm past caring. Byebye, Malou. That apéritif at the Deauville will have to wait. I'm about to make the acquaintance of the

Eighth Arrondissement police station. Let's hope I don't find you there. I forgot my deck of cards, and the night promises to be a long one.

After the customary amenities, they stick me in the tank on Avenue de Selves. It looks like an aquarium. I'm alone in it, gasping for breath. Around midnight another strange fish appears and brightens up my solitude. He's managed to slip a litre of twenty-two proof plonk past the guards – he must have hidden it in one of his gills.

'Here's looking at you, kid. How about a touch of red-eye?'

I hesitate before wiping off the neck of the bottle. His little grey eyes, with their penetrating look, never leave me. What a world of difference between those eyes and Lummox's! You've got to take the rough with the smooth.

'O big fish from the Red Sea, here's looking at you!'

The wine warms my innards. We raise our silent toasts in the shadow of the flatheads.

Indexed and put on file by the pussy patrol of the Ninth Arrondissement, and now listed by the vice bulls of the Eighth, there's nobody left for me to fool – except myself. It's about time I admitted who I am. But I can't take that step. Accepting myself would mean surrendering, and I refuse to do that. I'm too young to die. And so it's with a gay heart that I keep pounding the pavements of the Champs and the surrounding neighbourhood, dragging Malou along in my wake.

One night we recklessly venture into Rue de Presbourg. Oh, we're not asking the other girls for all that much: just five or ten feet and a little patch of moonlight. We're ready to supply certificates guaranteeing our probity, even witnesses, should they be necessary. We go so far as to invite them all for a drink. But we don't stand a chance. Those bitches won't even let us finish speaking. They pelt us with insults and give us a sound thrashing. They even – and this is utterly outrageous – they even put John Law on our tails.

With the disturbing, familiar sound of a siren ringing in our ears, we vamoose to Le Drugstore and collapse on its cold seats. We order two double scotches with plenty of ice.

'Those babies are really bad news.'

'Let's have a bite at Jour et Nuit and get our strength back. After that, we'll slaughter them.'

202

'No, we're going to the movies.'

'Later – we're going after them. I feel frustrated. We've been at it since three in the afternoon, our handbags are full of nothing, and on top of all that we get screwed up by bitches who are in with the cops!'

'But if we go back there, we're going to get busted.'

'Oh, you're still talking about *them*. When I said "going after them" I meant johns. Don't worry: some day, the girls are going to get their little surprise. There's no rush. I've got their mugs on file.'

We take our time as we do down the Champs. Our morale is low, the wolf is at the door. We've decided to call it quits when, by the traffic light at Rue Pierre-Charron, a TR-4 comes to a sudden stop. A youth who is barely out of knee pants rolls down the window. The driver would appear to be not yet dry around the ears. We feel that there's been a misunderstanding. We blush crimson, and start to turn away.

'Hey, you broads – what's the going rate for a group scene? We're not kidding. Come on over here.'

As I bend down, I discover a third infant curled up on the back seat.

'Usually it's two hundred for each of us, but with three of you – oh, what the hell. We'll charge you the student rate.'

'You're on. Get in!'

'I hope you have a place to go to, because no hotel will take the five of us.'

'Don't worry. We've got rooms near the Bastille. Get in.'

The Bastille is a long way off, and these boys are very young. I flash Malou an SOS. Her mischievous look answers back: these boys are young, the Bastille is two steps away from my place, we haven't made a bean all day – it's perfect! Afterwards, you'll come and sleep over with me.

The first two babies claim to be brothers. The third one, who's squeezed against the door, doesn't let out a peep. The radio's on full blast, the cigarette smoke is so thick it may pop the roof, and I feel a sneaky migraine boring its way into my forehead. When you think about it, we'd have been better off going to bed. That would have been more reasonable. 'Marie Mage, if this ever happens again, I want you to copy out "Be reasonable" a hundred times.'

I don't want to be reasonable. Never. I loathe reasonable

people. They're ugly, cold, and mean. Precisely, Madame Duplantin. You can shove my head in the inkwell and stick pen points under my nails and pull me by the ears, but as long as I have lungs I'll keep shouting 'Up with funny people!'

'Hey, Malou – yell "Up with funny people!"'

'Up with money people!'

We park on an empty street. Taking a package from under the seat, the little guy who hasn't said anything gets his voice back.

'My old lady's jewels are in here. Is it okay if we use them to settle with you?'

Silence. My knee grinds against Malou's.

'We steer clear of deals like that. We don't want any trouble.'

'We prefer cash.'

'Keep your shirts on. There's no blood on them.'

We get out of the car. I keep my eye on the boy whom the two brothers have addressed as Robbie. He's slipped the package of jewels – if they are jewels – under his jacket. I've made up my mind to get my hands on it. This objective serves to distract me, and for a moment I forget about the unusual aspects of the situation.

Malou is walking ahead, with the two brothers on either side of her. I try to turn Robbie on. No dice. I can't get to him. We must be about the same age, and my arguments, usually so persuasive, carry about as much weight as a sack of feathers.

We come at last to a fifth-class hotel. In the lobby, the night watchman is conversing with a bluecoat. The cop's presence reassures me. Robbie puts an arm around my shoulders, one of the two brothers takes Malou by the waist, and the other one unhooks two keys from the board. We go up to the third floor.

'I'll leave the four of you to yourselves. I don't feel like screwing.'

Robbie's statement is a relief to me. The situation is back on an even keel. To hell with the jewels. Malou is smiling.

'It's every man for himself. I'll stick with the redhead.'

'So I'll take the blonde. You coming?'

'Let's go. Want to watch, Robbie?'

'Maybe later.'

We leave Robbie and his jewels in the corridor. A number of half-closed suitcases are scattered around the bedroom.

'Passing through Paris?'

'Sort of. What are you waiting for – why don't you strip?'

I was about to say, 'What about my little present?' But this ready formula, suitable for the regular john, doesn't seem to fit in with the tone of our conversation.

'Pay me first.'

'I'll give you a cheque. I don't have any cash.'

No hassles, Sophie. Keep it light. Your infant is an extremely precocious one.

'A cheque's okay. You have some identification? I'm sorry if I seem mistrustful, but I've been burned before.'

My swain takes out a cheque and an ID that only Scotch tape keeps from falling to shreds. It's not something that inspires much confidence. I hold my breath as he writes in the sum of four hundred francs. His name is Idris.

'I'm paying for you and your girl friend, okay?'

'Let me see your ID card, please.'

I make a mental note of the last name, as well as the address, then write the number of the identity card on the back of the cheque. I'm ninety-nine per cent sure that I'm whistling into the wind, but I go through the motions just the same. I want to get it over with. I sense some vague danger. I fold the cheque, slip it between two pages of my passport, and quickly undress.

Idris makes love like a twenty-year-old: no foibles, and no refinements. He likes it dog-fashion. I compliantly arch my rump. He mounts me like a ram, and his rough thrusts dispel my fears. He's just a little boy who needed to make love, or so I tell myself as he gratifies me with a loud 'You're terrific' and pours himself into me.

He's starting to get up. I rub the nape of his brown neck before hurrying off to wash myself. Even if it was for nothing, even if you leave me empty-handed, a girl's got to take care of herself. And at least you won't have caused trouble. (In the life, as elsewhere, you have to take things philosophically.)

I've got into the habit of never sitting down on the bidet with my nose to the wall. You should always keep your face to the enemy. I have oldtimers like Brigitte at the Saint-Louis to thank for this bit of folk wisdom. She told us again and again how this precaution had staved off many a Waterloo. In spite of sarcastic remarks, I've never failed to honour the motto: keep your face to the enemy. That's what I'm doing now. Idris is in front of me. A cigarette hangs from his pallid lips. Unless I'm very mistaken, he's tensing up.

The cake of soap slips from my fingers as I take an uppercut to the chin that makes my head spin. At the same time, an unfamiliar sensation turns my throat to ice.

'If you budge – if you say a word – I'll slit your throat.'

My mind is working like mad. The menacing straight razor is making my lips tremble. Idris reaches out for my pocket book ... What about Malou? No time to think about her. There's that steel blade to worry about.

The bastard starts by taking back his cheque.

'You bitch, the ID card was some bright idea!' He spits in my face.

Not daring to wipe myself off, I drag my tongue over my lower lip, where blood and saliva mingle. I watch the bastard deftly disembowel my purse with one hand while with the other he calmly presses the blade under my jaw. I'm beginning to wish I'd had more dough on me.

'We sure had you figured. You're two really dumb little chicks. A lousy one-twenty!'

I swallow my saliva.

'If you move an inch, I'm going to carve up that pretty face of yours. You thought you were taking us for chumps, you and your girl friend. Well, let me tell you something: twenty-five of us have come up from Marseilles to straighten out little finks like the two of you. It's a stool pigeon like you who got one of our buddies put away for twenty. You know Michou?'

I shake my head as I let the tears flow. This misunderstanding has restored some of my nerve.

'I swear to you, you're making a mistake. We haven't anything to do with that. And since we speak the same language, you might as well know both our old men are in the same business as you.'

Mentally I repeat the name on the identity card.

The door suddenly opens, and Robbie bursts into the room, carrying a six-shooter fit for an epic Western. He wastes no time burying it in my midriff. I feel utterly tiny. I wish I were a man.

'The other bitch didn't even have fifty on her. We left her tied to the radiator. She's some lousy lay. We both humped her – it was like there was nobody there. What'll we do – go back out?'

'Go get the other shitbag. And keep the rod out of sight in front of the old guy. Got it?'

Here comes Malou, with a nose like a candle stub. I shrug my shoulders helplessly. I wonder whether, fundamentally, we may not have faces that just beg to be socked.

We go past the night watchman, who is dozing over the register. Malou buries her nose in her rabbit's fur collar. Outside, in spite of the darkness and my anxiety, I get my nerve back and stand up to the three boys. There's no denying I feel a little tight around the throat.

'I told your friend here we're both of us married. And not just to anybody. You're way out of bounds. So—'

The creeps are listening. Am I on the right tack?

'If you're married, we're willing to meet your men and talk it over.'

'You know Baro the Gypsy's place on Rue Descombes?'

'Who doesn't?'

'Be there at two. In case you forget, it may take a little time, but they'll catch up with you. I've got your name and your licence number.'

'Okay, we'll be there. Now beat it. And if we find out that you've tried to put one over on us, we'll get back to you real fast.'

With winged heels we fly off into a leaden sky. We don't know where we're headed, our hearts are heavy, and our mouths taste of blood. At last, drunk with revulsion and hatred, we stumble into the livid light of a streetlamp.

'Where are we?'

'Boulevard Beaumarchais.'

'What do we do now?'

'We find Gerry. No point in kidding ourselves, they won't be at Baro's at two. You have a pencil? Write this down and don't lose it: 3547 VM 75.'

chapter six

Now to start prowling through the night and find my old man. But where do I start? Hey, Gerry! Give me a hint. I need you urgently. Only your hands can soothe the lumps we took tonight. Only your hands can avenge me. Be at Carlos's place. Don't let me down once again.

Gerard isn't at Le Baudet, but the man from Nice is there, as well as a few of the other boys. They're all busy rinsing their tonsils with champagne, in the company of disco girls, hatcheck girls, and young rock 'n' rollers in search of advancement. When we two zealous little working girls come barging into their dung pile with our smashed mouths and black eyes, there's no doubt as to who the real women are. We abruptly bring them face to face with their manly responsibilities. Carlos tears himself away from a nymphet, clearly wise beyond her years. The law of the jungle reasserts its rights.

'Madame Gerard, please be seated, you and your friend. Make yourself comfortable.'

The teenyboppers are sent to the bar for refreshment.

'Here, have a glass of champagne. What happened to you?'

Malou bursts out sobbing. I grit my teeth. I have my dignity to preserve.

'A real bummer—'

The men cock an attentive ear as I recount our misadventures. The grapevine immediately goes into action. After an hour of comings and goings, discussions, and telephone calls, the punitive expedition has been put on a war footing. But where can Gerry be hiding? I ask the man from Nice. He answers evasively.

'I know he had business tonight to attend to. Madame, you mustn't worry. *We're* here. And that's as good as having your husband with you.'

Gerard, you're my protector, but I guess you'll never be around to protect me. It's a sad joke.

At this point, in come two men I've never seen before. Malou murmurs, 'That's Raoul, an old business acquaintance of my husband's. The other one's his brother. You've heard about the B— brothers? They're the ones who found me the job in Grasse.'

'The real stuff! Dry your eyes! We've got to look like women.'

The B— brothers – two truckdrivers disguised as gentlemen – warmly embrace the man from Nice before wrapping their arms about us protectively. Now start moving, you guys – I know you hate to crawl out of bed in the morning, but if you want to show you've got a dingus between your legs, it's now or never!

Malou in turn gives her version of what happened. I remind her of certain details not meant to make life any easier for those Marseilles creeps, if ever the men manage to lay hands on them.

It's half past midnight. We're put into a taxi heading towards Place de l'Europe. I'm dreaming of journeys and of bloody vendettas. We're expected at Les Trois Canards – the very heart of the Paris underworld. Gerry drools whenever he talks about the place. Cheer up, Malou, we're off to meet the elite, the top bananas. If what people say is true, it's in this apparently undistinguished bistro that the Solomons of the mob have their headquarters. When there's trouble between men – an agreement broken, a business deal that falls through for no good reason, a guy to be snuffed, a hooker to be fined, a madam to be brought into line – the problem is handled at Les Trois Canards. Nothing escapes these justices of the peace. The group at Les Trois Canards is composed entirely of men from Marseilles and Corsica. Parisians are very rarely accepted. They're liked well enough, but they're not taken very seriously, and Gerry certainly won't be the one to add to their glory.

Lou, you're not saying anything. Aren't you proud to be a member of this clan of outlaws? Good Lord, you're still crying!

'What's he doing, Sophie? They've been looking for him everywhere. I can't see what it is he does for you except take your dough. Where is he?'

'Malou, cut it out. What are you all trying to do to me? Kill me maybe? Can't you see I'm whipped? I've had it up to here. Let's get out and walk ...'

Unlike Le Baudet, there's nothing about Les Trois Canards to suggest a place of entertainment. As soon as you open the door you become aware of the old-school atmosphere. With a few exceptions, there are no young dogs, just old foxes; no teenyboppers with shadowy eyes, only duchesses whose eyes have gone dead.

The duchesses: they're the legit wives, the former chicks

whom others have relieved of their duties after fifteen or twenty years of good and faithful service. The duchesses are the ladies who've made it in the life. Or have they? And for how long? Each one of them has at least five years of welfare work behind her. Five years of letters, parcels, money orders, and Sundays spent looking through bars (but from the right side). Five or more years of loneliness, anxiety, and broken hopes. The duchesses are pretty much worn out. They're ready for the dump. And yet if anything went wrong, who better than they could ensure the survival of their men? The men know it and so they've started pampering them and giving them a semblance of independence and a share of responsibility. Responsibility? It's been grinding them down ever since the day they agreed to have a drink and sleep over. It's a really curious paradox – as a reward for their unflagging zeal, the duchesses now have the right to watch a card game through their drooping lids; hear retold for the nth time deeds that are barely interesting enough to make their eyelashes flutter; yawn silently; and stroke a curly-haired poodle while regretting the kid they might have had. That's the duchesses for you. And here I am striding towards them, wiggling my hips, flaunting my youthful capital through my sweater, and bringing Malou along behind me as if to confirm my arrogance. Despite appearances, we're bursting with life. Even if we don't sport diamond-studded watches on our wrists, even if our fingers are bare, the two of us together aren't old enough to equal the mean age of these women; and that's terrific. I say to myself, Me, a duchess? Never. I'd rather shoot myself.

On the threshold, we stop dead in our tracks and gaze on this mummified scene. Are they really expecting us? I doubt it – although this may be a particularly undemonstrative bunch!

Malou nudges me.

'Sophie, I've lost an earring. I think it was when getting out of the taxi . . .'

Embarrassed, we turn our backs on the big shots and go back outside. We keep our noses to the ground. There's not a glimmer on the sidewalk, except for the glow from the neon sign of the Tilbury, a nightclub for youngsters, where a noisy gang is shoving its way in. Malou keeps complaining as she searches along the gutter. Abruptly she disappears. She squats down behind a car and starts rummaging in her handbag. I hear her repeat in a low voice, '3547 VM 75.' The digits on the licence plate whirl in front of my eyes like pinwheels.

'Either I'm cuckoo or we're in luck. It's got to be one or the other. Don't move. I'm going for reinforcements.'

I stride confidently up to the gaming table, where ten pairs of eyes zero in on me. At the same instant, Carlos comes through the door, with his lieutenants close behind him. The avengers gather around me. No long speech is needed to fill the picture. In two shakes of a donkey's tail they reappear, armed with crowbars.

Malou and I settle down with the duchesses. Enlivened by our tale, these oldtimers start feeling young again. They pop a cork in our honour.

'Your husband's out of town?' one duchess inquires.

'More or less. He had business to attend to this evening.'

But where *can* Gerry be hiding? What a situation ...

'What about yours – he's not here either?'

'He's in prison.'

'Poor dears. They really gave you the works. Don't worry. Something tells me those little creeps are going to get their ears boxed.'

Then – like us, these ladies have enjoyed an active youth – one of them starts recalling an item from the past.

'I didn't have any hoods to thank for the biggest shellacking in my life. It was the hookers on Rue Godot. I was fresh off the train from Marseilles ...'

Malou and I grate knees. We can't stand women from Marseilles. They're all loudmouthed liars who brawl over the least little thing. Wherever they are there's hell to pay. In other words – troublemakers.

'I'm talking about fifteen years ago.'

Like an ageing coquette, she pats the back of her head, adjusts her chignon, and runs her tongue over her lips. As Malou and I listen to her, we keep one ear cocked for sounds from outside.

'It was four in the morning, and I'd pulled in so much change you wouldn't believe it. I couldn't get my purse shut. The others had been hanging around with nothing to do. So you know what? Five of them ganged up on me in an archway and stole my wad. Three years later, my old man got out. They'd forgotten all about it. Not me. So one night he went after them,

211

my old man did, with a whip. You should have seen them shell out – and nobody ever came asking for their money back! For a week I had the whole street to myself.'

Some broad. Some guy. That's real inspiration. Have I mistaken my calling? Can I have made that big mistake? Oh, Gerry, poor you. Poor me. Poor both of us. I have a hard time ever imagining you cast in the role of avenger. I can't see you as a Horseman of the Apocalypse, whip in hand, making those hookers at the Madeleine dance to your tune. Tonight, though you don't know it, you had a chance to prove your manhood – and, once again, you just aren't around.

Outside, the cannons are already booming: the dream-busters' militia is on the march. There's a sound of yelling, of crowbars bouncing off car bodies, of bugles pealing ... And what are *you* doing? I dismiss out of hand the image of you drying glasses at Le Tartare in Montparnasse, while you make eyes at Dominique, your favourite barmaid. You've been courting her for six months now. Every cent I make has gone into tips – and you still can't get her to come out from behind that bar! There have been a hundred and eighty nights that I've put up with your absence, ever since that evening when I made my little ruckus after catching you, dish towel in hand ... A hundred and eighty nights of wondering – but *you* can't count. Everyone knows that. Watch out: you're putting a big dent in your credit rating.

My, don't men look wonderful with their shirts open down to the waist and their skin all sticky with the hot sweat of combat! The duchesses, however, are overcome with indifference as they dully watch them lay down their arms and smooth back their hair.

The men's cheeks are bulging with champagne. They don't deign to look in our direction, but they speak loud enough for us to relive their glorious deeds with them. The first remarks exchanged lead me to the bitter conclusion that our creeps have got off easy, aside from a few assiduous applications of crowbar to spine.

'Did you see the bastards? They were jumping between the cars like billy goats.'

'Jumping? They were flying! Regular eels.'

I have a vision of flying eels.

'There was no way to keep your hands on them. And when you hit one of them, he'd start multiplying!'

I have a vision of all those Chinamen in China.

'One of them really got it, in the head. He went down like a ton of bricks, hollering uncle. Two of his buddies arrived to pick him up, and I was about to lay into them when five more landed on my back.

I have a vision of Indians.

'Well, now that we've got the car, they've had it. When we resell it, there'll be enough to make it up to the boys who lent a hand.'

This irony is too much for me. I take a swallow to assuage my pain. A prey to the glooms once again, Malou is fiddling with one earlobe and crying into her glass.

'You heard what the pit boss at the nightclub said? They're regular customers there. Finding them will be no problem at all.'

'The kids know they're in big trouble. The first thing they'll do is contact Blind Danny, and he'll call up Le Baudet right away. You agree, Carlos?'

'Unless they want total war, it's the best thing they can do.'

I imagine African tribes with their tomtoms. I dream of our little creeps stewing in a pot, at the camp of Big Chief Carlos. I dream of Blind Danny, the head of a hostile tribe. I imagine the two chiefs surrounded by their warriors as they negotiate the fate of the creeps under the broad-leaved baobabs. Meanwhile my husband, that great hunter, is exploring remote trails in search of game. In the shelter of our hut, Malou and I are dealing them out. Malou would like that – then she'd have earrings even in her nose!

'Madame Gerard, we'll get you a taxi. Set your mind at rest, and go home. I'll be seeing your husband later tonight, so there's nothing to worry about.'

We say goodnight to the duchesses, who had relapsed into speechlessness; and with lowered eyes, we whisper our parting thanks to the Solomons.

Just as I'm going out, I bump into a man on the sidewalk. I recognize him at once. Those snakes eyes, those sucked-in lips, that shiny pate can mean only one man: Jean-Jean the Cobra, France's husband, as evasive as ever. Whether he likes it or not, I casually ask:

'What's France up to these days?'

He stammers and his pursed lips utter the magic words:

'She's working at Le Boogie-Woogie.'

We ride in silence all the way to Rue d'Aboukir. It's cold in Malou's place. We warm up in bed drinking scotch.

'Tell me about France. What's she like?'

'I've told you everything already. You'll be meeting her soon.'

'You think we'll get along?'

'I hope so! Now we've got to sleep. I'm bushed.'

The fact is that I don't much feel like talking. I'm dreaming of Le Boogie-Woogie, of being warm and safe from shellackings and other bum raps. I imagine myself with France. We're the two nightclub princesses. We're dressed all in black – two gay, frothy shadows who caress men with enticing hands and sprinkle them with smiles. We wreathe them in our perfume as we raise our glasses high in our exquisite hands and lap up the best champagne in Paris with seductive licks of our tongues. Our legs will be sheathed in silk, our loins will be swathed in dollar bills. We'll be idolized.

That's how I foresee my near future – provided France gets me into Le Boogie-Woogie.

A violent knocking on the door wakes us up. It's noon! And here's Gerry, with his hands scrunched down in his overcoat pockets, his cheeks looking like a scrub brush, his eyes shrunken, and his nose glowing like a warning light.

'Baby! My poor little baby! I've heard the whole story.'

Carried away by his enthusiasm, he gives me a kiss. His saloon breath leaves me quite faint.

'*You* certainly haven't been sleeping.'

'Malou, be an angel and make me some coffee. How can you expect me to sleep? I've been going out of my mind ever since I heard.'

'I didn't see you going out of your mind last night. We looked for you every place in Paris – except Le Tartare. I guess your friends have been told not to disturb you while you're hard at work.'

Malou, behind Gerard's back, is making frantic signs to me.

'Listen, I didn't come here to get hassled. I tell you, I didn't get a wink of sleep last night. I drove to Brussels and back, fog and rain the whole way, to bring in a guy who's hotter than shit.'

'So you're a driver these days?'

And what if, after all, he was telling the truth? He looks like the old stray-dog Gerry: pathetic. I rub the nape of his neck.

'Okay, I'll drop it. Stop making such a face. Give us some news instead.'

'You can really be a ball-breaker when you put your mind to it. I've been talking to Carlos. The little punks who roughed you up are French Algerians. They hang out at a nightclub called Le Sentier. When they surfaced and realized what assholes they'd been, they immediately got in touch with Blind Danny and Roger B—. Your husband knows him, Malou – he spent six months in the same cell with Bébert when he started doing his time at Fresnes. Anyway, we're meeting them in an hour at Danny's bar near Place de la République. If it was all really a mistake, those little faggots will be there.'

'A mistake! That's a laugh. They knew exactly what they were doing. They were out to have a little fun with us. They deserve to get wasted. Talk, all you do is talk!'

'Do you mind letting me finish? We'll go meet them, and then see. Mainly, we'll see what they own – aside from their crummy car. We've impounded that already. According to the first reports, they do a little pimping on the side. Their women work the Saint-Lazare area.'

'It's a lousy neighbourhood.'

'So what? What matters is that they've got whores. Whores mean change. In that case, we just fine them. There – got that all straight?'

'I don't give a damn about the bread. I want them to hurt.'

'Don't worry about that. They won't be dealing with Boy Scouts.'

Gerry's face lights up. I actually think he's proud of himself.

'Slip into your finery, ladies. We're all waiting for you.'

A quarter of an hour later, everyone's feeling cheerful. Gerry is humming as he pours himself a *pastis*. Malou is whistling like a myna bird, I'm daydreaming of Le Boogie-Woogie, blue-tinged nights, and rich Americans ...

By one o'clock, we're on our way to République. At one-

215

twenty we go into a dingy little bistro. There's a fifteen-franc special posted up on the wall. Guys in overalls are finishing their lunch. Stocky women in smocks are having coffee. Two Arabs are playing poker dice. A mongrel bitch lies sprawled under a table. A lush is sucking the last drops out of her wineglass while she pokes a comb into her hair. The jukebox is playing a tango, the telephone's tingalinging, and a man in his fifties with lacklustre eyes is answering and saying, 'Right . . . right . . . Quarter of an hour's fine. The coast will be clear.' He hangs up and emerges from behind the counter. He hurriedly tots up the workers' bill on a greasy corner of the paper tablecloth. The women from the packing shop scorch their tongues gulping down their coffee. The Arabs have their dice cup taken away from them. The bitch gets a kick in the belly, and the lush gets one in the ass – she lets out a shriek. The tango comes to an end.

A scraping of curtains. Darkness. Fluorescent lights. And now, under the bright lights, Malou, Gerry, and I are standing face to face with the dull-eyed man.

'*Pastis*. Port for the girls.'

No offence meant, but I'd prefer a cup of tea. Still, since you neglected to ask our opinion, let's simply rinse our teeth with some fine old tawny. Malou laughs and rubs a finger over her eyelids. The men will be showing up soon.

All of a sudden I feel quite magnificent. Get this: on my account, they're closing down a joint at high noon, Gerry is actually working up a sweat, and a bunch of creeps, little players from the boondocks, is going to get braced. It all makes me feel pretty kicky. I'm out for blood.

Through a hidden door, Carlos comes in, followed by his lieutenants, among them Jean-Jean the Cobra. Next come the B— brothers, followed in turn by the creeps and their lawyers. All are carefully shaved, including the creeps, who seem to be suffering from severe headaches. Gerard looks like a wild animal. Knowing him as I do, I'm sure that nothing about his appearance has been left to chance.

The creeps are asked what they want to drink. '*Pastis*,' they answer with downcast eyes. 'A bottle of Vichy will do,' snaps Gerry, thus opening the hostilities.

They're off. Everybody starts talking at once. The lengthy

argument is washed down with *pastis*. The result is that after a half-hour's discussion, everyone is in agreement, even the lawyers for the defence of these prolapsed assholes. I find it incredibly nervy of them to have ventured this far in a lost cause.

The sentence falls like a slap on the table:

'A trip to the cellar may freshen their memories.'

Bravo, Gerry. That's telling them. There's no getting away from it, these jokers have plenty of nerve. They've denied everything. They've never seen Malou or me before. Last night they were attacked for no apparent reason as they were coming out of a nightclub. They went to see old Danny to be on the safe side. They wanted to prevent a shoot-out from taking place for no reason they could understand. Tough babies, these kids, with lots of heart.

As for Malou and me, we're not allowed to speak. I'm beginning to wonder what we're doing here.

'Shall we all go down?'

The man from Nice leads the way, with the Cobra right behind him. There's some resistance on the part of the creeps, for whom I feel no sympathy as yet, although I'm sure it won't be long in coming. A nudge in the ribs with a gun persuades them to go on behaving sensibly.

'Easy now. One foot in front of the other. No funny stuff – get going, boys!'

'Against the wall, the three of you. Now, which one of you hit my wife?'

No answer.

'Which one of them hit you?'

'The tall, dark-haired one.'

'Over here, faggot. Move it.'

'Monsieur, it's not true. I didn't do anything, I swear.'

'Hold him for me.'

The butt first smashes the bent elbows, then the crumbling knees. Screams, cracking sounds. My creep goes down like a sack of potatoes.

'Which one of you hit the other lady?'

'They took turns.'

'Tie them up together. We'll make them do a little dance.'

Each of the B— brothers picks up a crowbar.

'Okay, chickens, dance!'

Trussed up like a bale of hay, the creeps stumble and fall under the blows.

'Stop, stop, we'll do whatever you want, but lay off. Okay, so we're sorry—'

'Not that, not my head, please, monsieur, please, they had to give me stitches last night at the hospital – no, no!'

'You'll be back there soon – if you get out of here alive.'

'Now, get up on your feet like men. Stand up. We're going to have a little chat.'

'Danny, would you bring us down three *pastis*? These boys must be getting pretty thirsty, after all this talking.'

Backed against the wall, the creeps can't believe their ears. This expansive gesture encourages them to start giving their account.

'We got the wrong women. It wasn't our fault.'

'That's right. It was lousy luck. They look like two girls who work the Champs-Elysées and squealed on a friend of ours.'

'It's true, monsieur. Word of honour.'

'Don't talk to me about honour, you bastard. Drink instead.'

The glasses splinter against the creeps' teeth. Blood spurts forth. Malou covers her eyes. Dazed, eyes bulging, they cower among the cobwebbed bottle racks. I start wishing I were somewhere else, far away from this cellar filled with the stench of death, in some sunny country where it's siesta time. But here I am with Malou, standing erect on my own two feet among these men.

There's a sadistic gleam in Gerry's eye as he wipes the blood off his nicked hand with a handkerchief. Off to one side, the man from Nice and the Cobra are discussing business matters. Blind Danny condemns the younger generation *in toto*.

'We ought to put skirts on them and send them out to work the Bois de Boulogne. That's all they're good for.'

'You just gave me an idea. Stop carrying on like frightened broads. We're going to let you go. First, we're going to relieve you of your loot. Since your paws are so sore, my wife and her friend will help you out.'

Gerry passes me his handkerchief.

'Put it all in that.'

In spite of my memories of the previous night, it's unpleasant going through their pockets in front of the others. Three watches, two gold chains, eight medals – including one of the Virgin Mary. A pathetic haul.

'Maybe the junkman will give us enough for this stuff to pay our cab fare home. Carlos – catch! Now, before you leave, you're going to do us a favour. One last favour. The three of you, strip. And fast.'

Gestures of dismay among the creeps. Malou looks over at me: her eyes are like the wild flowers of some enchanted land ... Malou, I don't know. I have no idea what Gerry has up his sleeve. But if we ever get out of here, I'll build you a house made of cockleshells on the shore of the Red Sea. I swear I will.

'Putting on a little show for us, Gerry?'

The Cobra and the man from Nice come nearer, rubbing their hands.

'So strip.'

'Your shorts!'

'A little assistance from the crowbar? ...'

'You, the big fellow who's so handy with a razor. On your knees. Suck off your kid brother. After he's shot his load, suck off your buddy. You get taken care of last.'

'Please, monsieur, I'll pay you anything. I'll find the bread – I'll let you have my wife. I just can't do it.'

'Listen, creep, we've got money to burn. Your broad has got to be a real bitch to hang out with a guy like you. We wouldn't want her even if she volunteered for Dakar.'

'You see, baby, what we're interested in is having you suck off your little brother and your pal. Didn't you get that? My fingers are itching. Suck. Suck, I said!'

'There! You see? It's not so hard. That's it up and down. Keep going, you'll get there.'

'And you, asshole, just see you get it up. Get it up, or get slammed. Just imagine you're being blown by a girl – you're planning to snitch her handbag later, after whomping her on the head a little.'

'Hey, you – the one who's putting in for skull surgery: jerk off.'

'Look at them – aren't they real sweet? Reminds me of my days in the Scouts. Isn't it great being young?'

'That's enough. Now move over to your buddy – his cock's as hard as a rock. When I think we had to help you discover your true natures! Just think, if you'd been doing this last night, maybe you wouldn't have beat up on these two women here.'

'Jesus Christ, will you get with it, you son of a bitch? Go on, faster, come on, gag on it! Oh, wow! Swallow it, Idris, take it all …'

'Isn't that beautiful? Like little bees sucking honey out of flowers.'

My creep collapses sobbing at his brother's feet.

'Gerard, I'd like to go home.'

'Beat it, both of you. We men want to be alone.'

We slide along over the icy sidewalk. In less than two hours it will be nighttime and it will all have to be done again. I'll have to redo my hair, concoct a smile, and mislead Malou into thinking that things will turn out okay, that we're really lucky. We'll have to drink in order to confront the johns and all their subterfuges, drink so as to forget the cellar and the bloody-mouthed creeps trapped among the cobwebs, drink until we feel so disgusted that we fall into bed alongside one another.

'What'll we do, Sophie?'

'I'm going out to see my mother. It's been a long time since I took her to a restaurant. Don't wait up for me. I'll sleep at her place.'

The cockleshell house is engulfed by the surf. This time it's final, and Malou isn't going to change her mind: next week, she's returning to La Bohème.

'So that's definite? You're going back?'

'Yes. I'm sick of cruising the streets. I'm sick of getting beat up on. Anyway, all you care about is working at Le Boogie-Woogie with your friend France.'

'This is no time for scenes. You might as well know that if I've got a choice I'd rather stay with you. Give me forty-eight hours. You stay home and rest up. I swear I'll cop a spot for us. After that, you can do what you like.'

'It's the last time, Sophie. It's really the last time.'

A week passes. Malou is kicking over on one cylinder. She doesn't get out of bed any more and survives on toast and coffee. When I come home around midnight, after dragging around and making a couple of scores on the sly, she never asks questions. She's just waiting for me to be next to her before she goes to sleep. I start writing letters to Bébert again; she recopies them indifferently. You'd think that life was slowly draining out of her body, and that that was all she looked forward to. She cries, saying over and over that it's pointless for me to keep on looking after her, that the world is beyond her comprehension. I suggest she see a doctor. She refuses. I shout, 'You have no right to destroy yourself. Life isn't fun for anybody. You ought to face it instead of finding ways of avoiding it. If you go on like this, I'm going to end up thinking you're nothing but a filthy coward!'

Oh, Lou, I'm sorry. That isn't what I meant to say. Please, please don't look at me like that. Lay your head back on the pillow, and I'll fix you a scotch. Don't point to the door, Malou. I'm so beat myself. Are you really throwing me out? ...

chapter seven

On Rue Auguste-Chabrière, I'm held prisoner by a big alarm clock. It keeps painful track of the time; its second hand scratches my eye every time I open it. The telephone rings, but it's never Malou's voice on the other end.

Christmas is approaching. Gerard says I'm looking poorly, and he's offering me a month in the mountains to get my health back. A month at Chambéry. At Chambéry, there's a whorehouse hidden away between the fir trees and the avalanches where foreign workers come to spend their pay and their surplus affection. It was from Chambéry that Muriel used to come back to the Saint-Louis a total wreck – and she was a sturdy, hardworking girl. I'd like to put up a fight; but all my limbs ache, and my head is full of fog, as though I were coming down with a bad case of flu. Gerry turns out to be a good nurse. (It *was* his first trade.) You should see him putting poultices on me – and hear how well he can rub liniment into my sore spots.

'Now that little bitch Dominique is all set, I'm going to need your help. I know we're going to make a fantastic team. The only thing is, don't screw things up if some nights I don't come home. I've got to keep after her and see that she gets settled in her pad. She's a poor kid who's always lived in hotels. A little place of her own ought to give her a shot in the arm, right?

221

Anyway, I know you're big enough to take it. To get her started, I found her a spot at Les Bermudes, on Avenue de Friedland. Anybody who walks in the door there drops three hundred, at least. She needs special attention – after all, you catch more flies with honey than you do with vinegar. As for you, if you really give it all you've got, in a year's time I'll retire you. I'm counting on you. We don't want this little girl slipping away from us. Do you see now why it's better if you go away for a month? And in any case, you know that even if you are a pain in the ass, you're the one who turns me on.'

Oh, Gerry, do I ever see! Your business acumen is developing. You're broadening your scope! Odette, Dominique, and me. Watch it, buddy – you're tripling your risks. That means three meters to read now. You're really going places ... and I'm down in the dumps. I'm losing my aggressiveness. Still, how I'd love to get away from you and wander down memory lane. If I could avoid ever meeting you, I'd gladly go back to when I stood naked and terrified in my bobby socks, with my history book under one arm and incest staring me in the face. No, it doesn't make me suffer. No, I'm not jealous. And I won't leave you for Rue d'Aboukir, any more than I'll go to Le Boogie-Woogie and beg France for help. I'm too ugly, too empty, and too sick. You see, I'm contagious: I have no right to infect the people I love. But what about the others? You know, the ones I don't especially love – why not let them benefit from my leprosy, while I wait for passing time to swallow me up?

At the crossroads of two melancholies, a man brings his car to a stop. Take me away, Mr Angst! Never mind about the price. Let's hear that old sweet song. My breasts are soft pink blotters waiting to sop up your life story. Speak to me. But don't tell me your name, and don't ask me mine, because tonight I've mislaid my identity. Keep your hat on, and your glasses, too. Don't worry about it, just take me, take me and rape me, the way you're supposed to with a woman of the streets. Aha! So you don't want to talk to me? Are you afraid of seeing me smile? No, no, I won't make fun of you. Tell me all.

'I was in love with a girl in Italy during the war. Her parents wanted to keep us apart, but we used to meet secretly in an old abandoned farmhouse on the outskirts of Florence. While we were making love one morning, there was a bombing raid. She was killed. Her head was crushed beneath the rubble. Since then, you see, I haven't been able to make love indoors. I don't give a damn about the price, what I care about is fucking you on a demolition site.'

'You mean ruins?'

'They made her look even more beautiful.'

All right, Mr Angst, drive on. It'll cost you five hundred.

'Hold on – she used to smoke when she made love. I'll stop for some cigarettes.'

All this for a few berries. Mr Angst unleashes his horse-power down Uncertainty Avenue, then whips into Nowhere Lane.

'You're out of your skull driving so fast. Stop or I'll jump out the door!'

'I'll double the price – I'll double it! You look too much like her, I won't let you go. I'm taking you to Florence.'

A throughway in the rain looks like every other throughway. Low pink-tiled houses, umbrella pines, trattorias flashing by at seventy ... A light in the distance. Wonder of wonders, we're being stopped by motorcycle cops. There'll be no oleander or bougainvillea on my tomb, just ordinary cornflowers. I won't see Italy and die.

Mr Angst smilingly hands over his licence and registration. Well, Sophie? Don't lose your nerve. Tell them you're a hooker. Tell them what's happening. You rummage in your handbag, hoping they'll ask you for your identification as well. That might give you enough courage to start up a conversation; or, at least, maybe they'll remember your name, identify the corpse and the murderer, and avenge you. Because this guy is out to strangle you. Take a good look at him – he's really going to strangle you. Can't you see that he has the same sick look on his face as the German who did in the three girls in Pigalle two years ago? Think back to the face – the newspaper clipping tacked up in number 19 at the Saint-Louis. Think back to the terror you and the others felt. You even began turning down every Kraut that came along: you didn't want to end up like those girls you know on Rue André-Antoine. Ginoux – remember Ginoux? And in any case, from the very beginning you've been obsessed by two dangers: syphilis and being strangled. No sooner does a john run a finger across your throat than sweet, adaptable you become hysterical, and you're ready to shove him out of the room. You're afraid of death by strangulation. You dream about it, and you wake up in the middle of the night drenched with sweat.

So tell them what's happening. Just say: 'I picked up this man, I'm a panic-sticken prostitute, and I'm afraid he's going to kill me.' Speak up, or else you'll die at the cold hands of a maniac. At best they'll give you two lines in the evening paper. Speak up. Time's running out – Angst is already putting away his licence. The troopers are saying goodbye with a smile. (Always that smile!) Too bad. I'll have to take a flying leap at the first curve. Except there is no curve on this flat, straight road. In the distance appears a dark, threatening, mountain-like mass ... There's a forest lane, on to which Angst un-hesitatingly turns. Swing to the right, swing to the left, first gear, reverse. The night is all around me.

I take off with my head down and then run into something. The man nails me by the shoulders. The jig's up.

'Where are you running to? Come sit next to me inside the car.'

Don't struggle. Think ahead. Think. Not to die.

'You're shaking. Are you frightened?'

Think fast, Sophie. And if you want to see your family again, make it good. You've got a sadist on your hands; the more frightened you act, the itchier his fingers are going to be. Stay cool, baby! It's your only hope.

'I'm cold. This is no weather for walking in the woods.'

'Sit behind the wheel. Get undressed inside your overcoat. I'll turn on the heater for you. There. Now don't budge. There's something I have to get out of the trunk.'

A monkey wrench? A length of thick rope? A kitchen knife? Papa, Mama, little baby brothers, Malou – is this it? Will I never see you again? There were so many things left to do and see and understand. I needed so much time to learn more about myself and get better. How can I really be about to die at twenty-three? I've always dreamed of living to be ninety-five, with a cigar and a piece of toast and honey between my teeth, in a sprawling, draughty house, with a nest of blue chickadees in my bun, a brood of cats hanging from my shoulders, a red-headed bastard child at my feet, and all the brats in the neighbourhood ransacking my closets. What a bust my life has been.

'I found just the right thing. You'll read to me out loud. I'll hold the flashlight for you. Wait, let me find the right page and undo my clothes a little. There – that's where you start.'

My fingers are trembling as I turn the filth-spotted, blood-spattered pages and bleat out uncomprehendingly a tale of appalling cruelty.

'Your voice isn't steady.'

'I'm cold. Wouldn't you like me to touch you a little? Reading turns me on.'

'If you're turned on, you're going to get your jollies. When I stopped to buy cigarettes a while back, I also called up some friends. We come to this place all the time, so they know the way. They'll be here in ten minutes at most. Three buck niggers. They're going to fuck you up the ass.'

Three niggers! Shells, flames, sirens, bombs, Italy! Come, keep coming. That's it, big boy, give me all you've got; Now, Sophie, put his temporary lassitude to good use, and get the fuck out of here. Run. Run fast. By the time he recovers, you'll be far away. Make space between you and him. Forget about your clothes, and stop thinking about your purse. Just move those feet. The highway can't be far off. Lengthen your stride. Sing 'This little pig went to market, this little pig had none, this little pig ran all the way all the way all the way home ...' So long, Mr Angst. I'm hitting my stride, I'm digging my elbows into my ribs and keeping two steps ahead of life. With my belly bared to the moonlit breezes, I start waving both arms from side to side. Oh, sweet Lord, thank you. Thank you for coming along the highway at this very moment. And as for you, driver, forgive me for not saying thank you. You see, I have a communion wafer stuck in my throat, and it hurts. It's putting a cramp in my jaws. I can't speak.

When on one and the same night you've had both the Devil and the Good Lord for company, you need to get a firm grip on reality if you don't want to go under. My libido has its feet on the ground and it's tugging me by the sleeve – all the way to a beauty parlour on Rue Saint-Honoré. There for a few hours, I sip tea-and-lemon and play the elegant lady. With my neck bent under the shampoo spray, I catch fragments of a conversation between two housewives. As she massages my scalp, Vassilia unveils the mysteries of the *beau monde* to me.

'See that blonde broad next door? She's a high-class doxy. She works for one of our customers, who has a superposh town house in the Sixteenth – it's like Madame Claude's operation. She also has a little château a hundred miles outside of Paris where she throws weekend house parties to which invitations cost two hundred bills. It's exactly the thing for you. You shouldn't spread yourself around, honey. You're made for high society.'

Keep right on talking, dear, dear friend; and, between your next two shampoos, whisper the number of this sporting house to me. Tell me about this woman. A lot I care if she's a lesbian – I can manage. She'll get discouraged after a while. Naturally, I won't bring up the subject of pimps (such a nasty word anyway), and I wouldn't dream of letting her know that I was in transit between the sidewalk and a house in Chambéry.

I know I don't exactly conform to the requirements. My thighs are on the plump side, and I'm eight inches away from that magical five feet nine. I wish I had your optimism, Vassilia. You really think they'll let me in among those goddesses? Aren't you afraid they'll slam the gilded door on Rue Paul-Valéry right in my face? Maybe I should listen to you – after all, Madame Billy is just another madam, even if she does have a triple-A rating. Thanks, dear, dear friend. The climate in Chambéry may be healthier, but as long as I can choose, I'll take the Sixteenth Arrondissement.

What a shame it isn't spring! If only I could slip into my beige silk dress, I might captivate Madame Billy. In this beaver-skin coat I look like a vegetable dealer. Of course, there *are* those hot furs in the basement, but Gerard was very firm on the subject.

'Don't fiddle around with them, they'll blow up in your face. There's blood on them – I was there!'

Gerry spends too much time at the movies, and it goes to his head; and anyway he always ends up contradicting himself. Between scotches he confided to me that some guys had left the goods with him until they'd cooled off enough to be flogged.

Cooled off, cooled off – it all depends on how you look at it.

It's cold enough outside. Anyway, what cop, no matter how conscientious, is going to stop me on the street and ask me to show him the receipt? Sorry, gentlemen of the second story, but I must look my gorgeous best. You wouldn't want anybody to take me – me, Sophie, Mustang Gerry's wife – for some common hooker.

On Rue Paul-Valéry, the gilded door to depravity is opened by a dyky-looking woman who is gracelessly pushing forty. Carpeting, wall hangings, rugs, shuttered windows, and dark nooks and crannies muffle my footsteps and mask the tumult in my heart. I stifle my sighs and follow the ageing tomboy as we walk around to the far side of the castle keep.

We find fat Madame Billy slumped on one end of a sofa, just as I had imagined her: blonde, predictably bloated, well into her fifties, with dangerous-looking nails, a sharp eye, and a bitter mouth. The tomboy leaves me standing in front of my inquisitor and cuddles up against her mistress. Her respectable claws pluck at the mesh of her stockings, then grasp her ankle, and slide up as far as the adductor muscle of her thigh, which they stroke as she purrs away. She flashes every facet of her wide, Persian-cat eyes as her lascivious mistress caresses her throat and jangles the bells that hang from her neck. I wonder when this feline teasing will come to an end.

Blessed Virgin, forgive me. I have sinned by omission. I don't know the first thing about women; the only thing I understand is the blunt cock of the male. So now I'm scared. Are they going to do me violence among the cushions? Or spread me open on the Persian rugs? I can already feel their tongues thrusting between my lips, their teeth tearing at my earlobes, their knees cracking my ribs, their thighs crushing my spine. Help! There's been a mistake! I just came here to get a job, that's all.

Sophie, foolish Sophie, stop making problems for yourself. Those two don't really scare you, and if one of them was reckless enough to touch you, you'd explode in their mitts like a pinless grenade. You'd bust out of there leaving behind you nothing but shattered glass and a loud laugh dampened by a few tears. Go on, relax those clenched hands of yours – run them caressingly over your furs. And now, keep your ears open. They're accusing you of being too short. If it comes to that, lady, I can only use what I've got. First of all, there's nothing I can do about it. Mama Dédée brought me into the world like this, and, on the whole, I haven't managed too badly. Second, I loathe high heels. So make with the verdict. This pelt on my back is getting heavier by the minute.

'Show me your hands.'

I hold out my pretty hands. My nails are translucent, carefully shaped, freshly manicured.

'That's a very lovely coat you're wearing.'

Withdrawing my fingers, I smile. I was sure of it. It worked. It's the kind of ruse that never fails to impress bitches of her stamp. You know, madame, it didn't cost me very much. I could pass on a dozen to you from the very same place, and at a ridiculously low price.

'What are your breasts like?'

Now that, fatso, is something right down my alley. I've got a pair of pink marble boobs that are enough to tempt Maillol from the grave.

The tomboy is getting more and more kittenish.

'Come on, let's see them.'

Let's go, Sophie – make a gallant gesture, and strip. At least you'll have the satisfaction of making them dream. I lower my dress to the waist. My tits burst out of my bra like fireworks at high noon. That really takes your breath away. Never saw any like them before. Forgive me if I have to start weaning you, but I'm going to wrap them up again. Knockers framed by Somalian leopard skin aren't exactly to be found on every street corner. Anyway, they're part of my inheritance, and I wouldn't want them catching a chill.

And now listen, there's been enough fooling around. If I'm not the right girl for the job, just say so. No, madame, I'm terribly sorry, I don't have a little apartment with a phone. And I don't have any nude photos. But how generous of you to point out that some of your customers like short women. I was almost beginning to feel like a cripple. Do I move in or not? We're not playing games.

'What do you think, Vera? Shall we let her stay in the kitchen for a few days while she finds her little apartment? Be here tomorrow at two. I like you.'

I can't say as much. I don't like your type, or your mealy-mouthed ways, or that moist hand of yours – it oozes hypocrisy. And then you have such impractical ideas! Where's the money

supposed to come from for my 'little apartment'? I happen to
have a husband, madame, a husband who's counting on me,
since he's incapable of lifting a finger and he has three women
on his hands. Two apartments in just one week is a lot for one
man to handle. I could borrow from Malou, but she and I
aren't on the best of terms at the moment. And as for making
it up to her by bringing her into your place – not with those
wet-nurse udders of hers. No way! It's a black, black day: I
have the feeling that here, among the rare woods of your consoles and panelling, I'm going to prostitute myself more than
I ever did before.

Night falls as I'm on my way to Malou's. What have you
been doing, Lou, during these days of silence? Speaking for
myself, I cried, I laughed, I drank a lot, and I hardly slept at
all. In spite of your promises, one day you'll just disappear,
take off on some nobody's arm without leaving a forwarding
address. I'll be jealous of him and of his slack moist lips and his
reddened hands. He'll be the one to make you laugh, not me.
Don't ditch Bébert, Lou – and stick with me.

Tonight, to win your heart back, I'm offering you guitars and
sangría. Pin a rose in your hair, Malou. It's been such a long
time since we went to La Venta. And tonight I need courage
and sugared wine to break the news to you. That's the way it is,
Malou. A cloud is passing over our sun ... Let's drink every
last trace of thirst away. Let's drink till we drop. Let's drink to
the memory of the man who hanged himself yesterday in
Bébert's cell block. Let's drink to his mother's grief. Let's drink
the health of all the world's unlucky ones!

Off we go for the big thrill. Tonight, the Milky Way's the
limit. Raise your arm high, Malou, stretch out your hand, that's
it. Now clink the glass against your star and drink to mine, to
my lucky star, and all the other shooting stars that flash
through the streets before they lose their lustre in long, sleepless nights. Hang on to me, squeeze my hand, and behold the
fiery star that's tumbling among its shrouds as it settles de-
murely on to the couch of night.

Come on, Malou. Let's bear our burden lightheartedly. Happiness is hiding around the corner of some street – Unreality
Street. Let's go looking for it ... High above us, in the swirl of
the Paris sky, the stars are beckoning to me.

Goodbye, Lou. I have to look fresh tomorrow. The outing on

Vega was great, but now the sidewalk is sticking to the soles of my feet.

Tomorrow? How can you think about tomorrow when you've left your friend standing in front of her house, staring at her shoes? How can you think about today when greyness is clinging to the window panes like wet paint?

At two o'clock a phantom leads me into the large, dreary kitchen on Rue Paul-Valéry. A pretty, statuesque girl puts down her embroidery, and the point of her needle pricks me in the eye. I'm gasping for breath. I feel like shouting. I want to run away from these walls that are sweating with damp. I bite my lips so as not to start crying. Sophie, what are you doing here? What are you doing in this lair of hypocrisy? You – the girl who lit up the nights at the Saint-Louis, La Bohème, and La Hacienda. You used to leave men waiting for you at the bar – you'd whisper in their ears as you brushed past, 'Don't go away, darling, I won't be long.' They'd fondly watch you go upstairs with someone else as they faithfully bided their time. And now, how many hours are you going to have to stay here face to face with this sophisticated mummy? Where are all my men – the men from the other days, my private johns, and all the others? Come and rescue me! They're keeping me prisoner.

That's it! Here I am cooped up, hobbled by my body, standing across from this other, silently busy woman. Amidst what rumpled sheets did she forget her smile? Speak, mummy, speak. Stop playing high and mighty. We've both been caught in the same net.

The voice drones on like a worn record. It scratches against my eardrums. What is it she's saying? Am I hearing right or am I dreaming? It seems that the men here aren't treated like customers at all, but like friends. Here, no one questions the madam's right to pocket a hundred and ninety out of three hundred francs. Irony of ironies, everybody finds her pleasant and sings her praises. What ever happened to the solidarity of the old days? Whatever their gripes against one another may have been, the girls always banded together when it came to standing up to the women who exploited them. It's a bad house. A very bad house. If I ever told this girl that I had a pimp and that I was on good terms with the best of the life, she'd dash right out to the nearest police station.

230

What kind of world is this I've stumbled into? This lack of forthrightness gives me the willies. What sort of man is going to waste his strength tucking into a mummy like her? No doubt she's another smart-ass. Don't try and pull the wool over my eyes – I've been on my own two feet since I was ten months old. I gave up sweet talk with my diapers. Take off your mask, Cheops, I've seen through you: you're harnessed to a slippery handed purse-snatcher yourself. You may pretend to be above it all, but you're only a hooker. Don't forget, sweetie pie, that when you put down your embroidery it's to get fucked, just like me. And if the word 'customer' makes you gag, you ought to have the guts to change lanes and go sweat with the rest of them. You see, my name's Sophie, little Sophie, the girl who makes men feel good and makes no bones about saying so. Unfortunately, as long as there are twists like you around, there'll be turds who'll go on stuffing their faces at our expense. Now just pipe down, Miss Cheops, because as far as I'm concerned, you're just a piece of ass.

It's two minutes to four by the electric clock. One minute to. Four o'clock on the nose. The mummy goes on with her silent embroidery. I twiddle my thumbs and dream of ideal love. The phantom puts her head through the door, and Cheops comes to life. Unravelled, she reaches an acceptable five feet eight. Her pins are as dismal as a day without food or sunshine. Well, enjoy yourself, Monsieur X. After all, with that mealymouthed face of hers, she may know techniques I wouldn't dare to use. My mother always told me, 'Still water runs deep.'

A drink – that's what I need. My throat is dry. I feverishly make my way to the watering trough. The vodka burns my throat. Another slug, and then it's back to the servants' quarters, where I resume my thumb-twiddling. There's a place where the oilcloth is fraying. I pull out a thread, then another – and another, and another! I tie them together; and lo and behold, I'm back in my childhood: cat's cradle and all its variations ...

The phantom barges in unexpectedly. I hide my hands between my legs. She curtly orders me to follow her. I close my eyes for a moment and try to imagine my customer.

There's a man waddling up and down the downstairs hall and he has a greedy look in his eye. The stairway leading up to the bedrooms reminds me of a conveyer belt. My feet slide smoothly over the carpeting. I force myself to keep my hand off the banister. I let my arms hang loose and think about nothing at all.

The plush, still bedroom gives off a scent of violets. Perched in their frames, rakish lords and ladies are winking at me. The plaster cupids on the ceiling have given up beating their wings. At the head of the bed, there's a bell embedded in the wall velvet. Strange ... Does an occasional wild man show up in this select place? There's an abrupt silence. Am I the only victim? What ever became of the cardboard partitions at the Macao, and the girls' giggling, and the hybrid copulations that we'd laughingly dissect over a game of craps? Gone, all gone.

My partner isn't in the prime of youth. He's pushing sixty – well, let's be nice and say he was born in 1912. He won't do much damage.

'Mademoiselle Sophie: Etienne is an old man, and happy to be one. The time has come when he's able to enjoy all the pleasures that you and your little friends can provide. I have a comfortable pension, and I put it to good use. And you, pretty girl – what sort of work do you do?'

Shit. I'd forgotten to be prepared for this possibility.

'I do display windows – I do a lot of displaying!'

'Oh, what a naughty girl!'

My sixty-year-old waddles up and down, scratching his chin. His little eyes glitter with mischievousness as he lifts up my skirt with the tip of his cane. The basic rule here is never to rush the customer – if you do, you're fired. I'm not going to rush you, Etienne. I find you touching, and you make me laugh.

'Well, Mademoiselle Sophie, let's take our clothes off. But not too quickly. At my age, one needs to work up to things. One needs to warm up. I wouldn't want you to feel offended. Such a pretty little thing! Oh, Sophie, what do I see here? How naughty of you!'

'That's Sylvester, Etienne. I never go shopping without him.'

'Is one allowed to pet him?'

'Watch out, he's a real wildcat – and he only likes men without their clothes on.'

'Then I'll undress. I wouldn't want to vex such a pretty pussycat.'

Etienne certainly belongs to the World War I generation. Nothing's missing: stickpin, tiny-buttoned waistcoat, fob watch, suspenders, right down to long johns and garters. He smiles and stamps his feet when he gets them tangled up in the legs of his drawers. He keeps smiling as I discover with revulsion the reptilian skin – a kind of covering of dry scales – that stretches from his ankles to his belly. I feel like asking him about it. He anticipates my question.

'Don't worry, my dear, it's not a disease. You don't have to touch it if the notion displeases you.'

I find such thoughtfulness moving. I wish he'd explain and tell me about his condition. But faced with his anguished look, I capitulate – not very deftly, I must admit.

'You know, I don't find it in the least repulsive.'

My reply apparently satisfies Etienne. I try to convince myself by sliding my fingers over his rough thigh.

'Lie down in the middle of the bed. That's right. Now spread your lovely thighs a little wider. Stroke your honeypot, and tell Etienne about the first time you ever saw a cock.'

The first sexual organ I remember seeing as a child belonged to my dog Mirette, and I've never seen a sweeter one since. She was in heat and I used a toothbrush to try and lance the abcess ... Then I ended up under the footbridge with a young hood whose hands had grown soft from thieving. I was wearing my mother's black lace panties. With one hand he pulled this undergarment to one side (it was much too big for me) and with the other opened his fly. He took me standing up, next to the railroad tracks, without a sob or a sigh. After that I did it with a madman, and cracked open his head to look inside and see why he'd hurt me so.

As I invent a second defloration for Etienne, my mouth starts getting dry. To keep me going, he offers me a glass of bubbly. Here's to you, Etienne! Let's drink to the days when I was doing backbends on the embankment. The champagne sets me off again, and we finish our session with a story about a little girl who is half raped by a game warden.

'Mademoiselle Sophie! Everything you've just told me is so very improper ...'

Now, sitting on the edge of the bed, I empty my glass as I watch Etienne slip back into character as a respectable pensioner. He carefully fastens his suspenders with safety pins,

233

pulls up his garters, and conceals his handicap under his white long johns. I say a kind word to him, but he scarcely even hears it. For him, the game's over. It came to an end at the moment of ejaculation. Since he's polite, he gives me a pinched little farewell smile and then rings the bell by the head of the bed.

'What are you ringing for?'

'To find out if the coast is clear, naturally. It's always disagreeable running into someone in this sort of establishment.'

It's an electric world! The bells here are for the customers, not the girls.

There are three discreet knocks on the door. The phantom appears on the threshold and asks Old Snakeskin to accompany her. In the meantime I return to the kitchen. The mummy is still busy with her embroidery. I twiddle my thumbs some more until Vera abruptly bursts into the room:

'Time's up. You can go now.'

So at eight o'clock I find myself free as a bird on the sidewalk of Rue Paul-Valéry. I've been wondering why the hell they didn't give me my hundred and ten francs – and why I didn't have the nerve to ask for them, after an hour and a half with Old Snakeskin. Sophie, the reason isn't hard to find: they just want to be sure you'll be back tomorrow at two. Get it, baby? You were always quick to knock the Sandrines and the Fabiennes, but admit now that they're worth a hundred of the highfalutin bitches you're stuck with at Billy's. Well, if you need to plunge back into your own world and get a healthy reminder of what true character's like, why not have dinner at Le Baudet?

Is it indifference? Fatigue? Helplessness in the face of what's unfamiliar? It's been two weeks now that I've been letting the days drift by, hidden away in a corner of Madame Billy's kitchen. The first mummy's been replaced by a second one, a blonde giraffe weighted down with gold trinkets and serious problems. It would have been wrong to take this woman for a whore: she was in the house not to supplement her household allowance but to get her kicks. While her two little angels are scratching their heads over grammar and the rule of three at their boarding school in Neuilly, Mummy is having her cookies popped from behind. The front is reserved for Daddy. He's also enjoying himself, crisscrossing France in his Citroën with the adjustable seats, having a ball in Lyons or Lille or Grenoble, and not feeling an inkling of remorse. Supposedly he doesn't know a thing about his better half's favourite pastime. Talk like this tears me apart inside, and I feel truly sorry for Miss Nympho, with her tics and her latent anxiety. She keeps glancing at the door and biting her fingernails. At the slightest sound she repowders her nose, feels her breasts, checks to see if her chains and bracelets are all there, and slips one hand inside her panties.

It's a really strange place. Everything is done on the sly, with the greatest possible hypocrisy. Everyone has stashed her foibles, hopes, and fears someplace else. Everything hinges on frivolity. People act happy because they wear classy duds, have their hair done by whoozits, sport a bag and boots with a big name on them, and have accessories bursting with alligator hide. They act happy because they get fucked in violet-scented sheets, and because the customers – those sons of bitches who are allowed to have certain of their needs gratified on the strength of their well-filled billfolds and distinguished autographs – behave as though they were wenching with honest janes. But here no less than elsewhere they're just poor hookers, always ready to run and hide their beautiful faces behind the hangings in the downstairs hall.

One small consolation: Etienne has come back. And to celebrate his return, I invent a sixth defloration. Vera pays me every evening now. Unfortunately, my bank account has hardly got bigger; but for the time being Gerard is good-humoured about it, thanks to the income brought in by Dominique. She seems to have got off to a roaring start, and he's going to have a profitable year. Odette is about to be sold: the Corsican purchaser is waiting for his wife to come back from a house in Fedala before clinching the deal. Still, Gerry hasn't forgotten his promise concerning Le Boogie-Woogie.

Something about Gerry has changed. He doesn't look at me the way he used to. Even when he's drunk, he no longer has those moments of effusiveness I found so touching. Apparently Dominique has him thoroughly wrapped around her little finger. He's just ordered four new suits from his tailor; he talks of shaving off his moustache; and he's letting his hair grow. He's also leaving me alone for the holiday season, which he plans to spend with her in Megève. I suspect that they're in love and that on certain chilly afternoons they even go at it in my very own bed.

But I'm still the one who has to take care of our husband's laundry, mail, and bills. I'm the one who pays the cleaning woman and smooths down the bed. We must really seem like a curious couple to people who go to work every morning. Go make yourself a new life with her, Gerry. Let me get out while the getting's good. *La dolce vita* for her, independence for me. For starters I'll check on that little apartment on Rue Balzac tonight, and then I'll celebrate with Malou at La Venta. Afterwards, when she goes back to La Bohème, I'll slip over to Boulevard des Capucines and put in a little overtime.

chapter eight

What will my life be like next spring? I really wonder. It's three-thirty by Madame Billy's kitchen clock, and my purse is starting to squawk. Just then Vera beckons to me. I tiptoe after her. Her tall, mannish figure and Garbo shoulders hide me completely from view. Oh, if only this one was fun for a change!

'Monsieur Steve, this is Sophie. She's the miniature of our collection.'

I smile as I curtsy to his six foot three, which bends and kisses my hand. I like you, Steve. You're someone I feel like laughing and playing with.

'Okay, Vera, show us up to this dream room, and get the bottle open.'

'Easy! You're supposed to speak softly here.'

'But we aren't in church, shayree, we're in Paris!'

'Hush. Didn't you know that Paris *is* a church – a huge church full of lost souls? Madame Billy is the Good Lord, and Vera is the Holy Ghost. Don't laugh. It's perfectly true.'

'Then let's drink to Hell, shayree.'

An old man is coming down the stairs, bent over his cane. Steve asks him to join us for champagne. Vera looks unhappy. Dowager Billy herself emerges from behind a curtain, straightening her white collar.

'Please come with me,' she says in her driest tones.

The door slams.

236

'I'm afraid you shocked them. But it doesn't matter.'

'Nothing matters. Take this. Make me happy for a few hours. Last week my wife killed herself and our two children in our house on Staten Island. She was even smaller than you are.'

I study the green bill that Steve has placed on the table. I've never seen one like it. I do some rapid calculations in my head as I raise my eyes from it. No mistake about it, a real thousand-dollar bill. The equivalent of five thousand francs.

'Shayree, let's drink to the health of the Church.'

'To the Pope.'

'To our Good Lord Billy.'

'To the angel Gabriel.'

'To Vera, the Holy Ghost.'

'To Judas.'

'To the miracle of the fishes.'

'To the multiplication of the loaves.'

'To Mary Magdalene!'

' "Lord, forgive them, for they know not what they do." '

' "Forgive us our trespasses, as we forgive those who trespass against us." A-men.'

'Sophie, I can't get it up.'

'It doesn't matter. Aren't you cold? Don't you want to come in under the covers?'

'I want more champagne!'

I ring. Vera herself brings in the bottle. Her smile becomes more pronounced as she opens it. What a fathead I am – I forgot to slip the green bill out of sight. The tomboy's gaze settles on my breasts, lingers a moment on my thighs, and goes back to the bill.

'She's charming, isn't she? Sophie, you should come and spend a weekend in the country. I'm sure Madame Billy would appreciate your company.'

'No. *I'm* keeping her. She's mine. Out!'

After struggling until seven in the evening with a dead woman and two rosy-cheeked ghosts, I finally collapse.

'I've got to get out of here. I can't take it any more. I need air!'

'This evening you stay with me. We'll have dinner together. Afterwards I'll show you some Disney movies. I bet you'll like that.'

237

It's true, Stevie: I do love cartoons. But you and your three stiffs are weighing me down. You make me feel like snuffing it, in spite of the thousand dollars. You're making me feel unsure of everything once again. There's a stench of corpses about you, Steve – a stench of truth. Unless, of course, this family tomb is a fiction behind which you're hiding your impatience.

Brandishing a pen and a sheet of paper, Vera is waiting for me in the kitchen.

'He's a little loud, but nice, don't you think? Now, let's see: three-thirty to eight, that adds up to nine half-hours.'

The pen point goes scribbling across the page. The question is: if I strangle her, will they acquit me?

'So you owe the house exactly one thousand seven hundred and ten francs.'

If I strangle her, will they acquit me? Watch it, Vera. I've got claws, too – not to mention powerful backers. Forget it. You're not getting a bean, not a sou, not a kopeck.

So long, Rue Paul-Valéry.

It's sort of funny moseying around in a Rolls. My nose barely reaches the windshield. When I think how that old dyke wanted to brace me for seventeen hundred and ten francs! Those people don't even know what honesty means.

Steve is playing with my hair. What a strange man. If the 'studio apartment' turns out to be what I'm looking for, he'll make it possible for me to take it right away without having to borrow from Malou. He says he wants to look it over with me – and he won't take no for an answer.

'Handsome building with a hewn-stone façade,' says the ad. Let's go. My concierge looks like a good sort, and she smiles as she rummages through the pockets of her print smock for the key. The apartment is small but attractive, with a mixture of imitation Louis XV and Empire furniture. The windows, which look out over the street, are hung with blue velvet curtains that match the bedspread. The bathroom and mini-kitchen are less than perfect: the pale-green paint on the walls is peeling, and the tub is a trifle old-fashioned. But, on the whole, I have to admit that I've been won over.

Steve tugs me by the hand.

'Sophie darling, come and take a look. You'll have all Paris at your feet.'

'It's perfectly beautiful – but how much is the rent?'

238

'It comes to nine hundred francs a month. The owner insists on four months' rent down – three as a guarantee for the furnishings, and one month's rent in advance. I get four hundred and fifty francs commission.' The concierge spouts all this out without drawing breath.

'Sophie, look at me. I'll make you a proposition. I'll be staying in Paris another ten days and I don't want to spend them alone. You stay with me right to the end. After you take me to the airport, my chauffeur will drive you home. In exchange, I'll pay for the studio, and I'll throw in an extra month's rent.'

It's Mr I'll-Pay-the-Rent! I feel like kissing him. The concierge discreetly looks the other way. Big Steve literally sweeps me off my feet. It's a strange kiss we exchange. I always feel a certain revulsion when I kiss a man I don't love on the lips. I'm not particularly attracted to Steve, but I don't find him unattractive, either. He just leaves me indifferent, the way the others do. Never mind, his mouth is clean and I make my kiss a passionate one. I sense his surprise and joy. How else could I thank him? In the course of a few hours he's given me ten thousand francs. He must be absolutely loaded. And yet at this moment he's poorer than I am.

I much prefer the man who pays me fifty or a hundred francs, tears off his piece with no fuss, and splits. Customers like that usually don't talk; they don't have the time. They go to hookers the way they go shopping. For them, I'm just a hooker doing her job and giving them their money's worth. If there's any kind of warmth exchanged, I'm the one who makes it happen. If I start acting sweet, that's my business. Whether or not I take time out to chew the fat, smoke a cigarette, or have a drink is up to me and the man has to like it or lump it. But men like Steve and Maurice and Paul confuse me. They call everything into question. They somehow involve me in their problems. For them, I am no longer a hooker but a woman. They no longer make use of me – they need me. I'm touched by them, and I'm sorry not to be able to love them better. Nevertheless, I do love them in my own feeble way. Mustn't be soft-hearted or think too hard when you're turning tricks; you can't do that and stay in this business.

That evening we have a candlelight supper in an extra-ordinary indoor greenhouse. In the half-light filtering down through the glass roof, Steve even turns into a handsome, funny man. I find myself laughing unreservedly. Steve, I'd like to love you. I'd like to love all the men I've loved. I'd like to have ten lives, one for each of them. I'd like to have twenty or a hundred or a thousand lives. Perched up there on your big pile of dollars and Rolls-Royces, it's easy for you to smile, to tell yourself that other men are just like you, that they make love to me without being brutal, kiss my fingertips, and call me 'Sophie darling.' You undoubtedly think that their fingernails are clean, and that when they take me in their arms, it's between satin sheets. Sorry. My grey matter is beginning to lather again. Just uncork another bottle, and show me your Disney cartoons while we wait for tomorrow ...

It's already noon. On the tray next to the bed, there's tea, almond croissants, and a note from Steve. 'See you tonight, *ma chérie*. Don't run away. I know where to find you.'

I stretch. I have a headache. If only I didn't have to get up, go out, stop at the bank, and track down Gerry. But I must deliver to him personally the price of my ten days of peace. The great thing about him is that when he sees the green stuff it makes him lose his voice. He stops talking and starts counting.

Someone's ringing at the garden gate. I dash out – I'm not used to having anyone answer the bell for me. I get there ahead of the astonished butler and, to my delight, I'm handed a huge armful of jasmine. It's a topsyturvy world! If I only knew where Steve was, I'd go jump into his arms and forget all about handing over my earnings to Gerry.

'Dreams can't fill your belly ...' that's what my father used to tell me whenever he found me leaning out of the kitchen window. I'd be standing with my feet among the pots and pans and my chin in my hands, gazing out at the patch of sky above the second courtyard. 'Listen, you better start moving your ass. Don't just go on hanging there uselessly like an old man's balls. You've got to jump right into the middle of life – otherwise you get nowhere.' I used to sigh and turn away slowly, telling myself that he didn't understand me, that he'd never understood anything about either me or my brothers and sisters. But nowadays I'm beginning to think he was right. I've followed his advice: I'm moving it.

Steve flew back to America two days ago. He kept his

promise. In the Rolls that took me back to town, I felt some kind of enormous void. Naturally I hadn't been in love with Steve. But I'd been so extraordinarily comforted by the ten days I'd spent with him: the armfuls of jasmine, the games he played, the intimate things he told me, his respect and consideration, the money he used to spend so lavishly. When he left, he gave me a chaste kiss on the lips and said, '*Good luck, Sophie darling.*'

He's gone; and for the past two days I've remained shut up like a recluse in my little apartment. I've cooked, done the cleaning, and listened to the radio – all in a kind of dream. But as my old man said, dreams don't fill your belly. So tonight it's back to the wars. Destination: Le Boogie-Woogie.

After a relaxing afternoon at the hairdresser's, a *choucroute* washed down with a Gewurztraminer at Lipp's, and a neighbourhood movie to keep the clock running, the right moment has arrived. At ten o'clock I walk down a corridor papered over with the photographs of striptease artists, jugglers, prestidigators, and celebrities, and make my way into the nightclub.

chapter nine

So this is Le Boogie-Woogie! The irony of it is that I've been here before. It was when I was nineteen. My fiancé had told me to meet him here one Sunday afternoon. In those days, people came here to dance. I remember the terror I felt when I found myself in the midst of a horde of cuties whose makeup, hairdo, and clothes were the latest chic. They were all busily doing the twist in their white stockings, and I just stood there, with my yellow poplin skirt sticking out under my duffel coat. I didn't have the nerve to confront all that gaiety, and I ran away in tears, thinking of the public balls at the town hall and on Place du 11 Novembre. Nightclubs were for other people, not me. That Sunday I walked all the way to the Louvre, where the afternoon slipped by like something in a fairy tale. I had come out of the museum with wonderful colours running out of my eyes, repeating at each step the names of the painters that had most struck my fancy. Then and there, I decided to save up enough to buy myself a book about van Gogh; if I couldn't buy it, I'd steal it. I was very pleased with myself, and some-what less in love with my boy friend.

It's weird coming back to this place. But what a gas it'll be if France remembers me and can arrange things. Instead of one fiancé I'll be meeting with ten or a hundred or a thousand. Watch out, guys, little Sophie has just arrived. Dim the lights, and let the trombone start moaning! Loosen your ties, take off your jackets, keep one hand on your wallet, and the other on your bottle. Stop drooling, and hold your breath. Here she is – the one and only. Give her a really big hand. It's opening night for her all over again, and she'll need all the encouragement she can get. Hey, you girls, stop whispering and nudging each other. Applaud, because she really knows her stuff. Smooth those wrinkles away, you're starting to look ugly. Be patient. Just let her get settled here, and then you can indulge in your petty jealousies. Tonight, give her a chance to get into the swing of things. Give her a break.

'Hello. I'm looking for a girl named France.'

Whatever you do, don't answer all at once. Lord, if only my little friend Boondocks hasn't taken it into her head to change her name, now that she's working in a high-class place. The demi-mondaines reply in chorus: 'Never heard of her!' Bitches. They stare down at me from their perches on the bar-stools. It's their turf. I feel two inches high – just as I did that first Sunday. But today I'm ready for combat. What they don't know, of course (and I won't be the one to tell them) is that France aka Boondocks was born in Pantin, married Jean-Jean the Cobra from Corsica, and started out with fake IDs at the Saint-Louis when she was only seventeen. I might also add that she's for real, she is, and must be bored shitless from hanging around with zombies like them. But I keep my mouth shut – I'll stake my life on it that most of these girls are married to ball-less bums. I'm even sure there are at least two in the consign-ment who have pigs for pimps. I decide that it's better to be taken for a dummy and not get France into trouble.

When I insist, the demireps grudgingly chorus: 'Maybe she's looking for Linda. In that case, she'd better settle down and wait. As usual, Linda scored the minute she showed up here. I'd like to know just what that broad does with men.' You can cut the cackling and sniping. It's all clear to me now: France, Boondocks, and Linda are one and the same.

242

'Hi. I'm Linda's friend.'

A girl who has kept quiet so far smiles as she speaks to me.

'She was busy the minute she got here. She may be back, but if you want to see her, the best thing is to wait for her at the bar next door. Take a seat on the terrace next to the window and keep your eyes open. If she's the one you're looking for, she won't be long. Are you really a friend of hers?'

I nod my head. Betty has said all this quickly, under her breath.

'Is France – I mean Linda – in trouble?'

'Not especially. But the girls here are such shits. What's your name, by the way?'

'Sophie. If I don't see her, just tell her Sophie stopped by. Does this Linda like to drink *pastis*?'

'You bet. We go next door and knock back a few every night before we start work.'

'That's my girl? Thanks, and goodnight.'

It's her, all right. She shows up a good half-hour and two scotches later. She comes walking past with her head held high and her eye full of mischief. She's as cheeky as ever and ready to take up the slightest challenge. Not satisfied with merely working out of a nightclub, she's cruising the surrounding streets, ready with a snappy comeback in case she runs into a cop. She turns people on and off at will, utterly sure of herself, as pretty as ever, perhaps prettier. A few more steps bring her level with me . . . I rap on the pane, almost shouting 'France!'

She stops, manifesting her surprise with a slight jerk of her head. I'm already outside.

'Franzie!'

'Hey, girl, what are you doing around here?'

'Waiting for you.'

'Let's not stay here, it's too hot. Come on, let's go have a couple.'

We settle down at a corner table in the back of the café. France is still using the same perfume; and she's still as undemonstrative as ever. Nothing seems to surprise her. She looks at me and talks to me as if we'd seen each other last night. I feel a certain sadness at this, but what the hell had I expected? She isn't the kind to throw her arms around my neck and look at me with shining eyes. Had I forgotten what she said to me one night as we watched the girls at the Saint-Louis hugging and kissing? 'Just look at them licking one another's ugly mugs. The first chance they get they'll be dragging each other in the mud.' France and I never kissed. I don't like effusiveness either. All the same, it would be nice if tonight she dropped her customary coolness just for a moment. Can't she understand that I need her? Can't she show me by one gesture or look or word that she's still my friend?

To conceal my anxiety, I say as we touch glasses, 'It's been years.'

'You're telling me. The last time was at Saint-Lazare. You still up at the old place?'

'Not for ages. Franzie, I'm on the street. My pimp flushed a quail prettier than a day in spring. He wants to get rid of me and send me to the Casbah in Chambéry. If nothing turns up within a week, I'll be sold down the river.'

'Forget about Chambéry. Tonight I'll get you into Le Boogie-Woogie with me. Don't look so worried – the boss has the hots for me. But let me warn you – he's hand in glove with the cops, and the broads have got shit for husbands. The only one on the level is Betty. She's my buddy. And her husband's from my old man's hometown.'

'She's the one who told me to wait for you here. I can handle the others, now that I know what I'm getting into. What's the setup here?'

'Three hundred for going upstairs. Once you're in the room, you can fend for yourself. It takes three bottles to be able to leave the bar. There's a forty-franc commission for you on each one. If the john doesn't want to drink, try and manage a hand-job under the table and get one-fifty from him, or at least a hundred. But stay on your toes; and don't get caught. The regular help tells all to old man Claude. Some girls give head under the table, but I'm against it.'

'Well, nobody can accuse them of being too proud ...'

'Don't be surprised at anything. Some of them get themselves humped right on the banquettes. And then, you ought to hear them talk. They say girls with pimps ought to be sent to the gas chambers along with their pimps. You know the type. So I'm warning you, stay cool, and keep your mouth shut. If you make a fuss, out you go.'

'Great place. Where's upstairs?'

'Usually the johns are already registered in hotels. Most of the customers are foreigners. Since we only come in once a night, the desk clerks don't give us any trouble. Otherwise, you take them to your own place. Leave them your phone number. That way you can knock off a few in the afternoon. At any rate, that's how I work, and on the whole I come out way ahead of the game. Sometimes I also gander around on the way out of the hotel and manage to score. That's it. Be sure your clothes and hairdo are impeccable – and the less you look like a hustler, the better.'

'Where are you living these days?'

'Rue Balzac. Number three.'

'You're kidding! That's where I just found a place.'

'Watch out there, too. Everybody in that building's a hooker. Never take your old man there, be very careful on the phone, and see to it you're not tailed.'

'You'll really be getting me off the hook if this works out.'

In the street, even though it's only a short way to Le Boogie-Woogie, France never stops looking around. Is she worried? Is she hoping to find another customer? Beats me.

'I heard from Kim and Muriel. They're working on Rue de La Reynie and raking it in.'

'I could never work Les Halles.'

'It's my old man who doesn't want me to. He's changed, you know. For Christmas he's giving me a diamond ring. In six month's he's going to open a nightclub in Corsica, and I'll run it! I've earned it, haven't I? It'll soon be five years since I started working.'

France, France, you're breaking my heart.

'His mother's crazy about me. You should see the way they treat me down there.'

'I'm getting stage fright. If only I can bring it off . . .'

And I do. In less than a quarter of an hour I've been enlisted in the cock-sucking ranks of Le Boogie-Woogie. France congratulates me with a slap on the back, and Pointed Head – her gaga admirer – warmly shakes my hand as he bids me goodnight.

After I've left, I phone Malou at La Bohème to tell her the good news. Malou hears me out, then informs me that for the last week a certain Daniel has been spending all his evenings at La Bohème in the hopes of getting in touch with me.

I'd met this Daniel there. He's a man from out of town,

fiftyish, with a face so kind that when I saw him come in looking hopelessly lost, I left a customer with whom I was drinking
a farewell scotch to take him in hand. I led him to a back table
next to the dance floor, and when I mentioned to him that he
looked really out of it, he admitted that this was his first trip
to Paris. He'd asked to be dropped off at Pigalle because all his
friends in Metz kept talking about the place; and the uniformed
doorman of La Bohème had caught him by the sleeve and told
him that he'd find the best Spanish cooking in Paris inside,
not to mention guitarists, dancers, and everything else. Since he
hadn't eaten yet, and since he felt a certain nostalgia for Spain,
where he'd gone on vacation three years earlier, he had trust-
ingly come in; and as I went on teasing him and mischievously
playing with his moustache, he repeated in a voice that was
trembling with emotion, 'I didn't know. That's not what I came
in for. I'm going to leave. In seventeen years of marriage I've
never cheated on my wife.'

I was intrigued. The harder Daniel tried to defend himself,
the more I played with his moustache and flashed my legs. I
told him that he was a rare bird indeed. He still wouldn't relax.
He sat there perched stiffly on the edge of his seat, his hands
clenched on his knees, his eyes moving from one girl to the next
and always coming back to me. So I said to him, 'Perhaps
you'd prefer one of my friends?' He almost shouted, 'No, no –
you're the one I want!' He exchanged his Coke for a half-bottle
of champagne. Thirty minutes later we started in on the Dom
Pérignon. At eleven, Daniel grabbed my shoulders like a kid
and asked me to take him in charge and make him happy. He
was sobbing between my breasts:

'My wife beats me up, and she cheats on me with my
brother-in-law. She's a real shrew. Just imagine. I have a chance
of being transferred to the Paris area. It's the one thing I've
always wanted. I put in my request six years ago, and it's just
been approved. Well, you know what she did? She tore up the
transfer. She doesn't want to leave him. And my poor sister –
she's never noticed a thing.'

I dry his tears on my blouse and fondly stroke the back of his
grey head.

'But now that I've met you, all that's going to change. Tomorrow I'm going to the department to sign my transfer. I
won't be a bother, you know. I'd just like it if we could spend

an evening together from time to time. I'll make it worth your while. There'll be that much less for her to spend on those lousy candies she keeps ordering – nougats from Montélimar, prunes from Agen, sugared almonds from God knows where. Around where we live she's known as the Old Sow. She's as fat as she is mean. But all that's going to change. She'll see I'm not the failure she says I am.'

Nothing was less certain than the prospect of making one nickel off this guy. No doubt I was wasting my time, but it was a quiet night – it was a Saturday, and my steadies were away for the weekend. I felt more like listening to Daniel's tale of woe than to the inanities of the other girls. Around two o'clock I dragged him staggering to the Macao. He said my breasts were ripe melons as he put the envelope containing his month's pay on the washbasin. I felt cruddy. I felt like telling him, Go away. Beat it. You give me a pain, you and the thirteen hundred francs you earned slaving behind your post office window. I'm no better than that wife who stuffs herself with pastries. All I want is your jack. I'll never give you a thing in return. You're not rich enough for me to devote a whole evening to you. You're too kind. Scram. Get out. Hightail it back to Metz – putting up with a fat pig is better than heartache.

But I didn't say a thing. As I stroked and soaped Daniel's hard cock, I kept glancing at the envelope. I'd had time to check its contents while he was undressing. Thirteen new hundred-franc bills neatly clipped together. They smelled good.

We made love family style, with him on top and me underneath. Afterwards, he said he felt like he was twenty again, so we went at it again, this time with him underneath and me on top.

Later, we went back to the bar. He very much wanted to buy me one last drink. He was happy. At that point Simon walked in with a Lebanese, and Josepha came over to whisper in my ear, 'Sophie, this is one for you.' I said goodbye to Daniel and gave him a kiss on the cheek. We hadn't even started on the half-bottle. When I came back down, he'd gone.

When I left at five-thirty that morning, I saw him standing by the Métro entrance on Place Pigalle. He looked sick.

I said, 'What the hell are you doing here?'

He replied in a timid voice, 'I haven't got a centime left. I don't even have subway fare.'

I towed him into a nearby *brasserie*. We drank coffee and ate croissants. I slipped a hundred francs into his pocket and walked him back to the Métro. He said, 'Don't forget. I'm going to be transferred. I'll come back.'

We said goodbye. No doubt he has been transferred, and he has come back. A nice guy. Someone I'd like to see again.

How pleasant the night is all of a sudden! How lovely it is walking through the falling snow! The apartment's empty. On my pillow I find a note:

'Dear doll, I'm going to Brussels for a week on urgent business. Stop by at Les Bermudes while I'm away and see how things are going. I'm counting on you. You're the best of the bunch.'

So Gerry wants me to get to know my little in-law better. He wants me to act as his messenger. He wants me to back up his tall story. The time between reading these lines and seeing Dominique is no fun for me. How nice it would have been just to sleep ...

Dominique ... He calls you Domino when he talks to me about you – something he often does. He has very little discretion, let me tell you. I know what your favourite dishes are. I know you drink gin fizzes. I know that you have two beauty marks on your right breast, that your belly is as taut as a full sail, that you like to make love on your side, and that your shoe size is seven and a half. I also know that you're in love and want to have a child by him. So you see, I haven't been spared anything. If only you loved him a little less, I'd tell you how I was hooked when I was twenty. I'd tell you about the little hotel in Montparnasse, where I thought that poverty had thrust its ugly snout under my door for the last time. Thanks to him, I'd seen the last of it. And yet I've never seen more of it than during the past three years. You see how wrong a girl can be. I know it isn't the same kind of poverty. The other kind, with its hardships and hunger pangs, had something bohemian about it, a sort of gaiety that even beatings didn't destroy; whereas the new kind, with its promises of happiness that are never kept, is tragic. There wouldn't be any point in telling you about all that because you love him. So shut your eyes tight. The *commedia dell'arte* is about to begin ...

Christ, I'd forgotten how pretty she is! Give me a kiss,

Domino. I have news of our warrior. At this very hour, our guy is probably drinking our health in some bar in Brussels. Okay, Domino, let's hear it. I'm listening. Let's find out what tune he makes you dance to. I'll give you the pitch and get you started:

'It's true, Gerard's a swell guy. And let me tell you, when he starts talking about you, there's no stopping him.'

'I know things weren't going well for him when we met. This summer we're going to start a baby. He's happy about that. In the fall we'll buy a cottage in Normandy so I can have a quiet pregnancy.'

'Let me buy you another gin fizz. It's a real pleasure getting to know you.'

'You're nice. The girls here are such cats. I guess you know he's got another doxy. I certainly couldn't care less. The poor thing seems so dumb.'

Take a deep breath, Domino. Have a sip of your drink. I'm actually learning something. So the son of a bitch introduced you to Odette. Will wonders never cease!

'Can you imagine – he took us out to the country for lunch one day. Of course he cued me in ahead of time. You should have seen the way she was dressed – looked like something out of a sideshow! We really had a good laugh over lunch. He said I was his cousin, and she swallowed it. We were playing kneesies under the table. I don't know what you're going to think of me – anyway, the three of us made love together at his place afterwards. Obviously he only paid attention to me, so it all ended in a brawl. What a pasting she took! Seems she couldn't work for three days. Marcellin was fit to be tied.'

'Marcellin?'

'That's what I call him for a tease. It's his real name, yes, it is – ask him to show you his ID sometime, you'll see.'

Well, Gerry, you're really something. What a creep you are! You even showed her your IDs. Someone up there must love bums. If you don't end up in the clink one day, I'm going to have a pair of balls grafted on. And she laps it up like mother's milk! The cottage in Normandy, the kid – I'd heard it all. As for his sterile wife, he somehow forgot to tell you about her nine abortions. Marcellin is the name of his poor old father, whom he left to die all alone in Berry in a squalid shanty without heat or water. As for Odette being his wife – what a laugh!

249

Odette was a poor girl I had the misfortune of steering his way: nowadays she's running lines of North Africans somewhere near Barbés. He's on the point of selling her, and he'd like me to take over her job. Never. I'd rather die. But as for you, honeybunch, don't kid yourself. I give you my word, Domino, that your stock will fall just as mine has. Since he makes you feel so horny, enjoy him right down to the very last morsel, but don't expect any help from me. Now cut out the BS. I feel like spitting, or puking, or busting your pretty head in.

'Anyway, he told me he was getting rid of her.'

'I hope so, since I don't feel much like sharing, either.'

'Will you be coming back?'

I wouldn't count on it, sweetie pie. It's better not knowing anything than listening to this crud. Gerry is definitely one sweet pimp! I still don't know when or how, but I'm going to arrange a disaster for him that he won't forget for a long, long time.

Working at Le Boogie-Woogie takes me regularly into the world of the four-star hotels and group scenes. My first customer is someone I've seen before – a gentleman of elegant appearance whom I accompany to the Prince of Wales. I change my opinion of him as soon as the door has shut behind us.

'Don't get undressed,' he commands. 'Now squat down, make a circle with your arms, and bend your head back.'

He opens his fly and I barely have time to get out of the way. The gentleman is flicking his penis from side to side and spraying the carpet as he bellows, 'You're my pissoir. Do what I tell you! That's what I paid you for.'

You didn't pay me for anything, you creep, and if I wasn't afraid it would make you come, I'd spit in your face. Goodbye, monsieur – and you can call me thief and chase after me down these plush corridors all you like. My conscience is clean.

I'm starting to wilt in the twilight darkness of Le Boogie-Woogie. The men find I'm looking wan and peaked. Three days go by without my scoring. To pass the time, I drink and distractedly watch the dopey acts performed for the benefit of tourists. France treats me with affectionate disdain and adopts a protective attitude where I'm concerned – poor me, so ashamed of having a wife-in-law! She and Betty both commiserate with me, and I decide to meet her less frequently outside of working hours. I have the distinct impression that her future diamonds have gone to her head.

Still, after midnight on the fourth night, she's the one who connects me with two South Americans with a suite at the Plaza-Athénée. While our two hidalgos exchange gay caresses, we quietly rip them off. No cash-flow problem here – it's El Dorado. At three in the morning the fiesta is at its peak. Steering a table laden with dainties, a waiter makes his entrance. Just help yourself to champagne and caviar! We guzzle and smear slice after slice of toast. Then it's back to our frantic fun and games.

On our way out of the hotel, the night clerk thanks us for the free entertainment offered the staff. He adds, with a knowing little smile, 'During all the fun the young ladies must have knocked the receiver off the hook ...'

'I'll never dare set foot in there again.'

'What the hell do you care? Let's go count our winnings.'

France takes me to the small café on Place de l'Alma. Sitting in the back among the virtually empty tables, far from any inquisitive gaze, we spread our dollars out on the banquette. It's a triumph: two hundred honestly earned by each of us, plus what we ripped off on the side. That means a net profit of five hundred and twenty-five to be split two ways.

'Wow.'

'You said it, Goofy. You think they'll make a fuss?'

'Not a chance. They were stewed to the eyeballs.'

'You know, I feel so up tonight that if I knew where my little wife-in-law lived, I wouldn't mind warming her ears a little.'

'Drop it, Sophie. You'd only have to pay for it later.'

Those fabulous images of Le Boogie-Woogie that I'd conjured up as I lay next to Malou before going to sleep are getting shopworn. My muslin dress has become nothing more than a uniform; the headiness of perfumes is soured by the smell of cigarettes; the champagne has an aftertaste of hemlock ... and I can't say I'm turned on by the funny little Jew who is holding out his hand and running his fuzzy gaze over my legs.

But from somewhere in the shadows, Pointed Head has his

eyes trained on me. I jump from my stool with a smile and follow my elf into the darkest part of the room. There he introduces me to his wife, a lady who is collapsing under the weight of her trinkets. She has bright eyes and shiny lips. Her chubby hand squeezes mine: I immediately smell a group scene. As soon as the prescribed three bottles have been consumed, Lizbeth starts swaying rapturously back and forth between Gunther's shoulder and mine. She murmurs to me how much they both enjoy sociable copulation.

Since his wife is having trouble negotiating the steps of Le Boogie-Woogie, Gunther offers her his arm. I've clinched a deal for six hundred francs. Settled in the back seat of their Rover, I wait for my elf to inform me as to our destination.

'Do you know Les Marronniers?'

'I've never been there.'

'It's the place Liz likes best. You really have fun there. You'll see.'

And just what will I see? The few times I was involved in the orgies on Rue Boursault, I never saw anything to write home about. My colleagues spent their time sitting on the edge of the bed chatting, smoking, counting their change, and issuing an occasional slap. They were as much at ease in their total nudity as they would have been fully dressed. But have no fear, Monsieur Gunther. You'll be able to spot the respectable ladies on a spree. Freed for the time being from their hypocritical inhibitions, they'll be the ones who raise their wide-open thighs towards the ceiling as they perform their twirls, scissor kicks, and sly tackles. Keep your eyes open, and watch out for dirty tricks: those gluttons snap up everything that comes their way, whatever its sex. Learn how to protect yourself – unless your aim in coming is to be reduced to a shambles before you leave. Don't let yourself be carried away. Stay master of your desire. Remaining cool is important when your crotch starts itching. If you keep a clear head, you'll become aware of an entire underground fauna. It nests in the honeycombing of towels, and even in the suds of the bath soap. Take a good look at the sheets: each fold conceals a wrinkle, a grief, a loss, a revulsion. I have to confess, however, that these theatres of depravity have always stimulated my curiosity: I'd like to attend as a spectator, with my own box, from which, behind my lorgnette, I could behold the extravagant thaw.

*

Gunther discreetly slips a wad of bills into my hand. It feels nice. We'd agreed to the price at the bar. Apparently Lizbeth hasn't noticed a thing. What kind of game is she playing? No game at all. Whatever happens is simply her due. They go into a nightclub, they spot a girl who seems to be on the loose, they buy her a drink: that's all there is to it. Since she's being lifted out of the mire for a few hours, she belongs to them for the rest of the night. She's supposed to show her gratitude by making solemn references to Lesbos and Mytilene ...

Poor Lizbeth. She's climbing the front steps now, lifting up her dress with one hand, pushing an impatient finger against the bell that is to open the doors of organized debauchery. She can use her smile on the hostess all she likes, it's still a waste of effort: here they pretend *not* to recognize a familiar face.

So now we're standing, glasses in hand, in the very depths of voluptuousness. There's one panting squad engaged in frantic activity on a broad bed. In a corner, two men are tranquilly retrogressing towards childhood by playing yoyo with their cocks. One woman is smoking as she jerks off. Another, seated on the floor, is saying whatever comes into her head and licking out her glass.

The harsh light from the ceiling deepens the slightest wrinkle. The air is stuffy. From the next room a variety of sounds emerges: laughter, ecstasy, complaints, shouts, bottles being emptied into glasses.

Staring straight ahead of her, an abigail leads up to the cloakroom, which is crammed with clothes that their owners have hurriedly slipped on to hangers. Even there, people are at play, poking around and trying each other out. Seated on a table strewn with empty glasses, a woman is crying – her mascara has dribbled all the way down to her nipples. She's talking to herself:

'I'll never dare look my husband in the eye. I'll never be able to kiss my children again. I'm ruined.'

Lizbeth's unsteady voice echoes hers: 'The poor thing's had too much to drink. Gunther, darling, why don't you console her while we're getting undressed.'

I observe Gunther's tactics. His hands grasp the woman's fleshy hips, his greedy mouth flattens against her drooping shoulders, then follows the path of the mascara down to one nipple, which is now stiff again. His hands grope between her thighs, which she can hardly wait to spread, and she spreads them, uttering a hysterical wail:

'Armand! I want Armand – oh, yes, yes, it's starting again. It's wonderful.'

On his knees, dressed in a suit that makes him look like a penguin, repeatedly tossing his tie back over his shoulder, with his head buried between the man-eater's thighs, Gunther is grotesque.

Lizbeth latches on to my breast and starts sucking as though she were in the first hours of infancy. I think of Normandy, of the rough hands of my wet nurse grasping the substantial udders of sturdy milch cows … I think of white sand, mussels, cockles, and shifting sands; of Cabourg and the muddy Dive River; of my first strokes in the water, and the hands of my cousins gripping my stomach and chin …

Interrupting my daydreams, Armand looms into view. Lizbeth releases my breast, which comes to rest on the floor: Armand steps on it, without a word of apology. I bite my lips. Feeling a little weak, I follow the centaur's movements. Lizbeth is screaming into my ear, letting herself go, raising herself up and spitting forth her salaciousness in a subterranean voice. Go right ahead, dear lady, the pleasure is all yours. It doesn't excite me in the least. Lord Jesus, you who see everything from the summit of the cross, tell me: does the whole world live its life for a piece of ass?

Gunther is waltzing around among the scattered clothing without losing a millimetre of his superb erection. Armand lifts up the weeping lady and in one swift gesture sets her astride the table. Now that her hunger has been aroused by the centaur's thrust, Lizbeth suggests we move to the adjoining room until her turn comes. Oh – what a disappointment. My sisters-for-the-evening have commandeered the place. The bed has been transformed into one vast card table. The kids are playing gin as they down their Pimm's No 1. I greet them with a wink. Around here, introductions are pointless.

'If things get draggy, come and join us. No point going next door. The faggots have grabbed the limelight.'

As a matter of fact, I'd rather like to drop in there – at least I'd be spared. But Lizbeth wraps an arm around my waist, and we return to the cloakroom. The weeper, lying on the floor, has disappeared beneath the centaur's body, which is in turn straddled by a surly-looking old man who is beating his pipe against Armand's head. Gunther throws himself into the scrimmage. A slim youth draws his Galatea into a wild round-dance. Lizbeth holds out her hand and pulls me along, and we all gather in a ring. The room starts to sway and sing: *Sur le pont d'Avignon, on y danse, on y danse, Sur le pont d'Avignon, on y danse tous en rond* ...

The world is tumbling down and falling apart. I draw to one side and light a cigarette. How nice it would be to blow up the lot of them! An unknown hand strokes my rump – I duly apologize for burning it, then crawl over to the row of shoes where I've stashed my six hundred francs and seize my handbag. It would be easy enough to leave unobserved. I'd merely have to take my clothes into the bathroom and sneak away. They're all too busy to pay any attention to me. I unhook the hanger with my clothes on it – but Lizbeth lets out such a piercing scream that I drop everything.

'Sophie, my pretty little tramp, come and join us.'

Rotten bitch. You start whistling for me just as I'm about to slip off. I rejoin the procession, which is being led by the centaur. He carries Lizbeth impaled on his cock.

Her head is thrown back, and her gaping, gold-filled mouth makes her look like a carp out of water. Her eyes are shut, her nostrils are dilated, and her flabby arms dangle in complete abandon. Behind the centaur and his lady, the weeper, gasping for breath, is born aloft by four men as if to some religious sacrifice. On my right, the surly-looking old man is masturbating to the rhythm of a protracted coughing fit. On my left, Gunther's moist hand grips my wrist. His entire body drips sour sweat. Behind us, a Belgian couple is screaming inanities. The man's erection twice bumps against my backside; his partner snickers. I feel as though I were taking part in a procession of the damned. How, for whom, and for what reason do people become this depraved? I think of the six hundred-franc bills. The thought is like a warm compress on a swelling.

After Armand, exhausted, has dropped Lizbeth like a sack on to the bed, Gunther pushes me hurriedly between his wife's wrinkled thighs. He presses down on the back of my head, uttering every kind of obscenity. I'm greeted with the bitter smell of stale urine and heavy perfume as my lips brush the hairless crotch. She wraps her thighs around my neck. Be-

255

neath the assault my brow is flattened against her sagging belly, my eyes explore an old scar; I start to weep. Disgust mingles with contempt. I work away as I cry, while Gunther, poor impotent man, parades his limpness across my buttocks. That's enough. Keep your wads of bills and your rubber factories and let me get out. The price is too high.

When I leave Les Marronniers, alone, abandoning these lost souls to their slimy pleasures, it's three o'clock in the morning. I walk through empty, utterly airless streets. My arms caress the pleats of my dress through the torn linings of my coat pockets. If only I could go away – go away without a passport or a signed permission or having to ask anyone's opinion! Wait for me, Cabourg, I'm on my way. I want once again to see your shifting dunes aswarm with translucent sand lice, the grey water at low tide, the mother-of-pearlish razor shells that crunch beneath my feet, the pieces of driftwood that protrude from the cold sand like so many cries for help, the deserted promenade stretching out in the rain, the playroom in the flower pavilion (the first kiss I gave was through its misted windowpane); and beyond, the muddy Dive that flows past gardens, reeds, and bogged-down cows bearing the smell of apples and the savour of cider and wild cherries.

By looking forward to my coming trip I am able to survive three more weeks in the smoky atmosphere of Le Boogie-Woogie. Once again I have champagne, Gerard, and other hookers coming out of my ears. I'm tired of changing partners, of going from the Crillon to the George V, from the Ritz to the Claridge, from the Prince of Wales to the Plaza-Athénée. The only advantage of this routine is that I'm sometimes able to forget the acutely painful hours I spent in the police station not so long ago.

There's one small joy, however: every week, Daniel comes and visits me at my place. The dear man has been transferred to Épinay-sur-Seine. Unfortunately, now that they're suburbanites, his better half has gone on a diet, and Daniel is starting to miss her nougat period.

'She's worse than ever!' he groans among my pillows; and, as before, I mop up his tears.

France and Betty said goodbye to us yesterday. They're both going off for a tan and a week of winter sports at Courchevel.

Their friendship is phony, since it's something that's been imposed on them. Nevertheless, I've got a bad case of the blues. In spite of my determination to give up group scenes, I've gone back to Rue Le Châtelier with Lizbeth and Gunther. Oh, it wasn't as bad as Les Marronniers since the rooms are spread out over two floors. But poor Lizbeth got so drunk she tumbled down an entire flight of stairs.

At present we form a more or less complicit triangle of sorts. I'm frequently their guest at lunch. I become their niece for the nonce and thus discover the select restaurants of respectable Parisians. I laugh at all their nonsense and gently remind them that we first met in a nightclub and last separated in a bed.

Between two bottles of wine, Lizbeth, with whom I'm lunching alone today, makes a confession.

'You see, my little angel, if I let myself get involved in these silly games, it's to make him happy. I want to keep him. You know by now that he's impotent – too much self-abuse during the time he spent in concentration camps. That time in captivity is a depressing fact that has to be accepted Our evenings revolt me.'

The raspberry brandy has warmed my head, and I've begun listening to her with something approaching sympathy. But it's a lie! Lady, who do you think you're fooling? You weren't faking the other night. The sullen hunger in your eyes, your obscene language, the skilfulness of your gestures, the bitter taste in my mouth – remember all that? You weren't faking; and believe me, I prefer you in your role of conscious slut than as a tearful victim.

Goodbye, Lizbeth. Please don't tell me any more secrets. I was almost starting to find you likeable. No, you needn't leave with me. Finish your drink. Being alone in the street is nothing new to me.

I'm going off to meet Gerry. He seems to be sinking lower and lower. Gerry – my straw man, my lucky scarecrow. He's been preparing for the holiday he's going to spend with Domino at Megève by having himself outfitted with the wardrobe of a professional skier: magnificently quilted, custom-made parkas in colours that vary with each day of the week, from scarlet to lemon-yellow, from Kelly green to turquoise blue – and ski pants to match. Not to mention the mittens, toques, and scarves the worthy wife of his Armenian tailor has knitted for him. I think that if he had a pal who was a shoemaker, Gerry would have even had matching handmade boots run up for him.

No doubt about it: I'm stuck with a good-for-nothing. He's a weasel, and he's going from bad to worse: from little tricks to wholesale fraud. He's a nothing who night after night is dragging me down the soggy paths of his own failure.

Once again I find myself drifting along the steep, fog-shrouded shores of my own gloom. I'm groping forward with outstretched hands. I've lost my compass – it's been stolen from me. It's raining buckets. The sharp ribs of all the umbrellas in the world are piercing my heart.

I brush away the raindrops, raise my lips to the sky, and walk on, heady and beat, longing impatiently to find myself safe and warm once more on Rue d'Aboukir.

Stretched out near the stove, her fists clenched, the child lies sleeping. Malou is smiling as she opens the packages. What fun we're having! Our respective bosses, much against their will, have granted us a four-day vacation.

'You really went overboard, Sophie. If only they let Bébert keep everything.'

'As long as it's under ten pounds ... And if there's too much, he'll pass it around to the guys who have no parcels.'

'That's true. When you're on the inside, there's never too much.'

At one in the morning we finish wrapping the boned pheasant in silver foil. Malou, are you sure you've removed all the bones? You know they're prohibited in prison. Just think of all the things you could use a bone for – a toothpick, an ear-pick, a nailfile ... In other words, you can use it to do something for yourself, like keeping clean – unless you simply decide to put your eyes out with it. In any event, a bone becomes a forbidden weapon in the pokey. The pathetic drops of champagne you've been sprinkling over the caviar are forbidden too. Booze is forbidden, as is anything that comes in a bottle: that's the sort of thing that provides instruments for suicide and arms for rebellion. Women like you are forbidden, the women who burst with tenderness on the far side of the bars. Those lazy Sundays with their smell of coffee and hot croissants are forbidden. They've forbidden the affectionate impulse that makes us reach out for a shoulder to lean on. They've forbidden hope. They've forbidden life.

'Let's kneel down and pray. Sweet little Jesus, don't let some dirty-fisted screw stick his rotten nose into this. Don't let him drink up the few droplets I've poured in. Don't let him tear the pheasant open with his crafty fingers. Don't let my love parcel reach my husband in shreds.'

'Oh, Sophie – another Christmas!'

'That's right, Malou. And tomorrow we take off!'

On my return from Cabourg, I find an envelope under my door and recognize France's handwriting. Before opening it, I pour myself a scotch.

'Dear Pal: I hate to tell you this, but you're through. They gave you four days off, not ten. There's nothing I can do, although believe me Betty and I tried everything. As for *him*, he's in a towering rage. He's been looking for you everywhere. He's called me several times – from Megève as well as from Paris. He came tearing back here thinking you'd run out on him. If you want my advice, go to him as soon as you get back. I think you ruined his ski holiday. He spoke to my old man – but keep that to yourself, and tear up this note as soon as you've read it. In spring we're setting out for Dakar together. After all, a change of climate won't do us any harm. Betty will join us early in the summer. If you know of an okay girl who's willing to go, tell your old man about her. But make it snappy because openings are being snapped up. A friend of my husband's from Corsica has just opened the place. It's super-elegant – restaurant, nightclub, swimming pool, and all. You remember Martine, from Avignon? She worked for a while at the Saint-Louis – her husband had copped twenty for assault with a deadly weapon. Well, she's already down there. My old man and I called her two days ago. She says it's fantastic. There's more swag than you can count, and nothing to worry about. The only blacks who come in are all big shots who wear their hearts on their sleeve. Two girls like us could take over the place! I've already accepted. My old man is going to spend six months of the year there – and yours too. We could get tanned and go swimming. Lots of hugs and kisses, Sophie. I hope something turns up. Meanwhile, if there are any problems, I live two floors down! – France.'

259

Here at last is some truly heartwarming news. Nice going, France. I see you really learned the script – and have they ever snowed you! You've still got that exaggerated notion of how a 'real woman' ought to behave. Hats off to the pimp who knows how to cultivate it! But this time, old girl, you'll have to manage without me. This is one piece of misery you can have all to yourself.

Hey! Sophie! What are you doing there? Why are you sitting on the edge of the bed with your head in your hands? I'm thinking about Marie; and about how Sunday mornings, once my brothers were out of the way, I used to listen to the amateur hour on the radio. I'm thinking about this long exile. I'm thinking about the moment when it was too late to turn back, and about everything they've tried to make me swallow since.

I'm thinking about the Duratons, that model family in the radio serial my family loved to listen to. They used to sit down with us at dinner every evening at eight and drool on to our empty plates. In the Duraton household there were no insults, bloodshed, or beatings, and not the slightest hint of incest. There was nothing but hearty good humour. Oh, how I remember them – bursting with good health, settled so snugly in their spic-and-span home. You wouldn't have found one single bedbug at their place, not one tubercle bacillus hiding between the waxed floorboards. No grime, no vice, no adultery – nothing, in fact, that might foment poverty. When Madame Duraton spread her legs, it was only to be more comfortable as she leafed through her missal. When Monsieur undid his fly, it was only to read his paper. Monsieur Duraton had weak eyes and thin blood – not the stuff that trollops are bred from. On Sunday mornings, the whole goddamn family showed up for eight-thirty mass. Mademoiselle Ginette Duraton, who was knock-kneed, wore holes in her prayer cushion as she brooded about her mortal sin. Her brother George suffered from acne: he'd wait for the faithful to lower their noses before squeezing the pimples on his own. On the verge of menopause, Madame Duraton would watch moist-eyed as the priest swung the censer. Papa, fiddling with the plump beads of his rosary, dreamed about the clitoris of the lady downstairs.

I've always loathed sham, and I couldn't stand the Duratons; so every evening, at the first crackle from the radio, I'd take down the garbage.

Behind the benches next to the empty lot, I used to offer my hard breasts to the gentle hands of boys. I want to erase the Duratons from my memory, but I don't want to erase the marks the fingers of those boys left on my breasts. I want to thank my mother for giving the Yanks a tumble on the embankment at Rambouillet so that we could have butter with our bread instead of lard. I want to thank my father for keeping his fingers light. I want to thank my sister for renouncing great peace of mind and turning into a great piece of ass. I thank my brothers for having soft fuzz on their faces and no pimples on their noses. I thank his Honour the Mayor of Malakoff for finding us the two-bedroom top-floor walk-up in which we hardly had room to run around, but in which there was no room at all for hypocrisy to take root.

I want to get Gerard out of my thoughts, and all my dirty-fingered johns, too. I want to strike Dakar from the map of the world. I want to get up, stand in front of the mirror, say goodbye to my breasts, my womb, my father, my mother, my brothers, and my sisters. Goodbye France, Goodbye Malou! Now, Marie, shut your eyes and walk to the kitchen. Don't let your hand shake when you turn on the gas, just lay your head down in the oven. Show a little nerve, Marie-Sophie. This kind of asphyxiation's as good as any other.

part four

chapter one

There are certain streets of dubious fame where one always hesitates to stop, either because one is too puritanical, or not curious enough, or not at all imaginative – and sometimes simply because one is scared. Take the rectangle formed by the central markets, known as Les Halles. It's bordered by Rue Pierre-Lescot, Rue Berger, Square des Innocents, Rue de la Cossonnerie, and Rue des Prêcheurs; and it has nothing to recommend it at first glance – unless you've decided to tie on the feed bag within this forbidden area. When that's the case, everything looks different, and Les Halles shows not a hostile but a hospitable face. It turns into a vast port of call where everyone goes about his business in the misty glow of street lamps. You meet packers who look like sailors, sailors who look like packers, girls with sea legs, tough guys of every size, golden thistles mingling with chrysanthemums near pissoirs, young girls up to their elbows in lettuce who look just like their mothers, sealed crates, open cases, gleaming cobblestones, lofty plate-glass windows, merry tourists diving into their onion soup, oysters on the half shell, bent elbows, Dubonnet, butchers under fluorescent light, bloodstained butchers with their caps on backwards who look like tycoons as they stand in front of the anaesthetized calves' heads, whose tongues protrude through their clenched teeth. Les Halles puts the exotic within the price range of everybody – especially of anybody who keeps his eyes open.

You walk past the Restaurant Robert Vattier, a shipment of *belon* oysters, a woman gaping at a pig's foot, mounds of onions, a girl crying, Saint Eustache and its famous organ, a huge dance hall, thousands of garlic cloves pointing skywards, thick-lipped individuals of unsteady gait, a dog with a pipe in its mouth, three dead cats, barrows and blackboards, arcades and dumps, lightweights, heavy cruisers, imaginary cuckolds, scenes of carnage, a cluster of butter-and-cheese shops, birds on the wing, drooping shoulders, a ferreting eye, a groping hand, a day-old beard, a headcheese, pigs decked with flowers, sour-looking pike, a garland of fowls, girls in boots, flowering boughs, silver heels, a Square des Innocents, peeling house-fronts, billowing skirts, narrow hallways, a street cleaner with his broom, all the king's men without their king, a Negro in a wide-brimmed beret – he's picking up some Jaffa oranges that are every bit as red as this redhead, this butterfly of a girl who is fluttering by, fluttering around the baffled Negro, around the baffled old drunk woman as she pitches face forward into the bloody tomatoes. The girl keeps fluttering, and the more she flutters, the more she fills the street with her scent – it's a scent that goes to your head and makes you tipsy, a scent that you can feel with your fingers and your lips. She's scattering the smell of Les Halles: it's the smell of a gigantic orgy, the smell of fresh vegetables absorbing the Métro's air, of meat sniffing up sewer emanations, it's the smell of a dishcloth in which wine and beer have mingled, it's the flavour of laughter, bar tops, and tears. For those who know how to smell, it's a true perfume, and it's free to boot; and it makes you love the nighttime.

In Les Halles, nighttime has a different colour; it's navy blue. And anyone with a touch of wanderlust will have no trouble sailing down the River of Rue Saint-Denis. You need only a one-way ticket, and there's only one class of accom-modations. 'All in the same boat!' is what the fluttering girl is singing. And everything has begun fluttering with her: the meats and the orange-laden Negro, Saint Eustache and Res-taurant Robert Vattier, butchers and carcasses, the little girls among the lettuce, Pierre-Lescot and the pig's feet, the wino and the famous organ, the king's men and the headcheese, the tough guys and Les Innocents, the Métro and the carnage, the imaginary cuckolds and the narrow hallways, the dishcloth and the tears, the pint of red and the bar top, the tourists and the pissoirs, the dance hall and the glass of white wine. Things are fluttering and spinning: ships, neon lights, sirens – an infernal merry-go-round that when morning comes subsides on to a sidewalk washed down by a municipal sprinkler truck. And one girl and then another go on fluttering around the extin-guished street lamp. It doesn't matter if their lyrics have altered slightly – it's still the old, reliable tune, and it says: Come away with me!

*

'Tails, you go first. Heads, I do.'

'Tails!'

'Go ahead, Malou. I'll wait for you by the park. Move fast, but take a good look.'

'Let me have the shopping basket, will you?'

'Here. That's great. You look like a real little housewife.'

'Here I go. You don't think they'll tear me apart?'

'There are limits, after all – it would really be something if every dame who went past the hotel got knocked on the head. Come on, get going. I'll be waiting. Take a good look – I won't move.'

It's seven in the evening. Children are still playing in the park. A mother is belatedly pushing her baby carriage towards Rue Saint-Denis. Bright water splashes over the Fontaine des Innocents. Night is falling. The air is turning cold. I'd love to know what's happening behind each lighted window. Around me there's a general bustle. Rue Saint-Denis is palpitating. On the bank of the great River of Boulevard Sébastopol – it's hard to navigate at this time of day – a *café-tabac* sends out its beacon to those who've lingered. It's the end of the day, and the dawn of a great orgiastic night: the night of Les Halles.

And, if it's actually true that the girls here make a mint, I'll settle for this place instead of Dakar: even if it's rough, even if I'd rather be dead, even if – nothing. I no longer have any choice. For my twenty-third birthday I was given a one-way ticket to equatorial Africa. My only hope is to find a way out, which means, as Gerard likes to say, a good stall and a solid store. No more temporary arrangements: what we're looking for is something really nifty, a house where I can put in time for three or four years. Forever fluttering around is a waste of one's time, youth, and health.

Of course Gerard doesn't talk about health. He's never heard the word. Health? What's that? Who does it belong to? Where? When? Of course, one does need a minimum of feeling. Well, I can feel which way the wind is blowing. It's freezing. It's wearing me down. Sometimes, when I'm exhausted, I talk to him about it. I say, 'Actually, my health isn't everything it should be.' And he replies, 'You're talking yourself into it. You shouldn't do that. Anyway, it's not my fault they fed you only lung stew when you were little.' Gerard doesn't like responsibility. What he likes is cash.

He gets worried sometimes, all the same. He says, 'You're smoking too much. It won't do those rotten lungs of yours any good. All I need is for you to have a relapse. What would become of me without you, doll?' Gerry's so sentimental. When I complain of having abdominal pains, he says I'm imagining things – broads are known to yap obsessively about their ovaries. Gerry sure knows how to talk. And he has such a big vocabulary.

Health? He's drunk that of others often enough. Health equals prosperity. He's a practical man with a mercantile turn of mind. I'm shackled to an entrepreneur, that's plain as pie. I've made him a fortune with my hips – but I'm also planning to lose it for him, and I don't much care how I do it.

No time now to imagine what will happen after that. I see Malou, wreathed in a neon glow, walking past Le Croissant d'Argent. Her little meadow-mouse head is wrapped in a silk scarf, and she's clutching her Made-in-China shopping basket in one hand. She strides forward and stops in front of number 45. There she bends down as though to pick something up. Her eyes glance right, quickly take a count of the girls on duty, follow the walls of the hallway as far as the first steps, and at last return to the pavement in front of her. She's had her look. She straightens up. She's back.

'Well?'

'I'll never have the nerve to go in. There are at least fifteen of them. You ought to see the way they're dressed – leather skirts and whips.'

'Specialists, there's nothing strange about that! How's the hallway – not too disgusting?'

'It seems okay. There's a little niche at the far end with a statue in it.'

'To hell with the statue, just concentrate on getting taken on. We'll go put on a fresh face in that café down the street and then give it the works. If they hire us, try it for a week, and then if you don't like it, back you go to La Bohème.'

'What about Bébert? If he even hears Les Halles mentioned, he'll go through the roof.'

'Listen, I haven't got any choice. It's either this or Dakar. So make up your mind.'

'What do we do with the shopping basket?'

'We'll check it at the café.'

The lady who runs this café is a mischievous-eyed brunette. She welcomes us with a smile. The customers and the girls all call her Mimi. She reigns in magnificence, perched on a throne behind the marble counter. On the metal bar top beers are foaming, and there's a lovely smell of french fries. I suddenly feel like taking Malou by the hand and thumbing my nose at the Sands of Time. I want to sit down at that little table in the back, and, while I eat oysters and wash them down with beer, watch Rue Saint-Denis go streaming past. Say, Mimi, you know the neighbourhood: do you think we have the size and stamina to swim up the Saint-Denis River on our backs?

Finish your beer, Malou. We're going to darken our lids and paint ourselves new mouths. They're waiting for us at number 45.

'They don't look any too gentle. Have you really got the guts to go in?'

'Not exactly kittenish, are they? Come on. Let's take the plunge.'

'Fernande! There are two women in the hallway who want to see Madame Pierre. What do we do with them? They're in the way.'

'Send them on up.'

Hey, hear that, Malou? There's a girl coming down the stairs, and she's actually singing to herself. Maybe it won't be so bad after all.

'Whoever's doing that singing, call out your name. Well? I'm waiting.'

'It's Cleavage, Madame Pierre.'

'Okay, Cleavage, you'll do ten minutes overtime tonight. Maybe that'll help you remember what you're told, and maybe you'll be able to manage a couple of extra jobs. So far today you've been dragging your ass. How many tricks? It's you I'm speaking to, madame.'

'Nine, Madame Pierre.'

'That's going to have to change. Less than fifteen and out you go. Do you hear that, ladies? Out!'

'Let's not stay, Sophie. I'll never be able to work in here.'

'Shh, somebody's coming down.'

What kind of freak is this? She makes you think of the Witch in Snow White. She probably uses her tongue as a wicked wand and keeps her yellow eyes forever glued to keyholes. Malou, have you seen how hideous she is? Look at those grizzly cheeks, those gums riddled with tooth stumps, and the purplish knobs sprouting from her skull. What a weird-looking thing she is! I've never seen anything like her, and I'll bet you haven't, either. And her smell! It's exactly like the hallway. She's saturated with it. She stinks. You see, she's the one who cleans out the bidets, gathers up the used rubbers and towels, and collects the price of the rooms. She once dreamed of being beautiful – Malou, what do you think she'd have done if she'd been beautiful? Do you have the slightest idea? Some day, when we know her better, we'll ask her.

And you, Malou – what are you thinking about, right now? I'll bet you're thinking that there's a secret passage in the office. It leads out to an utterly dark shed where they park big windowless red trucks. They're going to chuck us into those trucks with a few other foolhardy girls, and then off we'll go to Zanzibar, Bahía Blanca, Conakry, and Dar es Salaam! The expendables ... Oh, Malou, the things you think about are so sad. You can't let those black thoughts get to you. Listen, take me, for example: I sometimes go to bed and no sooner is the light out than I start making up some sad story. Well, you know where that gets me every time? I start crying and sobbing, and I have to turn the light back on, have a drink, and read awhile. The next day I always wake up with my eyelids swollen and purple, just like the knobs on the lady. Then I have to spend a quarter of an hour with slices of raw potato on my glims. Sad stories don't help. Get it?

Now take a look at Cleavage. Her false eyelashes are sparkly with tears and she has two runny streaks down her cheeks. She's another one for making up sad stories. Now take a look at her customer – *he's* whistling. So you see, we've learned one thing already: it's only the girls here who get kicked around. You saw the Witch? She's pretending to count up those slashes in her notebook – maybe she really is counting them up. Did you notice that each row of slashes on the pad follows the name of one of the girls? For example: nine slashes = Cleavage. If you turn the problem around, that makes nine Cleavages = 81 little slashes. If you go still further, you reach the point where 81 slashes at fifteen francs a slash ... But I learned in school that you shouldn't try to multiply apples by pears.

'Sophie, I'm all jumpy. Did you hear that voice? Do you think we can smoke?'

'You're probably not allowed to piss when you go upstairs. Shh ...'

'Madame Delia, report the names of the women who were just talking.'

'The new ones, Madame Pierre.'

'You're a liar. You'll come half an hour early tomorrow morning – at seven instead of seven-thirty. Madame Gigi, see if you can do better than she did. Besides the newcomers, who was talking in the hallway?'

'Marie-Galante and Corinne Leather.'

'Good for you, Gigi. You know how much I like honesty. The three of you will report to turn tricks next Sunday.'

I'm so upset that I light my cigarette by the wrong end. If there's an intermediary stage between purgatory and hell, it's got to be here at Le Croissant d'Argent, 45 Rue Saint-Denis – unless we're already in hell. Malou and I must look like identical twins. She resembles a child who's just been punished and so must I. She's chewing on her filter and I'm chewing on mine. A little sigh that is as brief and deep as a stifled sob escapes her.

Down below in the hallway, the girls' beckoning, horny fingers snap, crackle, and pop on the cold door pane. How much? a voice asks. Twenty for me, fifteen for the room, another voice answers. It's a deal, resumes the first. If it's a deal, replies the second, follow me. With all your clothes off? implores the first voice. Forty! the other answers. Let's go, the two voices chorus. I hear them coming up. I watch them climbing the stairs side by side, then opening and slamming the door of number 1. Soon they'll start up an organ duet, the one inside the other ...

The stairway darkens. Madame Pierre, the sparrow hawk, has just settled on the banister. Her tail feathers are wrapped in a green cotton apron; her wings are encumbered with newspapers. She turns a dark, penetrating eye on us. Her mouth stretches and contracts like a cock's spur. The Witch is now pretending to dust the office. Hypnotized, Malou burns her fingers on her cigarette butt. Sighs have begun emerging from number 1. Below, fingertips are rapping against the pane.

'All right, ladies. You wanted to talk to me?'

'We're looking for a place to work. My friend's husband's on the inside, mine is on the run.'

'Has your friend lost her tongue?'

I wish she'd shut up. If she goes on talking this way, Malou will start crying and I'll start stammering. Dakar, palm trees, and exile!

'You're not new at this, are you?'

'We've worked everywhere – and we've made money everywhere.'

'You seem pretty sure of yourself, madame – Madame what?'

'Sophie.'

'Sophie, your husbands must have friends who are not in jail or on the run. See that I get a phone call this evening. You start tomorrow at seven-thirty with the daytime group. And since you seem to be inseparable, next week one of you will be transferred to the night shift – if you're still here. That ought to loosen your tongue, madame – Madame-whatever-your-name-is.'

'Malou.'

'Malou, you have to learn to manage in life without a mouthpiece. Right?'

Please, Malou, please. Clench your teeth and fists, shut your eyes ...

'And, of course, you agree, too, don't you, Sophie? In that case, get this into your heads. I've been madam here for twelve years, and around here, I'm the one who runs things. To begin with, I don't like your name. In my place you're going to be Fanny. Fanny's a pretty name, isn't it? Answer me!'

'Yes, madame.'

'I'll be expecting you tomorrow morning at half past seven. I said half past, not twenty-five to eight. If you're willing to work, your men won't have anything to complain about. Now say "Goodbye, Madame Pierre."'

'Goodbye, Madame Pierre.'

Wednesday, 12 January. The alarm goes off inside my head. What's happening? Where am I? What time is it – already six o'clock? In an hour and a half I start work at number 45.

272

Anxiety clutches me. And this one alongside me snores happily away as he sleeps it off, with his arms sprawled out in a cross and his spread legs protruding from the covers.

Just you wait, you bum. Now that the threat of Dakar is out of the way, all I need is time to gather a little stash together. Then wham! Got you! Oh, you were really beautiful last night – when I told you that one phone call was enough to get me into Les Halles, you started parading around as though you'd just won the sweepstakes. You positively twitched all over with enthusiasm. After telephoning old Madame Pierre, you waxed lyrical and tender. You pressed your drooling moustache against my lips; you said that I was worth my weight in gold, and that I'd just given you a finer proof of my love than any man had a right to expect. You're such a jerk! Don't you understand that I'm only staying now so I can make a faster getaway later? Or am I the one who doesn't understand anything?

Worth my weight in gold, you said. You might have added that I'm all sugar and spice, that I melt in your mouth, that I'm a regular jackpot, that I'm a regular cash register: in other words, a piece of shit. Wake up, Gerry, you pimp, stop pretending to be asleep. Let me tell you what it feels like to be transformed overnight into a turd – into something stinking, gooey, and slippery. Let me tell you what it's like to have hundreds and thousands of feet trampling you as you lie on the sidewalk. Whenever people step in shit – left foot, right foot, it doesn't matter – they invariably comment insultingly on the fact. It's not fun, you know, being a piece of shit. Pieces of shit are squashed, scowled at, and held responsible for what's happened – yes, held responsible.

For example, imagine that through some stroke of luck, after you've got out of bed around noon, just as you go out, right under the concierge's window – at the very moment you're preparing to get into your big car, bang! Your right foot slips out from under you – your right foot, please note, not the left one (that would mean good luck). So your foot slips and your neck bounces off the kerb. Pow! Your waterlogged puss explodes and spatters the concierge's window. She comes out screaming. But you don't make another sound. Everybody's there – the butcher, the florist, the woman from the beauty parlour, the cop on the beat. They're all bending over your pimpish remains. Then's when the piece of shit touches bottom. Because all these fine people, who now, out of sympathy for your lot, are giving you artificial respiration or slapping your cheeks, should really just have fleeced you of every penny you had, gathered in a circle around you, and sung 'Glory Hallelujah' to the tune of 'Drunk the Night Before . . .'

Unfortunately, things don't happen that way. As soon as the victim is pronounced dead, people screw things up once again and perform a miscarriage of justice. They unanimously denounce the turd and start vilifying it. They then proceed to stomp on it with the hobnail boots that they had carefully concealed underneath their aprons, smocks, uniforms, slips, and wigs. The poor piece of shit defends itself as best it can by spreading itself thin; but its accusers are stubborn, and they finally manage to restore it to its original shape by dint of effort. The poor turd now looks something like a Big Mac. It has lost every semblance of humanity. And wham! It's begun to smell bad, so they finish it off and shove it down a sewer hole, without benefit of flowers or dirges. Have you ever seen a marble slab engraved: 'Here lies a piece of shit'?

I've already drunk three cups of coffee. I'm shaking. I've got stage fright – the stage fright that's a part of every opening night. I'm playing the role of Fanny. Forgive me, Marcel Pagnol, but it's a name I loathe. It suits me like a moustache. What can I say? I'm blonde and not exactly on the buxom side. My wrists and ankles are slender, and I speak with the accent of the working-class suburbs. I've never been to Marseilles. Fanny is a name that was given to me by chance, or whim, or contrariness. I used to be Sophie and my literary customers would explain to me with a simper that Sophie was a word that meant wisdom – the assholes. But I was fond of Sophie. I'd grown used to her. We'd become buddies. Whereas I don't know the first thing about Fanny. We're going to have to get acquainted. We'll have to win each other's trust, and get to know each other well so as to keep from getting hurt. We'll have to take a good look in the mirror, then invent new faces, a new language, and a new way of putting on makeup. We may have to act tough – and act tough with ourselves. Each may have to forget the other without losing sight of her.

Goodbye, Sophie. Goodbye, wisdom. Hi there, Saint-Denis! Hello, Les Halles. Rack up your fruits and vegetables. Get rid of your hoodlums. I need room. Show me a brand-new side-walk. Make way for love in the open air ... I can feel my feet in the clover, my breasts resting on alfalfa, my eyes full of moss, and thousands of ladybugs on my back. Fanny, you dizzy girl, if you start daydreaming, we've had it. Any pimp can tell you that. A hooker who starts thinking has got to be thrown out or shipped as far away as possible. Otherwise she might become dangerous.

You see, they're expecting us. The gate of the château is ajar. Hi, Miss Polack. You're looking quite pretty with your hazel eyes and blonde pigtails. Too bad you're gussied up in that shiny plastic. I see you more in a peasant gown unbuttoned down to the heart, with espadrilles on your feet, or perhaps in Tyrolian dress – why not? You'd look fantastic. And I'm sure there are guys who'd be turned on by that. With guys, it's all in the mind. Ah, but Aline, what's the use of talking to you about mountain shrubs and edelweiss? You've taken on the colour and smell of these walls. You're incurable. I wonder who the bastard is who keeps you cooped up here, and since when. Why don't you try jumping out of the window? There are thousands of arms ready to catch you. I assure you, you wouldn't be hurt – provided, of course, that you pick your time. Saturday night, for instance, between six and seven.

'Fanny, you're supposed to report in on arrival.'

Pipe down, Witch. I'll be the first one behind the peekaboo door.

'Find yourself a free hook in the coatroom, and be sure you don't step on the shoes of the night gang. If you do they make a fuss afterwards. They're always saying they've been robbed. I sleep here, I get to hear them every night. They hate us because there are more customers during the daytime. Why did you come to this place? Now watch – Fernande is going to make the girls who are late think that Madame Pierre is upstairs. Your pal's late. She'll be penalized.'

'You're out of your skull. Let me by.'

'Don't be disrespectful. Walk downstairs behind me. Here come the Estienne sisters. Listen to them – they'll say they were stuck behind a truck at Rambuteau. Listen. Fernande's about to start shouting ...'

'Corinne! Delia! I'm marking five minutes. Who's that coming in now?'

'It's Malou.'

Malou – she'll never change. Her alarm clock must have forgotten to ring, as usual.

'You talk to the boss about that. On time means on time here. I'm marking a quarter to.'

'Sophie, I didn't wake up on time, and I had a nightmare.'

'Tell me about it later. Go up and get into your outfit.'

'You new ladies, into the hallway. No yakking allowed here. Who's coming in?'

'The Resner trio.'

'Cleavage, I'm marking three-quarters of an hour for you. Twenty minutes for Christine and Marie-Galante.'

'It's that other bitch Gigi's fault. I'm going to scratch her eyes out as sure as my name is Marie! As for you, Corinne, stay out of it, fatty – anyone who's got her husband to pimp for her kid sister ought to keep her mouth shut.'

What a scene! Our girl friends are as gentle and cuddlesome as bricks. The Witch ineffectually starts yelling her lungs out. She's turning bluish-green as she hangs on to the worm-eaten banister. She's shitting in her dirty frock and squealing for Madame Pierre-the-Rock as she adds up the time lost. Half an hour's work loused up means six bidets less to scour and a lot less scum to clean up. As for Malou and myself, our ears are ringing from all the sweet talk. As old defenders of lost causes, we're ready to leap into the fray on Marie-Galante's side. Outside are the customers – the poor guys who only have fifteen minutes of free time to get their rocks off, the poor proles who've just had the door slammed on their flies. Malou, listen to those billy goats demanding their rights. Can you hear their cocks grumbling? – Watch out for flash floods! Witch, you better move your buns out of the way or even *your* ass may get a workout. The levee holds. In the scrimmage, Gigi has just taken a boot heel between the eyes. It's darkened her outlook. You'd think she was having trouble finding the stairs. She's staggering out of bounds ... Malou, what about switching sides and giving her a hand?

'Sophie, I can't stand the sight of blood.'

'Then how about taking on the other girl – the one who's tossing up her morning coffee?'

'Hey, open up! It's been half an hour since we started cooling our heels out here. Especially with our johns in tow.'

276

The two girls who've just come in have nothing in common. Kim, an ageless, square-shouldered brunette, is pushing a red-faced little man ahead of her.

'Keep moving, scout, I'll explain everything in the room.'

The other, blonde and pretty, is telling her customer in the gentlest of voices that he has to pay the twenty francs in advance. Her voice is drowned out by the screams of Gigi and Marie, who have locked themselves into one of the bedrooms. There's blood on the stairs. Alarmed, the man changes his mind. Looking at his watch, he says, 'I have an appointment. I'll come back and see you tomorrow.'

Brigitte's expression hardens. The gentle blonde is turning vicious.

'See he has a good time, girls – here he comes!'

A kick in the backside pitches the man forward. His brief-case goes tumbling down the stairs. The Polack grabs it.

'Darling, don't tell me you're planning to run out just like that? After taking up a pal's time for nothing?'

Standing halfway down the steps, the man is utterly bewildered. He rubs his forehead, fiddles with his glasses, and stutters:

'Come on, be a nice girl, and give it back. My work's in there. Let me out – I'll come back another day.'

Time has stopped. The girls have moved away from the display window. Squeezed together in the middle of the hallway, they're waiting. Corinne is twirling her cat-o'-nine-tails. Nicole is lacing up her boots. Cleavage has taken a saddle strap out of her handbag. Christine and Delia are muttering obscenities as they tuck up their skirts. From her lofty throne, the Witch fulminates threateningly. Huddled against the cellar door at the bottom of the stairs, Malou and I aren't letting out a peep. We must look like orphans in a storm.

'Come on, Brigitte, be nice,' the man begs, 'tell them to step aside. I'll go up with you another day. I haven't got the time this morning. I'm going to be late at the office.'

'Nobody's keeping you.'

Hesitantly he starts down. The girls step back, but just as he is holding out his hand to take back his briefcase from Aline, the Polack hits him in the face with extraordinary violence. The man staggers. His glasses fall off. He bends down to pick them up, but his hand is slower than Corinne's foot. She bursts out laughing as she crushes them, while Nicole kicks the bejesus out of his behind.

'Why are you doing this?' asks the man, in tears. 'Why? You're all insane.'

The double-leaved swinging door abruptly opens. One last kick expels him on to the sidewalk followed by the crumpled metal frame of his eyeglasses.

'Next time, put on bifocals before you start bothering one of the girls here for no good reason!'

The door panels bang shut. Poor guy. Though he doesn't know it, he paid for what others have done. Fanny, you better get set. It's going to be a hot spring.

'You – the two new ones. Next time you'd better lend a hand. There's no room here for Girl Scouts.'

Hitting a defenceless guy just isn't my thing. I'd have preferred helping him get out of there. If I had any guts, I'd tell the lot of you what cute bitches you really are. Cowards! Doing to your johns what you haven't the guts to do to your pimps. You're losers, that's what.

'Sophie – are you crying?'

'No. I'm having a real ball. It's killing me. Lend me your handkerchief.'

Only three-quarters of an hour have passed since I entered the hallway of number 45. It's eight-twenty. Everything has settled into place. The girls are all smiles. The little blue hole between Gigi's eyes gives her an exotic look. Marie has stopped vomiting. She sings a Creole song from her homeland as she arranges the golden tresses of her wig over her crinkly hair. Their breasts pressed against the display window, Aline and Corinne are performing an enticement duet. The others are quietly lined up in single file, awaiting their turn.

Since Malou and I are not particularly aggressive, we have docilely got in line. From her high-perched throne, the Witch reads out the muster. In passing she reminds anyone who may have forgotten that it's forbidden to lean against the hallway walls, and that the two girls at the door mustn't ever stop knocking on the pane because Madame Pierre can always show up unexpectedly. Kim's customer is going down the hallway with his tail between his legs. The girls all give a cheer.

With a lump in my throat, I follow the initiatory lesson. Kim has started the crib off for the day. She has the reputation of being a good starter. Great. It'll be a profitable day for everyone. I have the feeling that the girls are more superstitious here than elsewhere. Am I going to become like them? Will their behaviour contaminate mine? Have I got the spunk to handle fifteen jobs a day? Will I ever manage to stomp on a man's glasses in the hallway? Will I someday be one of Madame Pierre's oldtimers? What a joke!

At nine-fiteen I emerge from the shadows. Here I am in the display window at last, standing at the head of the line beside Delia.

'Say, Fanny, how about doing your share of rapping? You expect me to go out and cruise for you?'

Delia, there's going to be no love lost between you and me. I don't like your kisser. You remind me of those floppy dolls they put in the show windows of department stores at Christmastime. Knock, knock – it's quicker said than done. My fingers are stiff as boards. Malou was really lucky and latched on to a young fellow. Hey, look – a cruiser. Dear little Jesus, make me look good to him.

'How much with all your clothes off?'

'Fifty.'

Zap! I just raised the ante.

'Hey, fella, don't go up with her. She's all syphed up.'

'Don't you believe it! I haven't got syphilis, I'm just new here. Corinne, get your foot out of the way. We're not in kindergarten. Just watch what you're doing, damn it, all of you. I'm here to work.'

What a speech. Nice going, Fanny. You hit the nail on the head. You remind me of Sophie. You tremble just the way she did every time she opened her mouth. Now get upstairs fast and lock yourself in with your customer, so that if you have to cry, they won't see it.

First stop is the door of the office, where the customer settles for the room: fifteen francs plus a compulsory service charge. The Witch takes the money without a smile and hands the customer a tiny white towel.

In his overalls, with his workbag slung over his shoulder, this guy looks really dumb holding the towel; so, since I'm the soul of charity, I carry it for him with a smile. All the second-floor rooms are taken. (Malou is romping in one of them!) My plumber tries putting a hand up my skirt. I take the steps four at a time to the third floor.

One of the doors is open. Surprise, surprise – the room's clean. I pull back the curtains. The window overlooks the courtyard. Close them quickly – it's a dreary view on that side.

'Say, your girl friends aren't very nice to you. You haven't got syphilis, though? They *were* kidding?'

'Of course they were. You want me to get completely undressed?'

'Uh huh. Anyway, with me you'll get a hundred. I get fucked up the ass.'

Here's one man at least who gets straight to the point. Usually, men who want to be corn-holed have to go through all kinds of phony preambles. It's always the first time. They just want to see what it's like at least once in their lives, and of course only if you go real easy. You have to reassure them and promise them that their wives won't notice a thing. But when they pull up their pants with a roguish look in their eyes, they casually say to you, 'I hope you don't take me for a fag. I only go for women. And anyway, it gets you out of your rut.' 'Sweetie, it certainly gets *me* out of my rut – but why don't you do it with your wife?' When I ask this question, they pause for a moment as they run their combs under the cold-water tap. 'My wife's always tired. She's never given me a blow-job. She doesn't even know what the word dildo means.' You smooth down the bed while you listen to them. It's part of the profession.

With Roger, there's no beating about the bush, no time wasted, no need to ring for the Witch to bring up the special equipment. In front of me stands a candid man who is now taking a huge rubber dick out of his work bag. Its black straps are entangled with the monkey wrenches, pipe fittings, and other tools of his trade.

'Holy mackerel, you stash that with your other stuff?'

'Why not? Keeps it greased. Take your dough, and tie that around your hips. I hope you enjoy being the one on top for once. Fuck me the way your lover fucks you. If you do a good job, I'll come and see you every Wednesday.'

Jesus. Here I thought I'd seen everything, and I feel like a newborn babe! And to think that I took the towel out of his hands! My credulity has no limit.

Nothing in the world ever bothers this kind of character. All the same, with most men, when a sympathetic spark is lacking, I've generally felt only indifference; certain men have astonished me; some have touched me; others have revolted me. Roger leaves me feeling nauseated – not because he's decided to get himself buggered, or because he keeps his soiled instrument in his work bag – because he never stops whistling, because he pinches my behind as he kisses me on the cheek, and because he goes away absolutely certain that I've just had a marvellous time with him.

It's a hairy world! Leaning over the banister, the Witch hands me a towel.

'Your friend's waiting for you in number one. The room's been paid for.'

In the hallway I pass Corinne, who spits at my feet. I go by without reacting. Luckily, behind that door I'll find nonviolent Malou.

Malou is smiling. She's preposterously got up in black mesh stockings and black garters, and she's wearing turquoise-blue shoes. Malou dressed up as a fladge queen is hard to take seriously. For starters, she should stop grinning. Her skinny legs are lost inside the mesh; her big-momma tits are swaying in time with her whip. The guy who's being punished is wiggling his rear end as he waits hopefully for a beating. He's quite a sight himself, with his stevedore's shoulders emerging from a pink lace bodice ...

What's the matter with everybody? It's enough to make you blow your brains out. But wait a minute – Malou is *still* smiling. With a flick of her eyes, Malou brings me face to face with reality. Reality is lying on the table. It's taken the form of *two* hundred-franc bills. No comment needed! The situation is clear. All I have to do is join in the game – that means putting on the nurse's uniform draped over the armchair – and start improvising. The performer's life is a hard one, especially when you have to work without a net! Anything goes as long as it works: that is, as long as the guy is satisfied. Professionally speaking, I'm really damn conscientious. Anyway, why would a guy like this pick Malou? There are four girls in the hallway who are more the intellectual type.

'Malou, drop the whip. You look like you were tickling him. Come over here and help me on with my cap. Now, as for you, you bad little girl, crawl out of your corner and buckle my Mary Janes. What's your name again?'

'Laura, Madame Head Nurse.'

'Laura? Why?'

'It's my mother's name.'

'An interesting case, Mademoiselle Malou.'

'Very. Before you got here, I had to confiscate a lollypop he was hiding in his socks. He still has his gumdrops.'

Poor you. The worst part about it is that I don't feel like beating you.

'I'm confiscating your gumdrops. Now take the towel, and shine up the plumbing fixtures. When you've finished, you can start with the dusting. While you're busy, Mademoiselle Malou and I are going to make love.'

'If it's nice and clean, you'll let me have my candies back and give me my enema?'

'What? Nice going, Malou. You might have cued me instead of letting me rack my brains.'

'Don't make me laugh – I didn't know anything about that myself.'

'Listen to me, you dirty thing. This little fantasy of yours is going to cost you double, and you're going to have to pay for the room twice over – right now, or I'm letting you have it. Shut up! Creeps like you are supposed to do what they're told without back talk.'

'Oh, you're wonderful! I like you. Take my wallet – it's in my pocket – and help yourself.'

'Say "Madame" when you address me, and lower your eyes. Malou, start whacking him while I relieve him of his jack. I'll ring for Fernande and pay her the double rate.'

'What about my gumdrops, Mademoiselle Malou?'

'Don't worry about them. We'll stick them up your ass afterwards ...'

When I leave number 1, Fernande hands me a towel. A customer who caught a glimpse of me in the hallway is waiting for me in number 3. After the customer in number 3, there are seven others. By noon I've used every room in the hotel. My success has given me confidence, and I look the girls right in the eye and make them smile back.

I'm hungry.

As I settle down at Le Croissant d'Argent, I have the unpleasant sensation of having a rock in the pit of my stomach. I gulp down a scotch to dissolve it: no dice. I grit my teeth to keep from screaming. Brigitte, who's at the table next to mine, whispers to watch out for Harry and his friendly smile. He's on Madame Pierre's team. His task is to report girls who refuse to get up after the hors d'oeuvres and before the cheese when a potential customer gives them the high sign from the bar or the street.

Lunch hour at Le Croissant d'Argent is really a wild scene. You eat under the voracious gaze of a dozen knowledgeable drinkers. They're sipping their apéritifs with trembling lips while their hands seem to be feverishly searching their pockets for a key, or perhaps for a few coins to pay Harry. (He never fails to freshen a drink the second a glass is empty.) The girls refer to them as Hand-Jobbers Incorporated. Their pants pockets are said to have no linings so that they can communicate directly with their pestered crotches. Actually, these men do no harm.

But there are the others – the tormentors, who haven't got a sou in their pockets but who get their kicks by making girls interrupt their lunch. They pass back and forth in front of the bar, finally position themselves on the sidewalk, and give you the nod. You acknowledge it. A dialogue commences, consisting of sign language accompanied by lip movements. You state your terms by breaking down the number twenty into four fives, following it with a plus sign, and following that with the figure fifteen. You conscientiously point your finger towards the ceiling: fifteen is the price of the room. He scratches his head. So he hasn't understood? Erase everything and start over. Unfortunately, at the end of the third try, for all your goodwill, patience, and devotion to duty, your interrogator still hasn't managed to understand – or he pretends he hasn't; and your steak-and-french-fries is beginning to congeal on your plate. Nevertheless, he seems so sure of himself that you suddenly panic and start wondering: what if he's a dickeybird?

With lowered eyes, you bite on a french fry and make a face. It tastes like brick dust. To calm your anxiety, you start fiddling with your feet under the table and grasp your glass with all five fingers – you'd like to crush it. All of a sudden, the hand-jobbers stop looking for their keys, the dishcloth in Harry's hand freezes in midair, the girls clam up: everyone is looking at you. You put down your glass, cast an imploring look towards the street, and raise your eyes to heaven – just to see what the weather is, of course. If it's a dickey-bird, you have to go through with it. My old man used to say, 'Even with your head in the noose, don't confess.' One eye on the sky, the other on the sidewalk. Take it easy! You're not confronted with John Law but with a jism-and-blood john. The heavyset little fellow is getting agitated, and his impatience reassures you. Okay. You shoot off an all-inclusive gesture at him, twirling your fingers to indicate, 'Got you. Thanks.'

The trouble is that in your enthusiasm you've forgotten that you're dealing with a pain in the ass. He at once reminds you of this fact by asking for details. 'Fifty? Why fifty?' His head has turned into one big question mark, and his five fingers into as many smaller ones. His hands open his raincoat and simulate removing his trousers and his clodhoppers. You play right along and pretend to slip the straps from your shoulders and raise your skirt up to your waist. Your fingers keep busy, declaring 'Seventy.' You say out loud to yourself, 'It's seventy with no clothes.' The others are by now well into dessert. You're still on your steak-and-french-fries.

The hand-jobbers look as though their eyes are going to pop out of their heads, and their hands are frantically busy behind their flies. You leap from your seat. Full steam ahead! The temperature outside is in the thirties. What the hell, you're not the only girl here, and the main thing is to beat them to it. You want to accumulate the greatest possible number of slashes in the Witch's notebook.

Too late! The second you come out of the door, he takes off. He grandly thumbs his nose at you, underlines the gesture with an insult, and splits. There's not even time to get your foot into his backside: he's already turned the corner of Rue Berger. You just stand there. You no longer feel the cold. All you feel are the stares of the gawkers, the housewives, and the kids who have come home from school for lunch. You're no longer hungry. You'd just like a cup of coffee. You understand the aggressiveness of the other girls a little better. Mortified, you return to your table. They're laughing at you, and in order not to seem out of place, you start laughing, too, and you mime the kick in the ass you wish you'd actually given.

There's barely time for a brandy, then it's back to the hallway. You paint yourself a fresh mouth and smooth away a few wrinkles under the glassy stare of the Witch, that guardian of Madame Pierre's interests. Confronted once more with the peekaboo door, the street, the johns, and myself, I tap on the window, softly, timidly at first, then more and more vigorously. A man pushes the door open, looks at me, asks a few questions, and takes me upstairs.

chapter two

During the hours I spend in the hallway, I get to see the hidden side of number 45 – and of Madame Pierre as well. She's a brunette who carries her forty-odd years with ease. She has lively, intelligent eyes and an acrimonious mouth. For fourteen years, in all seasons, she used to pound the pavement on Rue de la Grande-Truanderie. She was a glutton for work. She proudly describes how on certain February nights she had frost on her nipples. She gives me the shivers, she fills me with dread, and she fascinates me. This virago wields unlimited power, thanks to the men who have put the fate of their wives in her hands – with no questions asked. The women shrink, shrivel up, and fall apart when from her glorious eminence the Curse hisses at them: 'Ladies, you're cattle – nothing but cattle. And don't you forget it.' And my heart grows faint when I hear the disillusioned tenants of number 45 surrender their rights in humble unison: 'Yes, Madame Pierre.'

Yesterday was the feast day of Saint Paulinus or perhaps Saint Melanie, but certainly not Saint Brigitte. In spite of ourselves, we celebrated it all the same. It was early – eight-twenty – and we hadn't heard the Curse come down yet. But she was there, standing barefoot on the first step of the stairs. One corner of her mouth was twisted in an unpleasant grimace.

'Brigitte – are you feeling well, Brigitte?'

Brigitte smiles in astonishment. She isn't wide awake yet, hasn't completely recovered from the twenty-five jobs she handled yesterday. She still feels a little sore; but she's caught on. It's not the first time that she's seen this act. She smooths her work outfit, more to keep her anguish at bay than to take the wrinkles out of her clothes. She refuses to raise her eyes. She hopes that the Curse is talking to someone else.

But the Curse goes right on.

'They collared your old man last night. Now isn't that terrible news?'

No doubt she'd been informed during the night of Brigitte's husband's arrest. Brigitte is now wide awake and mumbling incoherent phrases. She's beginning to wonder whether she should strip or get back into her street clothes. She's tearing her working dress and her street shoes apart with her teeth, foaming at the mouth as she tramples on the night shift's shoes, impaling herself on the coatroom hooks. It's not her but her husband who's suffering. The cops have got him. He always counted on her for his first cigarette, for his midmorning snack, maybe even for the last kiss of the day. She refuses to accept the fact. Her innards start hurting again. She starts weeping, softly at first, then louder and louder. Now she's shouting, shrieking, and beating her fists against the wall while sweat pours down her body. We watch her go to pieces without saying a word. We don't know how to help her. But fortunately Madame Pierre is on hand. She reminds her that a woman should keep her dignity at all times, that what pimps need is bread, not tears, and that her proper place is behind the display window.

At number 45, the days follow one another indistinguishably. The Curse controls the flow of time's hourglass; she makes it rain or shine. In the hallway, it rains frequently. Madame Pierre is not only a destroyer, she's a businesswoman, too. Under her brown tresses a diabolical machine is constantly on the go: it's a lie detector, a machine designed to inflict humiliation and punishment, an adding machine. Today or tomorrow Gerry will phone her, and the machine will coldly reply that if I give him less than a thousand francs a day, I'm robbing him. That night, he'll take me in his arms and announce that I'm off to a good start.

Gerry and the Curse cultivate a mutual aim: to turn me into a caricature of a woman. But if he's a sucker, she isn't. She knows in her bones what her fillies are like. She senses my defiance, and that excites her. She orders me to wear lipstick, then sends me out three days in a row for a new brand, claiming she doesn't like the colour – and three days in a row I just happen to forget the new tube on the washbasin. Three days in a row someone steals it. Isn't that tough? The Curse doesn't give up. Four times in a week she interrupts my lunch, four times I'm obliged to have my hair done in a cruddy beauty parlour she gets a kickback from. Four times I come back singing happily, and four times I brush out the curls under her furious gaze. In two weeks, I accumulate fifteen hours' extra work as punishment. I become used to unlocking the hallway door, having a cup of coffee with Fernande, and taking the first customers. The girls are pleased: it seems that on the days I start the ball rolling business is good.

As for me, my morale is shot to pieces. Once again I'm at the end of my rope. When a guy goes to bed with me, I'd be happy if he quietly strangled me. But that would be too easy; and the Curse is lying in wait for me, with her razor blades and her demands, jeering at me and tripping me up. Somehow she knows I'm a holdout, and she won't stand for it:

'Fanny, you may be a rebel, but I've broken other girls, and I'll break you in two.'

Her voice – that appalling brain-grinder – haunts me far beyond the hallway walls. But it's only when I'm once more between my own sheets that I muster up the courage to answer her back: 'Yes, Fanny's a rebel. Fanny's not about to start kowtowing. Fanny doesn't belong in your stable at all. She doesn't like your kind of oats. And anyway, she finds the trough revolting.'

Yesterday, as I was emerging from one of the rooms, she had me come to her office. From her tone, I realized right away that she wasn't interested in hearing my singing voice. (She nevertheless says that I can sing on-key. Sometimes, during the brief intervals of quiet, I've had the privilege of re-creating the same warm atmosphere you sometimes find in prisons by breaking into the lullabies of my childhood.)

Without deigning to look at me, she started talking to me about condoms. She said I had a bad habit of throwing them into wastebaskets. As she counted up slashes, never raising her voice, she went on to say, 'Fernande is tired of having to straighten up after you. You'll find tin cans next to the bidets which have been put there for that very purpose, and I want it made very clear that you're to use them. The cans aren't there by accident. I have a purchaser for my rubbers, a gentleman who buys them up at one franc apiece. This gentleman arrives every evening at eight. He selects a dozen or so of them and sucks them clean on the spot; he takes the rest home with him. I'm sure, Fanny, that you'd find it interesting to watch him.'

I'm interested in everything, madame. I'm capable of looking at, and listening to, everything – that's because I've become indifferent to everything. It was only yesterday (I had to stay after school till eight o'clock) that I made the acquaintance of the night crew and the guy who sucks down embryos.

At noon today, at the Curse's command, Aline took me to a fancy shoe shop, in order to buy the highest pair of heels in Paris. At last I look like a 'real woman'. If Gerry happened to be cruising Saint-Denis, I'm the girl he'd take upstairs. And so, thanks to my guardian angel, I've risen in the world. Four more inches really make a difference. Now not only do my back and innards ache, my feet ache as well. At seven-thirty this evening, when I set my dogs free, it was all I could do to keep them from jumping up and licking my face in gratitude. My fancy clogs were supposed to have been red, but they're orange. Nevertheless, Madame Pierre had proved indulgent: Sunday, I'll be allowed to sleep late.

How can I look forward to Sunday? I have a hard enough time simply climbing into the back seat of a taxi. As soon as I get home, I jump into a boiling-hot bath and expend what energy I have left in mortifying my body with a bath mitt. How can I look forward to Sunday when I eat take-out dishes in bed, when the mere fact of speaking exhausts me, when the phone rings and I hear Malou's voice trembling on the other end? Malou whom I avoid in the hallway of number 45, who racks up her fifteen slashes a day without any fuss, who's losing her hair by the fistful and drowning her sorrows in the bottle? If I avoid you, sweet soul, it's because I'm running out of steam. Up there on my clogs I tend to lose my balance. But set your mind at rest – despite appearances, I've kept my feet on the ground and my eyes wide open. My whole world isn't going to end up being crammed into that hallway. My horizon isn't going to be limited to the bar across the street. With all due respect, to Gerard, the Curse, and that jailbait husband of hers, we aren't going to spend the spring in the display window of number 45.

Her husband is another wholesale fraud. He doesn't mind assuming his better half's duties when she doesn't feel up to them. With my own eyes I've seen him unsmilingly hand out those little towels. I've seen embarrassed customers pass humbly in front of this tough bastard, who unhesitatingly presents an upturned palm. What a farce.

I've seen him twice in two months. The second time was on a Sunday. Malou and I had been given orders to work until noon, with no further explanations. On one side of the office, the girls were standing erect and grave in their Sunday best, looking as if they'd just come out of church. Were we about to be told that the hotel was closing for the holidays? Would the class of oldtimers be sent off to the mountains under the auspices of the junior high school skiing programme? Or would these young ladies be taken to the seaside for the day, as was done in the time of the famous old bordellos? I could have spent the entire day scratching my head if Madame Pierre's husband hadn't burst into the office clapping his hands:

'Let's go, ladies! It's time to perform our duty as good citizens.'

I wasn't dreaming. On this Sunday morning, Slugger Pierrot was really planning to take his fillies down to the polling booth.

He knows nothing and cares nothing about these twenty-four women, the ones who night and day provide grist to his mill. We in turn know nothing about this wretched biped – except that he no longer takes risks. You can keep your nose clean and go on living very comfortably when you finger a cool ten thousand a day. You develop a liking for real estate. You mask your origins behind a house in the country, private hunting grounds, a racing stable, and well-stuffed payoff envelopes ... Oh, sorry – I forgot to mention that at number 45 we never see a plainclothesman. No, it's not merely by chance that number 45 stays open when all the other hotels on the street are closed for repairs. A curious character, this Slugger Pierrot. They say he's supposed to have saved the life of a high government official during the Resistance. Well, it's nobler than passing bribes, as far as the underworld is concerned. A lot of bosses must sincerely regret not having taken part in the Resistance ...

When you close your eyes for sleep – whether you work in a

department store, a factory, or an insurance company – you always take with you some part of your fellow workers' lives. A manner, a gesture, a word, or sometimes an entire way of being, an entire hallway, can set us thinking, can drag us so far down that that very night we find, waiting for us in the recesses of our pillow, the dread-splotched faces of ten women.

Take Aline, the Polack. Her Polish origins were the gift of a father whom she never knew. Her first address in Paris? 45 Rue Saint-Denis – where, for nine years, she's been living in a room sixteen feet long and ten feet wide, with a washbasin and a view of the street as her only furnishings. She's made one trip: a one-year stopover in a crib in Algiers. She hasn't budged an inch since then, and her behaviour has been exemplary. I sometimes feel like giving her a good shake, but she's too big, and too empty. I'd only be wasting my strength.

When I find myself next to her behind the display window, I hum bits of songs for her. She likes hearing me sing. She says the day I leave she's going to swallow a quart of ether. Meanwhile she uses me as her assistant. She has the knack of getting her special-fetish customers to accept me, but she won't let them lay a finger on me. She's even managed to get Jacqueline to accept me, a customer who for five years now has arrived at eight every Tuesday morning and – after paying the trifling sum of six hundred francs – docilely allowed a dildo to be inserted into his bottom. He keeps the dildo nice and warm all day long and returns at six p.m. on the button to have it removed – in exchange for a small consideration. At the end of sessions like that, I feel like snuffing it. I think they've driven her insane. That's it. I've sensed it from the very first day: Aline is insane.

The Slugger, the Curse, and her Arab pimp are the responsible parties. What are Aline's pleasures in life? After twelve hours in the hallway, she has the right to walk the Curse's two Scottish terriers around the Square des Innocents. Of course the little darlings have to get some fresh air. It's not healthy for them to stay cooped up in a brothel all day long. Aside from that, nothing. Except going out to a restaurant once a month, provided they haven't forgotten her up in her sixteen-by-ten room. I've seen her the day after one of these monthly outings. She must have stayed up very late: her eyes have big blue circles under them. And she apparently did a lot of laughing, because her lips are split. That was the same day Madame Pierre congratulated her – the day when Aline broke the all-time record: twenty-seven tricks.

Gigi is better off than Aline, since her window overlooks Rue des Lombards, and thus has a view of the Bar des Roses, which is where she dines every evening under the attentive gaze of her husband's partner. All in the family, right? Lunch at Le Croissant d'Argent, dinner at the Roses – that's real poetry for you. One evening we went upstairs together with a late customer. On the way out, I invited her for an apéritif. She indignantly refused. There was nothing sacrilegious in my offer, but I didn't insist, and I amicably suggested strolling down the Boulevard Sébastopol, since we were both going in that direction. She grabbed my arm and, quickly glancing left and right as if she were afraid of being observed, said in an altered voice, 'You see, I live on the far side of the boulevard. I cross it every night when I leave here. Every night I turn here – it's the second street on the left. I've been going back to my hotel this way for the last eight years. If one day I decided to walk on the other side of the street, go right instead of left, or make a detour by way of Rue de La Reynie, he'd know about it. He knows everything.'

She left me standing on Rue Berger, and I anxiously watched her hurry off, her tight little steps leading her towards her imaginary home. Since that day, she's never spoken to me again about anything except work. She's a strange girl. Every Monday she disappears for two hours. Now where is it that Gigi has to go every Monday? She goes to the hospital – everyone in the hallway knows that but why? No one knows why. They say she's got TB, cancer, syphilis, and bats in the belfry. The diagnoses are highly varied. My own feeling is that she's in the hands of some sadist who's driving her insane.

Marie: Marie-Galante, or Black Marie, depending on the Curse's disposition. Marie: a living flower with eyes that shoot rainbows. Marie: an uprooted flower stuck in a greenhouse. In this nauseous warmth, behind this glass that the sun will never penetrate, your corolla has lost its vividness. You've wilted, poor Marie – and yet you and your gardener lived in the same village. But as you say, 'Down there where I come from, it's too small. There's no way to turn a trick. If I went back, my little angels would die, and I'd die too.' All that remains of 'down there' are a few photographs, which you show to your customers, sitting on the edge of the bed, Marie-Courage, Marie the Madwoman!

Christine doesn't share your devotion. When she first landed at number 45, she didn't hesitate to lighten her wings of her fledgling. She dropped him in the courtyard of a public orphanage. She had to choose: it was either her brat or her revered Corsican. Making this sacrifice didn't prevent you from losing out as his senior woman. You're in a bad way. For the rest of us, you'll always be the informer, the woman who spends her Sundays in the country eating out of the Curse's hand. Meanwhile, poor fool that you are, your Corsican is performing his pater-familias act with another girl.

As for you, Corinne the Brawler, always squaring your shoulders in your all-leather outfit, always ripe for a fight, always ready with a hand when it comes to whopping anybody's who's down, I know you fantasize about doing me permanent damage. My fantasy is to hear you tell all. I'd like to have you explain what kinds of shit you have inside your head that made you persuade your sister to take your husband as her pimp. Was it because he told you that you had to come up with seven hundred francs a day and you couldn't make it? Or was it, as I think, for sheer love of lucre? Tell me: have you ever asked yourself that?

And you, Delia: how did you persuade yourself to march under the Brawler's dubious banner? I can understand her guiding your steps through childhood, but not her guiding them through the hallway, as she's been doing for the past five years! ... You're a perverted little exhibitionist: between jobs you get your kicks by washing your dirty linen in public. You become somebody when your sister's mouth starts twisting and she shouts, 'I keep asking myself, what is it that you do to him, with all your phony ways! I've spent two Sundays now being fucked here while you're getting off with my husband – and in my own bed at that!' Tell me, Delia: when he leaves you there, one after the other, in the bed you both paid for, and you bite your lips and there's a taste of blood in your mouth – doesn't it ever occur to you that it's time to leave him?

Claudette, aka Cleavage, wears number seven in the Curse's stable. She'd seen a lot of country before she touched down on Rue Saint-Denis. Her tale is not without its comic aspects ...

One day Claudette meets Prosper on the beach at Sidi Boussaïd. She's found the love of her life. But Prosper, unfortunately, is soon obliged to go back to his business. Heavy at heart, Claudette begs him to write. Two months later, when she's abandoned all hope, a letter arrives from Paris. In the envelope is an airplane ticket. Claudette is overjoyed. She'll now be able to continue her university studies in Paris. Life in Sidi Boussaïd has become so dull ... Her parents are dismayed. She silences them by reminding them that in February she'll come of age.

In Paris, she has no time to marvel at the beauties of the capital or even catch a glimpse of the Sorbonne; Prosper is having problems with the police. He needs an immediate change of scene. Claudette starts seeing the world: two months of *la dolce vita* in Rome, followed by a three-week stay on the Costa Brava, which they are obliged to leave in a hurry – bad news from Paris. They then journey north, towards Germany. Their pockets are empty. Prosper is in a black mood. He hardly speaks during the trip, but he does say the indispensable minimum:

'You could go to work, Claudette. It's our only hope. Otherwise they'll nab me sooner or later, and the only place you'll ever get to see me is behind bars.'

Germany means Düsseldorf and its huge, dreary, regimented brothel. Girls from the four corners of the earth wander through its grey courtyard. They wear peppermint-pink negligees, or red merry-widow corsets, or black-panther tights. Some sheathe their legs in black, or in close-fitting leather. Some wear Chinese gowns slashed to the hip, or transparent saris, or pleated skirts and bobby socks, or ball gowns, or rubberized raincoats. In this courtyard, which soon becomes her entire world, Claudette cries softly as she remembers the blazing beaches of her native land. But whenever Prosper appears, sunshine floods the yard. What's the difference if he makes love like all the others, wasting no time, using the same bed? What difference does it make, since he loves her? Between kisses he easily manages to convince her that he had been incredibly victimized and that she is his one support. What Claudette doesn't know is that there are two other women supporting him. One is in Marseilles, the other at the Madeleine. And so this gentleman is able to go on enjoying himself, even now that he's on the run; that is, until the morning when the German police, booted and helmeted, handcuff him and take him off to the frontier.

The situation is serious. So what? Claudette is in love. She swears that she'll find a way out: and so, a week later, she finds a way in – into number 45. She owes her opportunity to the goodwill of his friends who, after her return from Germany, succeed in getting her past the hallway door.

For an entire year she keeps out of sight; but on the day of the trial she hurries off to the courtroom. Let his friends get angry if they want to – she needs to see him again. She needs that one little kiss that her lips can treasure until the hour of freedom is at hand. It's a kiss that's worth risking everything for. Imagine her surprise when, in the midst of the bustling corridors of the Palais of Justice, she finds her beloved Prosper with handcuffs on his wrists and two women clinging to his neck and lips.

It's a hard knock; but his friends were there to sustain her and guide her back to her post behind the display window.

Prosper was sentenced to six years; he still has two to serve. Of the three women, one is still waiting for him: Claudette. You're a small diligent ant, out of your mind with love. You go on saving every penny in order to buy that little French restaurant in Tunisia. Aren't you worried that some day Prosper, always something of a rover, will run away with the till?

Big Nicole, daughter of a concierge on Rue Sainte-Apolline, learned how to toddle by running errands for dressmakers. By the age of ten she had a precise notion of the value of money. The young seamstresses who sent her on errands would give her candy and even slip her some change. By the age of fourteen, she's started wearing their threads; and at seventeen, she slams the door and walks out of the concierge's ground-floor rooms: 'So long, old lady. I'd rather do the split than kill myself scrubbing the stairs.'

But she doesn't desert those rooms altogether. From the bar across the way, she watches for the moment when her mother goes upstairs to do her cleaning; then she dashes in with her first customer. What had to happen happens. Her mama catches her in bed with a man. Now her mother isn't the sort to let suffering bow her down. No, she's a woman, still young, who feels that life has given her a raw deal. She's a realist. If her big

294

girl now feels like giving her a hand, why, it's the least she can do. It's been a hard enough business raising her all alone.

Time was on her side. She succeeded in turning Nicole into a real kook, one so sick that she sleeps with her whip. When the vice bulls drop in, she hides it in her thigh boot and snickers. Nicole has the most formidable pimp of all, one that she'll never ditch: her mother.

There's also Kim: an old trouper who knows every port in the Mediterranean. She's dropped anchor in Genoa, Toulon, Golfe-Juan, and Naples. She finds life dull behind the display window at number 45, where the sea spray never fills the air. So she drinks: she drinks to forget the offshore breezes, the sailor hats, and Tony, her GI. She drinks in order to work up enough courage to toss the dog tag he left her to remember him by down the sewer. She drinks in order to forget that it's been five years since they last saw each other at Golfe, that she's married, and that her husband doesn't fuck her any more because he finds that she's turned sour.

One night Malou and I went out with her. From number 45 we weaved our way to number 194, where she introduced us to the girl friends she used to go out drinking with. We got higher than kites talking about the good times, the joints we used to dance in, and the sailors we never knew. And then I saw Kim take a poor old guy upstairs – he'd just flashed an empty wallet, and she'd said to him, 'The bills come and go. They're not the only thing in life.' Kim, remember it's never too late to catch that ship.

As for you, Brigitte – you with your jade eyes and opal cheeks – what the hell are you doing at number 45? I know, you don't have to stand around like the others and wait your turn in the doorway. Every morning the hunting horns sound for you. All your men are always there, slumped down behind their steering wheels, leaning tensely over their handlebars, or standing with their backs to a nearby wall, out of breath and biting their fingernails. Their alarm clocks ring half an hour early on your account. They want you fresh out of bed, all hot and muggy with sleep. At seven-thirty every morning, the hounds move in for the kill. They don't even leave you enough time to change.

So you stay on because you make a good living. Still, they've managed to snarl your nerves – during your year in the hallway, you've made three serious attempts at suicide. It would be a blunder on their part to treat you like Aline and Gigi. So how does your charmer manage things? It's simple : he buries his oversensitive breadwinner in presents. His bracelets mask the scars on her wrists. He knows what he's doing. He figures that in the long run a small diamond costs less than a stomach pump. And you – you soak your sparklers in soapy bidet water and say, 'Might as well wear them now. You never know. Tomorrow it may be too late.'

Back to your holes, girls. Fanny is starting to see black butterflies in front of her eyes. Fanny's in a bad way. She's sinking fast.

She gets drunk all the time. Her throat is full of gravel, and she never sings any more. She makes childish imitative sounds and little animal cries instead. She keeps raving, 'I don't want to end up in the infirmary, like the man in the blues!' Nevertheless, during her two months at number 45, she's built up a solid clientele. She couldn't care less. She hates herself. The eighteen pounds she's put on don't help matters.

The fatter she gets, the more she eats. In the morning she starts off by joining Kim and Malou for a croissant cum café-au-lait cum calvados. At ten it's a salami sandwich washed down with a Côtes du Rhône. At noon it's a four-course lunch, with her back to the street. At five it's a cream pastry she'd bought that morning. At dinner, which she has either alone at home or with Gerard in a restaurant, she eats and eats ... And at night, in her bed, as she tries to untangle the lines of print in the book she's reading, she's still eating, and getting the Camembert mixed up with the cake.

Her mirror is merciless. It reveals the image of a bloated body. The skin of her hips and thighs and even of her arms has taken on a resemblance to orange peel. She now wears a size 12 instead of size 10. In his amiable way, Gerard has suggested that she go on a diet of vegetable broth. The girls are having a field day. They call her the two-legged dumpling. Customers have begun asking for that 'chubby little girl'. *They* think she looks stupendous. They've even started pinching her behind.

The danger level has been reached. Tough luck for the men who so admire her ample charms – if it really bothers them, they can change fuckeries. Anyway, she's tired of being screwed dog-fashion three times out of five, on the pretext that she has such an inviting rump. So she decides to see a specialist, hoping that he'll help her get her teenage figure back.

Spring is here, and with it the start of my third month at number 45.

It hasn't been easy enticing France off the road to Dakar. I've had to turn somersaults, produce earnings reports, make phone call after phone call, and sweet-talk Gerard so that he'd intervene with Jean-Jean the Cobra. The latter had been firmly counting on this charter tour: Franzie, who makes it a point of honour to camouflage her setbacks, has confessed to me that Jean-Jean may in fact have wanted to get rid of her for reasons she doesn't know about.

'I think,' she tells me, 'that he's got the hots for the new barmaid he hired. I'm not positive about it yet, but I've caught them giving each other the eye. They're up to something behind my back. If that's true, Sophie, I swear I'll kill the two of them. I didn't screw away my youth to have some straight chick beat me out.'

I've learned to be mistrustful of girls who pour out their hearts on nights when they're feeling depressed. Usually their self-respect quickly reasserts itself. I have to keep myself from telling her, 'It *is* true. It's been five years now that he's given you the runaround; Franzie you should jump at the chance. Pack your bags. I'll always be around to give you a hand. I still love you the way I did at Saint-Lazare.'

France isn't the only one to enlist in the ranks of the 45ers. Lulu has said farewell to the Medina and to the love of her life: next month, Yves is marrying the woman who owns the ice-cream concession down at the port. Lulu has been left a psychological cripple. I swap my Sunday off for a Saturday, which I spend with her at the hairdresser Carita. We get three years taken off her age. We invent a story about her pimp being out of the country on the run. And Gerry acts as her sponsor. It's in the bag. As far as the Curse is concerned, Lulu still belongs to Yves-from-Toulon.

Yay! I've lost four and a half pounds in ten days and won myself two solid allies. But deep down inside my head, Malou's frail voice keeps chiming: 'You wait and see, Sophie. They'll end up making you do things their way. They don't see things the way we do. You'll find it getting harder and harder to break loose. We don't even speak to each other any more. We're turning into regular machines.'

Malou, I know all that only too well – but don't spoil my pleasure. As it is, it's only dangling by a thread. Perk up your ears and listen to the god of spring! Rub your eyes and watch him stretching and yawning! Don't be discouraged – we'll soon go moseying off on his arm.

Meanwhile, this evening I'm going to press my nose against the window of real life. Gerard has invited me out for dinner. It's a business occasion. This evening I'm to meet Evelyne, the wife of a friend of his. It'll be up to me to educate her, that is, to sing the praises of prostitution and all its advantages. It's an important task: after all, a man's future is at stake. So, Fanny, why aren't you smiling? It's only one day's turnover going up in smorgasbord. They're expecting me at the Cutlass, or the Cutlet, or something like that – at any rate, in the taxi that's taking me to this cutthroat place, I start dreaming of being elsewhere: of sitting down under the trees of La Constrescarpe among the ragpickers, blowing on their harmonicas, drinking vinegary wine until daybreak. But duty calls. It's a good thing Igor will be there tonight. Igor's the brains of the little group. Igor's no pimp: he's a fox. It doesn't take a split-second glance for either of us to understand the other. Still, before I go into that restaurant, I'm treating myself to a half-bottle of white wine – just to clear my throat, of course.

I approach the jubilant gathering in a belligerent frame of mind. It's just crazy how much everyone's enjoying himself tonight. Gerard's sense of humour is certainly irresistible. And then there's that other rube, who's pretending to understand, not to mention the aspirant pimp, who keeps nodding his head and stuffing himself with *crêpes au fromage*. And I have to get up at six-thirty tomorrow morning!

All this just to bring one poor broad up to date. Some day sooner or later she's going to find herself right back where she started, minus her youth and her illusions, and without a sou. No – I haven't the right. No way. I'm as screwed up as she is.

Those others are the sharpies, with their same old script, their same old stories, their same old words. All the dream busters have to do is walk by, and girls fall down in a faint. Jesus Christ! There must be a breed of women that can stand up to them. These guys never try any new gimmicks on us. Most of the time they hardly bother to fuck us. Evelyne is twenty-one, beautiful, a teacher in a commercial school, living with her family in Argenteuil: why is she taking the bait?

Well, do *you* know why? Okay, you're beginning to see things more clearly; but don't forget that three years ago, when you decided to give it a try one night on Rue Godot-de-Mauroy, nobody was forcing you. You weren't exactly unwilling. You knew what you were running away from when you turned to hooking. What you didn't know, on the other hand, was what you'd find. It's the same thing for her. And as long as there are pimps and credulous girls who haven't made up their minds, there'll be hookers. Don't try to figure it all out: you can't do anything for her except drag her into the spider's web you're stuck in yourself. Unless, of course, you have the nerve to get out of line and risk a drubbing in public?

'Evelyne, you'll see. Les Halles are out of this world. Even a girl who's just starting out gets to knock off fifteen guys a day on the average – and I'm not counting blow-jobs!'

My! What's happening? You're not chuckling any more? You've lost your appetites? Something wrong? Come on now, smile. I enjoy telling funny stories at the end of a meal.

'You're lucky I'm with friends. Otherwise I'd be kicking your ass right out of here.'

'Listen, windbag, don't work up a sweat, you're not used to it. I can find the door by myself.'

Tonight's your last night, Evelyne. Tomorrow we'll be together in the display window at number 45. You'll be another woman, and I'll be the only one who'll know who you are. How strange!

Evelyne and I don't have much time for talking. We're upstairs all morning long. When I pass her on the stairway, I flash her a little signal with my hand, but she doesn't even notice it.

We meet again at lunch: two strangers sitting across from one another.

'You're not eating?'

299

'I'm not hungry. I'd like to talk to you alone.'

I lead her off to the ladies' room of Le Croissant d'Argent. I lock the door and listen.

'The last customer I took up was funny. He asked me if I was a beginner. He told me he had desert fever – his dream was to go off into the Sahara as a driller. He likes drilling holes wherever he can. He shoved it in the back way. I hurt!'

Instead of trying to show understanding, or reassuring you, or squeezing the hand you hold out to me, why is it that I grab you by the shoulders and start knocking your head against the shithouse door like a madwoman? Why, instead of speaking to you gently, am I screaming, 'Professional standards are going to pot. When I started out, I learned that my mouth and my asshole were about the only two things we could keep intact. You *never* use them, not at any price, get it? The next time a guy asks you if you're starting out, or if he wants to fuck you up the ass or preach to you, tell him not to overtax his brain: you're incurable. You just like being fucked. Right?'

Forgive me, Evelyne. I would have liked to say all this to you some other way; but they've managed to snarl my nerves, too.

Getting from Le Croissant d'Argent to the hotel is a real scrimmage. Evelyne's having trouble elbowing her way to the door, so I take her by the hand.

It's drizzling. What a foul day!

'Get a move on, Fanny. The guy with the beret is putting down roots in number seven.'

Okay, Witch, keep your shirt on, I'm on my way up.

That Albert is something. I'd forgotten today was his day. Can't say I'm jumping for joy at the thought of jumping into his potato sack and pinning on my Star of David. The hallway, the concentration camps ... you've got to have a strong stomach. Once a week I knock on the door of number 7, raise my right arm, and shout, 'Heil, Albert!' Once a week for two months now I'm fifteen years old and Jewish, and I lie face down and kiss your boots and the hem of your raincoat. With your whip you lift up my tatters, spread your legs, and pull the beret out of your fly. You use the beret to masturbate and to douse my face with an imaginary poison that I'm supposed to lick up. Once a week, I become your mistress in order to save my family from the gas chambers.

I listen to the sounds in the hotel. In number 6, my sister is moaning in tune with the bedsprings. The Bawler is shouting commands in number 3. Somewhere, Nicole is cracking her big whip. And look, there's Malou on her way up with her Thursday Ancient Mariner. It seems that at seventy-two he's still going strong. I knock on the door of number 7 and obediently go through my act.

You're one of my regular neurotics, Albert, one of my devoted chumps. You hump my head instead of my snatch. What are you like after you've left this place? Everybody, Mr Lonelyhearts? Whatever prompts you to act out your fantasies in this sordid hotel? With the money you shell out for me you could treat yourself to a high-class hooker in gilded digs. No, what you need, and what you want, is to go slumming. You pretend to be high and mighty, but you have a secret liking for what's morbid. It's nice knowing you have a girl at your disposal who's knocked off a dozen customers before she got to you and is going to knock off another dozen after you've left. You're no longer Mr Everybody: you're starting to compete. You vie with hundreds of thousands of other men. Poor Albert – if only you had a nice restorative orgasm from time to time!

I don't want to go back to the hallway straight off. So I sit down on the edge of the bed. I smoke a cigarette, try not to think too much, and turn my back to the mirror. It seems to be staring at me. Why are you looking at me like that? Who are you? Sophie? Fanny? That other one? I don't know you. You seem like a stranger to me. I feel like slapping your face, slapping it hard, like that! And that, and that, and that! Just the way I used to bang my head against the kitchen wall when I was little ...

I say a prayer for what I am – a snake that's keeping its head out of life's dirty water. I pray that it will grow silly little legs on its belly so that it can crawl on to the bank and roll around on the hot stone. I pray that it will turn into a great, glittering, green, muscular crocodile, one equipped with a huge mouth arrayed with golden teeth that can grind up unhappiness.

Come on, Fanny, get back to your shift. Listen – the lumberjack of my beloved boss-lady is caressing my eardrums. For whom can these tender words be meant? Let's keep our ears open and take our precautions going downstairs. There's no big rush.

It's raining torrents in the hallway. Winter has never seemed so long.

You should never give up hope. The twenty-first of March finally arrived – accompanied by the Vice Squad. The gentlemen came charging down the hallway at eight in the morning with Easter daisies in their lapels. The bitter taste left by coffee and a first cigarette still clung to my throat, and my eyes were still dreaming of sleep, when I found myself riveted to the wooden bench of a paddy wagon, between Evelyne and Brigitte.

Just like the first time, I look out at the wet street through the window gratings; just like the first time, I start dreaming of the sea. Meanwhile Evelyne's head is bouncing against my shoulder, and Brigitte is slipping a piece of cardboard underneath my skirt. Her hand pushes hard against my thigh, and I feel the round staples of her ID card pressing into my flesh. She whispers, 'I'll be eighteen in August ...' I start humming, 'It's the married man's month, it's the husband's salvation, with the kids and the missus away on vacation ...'

On our way into number 36, I slip the incriminating little card into my panties. Standing in front of the monkey cages, I briefly think of Ducretin. And in the office I come across my old friend Sophie ... How her hair has grown in three years! I wonder what she did with that striped sweater I liked so much?

It's crazy. The time has gone by like greased lightning. Franzie is still the same; but now there are Malou, Lulu, Evelyne, and the others. The others aren't knitting. They aren't doing anything – they're already dead!

After a routine interrogation, we're shipped to Saint-Lazare. I don't do my big number. My hand doesn't shake as I give the welfare woman the results of my VD checkup, and I follow the herd towards the dining room, where we'll wait for night to fall. Malou, France, Lulu, and I play cards while we wait; and Evelyne – but the Curse has rechristened her Ingrid – Ingrid, the girl from the fjords, tremblingly wipes her glasses on the hem of her dress. In this vast, unbearably dismal room, nothing has changed. The walls are the same hue; the benches are as hard as ever; and high above us, the loudspeakers can hardly wait to start their shrieking.

Suddenly, the claws of the striped tomcat – the one I'd forgotten, the one I thought I'd tamed – sink into my shoulders. Saint-Lazare is always a nightmare. Tomorrow I'll emerge from it whipped, drained, and covered with pimples. How I dread going to the dormitory, where I'll find the familiar pissy straw mattresses, the soiled sheets, the strong smell from the toilets, the clattering faucets, the cubicles covered with graffiti (including my old *nom de guerre* where Pat once scrawled it with her eyebrow pencil!). Seven o'clock is too early to go to bed, much too early. It's going to be an endless night for me, forever interrupted by the hysteria of women left to stew together. I don't feel like crying or screaming. I'm neither hungry nor thirsty. I don't feel like talking or playing cards. I don't really even feel like throwing up. Not mad about life, not completely sure of wanting to die, with absolutely no desire for sleep, what I *would* like to do is throw open the shutters and see what the weather is like in the courtyard below. I'd like to make sure spring hasn't passed me by. But there aren't any windows in the dormitory – either they're inaccessible or I've never noticed them. I wrap my raincoat around the bolster, and, with a cigarette in either hand, I attune my thoughts to the ten days that preceded the arrival of spring.

In the accommodating twilight of the Roll's Club, my dear sister succumbed to Igor on their very first date. When the fatal slow number had them dancing cheek to cheek, I tiptoed up behind them and heard them murmur, 'My bronze-eyed baby ...' 'My blue-eyed cat ...' 'This time it's for real, we're setting up house together.' – No, it's not nice to laugh, since Igor is already out apartment-hunting. Of course Lulu will pay the rent, but he says he can get the furniture wholesale.

As for Gerry, why, he's found the co-op apartment of his dreams. Yes, we're moving to another part of town – except I am not as carried away as Lulu is. I've waited too long; and I know for sure that in future years my windows will not overlook that park at Buttes Chaumont. I couldn't bear the idea.

Gerry's in a very good mood. The notion of owning real estate has sent the blood rushing to his head. In three years he sees himself with a house in Deauville; in five he'll be John D.

Rockefeller. Gerard doesn't know what the word 'unpretentious' means; he's ordered a Shelby, because he wants to be the first man in Paris to be seen driving one. Go right ahead, Gerry. Stick out your chest and plan for the millennium. You have no idea how well it suits me to have your name and not mine spread out in capital letters on the deed. I may be nuts, but I'm not nuts enough to sign on for another five years. I know I've got a strong back – no false modesty about me – but to have to carry five years of instalments as well as a hood there's no way of ditching when hard times come, that's not for little Sophie.

No, Monsieur Gerard, the season for posies is over. How happy I'd be if the one I gave you today, when I made the down payment on your new place, were part of my farewell bouquet. Each new day whispers that we're not going to grow old together; and you're going to need either guts or genius to finish paying those instalments, unless you start making a brilliant go of your career as a pimp. As for me, who knows? I may never own a house. But so what, as long as I can spend my life striding through the gardens of the world on some Gypsy's arm. Each night, when we pitch our temporary camp, my eyes full of moonlight, I'll at last be able to shout out, 'I'm free, I'm free, I'm free!'

I mustn't forget Paul. Paul has said *au revoir* to the coconut palms. Paul has moved in with his sister in Ville-d'Avray for six months. Paul wants to take advantage of his time in France to educate me. He wants to teach me how to eat properly with a knife and fork and find me an honest job. Naturally he'll slip me a little change: five hundred francs. A *month*. When he gives me three hundred to spend just one hour with him! He doesn't figure right. Well, I have one consolation: when we settle down on the Ivory Coast, I'll be allowed to start eating with my fingers again.

Dear old Popol! How, without tearing your heart to shreds, will I ever make you understand that behind the woman you've chosen for your wife looms the hawklike silhouette of a pimp? A pimp who is not at all inclined to abandon his prey. Even if we actually worked out a friendly arrangement, and you were prepared to shell out the price, whatever it was, I couldn't bear having to meet Gerry face to face. That's one confrontation I don't think I stand to gain by. Then what about running away?

Run away with you to Africa the way I could have with Jimmu to Japan? No. It would only be self-betrayal of a different sort. If I get out of this, I don't want to have anyone to thank but myself. The time for haggling and making dubious deals is over. *Alone!*

I mustn't forget my old man, either. He's returned to the fold still carrying his sack of troubles on his shoulders, still everlastingly on the run. Say, Pops, couldn't you just settle for a game of pinochle with me? Or you could teach me chess or tarots. Why do you have to start talking about the old days every night? And why is it that when I press my fingers to your lips to make you shut up, everything comes bobbing to the surface – your cap, suspenders, workbag, overalls; and you yourself, every inch of you, bending over me, your features drawn, wiggling your fingers under my nose and asking me to sniff them. And those feathers! All the feathers that keep whirling through the bedroom – a swarm of white sparrows just out of their nest, frail, warm, and mute, fluttering about my face, settling on my tears. I'd freed them with my very own teeth, biting into the bolster so as not to wake the kids. It was hard for me to realize that I'd slept so many hours, so many nights with my cheek resting on a nest.

Don't ever talk to me about birds, Papa. Don't ever talk to me about that night when everything went up in smoke. The wallpaper came unstuck from the walls, the walls made the most of the opportunity and ran off with the ice box, and so did the door and the door key, the casement windows, the bits and pieces – all those bits and pieces . . . You should forget about that night, and about the nights that came after it, and about that other night when you found me leaning over the footbridge, listening to the singing of the trains. It was a grinding, metallic singing, the drunken song that brings wedding suppers to a close . . .

Papa, don't ever talk to me about trains.

We're already well into the night. Calm has followed the usual tumult of the big shipments. Sighs, groans, and squeaks emerge from the cubicles. I get out of bed on tiptoe and rummage through Evelyne's handbag, looking for cigarettes. She sits up and looks at me wildly. I put my hand on her forehead: it's dripping with cold sweat.

'Oh, Fanny, Fanny – I was having this nightmare . . .'

She sits on the edge of the bed and vomits a copious quantity of bile. Around us the others moan and pull their blankets over their heads. The night's going to be a long one. It's spreading in every direction. Somewhere to my left or right, two girls are loving one another in the shelter of a cubicle. I stroke the frame of my bed until daybreak.

On my way back to the grind, I stop at the drugstore and buy a toothbrush and a tube of toothpaste.

Dressed like the Queen of Sheba, with her wig on askew, the Curse is standing halfway down the stairs, sharpening her skewers before she gives her fillies a speech. Go on, you harpy, let's have the poop. My glims are aching for beddie-bye.

'Things have got tight, ladies. So, starting today, Lulu, Kim, Cleavage, and all the others who don't regularly pull down their fifteen jobs are going to join the night gang. Quite a few of the night girls are eager to be on the day shift. As for the rest of you, I want you to listen. I'm not going to say this twice – but you can count on finding my fist in your face if you don't get it right. This is the way you line up: three in the back of the room – that means the *back*; two in front, at the bar, with your glasses filled from dawn till dusk; and the rest in the hall-way. Each of you rotates every ten minutes – back of the room, bar, hallway. Got it? One other thing, ladies. The first one who lays a hand on a customer, either here or in the street, is going to have to deal with me personally. Now, ladies, get to work. We're running way behind schedule.'

I brush my teeth as soon as I get my first job.

If other days at number 45 have seemed long, 22 March is endless.

chapter three

It will have been fifty years ago this noon that my grand-mother's labour pains began, that my father appeared on the scene, and that I started, as it were, paddling around in his balls. My unknown grandmother was an easygoing, absent-minded woman: on leaving Port-Royal Hospital, she forgot the baby on a windowsill between two pots of geraniums. This didn't stop my father from meeting my mother, or my mother from meeting Paul, or me from meeting Gerry.

You old scoundrel, you've left us down and dirty often enough. But I somehow feel the time has come to wipe the slate clean, and since up to now life hasn't made things easy for you, tonight I'm putting on a party in your honour. It'll be something to make your eyes bulge. I've rented a private dining room, and I've ordered snappers, streamers, flares, marinated herring, pointed hats, and paper flowers. You can dance with Malou and Evelyne. You can waltz with your daughters. Thanks to you, you old good-for-nothing, I'm not performing today. So long, all you greedy guys, on this eighth of April you won't see Fanny strutting her stuff at number 45. But this is no time for long speeches – time is short, Pops, and I first have to meet your son-in-law at his tailor's. This evening, in honour of the occasion, Gerard will be wearing a beautiful suit adorned with vertical, horizontal, and diagonal stripes: a real lounge lizard's outfit of the look-at-me variety. (And if you don't look at me now, I may be gone tomorrow!)

Yvan is a tailor and cutter by trade: that explains why he always has a pair of scissors in his hand. It doesn't explain his smile, however, which is less a smile than a birthmark. His wife is a rabbity mother and maid by trade. That explains why she's big as a tent, but it doesn't explain why she starts sulking when I refuse a Turkish delight. Their eight offspring are pretty children, but that doesn't explain why they latch onto my handbag like hooligans. The alarm clock may be a little off, but that does not explain Gerard's lateness. And I, who have come here to meet my husband, sit now with my rear end perched on a stool that's as sharp as a coral reef and with my eyes slipping down into the circles that number 45 has gouged beneath them; I am watching the holy family of Turkish Delight & Co tossing alpaca cuttings at one another's heads as they whirl about like dervishes.

At the centre of this dormitory, this one-room workshop, this one-room funnel, this low-ceilinged school yard where as they chirp the little brats get tangled up in lengths of grey cloth, Yvan's needle races ahead, pricking the circles under my eyes and riddling my extremities with its crafty little twists. The scissor blades are slicing up my nerves. The hands of the alarm clock are as soft and sugary as the Turkish delights. White, soft, and sweet. I eat the clock; it sticks in my teeth. I watch the alpaca dust fly; my eyes are filled with it. I drink Turkish coffee and pass my tongue over my lips. The grounds have a bitter savour, like that of a broken appointment, or a forgotten birthday.

Papa, maybe it's only a curious coincidence, but two hours ago I thought I saw Gerard's car parked outside La Ferme d'Issy. Papushka, there's something going on that I don't understand. It's not him I'm worried about, it's you. You may keep putting pointed hats on your heads and peeking through onion rings, the herring can go on marinating in the thyme and streamers: if I'm not there, there isn't going to be any party. Papa, tell me why I'm waiting for him. Tell me why this has been going on now for three years. And tell me also why you've never even lifted a finger to help me. I don't want to get angry on your birthday; I want you to be happy, even if I'm a bit late; but I also want to be sure that, if the going gets rough, you'll be there.

Mrs Rabbit-Maid, give me a glass of water. I can't get the alarm clock to go down, and my windpipe's sore. Any number of tiny screws are crunching between my teeth. Gear wheels are scraping my uvula. And then there's this three-pronged driver that's tearing the roof off my mouth. Yes, I know, I'm getting what I deserve. That'll teach me not to try and devour time.

A man is knocking on the glass-paned door of the one-room funnel. His hand is black as pitch, as black as coffee grounds, as black as the night that's quietly falling over the rooftops of Issy. This rabbit-maid opens the curtain. The hasp grates. Yvan puts down his scissors. The brats suck on a length of hemming ribbon. The long needle pierces my tongue.

'Madame Gerard, there are two gentlemen outside who want to talk to you.'

Judging by your faces, gentlemen, I'd say that you're very doubtful types. I'd say you belonged to a clan of hardfisted dealers. But I'm no longer for sale. I've already been sold on the Baghdad market; at Nogent-le-Rotrou the audience saw me drawn and quartered; and I was swapped for a canopy bed at the Chatou fair. I've been the mistress of Kemal Atatürk, the Emperor of China, and the stock supervisor at the Renault factory. There's nothing left to be squeezed out of me; I am –

one might say – empty. So let's hear the pitch. I never was good at word games. Oh, I see. You're *real* hoods. It really takes something to make you open up. But before I climb into your oarless boat, I'd like you to know that somewhere, in the back room of a restaurant, my Papa and my friends are starting to get sore.

And what about you, Gerryfish – what new sort of poisoned gift is this you're making me? What sticky business are you up to your neck in? Why have you put me into the hands of these two hoodlums? They won't let me say a word, and they're taking me away in their upholstered car to somewhere on the far side of my birthday party.

The automobile's fast, Papa darling, but don't worry, I'm not scared. I'm hardly even surprised. This is going to be my night. It's as bright as the winter night when you conceived me, and as clear as the mistake you then made. Goodbye, Pops. We're on the throughway, and they're gagging me and blind-folding my eyes and my heart. There's no doubt about it now: my guy's been taken for a ride. Underneath the blindfold and my crimped eyelids, I'm hallucinating. I see sunbeams falling vertically on dried-out embankments. I see Yvan's birthmark expand into a mouthful of laughing teeth. I see Gerry nailed stark naked to the execution post. I see the alarm clock's Roman numerals, bell, and winder as they slide down my lap. I see those brats with black moustaches stretching halfway across their cheeks. I see big scissors being used to sever time and cut people's lives short. I don't see anything else. The blindfold has wiped it all out.

If I no longer see, I can now hear, and much better:

'It's exactly eight p.m. here on Radio Vive la France. During the past twenty-four hours, there have been several hundred deaths between Blida and the southern outskirts of Paris. At Tlemcen, we advise you to follow the detour signs – traffic has been backing up at Sidi-bel-Abbès ever since a truckload of oranges let its nerves get the better of it. We also suggest you avoid the northern Paris area – there's a butcher's demo march-ing from Porte de la Villette towards Porte de la Chapelle. Well, here's the whole night gang of chimney sweeps wishing you a pleasant evening with Vive la France, and may we re-mind you that if you need a taxi, you can call 2–2–2 2–2 2–2 at any time of the night.'

This is it, Pops. Our junket's coming to an end. It smells like buds, cowpats, and duck shit. Two steely hands have lifted me up, and I'm pedalling through the dew. My feet are cold, my heart is cold – but don't get upset. If Gerry's been cut up into little pieces, it won't be a black ribbon I'll be wearing on my blouse but a bouquet of red carnations – and have a Happy Birthday!

'We've come with the goods.'

'Pull up a chair for her to rest her butt on.'

Papa, my teeth are chattering. I'm cold, I'm scared of the dark, Papa, there are voices moving all around me, and the sound of footsteps coming up from the cellar. My fingers have cobwebs growing between them, and I've peed in my pants. Papa, I'm scared. I'm scared of the hands that are fiddling at the back of my head and can't get the knot untied. Papa, I wish I were blind and didn't have to see their faces.

... Guy?

'Yes, it's Guy. Guy the Cripple. And to think that I watched you grow up! Your father used to say you had brains. You got your training in the old school – so whatever made you get stuck with a bastard like Gerard, when there are so many nice guys around who need to eat? Say, hooking seems to have done you good. You've turned into a looker. Not saying anything? Don't want to know what's happened to your guy? Maybe we wasted him? Stop sniffling, and stay cool. We're going to let you do a little thinking. Later, we'll have a chat. You'll want to have a clear head for that. Yako, tie her up until it's time to get down to business.'

Franzie, light me a weed, and pass a dustcloth over the furniture. Malou, throw out these rotting flowers and go buy some fresh ones. Lulu, open the windows so we can catch a breath of air. My God, it's been at least a century since a woman set foot in this dump. Papa, pour me a drink, and untie me – please untie me!

It's strange. Guy and Gerard were buddies. They used to play cards at Mado's together. That was when he was with his wife ... She was gentle, Helene, and he was a truly handsome young man. All the girls at the factory were after him. That was before his accident. Before he'd been nailed to his wheelchair. Before Helene took off. It's true I was just a kid and understood only half of what my father said. It wasn't until I opened the paper one day to the local news that I found out that Guy'd sent Sweet-Fingers Harry on his way to hell with a bullet in the gut. We never saw him at Mado's any more; but I knew where he was holed up. He was holed up in an inn on the Marne, and on certain Sundays my old man used to take me out to watch him play boccie. Let me have a cigarette, Papa. You've got to admit I don't forget things easily. Didn't you once describe him as the brains of a gang of awe-inspiring criminals? Lulu is my witness – as recently as yesterday you were telling us about him, and there was a mixture of admiration and nostalgia in your voice. You told me that he belonged to a vanishing breed of men. You said the new generation was barely capable of ripping off hookers' savings – when the broads were dumb enough to entrust their bread to these baby-balled bums. You should be pleased, Papa. Guy won't disappoint you. He'll follow the grand old tradition. The only thing is, tonight it's at the expense of your own kid.

According to the big broken-down alarm clock, it's one-thirty in the morning. The whole world's asleep and breathing its putrid breath in my face. I should be out there fighting ... but they swore that if I talked I'd get a stray bullet right between the eyes ... Oh, Father, I wish you weren't there, waiting for me, in your undershirt and with all that hair showing under your arms. As soon as you'd banged mother once you should have bitten off your balls. You should have backstitched her vulva with baling wire and a shoemaker's awl. But you were all for family life. Well, cheer up, you're about to become a grandfather again, with another little tike for a grandson whom I won't be breast-feeding ... Father, if you'd seen them all devouring me, this way and that ... If you'd seen your son-in-law's head, stiff as a stick crowned with barbed wire – he was weeping and asking for forgiveness. But everything was so mixed up, I didn't know whether he was talking to me or to the hoods.

And then at one point you spoke, and they all repeated in chorus, 'She's fresh meat, fresh meat ...' And everything in the closets of my memory came tumbling down. I was in ninth grade. Girls were then plucking their eyebrows, bleaching their hair with great dollops of hydrogen peroxide, wearing stockings with embroidery up the side and shoes with 'flowerpot heels'. I used to imitate them. I added a teaspoon of ammonia to the hydrogen peroxide. I stole a few flowers from Lulu to adorn my heels. For stockings I made do by daubing my legs with chicory extract. I looked too much like a woman for you to go on being satisfied with spilling your seed on the black-and-white, diamond-shaped kitchen tiles. You wanted me. The heady smell of chicory pursued you all the way to the factory. And so you started thumbing your nose at the time clock, and nothing else distracted you anymore – not even pinochle or boccie. You'd finally discovered a reason for coming back home: Marie's belly, Marie's thighs, Marie's slit! I belonged to you: it was thanks to you that I'd come sitting up and astonished into this world. And if you wanted me so much, it was because you could plainly see that I was capable of standing on my own, painted legs. You now sensed by the way I was holding my thighs together that I was on the point of giving myself to another man. This thought drove you wild. It turned you on to an extent you'd never dreamed possible.

You decided to subdue this proud, restive girl by making extensive use of your cock, by driving your fatherhood into her up to the hilt, by generously irrigating the channels of her brain, filling up the empty spaces, stuffing her belly and her head once and for all: then, later on, whenever she leaned her head on someone else's shoulder, the scar you'd inflicted between her thighs would ooze copiously and remind her of you.

'Marie, Marie – answer me! Oh, my poor baby, who upset you like this? Come and lay you head on your old man's shoulder.' No, Daddy, I'm not laying my head anyplace, ever. Each time I laid it down you took the opportunity to rummage around inside it. You stole it away from me. Oh, Papa, Papa, it would have been so much better if the first time I had taken off, head first, on my little girl's inky fingers.

So in forty-eight hours I'm supposed to come up with twenty thou! You don't find twenty thousand growing on trees. And yet, twenty thousand – Gerry's life isn't worth much really.

Why the hell did he have to go screw the wife of a guy in jail? Maybe Gerry's basically right. Maybe I was the one who corrupted him and made a chump out of him. It's thanks to my jack that he began hobnobbing with the upper crust and pro-pelled himself, through the deployment of hundred-franc bills and snakeskin shoes, into the bars around the Etoile and Montmartre. Previously he'd never dragged his ass any farther than Montparnasse – he was just a simp from the edge of town, a sociable drinker, a joker who'd been satisfied with his old wife's meagre earnings.

Gerry, all of a sudden you found yourself stuck with a winner. I was your evil genius. But if you get out of this, and if you decide to settle your accounts once and for all and make them pay in blood for the humiliation I've just undergone, I'll see to it you get the right gun for the job. It'll be a Luger equipped with padded stock and silencer. You can then perform your first gallant gesture in three years: a precise, quick gesture that will send the lot of them on their way to paradise. I'm sure the judge will show clemency. 'Victim of a grasping woman!' is what the defence attorney will shout. And the grocer and the hardware dealer will conclude: 'Victim of a woman of low repute.' A woman who wasn't a woman; a woman who at the age of twenty was always dreaming of distant lands ...

And now, Gerard, this adventuress, your very own woman, is getting the word out. She's summoned Marc and Igor, your friends of the moment, as well as Didier, your childhood friend, to make sure that everything is done properly and that there are no slipups. Gerard, you've just knocked a healthy slice off your lease on me. My cup runneth over – you've filled it with a liquid that tastes like holy water, neither salt nor sweet, just insipid. But in spite of everything, I'm plunging my lips into it with delectation: once it's empty, with a little luck, I'll be setting off on the journey that will lead me to myself ...

So, here I am, facing the gathering of the elders. My elbows are sinking into the table. My lips are split open. These old friends of yours don't seem exactly scintillating this early in the morning. Their eyes are puffy with sleep. They're keeping one hand on their wallets and starting to invent financial problems. Come off it! Your faces give you away. You're no different from other men, no different at all. Igor looks like an easygoing garment merchant, Marc like a PE instructor, Didier like a barman who's come up in the world, my father like a simpatico café owner, and you, my very own Lulu, like a gutsy but broken woman. An ordinary bunch, when you look them over, and a terribly sleepy one. I've lost my own way to the Land of Nod. Life for me has boiled down to a mustang race, and I'm ready to mount any horse in the world bareback ... Meanwhile, I listen uncomprehendingly to my dad giving his version of the facts. I'm fidgeting my feet under the table. I'm fiddling with my good-luck charm, with Gerry's life, with the cloth bullet and the lead bullet, with the twenty thousand francs I have to deliver to Guy within forty-eight hours. Time is short, so let's knock off the palaver. At 8.00 p.m. Sunday I have an appointment at Les Sports at Porte d'Orléans. It's no joke: I need that money. So talk. Say something. Say anything. After all, you've eaten at his table, drunk from the same glass, laughed with him, shared the same hopes. Just give me some sort of sign. I don't want to have to knock myself out for hoods. I don't want to work for anyone any more.

I've never asked Paul why he wears a crew cut, or why at the age of forty-eight he hasn't yet married. I've never talked to him about money, or hardly. I've barely spoken to him about myself. What *do* we usually talk about? Well, anyway not about his girl friends in Africa! A bit about his work, a bit about what we find in our plates when we're dining together, a bit about how Rue Sainte-Opportune got its name – and lots about nothing at all.

The time for polite chitchat is over. The moment has come to put the cart before the horse, take hold of the poles, release the brake, and, last but not least, shove Paul under the wheels. How about taking off my sunglasses very quickly, coolly looking him in the eye, and saying, 'I need twenty thousand right now'?

It's impossible. The words won't come out. We've already been circling the same bed of tulips for the last half-hour. For half an hour my heart has been as heavy as lead while his sparkling eyes have never left me. For half an hour he's been saying over and over, cracking the joints of his fingers:

'Well, what is it, Sophie darling? Since you came all the way out here on Sunday, it must mean you've thought things over. I'm in no hurry, you know. We can get married anytime you like.'

I can hear his heart beating beneath his Sunday shirt. I look at the tulips that rise firm and indifferent under a sky so blue it makes you want to shout.

'Paul, I need twenty thousand francs. I need them today.'

I turn and see a little, dismal-looking man sitting on the grass of the Ville-d'Avray park. He's gulping down hemlock and arsenic.

'Sophie, I haven't got the money.'

'Then forget about it.'

Now's the time to start running – knees high, elbows back. Just keep running till you're out of breath and, whatever happens, never see him again. But the sap that's rising in the trees has turned the pathways into swamps, and I'm knee-deep in hard luck.

Paul's hand lifts up my chin, slides over my cheek, goes limp against my neck. He's given in. I pluck off my glasses. The sky is as blue as Italian stained glass.

'Oh, Paul, you're so good. You never ask questions. We'll get married in June.'

'Hello, Daniel? Don't hang up. Meet me at two at the Deauville. You remember, the place where we went for drinks before going on to Rue Balzac? And bring your chequebook. It's a matter of life and death.'

I don't give him time to answer. I just hang up on him. In a moment of tenderness he had given me his phone number the way you give someone a rose. Poor old guy. You're going to have to turn somersaults to get away from that shrew of yours on a Sunday afternoon.

With you, there'll be no point in playing the big scene from Act Two. You're not in love with me. Something different is required. Stay cool, Fanny. This is no time to put your feelings through the tenderizer – it's half past one, and you're still short ten thou. Waiter, bring me a calvados, with a board from the Deauville boardwalk on the side ... Deauville, I can see you now: your Promenade des Anglais strewn with dog droppings, your grey roofs, your grey sea, your grey sky, and the milky beaches where I'd like to go to sleep and wake up dead, with a wave between my teeth, screaming, 'There's a woman drowning, a woman drowning!'

At the bar, a man is mopping his brow with his bandana. I didn't see him come in, and I didn't recognize him right away; but it's Daniel. It's my very own ten thou – and it's grown a beard. Please, let me relax. Let me unravel my nerves, brighten up my cheeks, finish my drink. Give me time to get used to the fact and realize what an incredible deal I'm pulling off. But you're trembling. You're hanging on to the counter as though it were your window at the post office. Don't worry. I'll still massage you with talcum powder and sing you tunes from operas. If it's what you want, I'll be the last bit of sunshine in your life. Yes, you'll still be able to bite into my pillows. And you're someone I'll pay back down to the last centime. Now come on, come over here ...

'Sophie, what's this about a matter of life and death?'

'I need ten thousand, right now.'

I look up and see a stricken man who's choking on his drink and letting his hands flop down on the table top. Ten thousand – it's ridiculous. How many hours would it take him to earn that by dying of boredom behind his window? How many letters to weigh and stamps to stick on? How many bags of cement for the cottage he's been dreaming of building in Daumartin, north of Paris?

My mailman is now crying buckets and dabbing his eyes with his carpenter's handkerchief; and all the shit-heads in the joint are looking at us threateningly.

'Please, please, you're causing a scandal!'

'How can you talk about scandal? *You're* the scandal, my girl. You're the scandal!'

Daniel has stopped crying. He orders his third brandy. I've just destroyed something. I'm left with the impression of a prodigious mess. But a scandal has no right to feel offended or upset. A scandal is supposed to remain scandalous to the very end, so I take careful aim and let fly:

'You seem to be forgetting that I have your telephone number.'

Go on, Daniel – sign the cheque. I'll massage you till the end of your days. My caresses will fill this gaping hole and cover this prodigious mess. I'll keep it up till it's you who are sick of having me around. But sign. You've got to sign ...

'Sophie, do you believe in God?'

'It depends on the day of the week.'

'Believe in God, and pray that there'll always be suckers like me around ...'

As I climb the stairs to Malou's place, a forgotten smell fills my nostrils. And yet this isn't the first time I've been to Malou's.

Where before have I smelled this mixture of cat pee, wasted time, garbage, and leaking gas?

'I've got it: it's the smell of Villa Paulette, where we used to sleep head-to-tail with one another, bunched together like sardines in a can. It's my grandmother's smell. She died in my arms while I was sleeping my grown-up-child's sleep. One should never imagine that poverty is always violent. It can be calm and tranquil, too, and noiselessly take refuge in children's hearts.

Someday, Malou, either I'll have to leave you, or you'll have to move; but when you're settled at last in a lovely house covered with slaked whitewash and chalk dust, and you've got a lyre-back chair to rest your butt in while you smoke your English cigarettes, don't forget to leave the key under the mat the way you did today.

'Sophie! I was just thinking about you. You couldn't have come at a better time. I haven't eaten a thing, so let's treat ourselves to a restaurant. Why did you stand us all up Friday night? Why didn't you come to work Saturday? Did you have a row with him? Ever since we started working in that crummy place, we never see each other any more.'

It's true, Malou. A lot of water has flowed over the dam. Do you remember – I used to call you Snowdrop because one cold night at La Bohème you'd broken through the frost and stolen my heart? It was during that blessed time before the exhausting hours in the hallway weighed us down. You haven't changed, Snowdrop. Your arms are still too skinny for your big, big breasts. The scar on your wrist still bleeds. You don't always take off your makeup before going to bed. But as far as I'm concerned, you'll always be the best, the purest, the least affected of us all. Malou, I don't know how to say this, but we aren't having dinner together. It's already five o'clock, and I still need five thou.

'Gerard's got a fine of twenty thousand francs hanging over his head. He's been locked up in a cellar since last Friday. I'm five thousand francs short.'

She doesn't look at me. She goes on grinding her coffee; she's using one of those old wooden coffee mills that you hold between your thighs. I listen to its musical creak. I see her leg muscles contracting, her little hand turning the handle faster, the mascara running down her cheeks.

'You see, I always get left out of things. I know France and your sister criticize me and say I'm a slob. I can understand why you see them more often than you do me – but I don't give a shit what you all think of me. You're one bunch of screwed-up girls. I'd never turn tricks for a guy. I'm helping out my husband because he's the father of my little girl. The rest of the money gets invested – it belongs to me, Sophie, and Bébert won't ever see a penny of it, do you understand, not one penny! Face up to the facts. Marry Paul.'

'Paul revolts me with all that business about his African girl friends he's so eager to have me suck off. I'm not giving up hooking to marry some kook. Would *you* get married with some frustrated nut?'

'I wouldn't stick with Gerard in any case. Sophie, take a look at yourself – a girl like you ought to have her pockets bulging with loot. Either you haven't got the nerve, or you actually enjoy the life you're leading ...'

It had been so simple with the other two. They paid up and eventually they'll both get over it. But maybe you and I won't get over it. Maybe we're going too far. I walk into the kitchen. The mirror hanging on the window hasp is cracked, and my smile shatters.

'If you think I enjoy having a plate of spaghetti forced down my throat ... They had me sitting on a chair with my hands and feet tied, one guy was pulling my hair from behind to make me keep my head up, another clamped my nose, and the third shoved the spaghetti into my mouth. He almost tore the roof off with his fork. You can imagine the rest. Do you think I enjoyed that? Do you really think so?'

'Don't cry, Sophie. Stop crying, I'll give you the money you need. The worst of it is, you're still so anxious to help him. I can't understand. I'll never understand.'

As in the old days, Malou slips fully dressed between the sheets and gives her two pillows a slap. I draw my chair up to the stove and let its warmth envelop me. As in the old days, Malou reaches under the bed for a bottle; and, as in the old days, we spike our coffee with scotch – and we fill our empty coffee cups after that, and they become big, beautiful, durable cups of sturdy porcelain. We smoke and drink, not daring to look at one another. Malou's hand slides under the mattress and emerges with a thick, sticky wad: five hundred ten-franc bills. That represents a lot of working-class tricks.

The rustling of the bills between my fingers is almost scary; but I have my twenty thou. So much money. So much jack. If only I'd known what lay in store for me when I was living at Villa Paulette. I used to hide behind a street lamp waiting for the grocer to start closing shop, then run in and humbly ask if I could charge a few things. It's a fogged-in world, and it's broken my dreams in two ...

'So your mind's made up? You're going? Listen, this may not be the right moment – but I would have told you sooner or later ...'

She inhales her cigarette, slowly swallows, and buries her head between her knees. Watch out, Malou. Be careful of what you're about to tell me. My eyes are burning, and my knees are shaking.

'You remember the time on Rue de la Faisanderie when I had the flu? Gerard came for dinner one evening – you'd made *lapin à la moutarde*. Afterwards you went cruising on the Champs. You said you were feeling lucky—'

'I remember. You were starting to feel better. The two of you played gin rummy.'

'Except we didn't. We went to bed together.'

The earth has started spinning cruelly. We look at each other in dismay, mortally silent. Gerry and Malou. Malou and Gerry. That's really killing. It's enough to blow your mind.

'Do me one last favour. Keep the money. I'm in no rush to deliver it any more.'

All I'd have to do is move my fingers a couple of inches, just a couple of inches, and I'd have the gun. Guy would have no time to react. He'd crumble up with an entire clip in his gut, and a 'Why?' in his glassy eyes. Why? Why not? Who cares what tomorrow will bring? Everything's collapsing. Everything's falling down in one big, lying crash. My best friend went to bed with my guy. Spring is here. A latrine-like smell hovers in the air. Just a few inches, and everything would be settled: Guy's miserable life, and Gerard's, and my own.

'Think you'd know how to use it? Watch it, now – I never fit them with silencers. I get my kicks from the bang. Come on, keep your hands on your ass. You didn't come here to play cowboys and Indians. The bread!'

The bread? That reminds me of Lola from Bordeaux. She sent her man a telegram that read: 'Yeast dead. Bread not rising. Love and Kisses, Lola.'

That got the point across, didn't it? No, it didn't: you and your sense of humour make a rotten pair. Still, if you took the time to look up and glance at the night-black skylight, you'd see it's hailing up there. The Almighty is in a fury. It's a day for frogs and fishes.

'Now what about the bread?'

'Give me a few days. It's hard reaching people over the weekend.'

'You little bitch! You must really enjoy being slugged. Beat it. Get out before I start messing you up. We'll be waiting for you Tuesday, same time, same place. Let me remind you that your guy's been on bread and water for the last three days. He's trussed up on a mattress in my cellar. And just so you know, one bullet more or less, it's all the same to us.'

Outside, the sky is hovering between day and night. The river Marne is cold. The little white iron tables are dripping on to the deserted terrace. Under my feet the sound of gravel unnerves me. Panic red flashes in front of my eyes. My anxiety's black and white and every other colour. My soles crunch in the cinders ... The night is filled with fiery bullets dancing and streaking through the air. They bury themselves in me. Fire in eyes that are heavy and warm, circled with blue rings. Loving globes of fire, heavy with milk and tenderness – Malou's breasts, in Gerry's hands. Ready, aim, fire! Why did I say 'I love you' the day I learned how to talk? Hey, you my father, don't you move. I've put on my track shoes and I'm running to meet you. 'Time!' I say –and the ball's in your court.

Since his scrape with what he calls the grand jury, meaning death, Gerry has been basking in euphoria and scotch. But it's the mere wreck of a man who now goes into local watering places and sounds off, standing at the bar:

'Gather round me, seedy gentlemen, and hear my tale of woe. I'm Mustang Gerry. I used to have three doxies knocking themselves out for me, night after night until daybreak. The first worked at Saint-Denis, the second in the Arab ghetto, and the third in the elegant parts of town. I had so much swag I could have declared war on the King of Turkey! Then my luck turned, and I fell among sharks – greedy, sharp-toothed riffraff who wanted my hide. They were out for my money and my life! Luckily, I had Marie – Marie, a girl on call around the clock. Marie, my whore, my floozie. Marie, my loving woman, who gave her all to get me out of a bind. Marie, my angel face – who now, since I've come home, as soon as we hit the sack, turns her back on me!'

Gerry came through with only minor injuries, but it was a tricky business. A lot of people had to be got moving; I had to resort to trigger specialists, professional intimidators, desperadoes with nothing to gain and nothing to lose, men out of nowhere who came galloping to his rescue without even knowing who he was. Matters were finally settled without rifles or rifle butts. There was a more or less friendly agreement. Guy silently pocketed the twenty thousand. Gerard gave his pimp's word that he'd never try to get Odette or Dominique back. They left him with just one working girl: me.

Meanwhile, behind the display window at number 45, I'd come close to insanity. But it's all over now. On the seventh day, I picked Gerry up in the street. He'd lost weight, and he was gasping for breath. I nursed him like a mother, with never a word of reproach.

I'm waiting for him to recover. He'll recover. There's no blood in his urine any more, and the marks left by the ropes that bound his wrists and ankles are gradually disappearing. (Scotch seems to stimulate the growth of scar tissue very effectively!) As far as I'm concerned, his days are numbered. Soon I'll turn my back on him.

chapter four

Then time started racing by. I resumed my old habits – or my old habits resumed me. I'm now witnessing the death of the hottest street in town. It used to be one of the guts of the city's belly, and by no means the smallest. I'm watching it being drained of its last drop of blood. It's being transformed from a river into a demolition site.

The flashbulb freaks, four-by-five fiends, and Rollei enthusiasts are using the fact that Les Halles are changing location as a pretext for shooting our portraits as we stand framed in the doorways of Rue Saint-Denis.

Ever since her picture appeared on the cover of *Paris-Match*, our very own Kim has become a national institution. She was shown front face, in close-up, drinking her coffee-and-rum as she leaned on the counter at Le Croissant d'Argent. If only she could lay her hands on the son-of-a-whore that did it! What's she supposed to tell her kid? After all, a ten-year-old boy can read, and his mother's entire life is summed up in the caption. There's much discussion of what hookers will do now that Les Halles are being moved to Rungis. No doubt the bastard who took that fine shot probably thinks that all hookers are orphans and that their reproductive organs have been totalled. It's no use our telling Kim that the guy was just doing his job without letting sentimentality get in the way: she persists in thinking that if this son-of-a-whore had known she had a kid, he would have picked somebody else. But she was the one, and ever since, she's been inundated with letters from all points on the compass.

'You'd think,' says Kim, 'that all the guys who've fucked me in the last ten years read the same rag.'

For over a week we've been spending our lunch hours ungluing stamps from Tokyo, Bangkok, New York, and Bordeaux, on behalf of our stamp-collecting little nephews, big brothers, and cousins. After lunch I read the letters out loud. There are some letters filled with insults and dried spittle; others, the anonymous sort, crammed with obscenities and smashed rosary beads; congratulatory letters with bits of ribbon; and a few love letters.

Things are changing though. I'd better leave Les Halles before Les Halles leave me. But it's hard to feel enterprising when you're standing behind that broken display window.

The Curse must have been hiding under the bed this morning when I went upstairs with François. She saw and heard everything. When he approached me and embraced me against the closed door, she shouted:

'Fanny, we have to change the sheets!'

The walls of the hotel started shaking. The sewers rose up in the bidets. My blood deserted my body and flooded the walls, the sink, and the landing outside. François looked at me in terror, pale as ivory, and then fled.

With my dunce cap on my head, I went back to my post downstairs behind the display window. Of course you have no right to be in love here. I began staring at a tiny, round bubble trapped within the glass. Gradually, I identified myself with this bubble, with this trifling thing, and I started banging my forehead against the pane as hard as I could until I'd knocked it out. I'd wanted to free that bubble and me in one go. Instead, there was a great crashing in my head, and I found myself lying down in one of the bedrooms. Lulu's face was hovering over me. Malou's fingers were gently withdrawing the glass splinters embedded in my forehead, and Franzie was offering me a week.

Thanks to me, there's air in the hallway now. Marie-Galante can start getting her colour back; Kim can breathe in the sea spray; Aline and Gigi can feel free. We're free – and do the men ever love it. Now it's not the pane they spit on, it's us. The girls sniffle and give me a dirty look.

'What ever possessed you, Fanny, to let in all these draughts?'

Standing behind the pane, I feel cold, and the men turn away because my forehead's such a mess. I'd take off, but Madame Pierre has announced:

'Nobody, but nobody, leaves here before seven p.m.'

Thursday is dirty-laundry day; so this evening I'm going to have to justify my lapse before an assembly consisting of the entire hallway, the regular help at Le Croissant d'Argent, Slugger Pierre, the Witch, Madame Pierre in person – and all the other flies in the ointment. All the high-and-mighties who crack their starched shirts whenever they draw breath. The ones who invented trench warfare, sidearms, sawed-off guns, slaps in the face, folding money, wordless meals, fertilizers, chair legs, sedan chairs, deodorants, and suburban cops! The narrowminded ones who always turn away from tenderness as it passes by, or else give it a kick in the guts and send it sprawling in the gutter. It's in front of this dumbbell world that I have to plead my case this evening and talk about the marvellous things that have happened to me here in this very hotel.

Well, gentlemen of the jury, you see it's perfectly simple. It all started just the way it does in the ballads, on the first Sunday in May. At first I found having to go to work on Sunday pretty dreary. I must say that Rue Saint-Denis on Sunday is not exactly heaven. The whole neighbourhood is sighing, stretching, and cracking its joints. On Sunday morning Les Halles are one big hangover, and people give the place a wide berth.

It's not until about two in the afternoon that the Sunday parade gets started. Leading it is the Trachu family. They haven't got the wherewithal for a movie or the instalments on a TV set, so they go to look at the hookers. Madame Trachu, wife and mother, leads the way, pushing ahead of her a dilapidated baby carriage in which the last little grey-cheeked Trachu is napping. She's followed by Monsieur Trachu, husband and father. Every ten yards, choking with laughter, he gives a tremendous nudge to Trachu junior, a pimply adolescent, who once again is going to soil his sheets dreaming of all those dolls, whom he certainly hopes to fuck someday. Immediately behind them come Aunt Rita and Uncle Gustave. Aunt Rita has harpooned Uncle Gustave by the sleeve, and she obliges him to look down at the ground each time they pass a hotel. Gustave sighs and sneaks a hypocritical look at the forbidden fruit. He's just turned fifty-three. He's never gone upstairs, and he's not about to start now. That pleasure is for the perverts.

Gustave, you're such a liar. I recognized you the way I recognize all the Gustaves who spend their Sundays wandering up and down Rue Saint-Denis. You belong to the legion of hand-jobbers who fill Le Croissant d'Argent during the week. You're the ones who make business good for Harry, the ones who keep your little grease-blackened hands frantically busy in your bottomless pockets. True enough, Gustave Trachu, you don't often go or get it up. I understand you a little better now. Your better half's anything but exciting – it's a wonder she ever hatched the two gorgeous children who are walking directly behind you. The little girl couldn't be more than twelve. Her eyes aren't big enough to take in these ladies. She can't get enough of them. To her, they're beauties. She grabs hold of your jacket to find out what they're all doing here, and she keeps yanking it until you condescend to reply, with gross stupidity, 'They've lost their keys. They're waiting for their husbands to come home from work.'

The little girl shows concern: 'That's awful – they'll catch cold!'

At that very moment, Rita turns around and gives her a nasty look out of the corner of her eye.

'They're whores,' that's what Rita says; 'they're dirty whores.'

The kid doesn't get it. She sniffles and looks down to see if she hasn't stepped in some dogshit. No, it can't be that – her carefully whitened Mary Janes are absolutely clean. So she tearfully looks up at her brother, hoping to learn the meaning of her mother's angry outburst.

But the son doesn't notice. His eyes are as bright as the Japanese lanterns on Bastille Day. He's staring at the girl behind the display window. She's bending over and showing her breasts. The way kids look at you can be a verdict and a sentence.

A few yards farther back, Grandpa and Grandma are leaning on each other's arms as they drag along. These Sunday outings no longer amuse them. They feel as the children do and would rather go to the zoo in Vincennes or the one at the Jardin des Plantes. There, at least, Grandma would find an outlet for her stock of stale bread, and she'd cluck and chortle as she tossed it to the animals. But what can you toss a whore? Of course, Grandpa spits a lot, but Grandpa spits all the time, here or elsewhere. He'd be doing the same thing at the zoo. So they feel no enthusiasm as they walk down the street. They just follow along, and they don't complain when the entire family comes to a halt, either at the first bistro they reach or in front of a stand that sells hot dogs and french fries congealed in cooking oil. And then the whole goddamn Trachu family, wobbling from side to side, with their mouths full of grease, wanders off towards the Châtelet.

On the other side of the street, moving in the opposite direction, is a colourful stream of Arabs, Italians, Spaniards, and blacks. On Sunday, Rue Saint-Denis is a little like Barbès: it's killjoy alley. And yet it was on a Sunday, the first Sunday in May, that I met him. I was charging head down from the hallway to the bar when I bumped into someone. He smiled at me, and the street abruptly emptied. The Trachu family went back to its housing development. The foreign labourers went back to their hovels, with their pockets full of grief. There were just the two of us. I'd forgotten there were guys my own age who could look at me the way this young man was doing.

We went upstairs without a word. I was trembling as I had on the night of my first dance. He came to my rescue and put a hundred-franc bill on the table. His voice was as soft as his lips. I drew the curtains on all the windows in the world. As he lay down on top of me, he called me Mimosa, because I was wearing a yellow dress. His lips were even softer than I'd guessed. Beneath my eyelids streamed thousands of motes of sunshine.

He came to see me regularly every day in May; but not until the door shut behind us did he become my lover once again. I hadn't been in love for so long that it left my heart in a muddle. I felt utterly lethargic, bashful. I started going haywire. Instead of laughing, I wept. I'd have my sensible moments in which I'd say, 'Basically, it's an abnormal situation. Love and money don't mix. It's not natural for you to cut classes and spend your afternoons at Le Croissant d'Argent watching me disappear upstairs!' He'd reply, 'None of that matters.' I'd say, 'Try to understand.' He'd get angry: 'There's nothing to understand. I love you and only you – and after all, it's your job.'

My lover was a very classy dresser. France said that he was the typical rich man's son – neurotic enough to fall in love with a hooker. Franzie knows the score:

'Drop it. It's a waste of time. Everybody has to stick where he belongs.'

Well, exactly – I can feel at home anywhere except behind the door pane. So I told François I didn't want him coming back to number 45. We'd meet in the evening at his place.

Our first dinner lacked intimacy. The table was far too long. It was a formal occasion, not a lover's feast.

François was very talkative that evening. He told me about the woman he'd lived with for two years, a fairly well-known actress.

'She's the one who taught me all about love.'

I stiffened. 'I always thought that was a subject that couldn't be taught. I'd make a very poor coach.'

With an unpleasant smirk he replied, 'That seems a bit paradoxical.'

I'd been dreaming of romance, and I found myself confronted with a dirty-minded young man with his mind on just one thing. I should have walked out that very evening and never gone back to Rue de Bourgogne; but I fell asleep. And the subsequent dinners were cheerful affairs. The smoked salmon and the Camembert were excellent. François was attentive. He'd get up and go to the sideboard whenever my glass was empty. His drinking nothing but water seemed somewhat gloomy, but I couldn't move him: 'I never touch liquor.'

One evening, after dinner, he took me in his arms and carried me to the bed. Raising one finger to his lips, he said, 'I have a treat for you,' and disappeared into the bathroom. I went into the kitchen and poured myself a cup of coffee, then went back to bed and waited, propped up on the pillows. I felt fine. When he opened the door, I burst out laughing. I make a good audience, and in any case there's always something comical for me about a man in drag. He stepped forward wiggling his hips, dressed in a magnificent silk negligee trimmed with ostrich feathers, my handbag swinging from one arm.

I didn't recognize myself right away. I guess I didn't *want* to recognize myself. But he said, just the way Fanny does, 'Like to spend a little time with me?' I dropped my gilt coffee spoon into the cup and watched it drown. A storm was brewing inside my head. He didn't notice a thing. He ran his hand through his hair like Franzie; imitated to perfection the way Big Nicole pulls her bootlaces tight; smoothed the tips of his pigtails between his lips even better than Aline – and Marie-Galante would have blanched at the way he swore as he scratched his backside.

He would have gone through the entire hallway crew, but I shouted, 'Stop!'

He buried his head in my lap.

'I only wanted to make you laugh.'

So there you are, ladies and gentlemen – and you, too, Madame Pierre. It's as simple as playing tiddlywinks. When you caught us this morning in one another's arms, standing next to the warm radiator, François had simply come to tell me goodbye. He was taking back the key to dreamland. He's getting married in Geneva next week. It's nothing to get all excited about, no reason to point an accusing finger at me. It was only a minor lapse.

I've even come close to dying at number 45. What more does this bitch of a madam want of me? Why has she publicly accused me of refusing work? She'd better watch what she says.

I've been carrying a pair of scissors in my purse for the past month. If she dares point a finger at me, I'll put her eyes out without a shred of remorse. I've been humiliated and treated like an animal in this place. I've demeaned and degraded myself to the point where one customer used me as a mop (I had to wet my entire body the better to sop up the filth on the floor). I've seen decent-looking men come into my room and spread themselves so wide that they'd leave with a whole newspaper rolled up inside their rectum. I've seen others overturn splintery wooden chairs and impale themselves on each of the four legs one after the other, without wincing, without groaning, and with unbelievable dexterity. I've seen friends look at each other first with mistrust, then with hatred, until they finally leaped like sheepdogs at each other's throats, each calling the other a thief, never suspecting the two girls they'd just been upstairs with. I've seen an Italian crying as he sat on the edge of the bed because all his lire had disappeared in the depths of some mattress. With his head in his hands, he kept saying over and over, *'Due giorni a Parigi, due giorni soltanto.'*

I've seen mothers drag their sons in to see me and beg me as they dug into the pockets of their skirts, 'Take him, Mademoiselle Whore, he's forty years old, and I'm the only woman he's ever known.' After resting my eyes on the rolling stone that had gathered a grimy moss, I'd answer, 'Don't say another word, madame. You don't need to fill in the picture. I've had so many children myself that I can sympathize with your feelings. Our wombs are so insistent – and yet they bring forth nothing but sorrow. Entrust your son to me, and, if it isn't too late, I promise to try and give him a new start in life. I'll try my utmost to help him learn in my bed how to be his own master.' And then I've seen the sons take off their swaddling clothes and slide down my groove completely out of control. I've pressed their mouths to my breast. I've stroked their backs and sung them lullabies: 'Sleep, sleep, sweet little thing. If you bruise yourself inside me, don't forget it's not my doing. If you bleed like an orange, don't lose heart – it's only a little vessel, and it's weaning you from your cradle. Sleep, sleep, sweet little thing. Hey! Where are you running to without any clothes? Come back here. You'll catch cold!'

Behind the door pane, I've gone to the ends of the earth; I've gone to the ends of mankind; and this morning I nearly died.

The session lasted a bare three-quarters of an hour, but the indictment fell sharp as an axe blade:

'Fanny, this slip-up is going to cost you. Your husband is going to cut you up into little slices. What were you thinking of? Where was your head?'

Why, I was holding it in my hands. The crowd in the grandstands has risen, and it's stamping its feet. In front of its eyes it's waving bloodstained handkerchiefs, branches of violet-coloured lilacs, paper flowers, and irrevocable verdicts: 'To the lions, to the lions!' I set my head down in the middle of the arena so as to have my hands free. Just the two of us, Madame Pierre. Just the two of us, Madame la Curse. If your storekeeper's apron is bothering you, take it off. We'll be on equal footing: just us two hookers. We can have a real fight.

Who are you anyway? Who are you to treat the women who work for you like cattle? What gives you the right, just by making a phone call, to have a woman beaten to a pulp by her manager? In the name of exactly what do you force us to spend twelve hours a day in the hallway and turn at least fifteen tricks? By what authority do you claim these rights over us? Am I guilty of being in love? How can you judge, when you're nothing but a disgusting old whore, informer, and freak?

It's all over. The time has come to forget about the broken pane and the six-month nightmare. It's time to think about something else. Time to laugh – time to laugh a little or laugh a lot!

part five

chapter one

Capri in the summer is like an orange that has been cut in two. At Marina Piccola, people spend their time sizing each other up or carrying on about a new brand of suntan lotion. They drink exotic cocktails; they change their bathing suits three times a day to keep them from fading; and everyone has a yacht floating in his head if not in the bay. At Marina Piccola people say hello to each other only every second time they meet. They speak condescendingly about the hoi polloi splashing about in the dirty waters of Marina Grande. They put on airs. And yet on the other slope of vacationland the sun shines just as brightly, and when the summer's over, everybody will have the same tan. If there were a third beach, I'd rush right off to it and roll in its sands. I'd lick its salty pebbles, make eyes at the sun, and drink up the sea in little gulps. I'd reinvent the world: What's your name? 'Eve.' How old are you? 'Old enough to love.' And what sort of business are you in?

Oh, my business is to be free as a bird. I leave my door open to every wind. I like these noisy Italians with their white wine and their proliferating brats. I like garlic and the evening breezes. My friends don't go off to loaf in the Virgin Islands – one of them's trying to get her health back in Corsica, another's working the summer season in an up-and-coming bar in Beauvais – you wouldn't happen to know it, would you? As for me, before I came down to Capri, I worked in a cathouse on Rue Saint-Denis. Last Thursday I decided I'd had it (or they'd had me, if you prefer). So I stood in front of my mirror completely naked, brushed away my false eyelashes, and wiped off my eyebrows and all my powder. My cheeks were pale, and my lips were white. I scrubbed my teeth with purple toothpaste, and after smiling a big violet smile at myself, my mug looked pretty good to me. It was at that point that I began bouncing my knockers on the mirror. It was wild. There were thousands of warm little spheres bouncing between the floor and the ceiling, and I'd barely needed to get them going with my fingers. All of a sudden, one of the balls got away from me, and I looked at my hand. There was my lifeline staring me in the face. I dropped my tits and pressed my mouth to the mirror. I gave myself a real lover's kiss. It tasted salty; and it gave me a longing to have waves breaking in my mouth, to dance the tarantella, and to do cartwheels in the sun. It made me long to yank the door bolts wide open ... You've heard about freedom, haven't you? You've got to admit, Madame Cheque Stubb, that it would be a crime to keep the rabble off the beaches during the month of July.

If only you knew how many suns I'd traced on the pane in the hallway before I broke it. If only you knew how that place was killing me. Well, since all this seems to interest you, you see the brunette over there who's absentmindedly skipping stones? That's my sister. And the pudgy guy with the newspaper over his head, the one who's digging a tunnel with his feet, that's my future brother-in-law. And the tall wiry man with the rope-scars on his ankles is my uncookable macaroni. Do you find him attractive?

But to go back to last Thursday. When Mr Hot Shot dropped in at home between bar hops, he found me with all my clothes off and my head in my hands. Now, Madame Cheque Stubb, what do you think he did? I'll give you a thousand guesses. He lunged at me with everything he had. All at once I felt this violent shock in the small of my back. I kept my cool. I wrapped my legs around his neck. Never once taking my eyes off the mirror, I rubbed my thighs against his beard, I purred softly the way cats do when they're happy, and I put my heart and lungs into getting myself off, because they say it's good for your nerves. Right afterwards I felt horribly nauseated – I had a sort of longing to be done with it all, you see what I mean? He didn't notice a thing, of course. He was just lying there happily on the waxed floor with all his buttons undone, sleeping it off.

I flung the shutters wide open and rested my tits on the railing, which was white-hot from the summer sun. I beheld a vast indigo sky and towering silver poplars. I saw dogs sniffing each other, and concierges who were kicking them on the sly. I saw little tots who'd decided they'd had enough cram their mothers into rusty strollers and send them flying down the steep slopes of the park. I saw lovers numbly tearing at each other's mouths with kisses while they exacted mutual promises. I saw glaziers bent and broken beneath their sheets of glass. I saw a man selling rabbit skins. But when I saw the knife grinder standing underneath my window in his big black shroud, I thought it must be some kind of miracle.

'Hey Mr Knife Grinder, look up here. It's Whosits's daughter – my old man used to know yours. You wouldn't by any chance be kind enough to have a big sharp shiv for me, would you?'

The knife grinder came running noiselessly upstairs. I was waiting for him on the landing. Steadying ourselves against the tempered-steel banister, we kissed each other passionately on the mouth. He slipped a large knife between my breasts. It hurt like mad. Then he calmly went off, as if nothing at all had happened. But I heard his voice floating up the stairwell:

'To become beautiful you must first learn how to suffer ...'

Just imagine the face my husband made, Madame Cheque Stubb, when he saw me all covered with blood. I really was bleeding like a pig: both wrists. I hadn't been messing around. I have to admit that for once he kept his head. He bundled me up in a blanket and honked his way like a madman all the way to Hospital Silence – you know, emergency ward, blood pressure, injections, bandages, the whole bit.

You can believe it or not, but checking out isn't all that easy. Thank heavens, even with this adhesive tape on my wrists, I can still go swimming.

'Who was the dame you were talking to?'

'Some rich bitch. She asked me for drinks this evening at her hotel – she's staying at the Philippe-Auguste. Say, Lulu, do you think you can fall in love more than once?'

'I should hope so. Mama says it's never the same twice in a row. Oh, Marie, isn't it nice being on vacation? And you know something – I can't believe it, but I think I won't be going back to work. Igor's been talking about retiring me.'

Not going back to work ...

Lulu turns over and presents her face to the sun. It's hot. As they moo their way into port, the sirens of the *vaporettos* chill my heart.

There's no denying it. For the last two months we've led a wonderful life. We've shut our eyes at daybreak and reopened them at nightfall – and we're tanned to boot. It's astonishing how well arranged life is.

Gerry is now his old self again – a pimp. As his Shelby burns up the roads along the Côte d'Azur, he makes elaborate plans for the future. We musn't forget that those instalments are still falling due. Of course, those last months had been rough, and we'd all been in need of a well-earned rest. But matters must now be taken in hand without further delay. Just the same, before we go back to Paris to fill up our tanks, we're making a little detour to the Medina. Lulu's feeling a mite nostalgic. Before she hangs up her spurs, she wants to kiss her old buddies goodbye.

Since the wherewithal is in short supply, we start looking for a little hotel. We find one that overlooks the port, the boats in the water, and infinity : a nice little one-night hotel. Tomorrow, while Lulu is bidding the life goodbye, I'll take my shovel and my pail and go down to the beach and build dream castles full of dungeons. When the first ripple brings them tumbling down, I'll drag my way back to the hotel with my back all sunburned. I'll return heavy-hearted to this hotel that overlooks the port, and I'll pack our bags.

Because of the heat, Gerard has decided to drive at night. In the meantime he's storing up energy for the big push ahead by relaxing on the dirty sheets of the big double bed. He sips a *pastis* diluted with warm water. My hands feel sticky, and before I shut the suitcase, I stare at the shutters thinking of Italy and its splendours, of the Blue Grotto, of the Emperor Tiberius, of the disturbing Faraglioni standing face to face in the water like one more doomed couple. I think of the twin beds in which I was able to sleep in peace. I lick up my saltwater tears and dream of Arthur Rimbaud.

'What would you do if I left you?'
'I'd have a good laugh. Take a look at me, doll. Take a good look. Once a girl rests her head here, she's trapped. Gerry is someone nobody runs out on.'
I silently turn my gaze from the shutters and see him smilingly tap his right shoulder. And to think that I'm the only witness of this cosmic nonsense.

In the old days, I didn't ask questions. I never used to say,

'If I left you ...' In the old days I used to scream and break wineglasses. In the old days, I'd get hysterical, and I'd push my thumb into the eyes of the doll that belonged to the butcher's daughter. It would always end in shouting and pain and the gnashing of teeth. I always felt cold in the old days. But today it's hot. As I fold up my bath towel, I quietly repeat:

'No kidding – what if I left you?'

He gives his pack of weeds a flip, a cigarette emerges, and he thrusts it between his lips. He starts tossing his lighter from one hand to the other.

'Just what are you getting at?'

'Doesn't it seem stuffy in here to you?'

'Stick to the subject. If you left me, it'd be a hundred and twenty thou!'

'I don't owe you a thing. I got you out of that cellar. Without me, you would have died like a rat.'

'You little bitch! You did what any woman in your place would have done. I don't know what's brewing in that dishwater brain of yours, but if you're planning on running out on me, I'll stick you with a hundred-and-twenty-thousand-franc fine. By the time you've paid it off, you'll have to go to work in a factory. They won't allow you on the streets. You're not thinking straight.'

'You've got some nerve talking about fines and my not thinking straight. Don't you remember your little trip down to the cellar for having fucked the wife of a guy in the cooler! Do me a favour – take a look at yourself in the mirror. It's not a man you'll see. You'll see a mouse.'

'I'm getting up, bitch, but it isn't to look at myself, it's to give you the stomping of your life. When I'm through, there won't be one bum in the world who'll screw you, not even if you beg him to. You're going to get it, and I mean really get it.'

The shock brings my belly to life. I feel a stream of lava thrusting its way up to my mouth, bitter and sticky, warm as blood. I feel drunk with it. I start staggering and clawing the air. I collapse, my breast crumpling against the edge of the bathtub. Beneath my eyelids, the grave countenance of the shadowy knife grinder looms into view; so I don't let go. I hang on to Gerry's pants with all my might. My pelvis is split with dull pain. I bite the tiles, and I start vomiting miles and miles of gauze, curdled milk, mucus, and slit veins. I drool all

337

over my belly button, I puke up my amniotic fluid in one burst. I feel deliverance rising inside me, and I sink my nails into life without a sound.

'Now that you've calmed down, we'll have a little snooze, a quickie, and then we'll be off.'

'There aren't going to be any more quickies. And no more scenes like this one either. Not *ever*.'

chapter two

My mind is wandering as I lie in Lulu's arms. We're on the Fogsville Throughway. At Montélimar she brings my cup of coffee out to the car for me. She gently soothes my bruises. Her heart is overflowing, and her voice sounds high and unnatural. It's a voice that speaks volumes – mournful, with tears welling up within it, breaking as it passes her lips ...

The drive back to Paris is as smooth and cold as rain. Great bright birds bang into the windshield. Each toll station is a frontier where revenuers in battle dress are ripping apart the pathetic shoulder bags of immigrants. We're driving towards the autumn and its plucked trees, towards hoarfrost, towards the trenches ...

At Buttes Chaumont, the park is full of sights. It's summer's end. The apartment has lain dormant, in perfect order. Nothing has moved. You can still see the imprint of my lips on the mirror. The bag of laundry to be ironed is still on the table, and our two coffee cups are still in the sink. The geraniums must have had a boring time. The bed is still undone: without us, it has certainly breathed easier and slept better. You're a bed of pitfalls, but you won't catch me! Tonight I'm sleeping on my feet.

With my eyes obstinately fixed on the windowpane, I watch the day break. Good morning, morning – say you'll be my friend. You look like a nice day, it's true: but I've known days that were black, days you couldn't pick up with tongs, days pierced by strange shouts, days that were like nights, days so thick you could slice them – in other words, days that make life what it is. Tell me you'll be my friend; because today is a big day.

'What the hell are you doing up at this hour? And what time is it anyway?'

'Eight-fifteen.'

'Going to the hairdresser's?'

'No, I'm leaving. I'm off.'

'Keep it down when you come back. I need some sleep.'

Gerry, *adieu*. I'm taking off to wherever my feet will lead me ...

No, that would be much too simple. I'm afraid. I'm shaking. Time will be on my side for only a few hours. After that you'll understand that this is no joke; and this evening, at nightfall, I'm afraid your vulture's soul will come to life. Where can I go? The horizon of my world is so constricted. You know in advance of every single place where I might hole up. And I don't want to get anyone into trouble. I know perfectly well that some sisters rush off and bury their heads in the lap of the cops; others pour out their hearts to the priests. Can you see *me* doing that? I'd rather die than turn myself over to people of that sort.

You bastard, why did you ever come to my suburb that summer evening? You cut me off from the world. I don't know who I am any more, and I'm groping around in a fog. But by God, you're going to pay for it! Don't forget, you can't count on those other men for beans any more. Your prestige took a beating when you let yourself get bundled off by the cripple and his gang. My old man was right when he said you were nothing but a bum – nothing but a fuckup. You didn't even have balls enough to fire off a few rounds, while I played my wife's role out to the bitter end, and until further notice there isn't a door that won't open when I knock on it. But, in the meantime, where can I go? Where? Thanks to you my self-esteem is so destroyed that if my face weren't a mess I'd go out and turn a few tricks to see if I couldn't get my confidence back.

In the taxi that's heading towards Aubervilliers, I look out at the round, round sun. I start thinking of Lulu's tits as she lies sleeping, with her lips resting in a sweet pout against Igor's hairy chest. Lulu – she yells a lot, like Mama, but she loves me very much. Suddenly I pinch myself. No, I'm not dreaming. The driver really is smiling at me. People really are running along the sidewalks, the meter is ticking away, and my first cigarette tastes a little bit like a gumdrop!

It was all too predictable. It was as predictable as two plus two is four. Gerry has shown up at Aubervilliers, and he's throwing a great purple fit. He threateningly announces:

'I'm not really a nasty type, but if she goes too far, I'm going to let her have it, and when I'm through they'll be calling her Scarface.'

Lulu, Igor, and my old man hang right in there. As for me, I've curled up on the floor of the clothes closet. I'm muffling the sound of my heart with both hands, rubbing my cheeks, crossing my fingers to ward off bad luck, and dying of fright.

Next day, bravado still holds sway. In my niche I choke down my claustrophobia and listen.

'After I read her the riot act in Toulon, she just took it into her mind to leave. It's not the first time she's treated herself to a little show of independence. She'll be back tomorrow – or maybe the day after, or maybe in a week. She must have holed up with her old lady. I'll let her stew in her own juice for a while. She'll be eating out of my hand when she comes back.'

Gerry never was short on wind, and his lack of imagination is a formidable weapon. But don't let that get you down. Just keep on eating Igor's trousers, not to mention the old man's belts – the ones he used to whack you with in the old days. Keep wiping your eyes on Lulu's slips, keep biting on the hangers, anything not to shout out, 'This time I'm leaving you for good!' You learn how to live: that means, how to keep breathing on the floor of a closet.

After a week the tune changes.

'I've forgotten what it's like to be sober. I went out to Malakoff. Her mother hasn't seen her. It's really getting to me. I hope to God she hasn't done anything foolish. She's just a kid, but when things get turned around inside her head, I don't know where to begin. Lulu: she's your sister! Lucien: she's your daughter! If you see her, or if she calls up, tell her to come home. Tell her I won't say a word. Tell her it's killing me.'

On the closet floor, I've just reached full puberty. My breasts are burgeoning, and there's down under my arms. At this rate, in a month I'll start having my period. By that time I expect to see him flatten himself like a pancake and come crawling under the door. In a month I'll be a woman; so when I see his lousy mitts scraping along the doormat, I'll squash his fingers against the jamb. I'll wedge his great snotty mug in the lock – and then like a little girl I'll slyly go off and masturbate among all these boots and shoes. I'll come like crazy – using my own hands this time, my own ink-stained fingers. It's going to be so good. It'll make me feel great as it spreads through me and floods every part of me. It'll shoot me right up to the stars. It's going to open all the doors that are shut. It'll go off in my little tummy like some gigantic fireworks display, or a real revolution, or a feast day on which they're commemorating the massacre of the innocents.

Since the family hasn't told him a thing, Gerry has started turning to my friends, and particularly to Malou. At the end of her season in Beauvais, she went back to her old job at La Bohème. She's coming to Aubervilliers tonight for dinner.

It's a hen party. Lulu keeps walking around the table with her hands buried in her apron pockets and her forehead all furrowed. Now that she's retired, she's taking her role as older sister very seriously. I feel like shaking her up a little, like tickling her hips, pushing her down on the sofa, and telling her that all these high-minded airs are just going to give her wrinkles. Poor old girl! Don't put too much stock in your new status. As soon as things get rough again you'll re-enlist.

What about you, Malou? Have you forgotten how to smile? So what's happened? Did he manage to bobble you again? After fucking your ass, did he fuck your mind? What a joke! I'd just as soon laugh about it: here I am up to my neck in muck, and you're the ones who are falling apart!

'Sophie, I'm telling you, he's a new man.'

'Stop it. You're making me cry.'

'He said if you come back, you'll never have to turn another trick. He'll go back to housebreaking, and he'll shoot up the guys who fined him.'

'Quick, a drink – I'm laughing so hard I may choke! Now listen to me, Malou. Gerard will never be able to shoot anyone – not unless I hold the gun for him. Thanks a lot, but I've got better things to do than worry about some creep's honour. I want to be able to sleep with a clear conscience. And as for his taking a jimmy and prying some back door open, if he's really got you to swallow that, you're not the girl I thought you were. Anyway, I'm not playing the queen of hearts any more. Guys who pretend to be big shots are handing out a line of bull that's strictly for chumps.'

'But all the same, you can't spend the rest of your life inside a closet. It's easier to take off when you've got a little dough. I just got another letter from Paul.'

'Use it to curl your hair with. Paul had better just forget about me. Let's talk about something else.'

'No, Marie, I want you to listen to me. You'd better get yourself organized, girl. The years go by quicker than you think.'

'I don't feel like getting myself organized. I don't give a shit.'

'Are you talking like that on purpose? Or aren't you feeling normal?'

'Normal, serious, reasonable – Lulu, I don't like those words.'

'Well, I'm tired of being in such a sweat about you, understand?'

'Nobody's forcing you. And now you listen to me. As long as I'm a hooker, I'll never be reasonable about anything. I'll never get myself organized while I'm turning tricks, because I'll always feel I've got a right to compensate myself for it. When Malou and I went off last winter, I needed to let myself go so badly that I blew all my savings. But in return, I was addressed as madame, and I didn't have to lift a finger. People did what I told them to. And at night I could sprawl between clean sheets and dream I was somebody else. It was so fabulous that every morning, while I was spreading butter and orange marmalade on my toast, I went right on dreaming. It used to make me cry. Malou, tell her it's true. Tell her how the first ten days we cried over breakfast.'

'You seem to have forgotten everything you've been taught.'

'Forgotten what, Lulu? I'm listening. Go on. We've got the whole night ahead of us. Would you like it better if I did the talking for you? You really want me to stir up all that shit?'

'Sophie, stop!'

'Stay out of it, Malou. This is between the two of us. I'd like to forget – I'm *paying* to forget – how when I asked for a franc to go to the movies on Sunday, they'd tell me over and over, "Right now, you're just one big drain – you eat, you fart, and you don't earn a nickel." You see, I do have a good memory.

342

And don't think I've forgotten why you took off, either. Don't think I've forgotten who your replacement was: me ...'

'Shut up, shut up!'

'Don't think I've forgotten how I used to steal from Mama's change purse to buy myself diaper pins so I could fasten the bath towels I always wrapped myself up in to keep Pop from fucking me.'

'Sophie, stop it! And don't shout – you're making your sister cry.'

For seven long years I shut up so as not to make anyone cry. For seven years I kept smelling his cock under my nose. Then one day, I saw that my old lady was in love. She was so in love I thought she'd die of it. Malou, you have no idea how beautiful and how mean she was. The least little thing would irritate her. She'd just as soon belt you as look at you. And I forgave her, because she was in love.

One Sunday, we went off to Meudon for a picnic. She introduced me to him. He was handsome, a little younger than she was, and he looked nice. It was hot that Sunday, so she took off her blouse and kept just her bra on. He hugged her to him as though she were in danger of drowning, and I remember that she cried. I said to myself that like everyone else maybe she had a right to a little happiness, and I made a big decision : on the bus that was taking us back to Malakoff, I told her everything. I didn't look at her, but as I got into my story, I saw that her hands were shaking. The bus stopped a first time, then a second time; but it wasn't until the third stop that she spoke.

'You're a liar. You're a little bitch. It's you who turned him on.'

I'll skip the rest of that ride, and the two years that followed. She never told him right out that she knew, but it was worse than if she had. She had a hold on the two of us. She toyed with us. And then her guy took a powder, left France, and Paul and Gerry came along. My old man took off about a year after I did, leaving her with the three youngest. Twenty-seven years of living together, and four years doing double duty with the other guy – isn't that enough to make you want to scream?

Do you remember, Malou, one day you told me you'd almost drowned in the Loire when you were little? It's a horrible feeling, isn't it? Well, on Rue Hoche I was going down fast, and so with all the strength of despair I grabbed the first branch that came floating along. I didn't want to go under. I wanted to swim as far as the lagoon and see the campanile and Piazza San Marco with its gilded pigeons. I wanted to float my fevered heart all the way to the Bridge of Sighs! Come on, stop bawling. Tears are just more water – and it's milk I need.

The day after our dinner, I asked Lulu to buy me a box of crayons. I've been drawing crosses on the inside of the closet door. Blue days are the ones when Gerry doesn't come. There have been two of those. Red is for the days when he cries, beats his head against the living-room wall, and knocks off a fifth of scotch while he stares at the TV long past sign-off time. There are already twelve of those. Black is for days when I hold my head between my hands in the depths of my niche, listen to him grind his teeth, and hear the hammer of his pistol clicking: six of those.

Though I'd been so positive in telling Malou that he was incapable of shooting anyone, now that I'm the potential target I no longer have any doubts as to his capability. I'm slowly sinking into terror and insanity. Between the legs of Igor's pants, I see johns snickering at me and running their tongues over their lips. Between the pleats of Lulu's dresses I make out the faces of the girls from the Saint-Louis and number 45. They're tearing their hair as they call my name. Pedro is there, with her cat's head and her scarlet claws. The Witch is there with her purple knobs and her decaying teeth, which she licks whenever she has to make change. Last of all comes the Curse, in a black wedding gown, slipping a ring on Gerry's finger ...

It's too much. I'm suffocating. Turn on the lights! No answer. Total darkness. So when Lulu goes down with the old man to do the shopping and Igor is busy elsewhere, I emerge from my closet, creep over to the telephone, grab the classified section (it's heavy!), and turn the pages to P. I shut my eyes for a moment and let my finger pick out some name at random.

'Hello, Dr Shrink? I'm twenty-four and a half years old and I've started wetting my bed again. It's urgent. Can you see me this afternoon?' No? T.S.!

I put down the receiver, close my eyes, and let my finger choose a second name.

'Hello, Dr Shrink? My period's twelve years late. I keep scratching the crotch of my panties, but so far not a sign of anything. It's not normal. Could you give me an appointment tomorrow? It's urgent.'

No? Turn the page and try again.

'Hello, Dr Shrink? For the past month I've been seeing cocks everywhere, big, red, smelly cocks just like my papa's. I'm scared. Could you see me in an hour?' No? T.S.!

'Hello, Dr Shrink? My sister's been keeping me alive on baby food, and ever since I heaved the iron into the TV set, they don't turn it on any more.'

'Hello, Dr Shrink? I scream whenever the phone rings. My pimp's out to kill me, and it's sending shivers up and down my spine.'

'Peekaboo, Dr Shrink! I have good news for you. Ever since they caught me talking on the phone, they've got this idea that I've gone nuts. They've been talking about electric shocks, and electroencephalograms, and electroencephaloflams. Instead of taking up a collection to send me to the seaside, they've made an appointment for me next week at the loony bin. They don't seem to notice that this is an emergency. I really need a change of scene. They're planning to leave me in the dark for another week. Another long week on the floor of the closet, hobbled in the straitjacket of my own anguish. Seven days and seven nights ahead of me. So many, so few. But hold on a minute – you haven't won yet. Don't be so sure they've recruited a new customer for you, while you were keeping your ass snug in your armchair, farting in the faces of your patients and half-choking them. I've still got a little over a hundred and seventy-two hours to snap out of it. That means a hundred and seventy-two hours for me to suck my nerve cells out through my thumb, one at a time. After all, a hundred and seventy-two hours is a long time. And even if they drag me off to the crazies and you get to rummage around inside my skull, you won't find doodly-shit. *Au revoir*, Dr Shrink, I'll be reseeing you. Uh huh. And a big kiss to you – a great big soul kiss in fact ...'

So as not to be carted off to the hospital, I promised Lulu I'd behave reasonably. I'm not making any more appointments with psychiatrists, and I get out of bed to pee. She's had the locks changed to make me feel safe, and she's had the TV repaired. They keep it turned down when they watch it now. Papa is again allowed into my room, and, if I'm not too tired, we play pinochle on my bed. Igor has bought me a record: Chopin's Polonaises. That music makes me cry.

Yesterday, Lulu got a letter from Malou, mailed from Beauvais. She's met a guy, and she doesn't know when she'll be back. She added a postscript:

'If Sophie needs a place to hole up, the concierge has the key to Rue d'Aboukir.'

I tore up the letter. I flushed the toilet. I broke the Polonaises into pieces and dropped them down the garbage chute. I looked at the calendar: there was a naked girl stretched out under the broad leaves of a banana tree. I stroked my breasts absentmindedly ... *Banana Dream* ... It was the feast day of Saint Pelagia yesterday. In three months to the day, I'll be twenty-five.

Aside from all that, yesterday was a red-and-black day. Gerry showed up at seven-thirty, his arms laden with food and drink. Listening to him at the beginning of the meal, you'd have said he was in a good mood. He told how he'd started making things up with Sandra, the mulatto girl at Big Suzie's. He said he'd also copped and locked the disc angel at the Club 65. Then there were long periods of silence. I heard Lulu say that I'd undoubtedly holed up with my old wet nurse in Normandy. There was another long silence. It was followed by a tremendous noise – a fist splitting the table in two. There were steps, a clatter of feet, and the door of my room was broken open. I smelled his breath, got belted, heard a bottle crash in the sink and my father's and sister's voices mingling:

'Out, get out of here, you shit, and don't ever set foot in here again!'

I heard sounds of breaking glass, dull sounds, sounds of splashing. I heard blood flowing and Igor's voice shouting:

'Stop it, stop it – what kind of family is this!'

Then I heard Gerry's rasping voice:

'I'll be waiting for her at the Playboy tomorrow at seven. If she doesn't show, the day after tomorrow I'll go out to Malakoff, and I'll pick up the youngest on his way home from school.'

After Gerard had left, they tried absolutely everything they could think of to get me out of the closet. To no avail. I lay there curled up among all the clogs and refused to speak. At two in the morning they gave up in exhaustion. The men were the first to go off to bed.

Lulu, in tears, cleared the floor of the closet. My eyes and mouth were dry, my body was drenched with sweat. She wrapped me up in a blanket, slipped a pillow under my head, went into the kitchen to fetch me a glass of water, and handed it to me together with a Valium 10. Finally she shut the closet door.

I closed my eyes and started breathing very hard. I unclenched my fists. I felt like smoking a cigarette. Then sleep abruptly caught me unawares, and I tumbled into the dark pit of my childhood dream. It was an obsessive, invariable dream: a violent start that wakes you up and gives you the feeling that you've fallen out of bed. You shiveringly grab hold of something solid – the sheets, anything. Sleep once again swallows you up. A gentle falling, during which the body becomes weightless and eyes stare out of the blackness. Then a fall down a dark shaft, and way at the bottom you see the mouth of a black cannon. I scream as I'm about to crash against it. But I never do crash. My body dissolves. There's nothing left of me but my eyes. They break through the shadows and seize hold of the word 'SALT' inscribed in white capital letters on a shelf – salt, sea, water, womb. O Mama, Mama!

As soon as the taxi turns into Place de la Concorde, I start hanging on to my seat and biting my lips. For a split second I have the feeling that he's starting to back into the Rue de Rivoli. Excuse me, driver – over a month on the floor of a closet is strictly for owls. I have to get used to daylight again.

Paris looks really beautiful. It sparkles, it floats in the air. Hey, driver, I'll give you a ten-franc tip if you'll drive someplace else. Instead of going to Rue de Ponthieu, why not head for the airport? You've heard people talk about coconut palms, banana trees, and shrinks? You haven't? Oh well. Drive on.

As I enter Carlo's new night spot, the Playboy, my legs are like water. Come on, Marie, don't lose your nerve. It only hurts the first time, as France once said on the way to the police station.

Seated at a table amid bags of plaster and cement, piles of wood shavings, lengths of wall mirror, and tools of every description, Gerard is holding court. Carlos and Antoine, the boys from Nice, are sitting next to him. Jean-Jean is standing with two other guys I don't know.

Gerard has shaved off his moustache and let his hair grow. I feel sick. On top of everything else, he's shooting off at the mouth. And the dirty pig actually has the nerve to look at me the way he did the first time we met.

'Why, it's the little runaway herself, gentlemen. You, come with me. The two of us are going to have a little talk before the meeting starts.'

I step over the piles of cement shavings, the bags full of wall mirror, the plaster tools, reinforced concrete, phony marble counters, lengths of bare pipe, psychedelic lighting fixtures, the bronzed wood of the dance floor, trip-hammers, pools of sweat, a mason's finger, the raw bellies of the girls they've been using to pay off the workers ... A door opens and there's the smell of manure. Now he's taken my head between his hands.

'Well, how about it? Don't you think your act's gone on long enough? After all, we both feel like hell. I'm willing to let bygones be bygones. I'm going to buy the guys a bottle for their trouble, and then we'll take a nice drive home. Come on, give your old man a kiss—'

I'd sooner be the rope than the hanged man. I'd sooner be the judge than the prisoner in the dock. I'd sooner die without a blindfold while my eyes stared into summer than give you a kiss.

'Get away from me. You disgust me.'

'You're my woman. I made you what you are. If you feel like running out, you'll have to pay up. Got that? Now I'm going to kick your ass back in there, and we're going to talk. Get moving.'

Standing in the rubble face to face with the grand jury, I let the snot dribble on to my hands. My heart is beating in my breast like a panicky animal, a rodent clawing at its cage, gnawing at my ribs. At first it hurts a lot, but I get used to it. The animal finally calms down. I use the opportunity to start playing with my snot – cat's cradle and all the variants ... The coif of the nun who's in charge of us casts its shadow across the dormitory: 'Marie! Marie Mage, you're going to be disciplined. You're not allowed to play with ends of yarn under your blanket during nap time ...'

I emerge from the isolation ward after forty days in quarantine. I'm no longer contagious. Lulu is waiting for me under the archway at the main entrance. She's smiling at me. She's holding a bouquet of buttercups in one hand and wiggling it beneath my chin: 'If it turns yellow, that means you like butter!'

The men are talking in low tones. The little rodent comes back to life and starts clawing again. Carlos takes a big swallow before he starts to speak. I sniffle loudly.

'Tomorrow, madame, you'll go back to the Saint-Louis. Pedro is expecting you.'

'Since you want to be independent, once a week you'll come here and deposit an envelope. You'll write on it, "For Monsieur Gerard." And try and get the amount right. Three thousand. Not two thousand nine hundred and ninety-nine. Now beat it. We've seen too much of you as it is.'

If the men from Nice and their clan are backing Gerry up, it's certainly not out of Christian charity. They're making something on the deal. I've won: I'm no longer just Gerry's wife – I've got a whole gang acting as my pimp. Nice going, Marie. You hit the bull's eye. A hundred and fifty thou? That's just one year's work. In a year I'll be twenty-six. Twenty-six, and free.

But will they really set me free when the time comes? My father says it's a declaration of war. Lulu's nervous. Igor counsels prudence:

'Until the situation clears up, the best thing for her to do is go back to Montmarte. It would be suicide to take on the guys from Nice.'

Since I'm the nonviolent type, since I hate beatings and shouting and cry at the sight of blood, I take up my bundle and set off once again to Pigalle-by-Night. I have this idea at the back of my head ...

My flight's taking off in half an hour. Even though Lulu, Igor, and my father are the only ones to know about my departure, I'm sure I won't start breathing easy until the plane is airborne. I stroke my glass with my fingertips as I observe the travellers who are setting out for far-off destinations. I feel no jealousy towards them. I'm going to be taking off myself someday – later, elsewhere, for ever. I too am going to leave and extend my greetings to the world. I'll be laughing when I do it, and there'll be friends waiting for me when I get off the plane. Someday, I'll no longer feel afraid.

The week I've just spent at the Saint-Louis has been rich in emotions. First of all, I had to get reacquainted with number 19 and the girls. Since I was there to pay off a fine, they looked at me as though I'd just arrived from another planet. They spied on me, and they pretended to ignore me. They were jealous of me because at the lineups I was always smiling. I was still little Sophie, and men still found me to their liking.

With the men it was the same old song: 'Hello, my name's Sophie. What's yours?' And when I'd leave the bedroom, I'd work my way upstairs against the rush of girls who'd bump into me as they dashed down to the next selection. In the old days, I would never have dreamed of missing one. Oh, how the men used to love me with my hair mussed, my clothes undone, my breast heaving, my eyes bright as mica, my lips half-parted ... They liked me dirty, those animals. That was easy enough to manage. And I knew how to pamper their special foibles. Who could sit up and beg for a hundred-franc bill better than I could? That was almost four years ago ...

On Tuesday morning, while I was on my way out at five-thirty a.m., my stomach turned when I saw Gerard's car was double-parked thirty feet down the street from the Saint-Louis. So now what? Isn't the jack enough for him? I jumped into the first vehicle coming up Rue Fontaine. The driver proved cooperative – he thought I must have had the cops on my tail. He dropped me off on Place Blanche without asking any questions.

As Arlette paid me off on Wednesday morning, she whispered in my ear that Gerard was waiting outside. When I left, both my fists were full of pepper. By the time he realized what had hit him, I'd taken refuge at La Cloche d'Or, from which I re-emerged at seven-thirty with a load on.

On Thursday I was amazed to learn from Arlette that the coast was clear. That was fine by me, because I had a letter to mail. The night before, Lulu had called up a girl friend of hers in the south of France and explained that I needed a place to work, fast. The friend in turn had phoned a madam, who'd replied that something might be arranged. But I'd have to write and supply a résumé, as well as a photograph and a birth certificate: at Cuers, they don't hire girls over thirty.

I spent part of the night making out my application. It had been with trembling fingers that I'd spelled out the address in block letters: Mmes Toudé & Risty, Hôtel-Bar Le Snack, 1 Rue du Purgatoire, Cuers (Var). I stuck the stamp on upside down because, when I was little, I'd been told that that meant Up Yours!

The coast was clear. I hugged the walls all the way to the post office on Rue Duperré. Just as I was about to slip the envelope from under my sweater, a car door slammed, and there was Gerard, dragging me into his car by the hair. For over an hour he appealed to my feelings. By half past six, the price of my freedom had risen from a hundred and fifty to three hundred thousand.

Friday, after she'd paid off all the other girls, Arlette went outside to take a look around. By the time she came back, I was lying sprawled on the ground, hugging the doll that served as house mascot, high as a kite. But even though I'd been drinking, I remembered that I had a letter to mail, and that it was important.

I was about to let the envelope drop into the mailbox when a familiar hand grabbed me by the nape of the neck. The letter trembled on the tips of my fingers. I let go of it, and it dropped in.

'Who are you writing to?' shouted Gerry.

'A guy.'

'You can't be in love. You have no right to be!'

When I recovered consciousness, I was stretched out on a banquette at Le Balto. The doorman from Le Fifty had carried me in.

On Saturday Gerry showed up in Aubervilliers behind a protective sheaf of flowers. He said they were his going-away present. Humbly and penitently, he got down on the floor in front of me and clasped my ankles. I followed the path of his tears as they ran across my patent-leather shoes and disappeared between my toes. They tickled, and I had to bite my lips to keep from laughing out loud. Just then I felt something warm between my thighs, something I didn't dare believe ... I dashed into the john: my period was starting, two months late.

Lulu had whipped up a scampi-and-rice curry. Gerard asked our permission to stay for lunch. He even went out and bought a couple of bottles of good wine. In spite of the migraine that was splitting my skull, I smiled and started to relax. I had my period, and Gerard was at last capitulating. He was giving me a chance to start life over again. To start my life over! ... Lulu gave me a kick underneath the table. By dessert, we'd lowered the price to a hundred and twenty thousand, and he had solemnly promised not to try and see me again, except every once in a while – as pals.

'Just pals – after all, we're not animals.'

It's true that we weren't animals. We were human beings stuffed with food and good wine. The old man, Igor, and Gerry lay sprawled out on the sofa waiting for their coffee. They were talking about how rough life had been and what god-awful low-down tricks it had played on them. They looked like three magnificent soldiers, covered with mud and blood, who had taken refuge in their bivouac tent to warm themselves with pointless words. It might have been touching, if there hadn't been a traitor in their midst – maybe two, and even, potentially, a third. Lulu washed the dishes, and I dried. I was thinking about the floor of the closet; she, no doubt, was thinking about Yves.

After brandy had been served, Gerry clapped his hands and said,

'Baby, it might be a good idea if you came and picked up your togs. I'd like to have your replacement move in, and after all there's no point in neglecting your property just because you're having a little heartache. I'll help you move.'

Lulu gave me the high sign to accept.

During the ride, Gerry joked a little. In the elevator, he brushed back my bangs. I felt as though a blade had gone through my forehead. He told me that he loved me.

When he opened the living-room door, I recoiled. My clothes had been strewn from one end of the room to the other. The razor blade had spared nothing, from my panties to my fur coat. My charred shoes lay piled up in a plastic basin. My passport, hardened by the flames, looked like a black-and-blue baby porcupine. Was I doomed to mutilation and death by fire, or did I still have time to jump out the window? People don't choose the way they die ...

Gerard lunged at me. He tore off the chain he'd given me for my twenty-first birthday and wound it around my neck, pulling it tighter and tighter until the head that was floating above me had doubled and trebled in size. The head became gigantic, at once monstrous and light, like an advertising balloon. It started getting away from me and gently floating up towards the ceiling. The string slipped from my fingers ... I was melting into the flooring – my groping hands felt every groove and unevenness, and the motes of dust rolled beneath my palms. For a split second I had a glimpse of the solar corona. Then there was nothing but darkness.

Gerry's voice was trembling like a candle flame in the obscurity.

'I love you, I love you ... You're not leaving me ... I made you what you are ...'

I could still hear him, while I listened to my cartilages snapping. There was a knocking on the door that grew more and more violent. Gerard let go of me – I actually think he was crying – and then Lulu, Igor, and my old man were bending over me.

After that, I remember the image of my mother busily making herself up. She was using the mirror that hung from the hasp of the kitchen window. She was dusting her beautiful green eyes with emerald-coloured eyeshadow. Her warrior's hands were knotty. Thick blue veins rose from her knuckles to her elbows. But I knew that someplace inside her there was a heart, and I remained quiet, loving, my wrists tied to the radiator, my eyes gazing intently at her mouth ... There was the water they kept making me swallow – it came back up in my throat in chunky bubbles ...

On Sunday I took the day off. I tried to hide on the floor of the closet, but Lulu wouldn't hear of it. From her apron pocket she drew an enormous gun.

'If he shows, I'll let him have one right in the gut, and that'll be it.'

We played pinochle late into the night.

On Monday, when I returned to the Saint-Louis, I had a scarf tied around my neck like an Apache. The men were their usual tactful selves: 'Hey, Sophie, where'd you get the hickeys?'

The girls joshed me: 'Been playing hooky?' I choked back my saliva and smiled.

That morning, Lulu, Igor, and the old man were waiting for me in the side parlour. When he saw the four of us come out the front door, stray-dog Gerry climbed back into his Shelby with his tail between his legs.

Tuesday was the day I was supposed to pay up.

With Gerard's three thousand francs squeezed flat inside an envelope, I started walking up Rue de Ponthieu towards Le Playboy. I went past the place once. The second time, I'd made up my mind. If Gerry wanted bread, he could sweat for it.

When I reached home, Lulu handed me a letter. It was from Cuers. The deal was on: the madams would hire a third girl at the beginning of November, provided she stayed through the Christmas season. Lulu was jubilant. She uncorked a bottle of old Bordeaux.

'You've only got to hang on five days more. And if that man starts making a fuss, we'll just tell him you're laid up.'

The jet engines are purring like a litter of kittens. I fasten my seat belt and stub out my cigarette. With my eyelashes glued to the window, I blend into the sun's trajectory as we drift towards the tropic of Capricorn.

chapter three

In the taxi that's winding its way up the Grande Corniche, I'm feeling like a still. I've successfully extracted the essence of five double scotches – three on the plane and two after landing at Marseilles. I know I'm perfectly fine since I can still manage to count, and I also remember where I'm going.

The driver knows what's up. Even though his attention keeps wandering off to my thighs, he's been talking to me fondly about the little town: 'Cuers, yes – "Charming Provençal village. Its inhabitants number five thousand one hundred and sixty-five and are known as Cuersois. Famous for its big cheeses." ' Who *are* the cheeses? Le Snack, it seems, belongs to the Combinati family – remember, Carbonne and Spirito, that American cigarette case? I thought they'd all been wasted. There must be a few surviving relatives.

If I come through this alive, I promise – I swear – that I'll run away and hide in the skirts of the whirling dervishes. Or maybe I'll settle down in the lotus posture on the banks of the Ganges and suck on a bamboo pipe until I get my health back. The thought makes me fall silent. I start meditating.

The taxi comes to a stop in front of a little bar whose windows are hung with red-and-white check curtains.

'So long, kid, good luck.'

Good luck, good luck. That's easy for him to say.

The weather's beautiful. Standing on the sidewalk with my suitcase in my hand, I look down the street on to a little square flooded with sunlight. Men with their caps pushed back on their heads are playing boccie. Two dogs are walking round and round a plane tree, whose yellow leaves tremble in the sun like candles on a baroque chandelier. Grey, gauzelike mists crown the still-green trees. A tuft of begonias sprouts from an olive-oil can. Water from a fountain rises towards an azure sky. The fringes of the parasols outside the *café-tabac* wave in the warm breeze. Young children dressed up as cowboys shout incomprehensible sounds as they chase after each other. A woman rides by on a bicycle; sunlight is refracted from the spokes of her wheels. Smells of huckleberry and *ailloli* emerge from behind closed shutters. Perched on the bust of a headless statue, a bird is singing its head off. Unless I'm dreaming – if it's all real – then peace truly does exist here.

A boccie ball ricochets off a stone. Everything cracks, splits, and crumbles.

'Are you planning to stand out there all afternoon? We were expecting you yesterday. Weekends are our biggest days.'

Without a word, I follow the horrendous matron up to the second floor. Which is it – Risty or Toudé? It's got to be Toudé.

'Here she is. She finally got here. Well, put down your bag. What's your name?'

'Sophie.'

'How does she look to you, Risty?'

'She seems nice.'

'She's not very plump. We're taking you as a favour to Renée– she worked here for years – and on account of your situation. How long's your husband in for?'

'He hasn't been tried yet.'

'Let me have your ID card. I'll show you your room.'

Another floor, and then another. Depression really hits me as I enter the tiny, impersonal room where I'll be living for the next two months. If less than half an hour ago I hadn't with my very own eyes seen a glorious sun exploding in a blue sky, I'd swear it was raining outside. It must be on account of the shutters, which are closed – hopelessly closed.

'Here's your room. This is where you work and rest. That's your bed. It's comfortable, and it's the best friend you've got. Open up your bag. That's all you have? You'll come shopping with me during the week. You're going to have to buy something better for the weekends. For today, wear that.'

Toudé points to the navy-blue crêpe dress I used to wear at the Saint-Louis.

'I wonder how you manage to fill out the décolleté? Let me see your underthings. We'll have to buy new ones.'

'But these *are* new.'

'Hold your tongue. I'm the one who gives the orders around here. You keep the shutters shut. You clean your room every morning and wash the floor with disinfectant. And don't forget the corners. Be sure the plumbing is always spotlessly clean. Keep the mirror wiped, the bed smoothed down, and everything dusted. A word to the wise – I sometimes make surprise inspections. In the morning, be out of bed at seven-thirty. Wash up. Breakfast's at eight, in the kitchen. Come down in your dressing gown. Where *is* your dressing gown?'

'I never wear one.'

'You'll wear one here. I'll buy you one tomorrow. At eight-thirty you go back upstairs and do your cleaning. At nine-thirty you come down to the bar and start work. Lunch is from twelve to one. After lunch, you have fifteen minutes to fix your hair and makeup. You're at the bar from one-fifteen to seven. Dinner's at seven and lasts till eight. You have another fifteen minutes to freshen up. Work starts again at eight-fifteen and doesn't end until the last customer has left. During the week, that's about ten-thirty – sometimes earlier, sometimes later. You go back to your room. You launder your towels – two a day – and hang them on the towel rack to dry. The toilet's over there. Disconnect your electric heater during the night. You're allowed to read for half an hour. Over the weekend, there's no special closing time. On Sunday we have lunch with the family a few miles from here. We come back around three. Now—'

Fat Madame Toudé runs her toadlike tongue over her thick lips. The lump in my throat is getting so big it's choking me. My eye sockets are itching with a terrible urge to cry. So the little square, the children, the two dogs, the bird, and the pools of sunlight were nothing but a mirage?

'The price of a trick is twenty-five francs. Twelve-fifty for us, twelve-fifty for you. We're determined to have everything fair and square. A job lasts seven minutes. To avoid any misunderstanding, I make a note of the time you go upstairs. The seven minutes begin at the moment you leave the bar with your customer. They include: both parties getting completely undressed, washing, and getting dressed again. They terminate when you come back to the bar. If you run over seven minutes, the whole twenty-five francs go to the house. Sometimes there are fifteen-minute jobs: thirty-five divided by two. Half-hours cost fifty francs, divided by two, one hour a hundred francs divided by two, and one-night stands are three hundred francs divided by two. Tipping is forbidden. And don't forget, the customer is boss here. Monday mornings you get up half an hour early, in other words at seven, so that Bert, who drives the house taxi, can take you into Toulon for your checkup. Have you ever had syphilis? Well, say something. Yes or no?'

'No.'

'Why knock on wood? Does the idea scare you? Say something!'

'Yes, it does.'

'Today, with penicillin, it's less of a nuisance than a cold. Anyway, it's a professional hazard ... For the time being, there are three of you here: two girls from Marseilles, who are oldtimers, and you. Their rooms are downstairs. They're good girls. Try and get along with them. I think that about covers it. Oh – I hope you don't drink. We don't serve liquor to the girls here. During the week, if a customer asks you to have a drink with him, order a coffee or a fruit juice. Your board comes to fifty francs a day, payable at the end of each month. Now, hurry up and get yourself dressed and made up. They're waiting for you at the bar ... No, no, none of that baby – I won't put up with it. I don't need any weeping willows in this place! Risty! Risty! Come up or she's going to get slapped.'

357

Toudé goes downstairs. My wildly beating heart drowns out the sound of her horrible baby-blue, swan-tufted slippers. I throw myself face down on the bed. Risty puts her hand on my shoulder and speaks to me gently.

At three o'clock, with my eyes still red, I make my appearance at the bar. There are two brunettes, each wearing identical tight-fitting print dresses. They gaze down at me from their perches on the barstools. Risty's hand is resting on my shoulder.

'This is Sophie. She's just arrived from Paris.'

'Hi, there,' say the girls as they roll the poker dice.

'Is it true,' asks the fatter of the two, 'that in Paris you have to be in with the cops to work the street?'

'Be nice, both of you. You're going to be living together for the next two months.'

'Hey, Risty – how is it you took her on? She's as skinny as a flounder. That sweet young thing's not going to make peanuts here. Why, if she gets any work, I'm going to have two big beautiful balls grafted on to me and turn out as a pimp. In a month I'd have a dozen women working for me between downtown and the old port. Right, Mado?'

'Shut up, both of you.'

'Yeah, Risty's right. We'll shut up. We're shutting up, right, Mado?'

'We're shutting up. Shh, shh! In fact, for the next two months, she won't hear a single peep out of us.'

Monday, 3 November
I don't know if I'll have the strength to write this diary in my memorandum book every night. It's the second time I've started a diary. The first was when I was fourteen. I'd hide it inside my mattress; nevertheless, one day my father found it. When he burned it, I felt as though I'd lost something of value. Maybe I'll be the one to burn this one.

It's a quarter to ten. I've laundered my two towels and plugged in the heater. I'd breathe easier if I could lock the door, but there's no key. Mado and Martine were as good as their word. They didn't speak to me once throughout the entire day. As a matter of fact, I don't know when they'd have found time to. I turned thirty-seven tricks. They must have done more than that, since I was often alone at the bar.

I'm beginning to grasp the meaning of 'slaughter run'.

Tuesday, 4 November
Toudé hasn't given me back my ID card.
Today I turned thirty tricks. It's not fair that the other two girls have the same amount of time as I have, even though I have an extra flight of stairs to climb. Mado and Martine still aren't speaking to me.

Lulu phoned. It gave me a bad case of blues – especially since I couldn't talk Toudé was standing right behind me. I could feel her dry breath on my cheek She tore the receiver out of my hands and told her not to call or write again. I heard Lulu's voice shouting, 'Her husband has to write her someplace!' Toudé shot me a nasty look. 'Tell him to write her at General Delivery, Solliès-Pont. She can take the house taxi there once a week.' She hung up. Lulu better write soon.

Wednesday, the 5th
Forty-three tricks. I'm whipped.

Monday, 10 November
Five days without writing.
This morning, Bert the Taximan took us into Toulon for our checkup. The infirmary reminded me of Saint-Lazare. In both places they use very fine needles for the blood tests ... I have a piece of adhesive tape in the crook of my left arm. Afterwards, Mado treated us to *pastis*. It was marvellous sitting at that sidewalk café. I bought a round, and so did Martine. I sang all the way home.

Yesterday – Sunday – we went out for that family lunch. I don't know who the people were. A couple. The girls called the man 'Uncle', but I wasn't given any details, and I asked no questions.

Lulu telephoned this morning, but I wasn't allowed to speak to her. Risty, though, whispered in my ear that there was a letter waiting for me at the post office at Solliès-Pont. Bert will take me there tomorrow. I'm so happy at the thought of reading Lulu's letter that I've forgotten the hundred and seven tricks I turned over the weekend.

Tues. – 11th
This morning, just as I was leaving, Risty returned my ID card. Something of myself, at last. I waited until I was in the taxi to hug that little piece of cardboard to my heart and give my photograph a kiss.

I picked up not one letter, but three. One from Lulu, one from Malou, one from my mother. If I hadn't controlled myself, I would have thrown my arms around the postmistress's neck. Even though I was longing to open them, I didn't want to do it in the taxi, and certainly not in my room. I told Bert I could use fifteen minutes of sunshine and a cup of tea. He said nothing, but three minutes later he dropped me at a café on a little pink square. There were two tables on the sidewalk. The air was cool. I shut my eyes and picked up one of the letters.

It was Malou's. She calls me 'Little Sophie'. She's gone back to Paris, and she's working at the Mephisto on Rue Pigalle. She writes that she had a drink with France, who's signed on at the Sans Souci, at the corner of Rue Pigalle and Rue de Douai. In a PS she adds, 'I didn't give her your address. You never know.'

Lulu, in her letter, included a recipe: headstrong horse stewed in its own juice! In the margin she's sketched a hurdle and, in front of it, a horse turning off to the side. Underneath are the words, 'This is you, my little runaway mare.' Not a word about Gerard.

My mother's letter starts out like the ones she used to write me in the sanatorium: 'Hello, big girl ...' She still talks about the same things: her colitis, how abnormal her discharges are, how hard life is, how selfish men are. She signed in the same old way: 'Your mama who adores you, Mama.'

As I read all this, I started sniffling. Bert, meanwhile, waited for me behind the wheel of the Mercedes, reading *Le Provençal*.

Thurs. – 13th
This morning, under the paper lining of one of the closet shelves, I found a calendar from a manufacturer of cheap perfume. It smelled of lily of the valley. Each day in May was crossed out, except for the weekends, where holes had been punched all the way through the cardboard backing.

Fri. – 14th
I feel weekend dread building up inside me.
This morning, Toudé came up to my room on her tour of inspection. She went away disappointed. You could have eaten off the floor. When she checked my sheets to see if they were smooth, I was scared she'd look under the bolster and find the flashlight I'd bought in Toulon. Thank heaven, she didn't notice a thing. She just went off with her head down, without one speck of dust she could get her teeth into.

Sat. – 15th
Two-thirty: seventy-five customers. I'd never have believed it. Especially in what Toudé made me buy – a brown jersey dress

from Ted Lapidus that's as draggy as a sleepless night. This dress cost me a weekend's take – too tired to figure it out exactly.

Sun. – 16th
We had *civet de lièvre* for lunch at 'Uncle's'. I didn't eat anything. Now that everyone's asleep, I'm going to sit by my window and count the stars.

Mon. – 17th
No news. I hope my VD test is negative.

Wed. – 19th
It's the first time a customer has paid for a whole hour. He was so sweet and gentle that I began to cry. As soon as the door had shut, he said to me, 'Lie down and get some sleep.' I didn't sleep, but he didn't touch me. He lay down beside me, and we talked. He'd never been upstairs with anyone before. Toudé and Risty were dumbfounded when he picked me. His name is Jean. He owns an inn at Vallauris. He held a finger to his lips as he handed me three hundred francs. He reminded me of Paul and Daniel. He's promised to come back. He invited me to come to his place and rest up when my two months are over. Dear Jean! Just what are *you* after?

Thurs. – 20th
I vomited up my lunch in the sink. I want to die.

Fri. – 21st
One a.m. The weekend's off to a bad start. Today a customer bit me in the breast. Pain and the sight of blood drove me wild. I don't know where I found the strength to kick the son-of-a-bitch out, but in any case, there he was, bare-ass on the landing. Toudé came storming upstairs. She was so red I thought she'd explode. If only her heart had collapsed, it would have meant one shit less on the face of the earth. She fined me the price of the job, and I'm being made to stay here Sunday as punishment. Well, it's no punishment as far as I'm concerned. Those family dinners depress me. All they ever talk about is hoods, hookers, cathouses, business, customers, and jails. Drives me out of my mind, and I never have anything to say.

Sat. – 22nd
Two-thirty.
A customer's in the alcove having a piss in the bidet. An 'all-night stand'. I'm dreading it.

Mon. – 24th
I'll be doing the rest of the month alone with Mado. Martine has syphilis. She went back to Marseilles today. I'm feeling very blue tonight. If anything like that ever happens to me, I'll shoot myself. Martine didn't seem upset. She broke the news to us over apéritifs. It seems this is her third time. She laughed and said, 'I've copped a chancre. That's okay by me – it means a vacation.' How sad!

Saturday's all-night customer didn't give me a moment's peace. He left at seven-thirty in the morning. Sunday, while I was doing my cleaning, I found a gun on top of the closet. I didn't say anything. But at noon today the man from Marseilles showed up again. He spoke privately with Toudé. They went upstairs. Later on, when I went upstairs myself, I slid my hand over the top of the closet: the gun had disappeared. What kind of guy forgets his artillery in a hooker's bedroom?

A letter from Lulu this morning. From it, I learn that Gerard, armed to the teeth and drunk as a lord, is scouring Paris with a gang of dream-busters. 'You're better off where you are,' she writes.

The days are so long. The nights are so short.

Tues. – 25th
Thirty tricks – a quiet day. It's nine-thirty p.m.
This morning, Risty sent me to buy the paper on the little square. I went wild with joy at the unexpected chance to go out. But I won't be picking up the paper any more. A kid called me a whore and threw a rock at me.

Wed. – 26th
I've been in this place almost a month. It's hard to believe. Right now, I feel like my brain's kicking over on one cylinder.

I went upstairs today with Julien, the son of the local druggist. He's twenty. He tried to kiss me. I thought of François's lips.

Thurs. – 27th
Telegraphed Lulu this morning from the Solliès-Pont post office: 'France or Malou must replace me December. Use any pretext. Can't go on. If necessary have Papa intervene as husband's friend. Marie.'

Well, why not? Why shouldn't I drag in the old man? He was my first john.

If I remember right, it happened on 1 January 1962. My mother had gone out on the town. The kids were asleep. My boy friend was waiting for me outside, leaning against the grating in front of Guilvard's, the funeral parlour. As I was doing the dishes, I pushed aside the kitchen curtain and signalled him to be patient. He was standing with his arms crossed, rubbing his biceps. What a crazy guy! There he is in only a black velvet jacket and bell bottoms on this snowy New Year's Day. Yes, I remember that it was snowing, and that after wiping the last dish dry, I tiptoed into our bedroom to get my duffel coat. The children weren't sleeping. They were standing naked by the open window with their hands stuck out and raised towards the sky. Sitting in the middle of the mattress, the smallest of them was swallowing the snowflakes that his brothers tossed at him. I shouted and cuffed the lot of them because that was how things were done in our house.

As I closed the window, I blew Jean-Paul a kiss: 'I'm on my way down.' I knocked on the old man's door to wish him a happy new year. He folded up *L'Humanité* and said:

'You're all made up! Got any money to go out with?'

'Jean-Paul is taking me to the movies.'

He pulled back the sheet. His cock was as hard as a stallion's. He'd put three one-franc coins on the stool he used as a bedside table.

He said, 'Suck it, and they're yours.'

I heard Jean-Paul whistling our song, 'Love Me Tender'. I knew that he was getting impatient, that he was cold, that it was New Year's Day – but I couldn't bring myself to suck. Still, I was dying to see the flick that was playing at the Miramar: *Les Régates de San Francisco*. So I jerked him off and picked up the three francs.

I can't go on any longer and that's the truth. When I start to flag, Toudé, that old enforcer, keeps me going on cognac, even though she's always saying we should never drink liquor. Now that there's only Mado and me, there are nights when we don't even leave our rooms. The guys line up on the stairs. I don't have time to wash, and I work with a tube of Vaseline in one hand.

Sat. – 29th
France is arriving tomorrow to take over as my replacement for December. We won't see each other: my plane takes off at noon.

In the Mercedes that's gliding with all its windows down to-wards the Marseilles airport, I fling open my arms. It's over.

I'll no longer have to cover my face with my hands whenever someone shouts into it. It's all over. Come hell or high water, I'm going to start living my own life. Never again will anyone make me tremble or lower my eyes.

Lulu really rose to the occasion. She not only persuaded France to relieve me on the spur of the moment, she also found me another place to work: it's in Evreux, and it's called Le Cristal. Malou's been there for the last two days. Igor is to meet me at the airport and drive me straight out there – there'll be plenty of time to rest up later on. I'll go to look at the sea again: not the all-too-blue one stretching away on my left, but the other sea, the one that's grey and real, with its white dunes and cold sand.

At Le Cristal, after the nightmare of Cuers, I just let myself flop gently down in the sack to the rhythm of the local farmers' billiard cues. It's not a bad place. Malou and I make Christine, the madam, do everything we want. She's a fat, blonde girl who has yet to learn that the alternative to yes is no.

We've got a good number going. We're teaching the farmers how the pleasures of the eye are far superior to those of the grope. We're showing them how an expanse of pink flesh can be worth as much as any plot of land. The big tips are spilling over the zinc-topped bar. We really know how to sew things up – and it's all hand stitching! After two or three scotches, Malou doesn't hesitate to rest her breasts on the bar and use them as a piggy bank. Meanwhile, I put my suppleness to the test and start turning cartwheels among the natives. It's not true that the Normans are tightfisted. True, they go to bed with their boots on and stroke our rumps as if we were their mares, but they're good-natured on the whole. I prefer them to those agitated Mediterranean types who sink their nails into our hips, their wavering virility between our legs, and then carry on like conquistadors once they've been satisfied.

Anyway, we're not whores here. We're up-and-coming bar-maids. Of course, there's a pane missing in the bedroom window, so that when it rains, it rains in our bed. It's a trifle damp. It's certainly the draughtiest house in Christendom. When it gets too cold, we bundle up together and start making plans. And on Christmas Eve, we closed down the place at eleven. We threw all the guys out to the tune of 'Adeste Fideles' and then hopped into a cab to go and sow a few wild oats in Paris, at La Venta. Naturally, we were pretty tired the next day, and by the end of the week the Christmas turkey was beginning to seem a little tough. Naturally, we'd like to spend another six months at Le Cristal. But it's 31 December, our replacements arrive to-morrow, and we've got to pack up and head for Paris. I've decided that, come what may, I'm not going to hide any longer.

On the corner of Rue Pigalle and Rue de Douai, the girls who are turning tricks are decked out in rabbit's-fur dresses, red leather boots, and silver foxes. They wear their hair loose and sport false eyelashes made of silk, tweed trench coats, Mercedes coupés, and handbags from Hermès. Some are cuddly, others are crummy. Some are nice, others are bitchy. There are even drag queens on the corner of Rue Victor-Massé who make the dykes from Chez Moune look as though they were back at square one.

During the cocktail hour, my pals discuss the latest best-seller as they twirl their glass straws in their beakers. Some talk about giving up the life. Others bounce around in time to the Beatles. Some show off their black-and-blues; some lift up their skirts; some laugh; others cry. And then there are the guys. They stare at the goodies, scratch their chins, and come in their pants. I have the street, and life, and Franzie: she's sharing a yard of asphalt with me and acting as my shield.

In a few hours I'll be back on my turf: the corner of Pigalle and Douai. That's where the independence I dreamed of is being worn thin by the long hours I have to spend at the Opéra police station. The bulls keep after us relentlessly. My purse is filling up with notices of fines, on the back of which Article 34 reminds me that any behaviour on a public thorough-fare conducive to depravity is punishable under the law. I'll have to pay them sooner or later, if I don't want to put in time. 'Bodily incitement', that's what the pigs call it. If only I knew what to do with my body, and my life – if only I had the nerve to get rid of them! One year. I've got to hang tough for one year, make some dough, and then head for someplace else.

But how can I hang tough when fear keeps gnawing at my guts? How can I hang on to this street corner when a simple look is enough to start a scrap? Last week a girl went rolling into the gutter with her forehead split open. She lay there for an hour before the police sent an emergency patrol to pick her up. The night was finished for her, and for me, too. How do you hang tough when you have to go miles to find a hotel that will let you in, when you have to go knocking on five or six doors before you find the right one, when you have to climb five or six flights in the dark only to end up in a room where there's no bell and you have a potential maniac lying on top of you?

Should I change my street, or my neighbourhood? Should I go back to Les Halles and put myself behind the shelter of a glass-paned door? But what boss-lady will take me on? I'm no longer anybody's wife. I've been outlawed. I really can't see going back to the supermarket grind and earning a thousand a month, when that was what I made in a day at number 45. Can I maybe catch an old man who's lousy with the stuff? That's the attitude I was raised in. I didn't think it up by myself, it was drilled into my head: 'She's so pretty, little Marie. What's she going to do when she grows up?' Little Marie would stroke her ringlets and answer, 'I'll find an elderly gentleman who'll fatten me up.'

Ech! I loathe my genitals. I discovered them too early. Or, rather, the man who passed for my grandfather discovered them for me when he pulled them open with his earth-blackened fingernails. I was four years old when I first had blood between my thighs.

Tomorrow I'll talk to Lulu and ask her to get me sponsored. After all, my references are good. I never sent anyone to prison, I'm the daughter of a hood, and I'm a hard worker. Nothing's lost yet. Franzie will follow along, and, who knows, maybe Malou will, too. Sooner or later there'll be happy times. On some nights my flag may fly at half-mast, but I never give up hope of seeing daylight again.

Nine p.m. France still hasn't showed up. Fifteen minutes have gone by, and I have yet to score. Am I losing my stuff? No! Here's a rolypoly little man waddling my way, and he's got a nice john's mug. Go on, Sophie. Flash your tits, turn on your running lights, sharpen your fingers, stick out one hip, and arch the small of your back. Let him have it:

'Hello, big boy, look me over – they call me Sophie.'

'What's your rate, sweetie?'

Ooh, what nerve! Either he's got the habit, or it's his first time out and he's forcing himself to make the plunge.

'Fifty francs, plus the room.'

And I add, with an intriguing little pout:

'With all my clothes off, natch.'

'For that price, do I get anything special?'

'Why, it's the very least I can do for you.'

This is the kind of question that puts my back up. It's going to hit you where it hurts, old man. I slip my hand in Roly's arm. I have a little hotel on Rue Henry-Monnier – I pay for it by the day and leave a few threads there, and I can use it three times a night. So to start things off on the right foot, since this is my first trap, I make him a proposition.

'I like you. I'll take you straight to my hotel. You won't have to pay for the room, but you'll give me an extra twenty-five and we'll spend more time together. Okay?'

'Okay, sweetie.'

I lengthen my stride. The hotel sign is cheerfully winking its welcome.

'Well, what is it? Don't be bashful, come on. Don't take your wallet out here – you can pay me upstairs.'

'Police.'

Rotten Roly's badge burns into my brain and brings tears to my eyes. A cop!

'Oh, no! It isn't fair. It isn't legal!'

'Your ID. Now follow me. They've been saving you a seat in the wagon.'

We go back the way we came, and this time he's the one who grips my arm. The intersection is so empty you'd think no girl had ever stood there. Men are pacing like wild dogs outside the Lautrec and the Sans Souci, where, in the neon light, girls are drinking to the health of John Law.

In the paddy wagon, which is parked on Place Pigalle, I start biting my knuckles. It's a good thing I laid in a supply of weeds for the night. The wagon starts up, and I'm on my way to another ten hours at the station, with Saint-Lazare waiting for me at the far end of the night. With an angry gesture I push away the hundred-franc bill that Rotten Roly is crumpling under my nose with a snicker. Thirty hours a week at the station is too much. I urgently need to change my street and go back to Les Halles. France, Malou, a few local girls, and I will start a new fashion: no more bosoms ambiguously bared, no more outrageous makeup jobs, no more laced boots, leather dresses, or wedding-cake hairdos. We'll all work in pleated skirts, blouses, and white knee socks. The customers will walk past number 45 without even turning around. The place will go bankrupt, and Madame Pierre will have to shut down. And who knows? Maybe that's exactly what I need.

Number 45 was Buckingham Palace compared to number 71. You need lots of heart to make your way through the swinging door, behind which girls out of some Fellini movie are sulking and scurrying. Fifteen minutes at the bar across the way were enough for Franzie and me to size up the situation. We're entering a den of immigrant labourers. It's a place where psychopaths of every known variety flourish. A smell of sperm tickles our nostrils. The sticky banister contaminates our fingers. We stumble over motheaten carpets. We're going to have to hang on tight.

Gaby the Crooner is standing outside the office door. A handsome, candid-looking man, he's a prewar pimp with rugged shoulders and lines of princely elegance. Old Gaby has style.

'So, from what you told me over the phone, you're looking for a house? Your husbands are the right sort? You're hard workers?'

He smiles as he hears us out. Our proposal is highly attractive. Franzie and I are providing him with young flesh that's nifty and brimming with heart. We're two broads who want plenty of it, and fast. Everything could be for the best in the best of all possible worlds ...

Alas, alas! Rue Saint-Denis has become infected with gangrene. The hotels are shutting down one after the other. Even number 45 hasn't been spared, and here the girls are on their final shift. (The expression 'condemned hotel' has never seemed more appropriate: at Madame Pierre's, the girls spend their twelve hours imprisoned in their rooms. They even eat their meals there.)

'Ladies,' says Gaby, drawing on his Havana, 'your old men's

daily bread is in danger. The black flag of disorder is casting its shadow across the kitchen table!'

'But there must be a way, monsieur ...'

We turn kittenish and imploring. The point is, we don't want to go back to Pigalle: we have no intention of paying those fines, nor do we feel like wasting our youth playing gin rummy at the Opéra police station. We want bread, heaps of it; and there's still a lot left to be made around here. We want to be the last women to reap the benefits of the street before steam shovels and bulldozers gut Les Halles and fat developers ruin it for good.

Give us two ringside seats, Monsieur Gaby! We promise to be discreet and couth; but we do want to watch the hottest street in Paris in its death throes. We want to see it bleed as it trips over the demolished sidewalks. Give us a chance to slake our thirst and take nourishment from its last corpuscles. It'll be too late afterwards. They'll have wrecked it.

Aha – I had the feeling Gaby was the sentimental type. We've got to him. In the midst of the Havana haze a promise is taking shape, and Franzie and I bite our knuckles as we wait for it to materialize.

The deal is on. There's one condition: we'll have to set our traps out of doors – on either Rue des Prêcheurs or Rue de la Cossonnerie. If we keep our asses glued to the hotel, out we go. Gaby slips each of us a key. He feels that things will settle down in a while, and we'll be able to bring our girl friends, too.

May Day – that's my day!

For the past three months I've been rushing off to Rue des Prêcheurs every day of the week, Sundays included. I thought I'd seen everything and been through everything: I now find myself buffeted by the rough winds of biting sarcasm. Yesterday, it took the form of a rotten egg thrown from an anonymous window. Today, it's a boy's schoolbag dragged across my shins. Tomorrow, it'll be someone spitting at me, and the day after that an insult, a blow, a stone – or dreary hours spent hunched up in the police station on Place du Marché Saint-Honoré.

Today could be a beautiful Sunday. The bells of Saint Eustache are happily soaring into the noon sky. But on Saint-

Denis River, alas, there's not one skiff in sight. The street is empty. What's going on? The morning light is thin, the city is dead, and I hear misery knocking on every door. Looking up, I see a woman in the adjacent building shaking out a rag with her flabby arms. She seems consumed by hate. Dust and lice rain on to the sidewalk. I go past a churl who has come out to slake his thirst. It's a glum morning. A drizzle is streaking the dirty windowpanes ... Farther off, towards Rue de Rambuteau, a child's sob is choked off in a fit of coughing. The grating noise of a storefront iron curtain that a little boy is laboriously hoisting fills the morning air. A shivering old man trips on the pavement, and his bottle of milk comes crashing down with him. This morning is an animal who grasps my breasts as he passes by. It's my foot in the seat of his pants. It's a dog howling in the distance, over by the canal. It's me, standing by the streetlamp in tears.

I'm shrieking, biting, begging the bulls not to take me in: I haven't done anything, it's noon, and I don't want to wake up tomorrow morning in the tank, all crumpled and torn, with my glims aching. The cops chuck me into the wagon like a sack of rotting potatoes. Three guys are sitting on the benches, handcuffed, their faces bloodied. The cops are rubbing their hands underneath their capes. I feel a longing for revenge against all this rottenness welling up inside me.

In the monkey cage next to mine, the cops are beating up some guy. I can't stand his screaming any longer, so I get up and shout:

'Stop it, stop hitting him, please, don't hit him any more, make him be quiet ...'

I'm knocking my head against the bars. The girls grab me, push me down flat on the bench, and stuff a handkerchief into my mouth. They call in the sergeant and tell him I'm having an epileptic fit. I'm led off to the john. They yank me by the hair and shove my head under the cold-water tap. The man is still screaming.

There's a glass on the sink, the kind we used in the school lunchroom. I promise to calm down, and I ask for permission to drink. The cops let go of me, the glass shatters, I watch my blood flowing over the white stones, and my left hand starts to get numb.

I couldn't stand those shrieks any longer. It was my only way of getting out of there. Lying on a stretcher in the police van that's heading towards Hôtel-Dieu Hospital, with my arm wrapped up in a cop's handkerchief, I feel myself coming back to life.

May '68. The country is paralysed by strikes – including the garbagemen's. On the corner of Saint-Denis and Rue des Prêcheurs, Franzie and I are up to our knees in potato peels. We're also hopped up – which doesn't stop us from going upstairs, on the contrary. We're beginning to think that in times of crisis men must need more affection. But we have to stay alert. It's not just in the Latin Quarter that they're throwing cobblestones. There are demonstrations going on pretty much everywhere from the Etoile to the Bastille. After work, we take off and join the ranks of the revolutionaries singing the Internationale. It's a natural reaction for anyone who's grown up in the working-class suburbs. I certainly haven't forgotten those Sunday mornings when I used to get up early and sell *Humanité-Dimanche* on street corners. At number 14, Sunday morning was a time for heavy sleeping, especially in July – there was all that back sleep to catch up on during the period of paid vacations (inadequately paid, evidently, since no one went away). All the way to Rue Avaulé I could hear their noisy sleep. It was an industrial sleep filled with utopian dreams.

'What does the worker dream about?' That was the question given to the students of a technical high school in the Paris area on their final exam. 'The worker doesn't dream. He's too tired. The worker works and snores.' The girl who wrote this answer passed the exam with flying colours; and at the end of summer vacation she came back to a job in the marketing department of a pharmaceutical laboratory – a clean, solid job located two minutes away from where she lived. (Its only drawback was that she had to supply the indispensable white smock herself. They don't kid around in labs when it comes to the way you're dressed.) The other students failed. They were the faceless ones in the back rows, the ones who dared presume that a worker actually dreams, just like everyone else, except that he's lulled to sleep by the stultifying drone of his lathe, the earsplitting whine of his milling machine or his drill, the instalments on his TV set, his everlengthening debt at the grocer's, his gas and electric bills. (They've cut him off once, twice, a third time ...) The worker is doomed to live in the shadows, to survive in a tidy but dark little apartment. He and all his brood have affectionately dug themselves into their poverty: the sort of poverty that pounds on the table and dances jigs in front of the sideboard, the sort of poverty that bares its teeth and threatens to wreck everything if it isn't fed. They failed the students in the back of the classroom when they inscribed the worker's dream in clear letters on their white pages.

I wish I'd been drawn to rebellion, like these young people with whom I link arms as we march. I identify myself with them. I'm their age, after all; I could be a college student myself. So down with lying and hypocrisy! I'll never let filth get the better of me. If sometimes I have to bow and scrape (just like them), it's only so I can rise up all the stronger and deliver the decisive blow. 'She's a marginal type,' say the stuffed shirts – the ones who have been trapped in their own idiotic, dehumanizing comfort. 'That's right – a marginal type. She's unfit for society,' others murmur disdainfully. And they're right. I *am* unfit for the cockeyed, lying society that 'they' have propagated and from which they have systematically and carefully excluded everybody but themselves.

O you, Wild Heart whose name I cannot guess, you who, somewhere, love me without realizing it: the first thing you need to know about me is that I'll never be broken or tamed. For me, and for all those now marching alongside me, there are no such things as traffic lights, grass to keep off, or automatically closing doors. We'll blast through the tactics of repression. Who cares about their flags? Who cares if we lose a few feathers? Those who come after us will have sturdier wings. I'd like to write you words of love, but aren't these words the loveliest of all? Listen: the jailers will never have prisons vast enough to confine those who love freedom the way you and I do. We'll grow faster than crabgrass, and we'll burst through the prison walls to enter at last on to the majestic plains of the truth.

Yesterday, a girl jumped from the third floor of a hotel on Rue des Lombards. She'd been ordered to produce two thousand francs a day. Wild Heart, it's time you gave me a sign. I don't want to spend the rest of my life slicing into my veins. I know I gave up the other day, but it wasn't because I felt like dying. I just didn't want to see the submissive faces of the girls any longer, or the sarcastic facets of the cops. I couldn't go on listening to the shrieks of the man they were clubbing on the other side of the wall. That man might have been you. I couldn't stand it. Give me a sign, show me that you exist – and, above all, don't be afraid when you see me approaching. I may be a little violent. But when I lower my eyes, take me gently, hug me, stand me up against a wall – any wall – and kiss me. Kiss me for a long, long time. But don't wait too long before showing yourself, because to tell you the truth, I've lost faith. I just long to sleep: to sleep until the day we meet, and then awaken at your side, once more fresh and virginal.

Summer has arrived, accompanied by its smells of corruption. I watch it as it flows, warm and sticky, down Rue des Prêcheurs. France has gone off to Corsica to recover her strength. As for Malou, she surprised me one July evening by appearing at Rue Pergolèse, where I now live, with a flabby-faced ape in tow. He is, as far as she's concerned, the very personification of love. Bébert will go on receiving his money orders and his parcels at Christmas and Easter, but from now on there'll be no more letters or visits. Five years is a long time; and when love takes a holiday, it's endless. To each his illusion, as Bébert has learned the hard way.

For Malou, the struggle is over: she's giving up the life. For July and August she's taken a job as barmaid in a place on Rue Claude-Terrasse. I stop by there every day and roll the dice with her. Malou now speaks another language. Is she happy in her new life? I doubt it. While she's drying glasses, her ape lies sprawled out on the marital sheets. He's unemployed. I warn her, timidly, but she's all confident smiles.

'He'll find a job soon,' she replies, 'and then I'll be able to stay home and look after my little girl. I'm bringing her here to live with us.'

Since Malou is already talking about 'us', further advice seems superfluous. So let her live her life. I have my own to live.

I start dropping in less frequently at the bar on Rue Claude-Terrasse. I let a week go by without a visit. Then one day when I'm in the dumps I go back. Instead of Malou, there's a plump little woman drying the glasses. I leave the bar without touching my drink. With a heavy heart, I go tearing off like a crazy woman to Rue d'Aboukir.

'Madame Langlois has given up the apartment for good,' the concierge tells me.

'She didn't leave any message for me? Or a phone number?'

Nothing. Malou's gone. She's gone, and left no address. There'll no longer be a key under the mat up there on the third floor. The time has come to cross out Rue d'Aboukir and strike it from the map of Paris.

After a hectic spring and an up-and-down summer, good times have returned to the sidewalks of Rue Saint-Denis. A chill autumn wind has burst open the brothel doors. New recruits have taken their places on the sticky benches of number 71.

In his new capacity as master and auctioneer, Gaby the Crooner is standing on a platform rubbing his hands and vaunting the qualities of his new string of girls.

'Please come right in, Mr Mayor. Come right on in, young man. Save a seat for the elderly and the invalid. Make way for the deaf, the dumb, the plain, the polio victims ... There's room here for anyone who's got cash. Come right ahead, Doctor, and you there, the guy with one arm ... Artists, dumbbells, youngsters who still have their cherries ... You, the gentleman with the wooden leg, and the TV man: just push your way in, that's it. The girls here can handle anybody. They only turn down Arabs. From the tiniest among you to the fattest, you all can enjoy the *jus primae noctis*. So fly at it! Step right up, have your money ready, and let youth have its day! The year of the highest bidder has just begun.'

As the end of September approaches, Gaby starts pulling in the change. To hear him talk, he's never had it so good. Neither have I! And there's nothing like it to keep you hopped up. I'm by no means alone on my street; there are sixteen of us pacing the asphalt between six in the afternoon and one in the morning. The cops are lying low. For a few months more we'll still enjoy the cooperation of the market people, who never hesitate to hide us in the back of their shops at the slightest alert. Paradoxical as it may seem, this period has something marvellous about it. There's the complicity of the nightime, the vivid smell of fresh vegetables, the mountains of oranges dumped on the sidewalks, the friendly cafés, the neon glow, and, underfoot, the crates of eggs and wheels of Swiss cheese. The multicoloured chaos of Les Halles reassures me, and the night protects me.

Nevertheless, when Christmas approaches and Gaby starts talking about organizing a daytime shift, I immediately volunteer for it. Work will begin at nine and end at six: that means nine hours behind the pane. The sidewalks are to be cleaned up and returned to the honest folk, their rightful owners.

On the afternoon of New Year's Day, Gaby, who's certainly unlike any other bordello-keeper, invites his girls into the office for a snack. Jars of caviar burst open – we eat it by the spoonful – and champagne corks pop. In an atmosphere of general festivity, the Crooner wishes us a Happy New Year.

'Ladies, the best thing I can wish you is that a year from now you won't be here!'

Moist-eyed, we all applaud. It's really a touching way for a man who runs a whorehouse to talk. As for myself; I have no doubt whatsoever that in a year I'll have completely forgotten number 71.

After the inevitable hugs and kisses, Gaby goes into action. Eleven of us will make up the *beau monde* of number 71. The day shift has become a reality.

I call it the '*beau monde*' because it seems to me that something has changed in the thinking of these girls, whose average age is twenty-five. At bottom they may be the same, but at least they're dressing better. The word 'fashion' appears in their vocabulary whenever the talk turns to clothes. Some of them now go out to dinner together, with no men present, and others have even gone as far as visiting discotheques together. Owning a car and having their hair done at Carita's have become matters of necessity to them. They all dream of mink and leopard skin. They find it perfectly normal to have a bank account – a woman who doesn't have one is a chump. The only watches that can tell time correctly are those from Piaget or Cartier. The *ne plus ultra* of success is, of course, to flaunt a diamond on one's ring finger, whatever its size and provenance.

Are the girls becoming emancipated? Is prostitution going to be run on a democratic basis? I doubt it. The better I get to know the day gang, the faster my illusions wane. The tenacious whore mentality is still there. These women resemble their elders and speak the same language. The old and new schools are one and the same. Reform is not likely to happen overnight. Still, despite this, I somehow have the feeling that the girls are imperceptibly but surely becoming conscious of what they are – and of what they could have been. I can't be the only one who feels like kicking over the traces.

And then there's Franzie. She's decided to stay on the night shift. For several months I've caught only occasional glimpses of her. She seems to prefer Kim's company to mine. (Kim had walked out on the Curse.) She spends a lot of time sitting with her on the terrace of La Bistouille, a café on Rue de la Cosson-nerie that attracts a somewhat unusual clientele.

(There's no denying it: Les Halles may have moved out bag and baggage, but a new breed of animals has already started romping on the old stamping grounds – riffráff out of nowhere. Ragpickers, braggarts, and, as my father used to say, baby-balled bums ...)

'Hey, Franzie – since Kim is away tonight, why don't the two of us have a drink together on the terrace of La Bistouille? The sun's still out, and we could bring each other up to date. Just take a gander, Boondocks. The new girls are taking over the street. They're streaming in from Avignon, Marseilles, Limoges, Lyons ... Look at the way they come on, all snappy and happy, with their purses between their teeth! They're oozing dreams from every pore – they still believe in them. And we don't; not any more. They've come to barter closed shutters for a little fresh night air. Look at the way they're un-packing their lives and laying them right out for everyone to see!

'Oh, Franzie, time's running out on us. It's pummelling our bodies. Take my hand, squeeze my fingers, and let's head some-place else before our thighs start going out of fashion. Come with me, Boondocks, I'm your sister. I'm your double. I don't give a damn if I didn't cut my milk teeth on caviar eggs, any more than you do. (And I don't think I'd have appreciated them!) Now that men have skimmed the cream off our dreams, now that we have our cars and fur coats and our big-name shoes and handbags, don't you think it's time we traded them all in for a little lucidity and started leading our lives as women? Wouldn't that be fabulous?

'Come with me, Boondocks. Time is against us. I feel its breath on my neck – don't let it get ahead of us. Do you remember, Franzie, when you and I were sitting astride a cloud with a forty-five pointed at our jugulars? Do you remember our plans and our betrayals, my first smoke, and my first beer, and that night at the Vice Squad? Remember the fireworks in Ducretin's eyes? and then Saint-Lazare? France, give me your hand!'

'Sophie, you're dreaming on your feet. Sophie, I can't bear it any longer. Two months ago I started shooting up – and you didn't notice a thing. Six months ago I started making it with Kim. You see, I'm just not normal. In six years I've never got off once with a guy. And Sophie, I have a lover. It's not Mustang Gerry I've got for a pimp, it's Jean-Jean. My man is no small-time pimp. He's a bloodletter. He just isn't going to throw in the sponge like your old man and decide to become a taxi driver. My guy's a madam, a real pimp, a killer hawk, someone who'll stop at nothing – and someone who's good for nothing at all! Sophie, he's dangerous. If I ditch him, he'll plug me.'

'Have a joint, girl – it's your turn. Breathe in deep, close your eyes, and Franzie, I promise you the world won't seem all that crummy.

'I'm leaving tomorrow. I heard about this little town in the south of Italy. It's on the side of a cliff, and according to legend all its windows overlook the sea. You say you feel like a bird – so come with me. There's no limit to where birds can go. I'll tell you the story of Jonathan, the wild, wise sea gull who didn't want to fly the same way the others did. I'll invent long-stemmed flowers for you to land on, and when you land you'll be like a newborn baby, all wrinkled and wet, both pretty and ugly – the child of hope, utterly mute, blind, and deaf, and with bloodied wings. Come with me, Boondocks. Let's head for the land of the sun and not look back. Behind us there's nothing but darknesss.'

My eyes are full of smoke as I leave Rue Saint-Denis; and I do not look back. I fall into step with ordinary folk. At number 45, the girls are still tapping on the pane. Oh, Franzie, *per pietà*! How can you endure it any longer?

chapter four

Viewed from the cabin window, the sky is nothing more than a vast bubble of coloured light. We fly over the Gâtinais, the Grande Chartreuse, the Gran Paradiso, the Alps and Mont Blanc, Esterel, and the Mediterranean. Next comes Italy: Pisa, Civitavecchia, Latina, Napoli, and the plunge down towards the bay and its kingdom – umbrella pines, thickset fig trees, rocks breaking the surface of the sea, house roofs round as breasts, spent lava, jasmin, bougainvillea, and white and purple oleander entwine themselves above the raucous streets. The sun rebounds from the white bosoms of mamas; it gives the sea its rough, metallic sheen. The laughter of the *guaglioni* spills over on to the landing strip. My suitcase is snatched from my hands, voices start singing into my ear, hands caress me and carry me away – and I let myself be carried away. They toss me into the sea, and I swim through the foam that blurs my gaze. The street disappears beneath the soft blue wake of the propeller. I arch my feet in my sandals, grip the railing with both hands, and gently shut my eyes.

I'm not dreaming. I'm no longer leaning out of that top-floor window with my feet on the kitchen cupboard. I'm really out at sea, cruising away from the shores of my life. Wild Heart's breath is caressing the nape of my neck, I'm sixteen years old, lapping up the pistachio ice cream like a greedy kitten.

Above Amalfi, a sung mass is being borne aloft by the voices of children. They're bowed down under brocade and antique candles. The procession advances in the shadow of covered passageways and stretches all the way to the beach. Amber is mingling with incense. I see three blond heads among the brown: small heads, with wide green eyes – in their rose-coloured smocks, Bernard, Christian, and Patrick are striding over the waves. Their lips are rounded, as if they were singing a hymn. They stretch out their hands towards me, their fingertips brush against me. A piercing, familiar voice emerges from the deep: 'Marie, relish this mass, relish your sky-blue days. Let the blue drive out the black!'

I threw my watch into the sea, and with it the calendars of the years to come. I buried the key to daydreams at the foot of some outlandish tree. I live from one day to the next, from one night to the next. I'm swimming through all the days of my life.

The *pensione* in which I'm staying hangs from the rockface. I have a white room where I dream waking dreams. I'm speaking a different language now. My feet, which have always wanted to be in on everything, have lost all sense of direction. Some nights they even admonish me – they go to my head! 'And just where will we be going after that?'

The people who run the *pensione* are friendly and considerate. Three times a week I find a French newspaper on my breakfast tray.

I glance over the headlines in *France-Soir*.

SURVIVOR OF CREVECOEUR FOREST MISHAP RECOUNTS INCIDENT

YOUTH SHOT FIVE TIMES, LEFT FOR DEAD

Investigations by members of the *France-Soir* staff have established that Philippe V—, whose bullet-riddled body was discovered last Monday night in Crevecoeur Forest, was the victim of a jealous pimp. 'Jean-Jean', his presumed aggressor, had been trying to learn from Philippe V— the whereabouts of their mutual girl friend, France. As of yesterday evening, Jean-Jean was still at large ...

The article went on to tell in great detail how Philippe, the young executive in love, had attempted to make France quit her profession, to Jean-Jean's rage. 'The officials express the gravest concern as to the fate of Kim and France, whose trail, according to the latest reports, has been picked up.'

It's barely three months since we said goodbye, Franzie. The sky may not have been blue as it is today, but since it was hot, we had a drink together on the terrace of La Bistouille. We celebrated my going away on vacation; we watched the street flowing past us as we rolled ourselves a joint; and, if I'm not mistaken, we talked about birds. You said to me, 'I know it sounds dumb, but some days I feel like a bird whose wings have been clipped.'

People are always talking about the permanently crippled – those whom war has permanently disabled, or those permanently scarred by fire. They forget the ones who are forever drowning. The permanently drowning live in a state of frenzy – they'll grab you by the throat and try to drag you down with them. Franzie, if you ever rise to the surface again, start fighting as hard as you can. Fight the way you used to at the Saint-Louis in the black dress I gave you. Fight for all the little budding hookers sprouting up on the outskirts of the city who are dying of boredom. Fight for Malou. Fight for Lulu. Fight for Sophie.

I've passed the Cape of No Hope. I now know that I wasn't lied to, and that the earth is truly round. I now know that I've said goodbye to my childhood once and for all. I'm floating down the river that flows into madness – the one great, grey madness, with its surge and ebb, with its vanishing waves that will beat against my brow all the days of my life.

I'm strolling along Quai Malaquais. The secondhand booksellers are hiding from the wind behind the works of others. The Pont des Arts stretches out beneath the late-afternoon sun. As I cross the Pont Neuf, I play at not stepping on the cracks between the paving stones. A bus comes tearing out of Rue Dauphine: I promise myself I'll reach Quai des Orfèvres before it does.

At number 36, on the left-hand side of the courtyard, there's a metal plaque that reads: Vice Squad. This time I'm here of my own free will.

On the vast stairway that I've climbed so many times swearing at the goddamn cops, I pass three men. They smile at me, and I smile back.

'Monsieur, could you please direct me to the office of the Vice Squad?'

'Third floor, on your right, mademoiselle.'

These corridors are so creepy. Vice Squad, Vice Squad – here we are. Should I knock? I knock.

'Come in!'

The setting hasn't changed: desks piled high with official papers, old-fashioned typewriters, the smell of stale tobacco that makes you gag, the lack of light, the metal cupboards, and the cops. I know them all, almost: all except for the one who's motioning me to a seat. Funny, I never saw him here, but his face reminds me of someone. Who could it be? It's a face I know all right – two peepholes, a florid nose, and a lipless mouth. I've got it. It's the priest who used to come to La Hacienda, the bastard who used to confess us one after the other behind the red curtain. Either it's that priest dressed up as a cop, or he was a cop dressed up as a priest.

'What can I do for you?'

'I've come to have my name removed from your files ... No, Father: I want to confess.'

'On your knees, sinner! Lower your eyes, and lift up your skirts! Have you come for absolution?'

'Yes, Father. I repent. I've seen my share – in every possible size – and did I ever handle them! I handled a few, I handled a lot – fine-looking ones, peaked ones, little ones, and fat ones. Ones that were pointed, webbed, broken, and unshod. Ones that were bare, black, dirty, arched, warm, freezing, or purple. And the others, the ones they call club, athlete's, and pig's ... I've come face to face with ones of every known size and colour. I've dealt with ones from every known planet. I've advanced from footpaths to footpads, from flat feet to flat-foots by way of footholds, foothills, footlights, footnotes, and hot feet! But I'm through with all that. I've given up feet for good. You mustn't imagine, Father, that during my foot period I was a practising podiatrist. Not at all – I was merely an obedient, conscientious girl. I made my men get undressed so that they could keep cool.'

'Sinner, tell me one thing: did you love these men?'

'I tried my best. There were some I would have been glad to see drop dead as they lay on top of me. But with others I was gentle. For those who were hungry I'd snitch something from the brothel kitchen. I returned the money to some; others I robbed. For a few I felt affection: that had nothing to do with their status or station in life. They could be plumbers, chroniclers, or princes, they could be surgeons or private chauffeurs, they could be plasterers or on welfare. They could have been born on the edge of town, in the ghetto, or in Tokyo. My affection was nothing more than a response to theirs. When they tore themselves away from me, I always saw in their eyes that trapdoor look that opens on to the depths of loneliness ...'

'Sinner, tell me: what is your name?'

'Marie Madeleine.'

'Fine. Now don't move. Stay right where you are. I'll go and get your file. Marie Madeleine, Marie Madeleine ... You see, there are so many of them. Ah, here we are. I've found you. This has to be you. You've got prettier, bitch.'

'That's love, Father.'

'Silence, blasphemer! To summarize your career: you were picked up by the Vice Squad on 13 February, 1965, in a brothel located at number 59 Rue Fontaine. The Saint-Louis! Brazen hussy! Do you feel no shame at having chosen a holy place for your first iniquities?'

'I do not.'

'You are a lost soul! We next find you at La Hacienda on Rue Victor-Massé.'

'Father—'

'Silence, miscreant! Later you are to be seen at La Bohème; at a bar on Rue Frochot; and, finally, at number 45 Rue Saint-Denis – the hottest street in town. I suppose you considered that a "good" house! ...'

'It all depends for whom, Father.'

'You then disappear. When you re-emerge, you're overcome with contrition, and so you return to Pigalle forthwith. The Lautrec and the Sans Souci become your bailiwick – right?'

'Right, Father.'

'Once again you sink into sinfulness and sell yourself to all comers on the corner of Rue des Prêcheurs—'

'We must try to love one another.'

'And now that you have made your confession – you who are covered with spittle, filth, and dung – what can you possibly expect of me? Redemption?'

'No, Father. I simply want to sign my name at the bottom of this page, declare that from this day forward I shall never again indulge in prostitution, and leave this card with my photograph stapled to it in your wretched files. That's all.'

'Very well, sinner. You're not asking for all that much. Just the same, you must say a prayer before I can give you communion.'

'I've forgotten my prayers.'

'Then remember them!'

'Blessed am I among women ... My sins, which are many, are forgiven; for I loved much.'

'That's fine, Marie Madeleine. Now stick out your tongue. Farther – I want to set the wafer right on it. Come on, farther than that – in remembrance of things past! There! Now don't move, just wait. Keep your eyes closed. I have to get my shears in position. There, that's it: snippety snip snip snip! You see, your tongue was too long for your own good. And now, young woman, you can leave. Public morality is safe: I've tucked your tongue away between the pages of my prayer book.'

Now I mustn't go kicking and wheeling down the stairs like a young filly. I must act dignified and keep a solemn, obstinate look on my face. And as I pass beneath the archway, I must nod respectfully to the representatives of law and order. It's the only proper way to behave. And then I'll blow a kiss to Ile de la Cité and discreetly spit on the icy shadow of the cellblock. I must at all costs remain respectable until I round the first corner – and then I'll take off! Anything goes, I'll tear off my threads as I run, and I'll leap naked from the top of the Pont Neuf into the gardens of the Vert-Galant. Let's hope I land in a budding grove!

And what if I crossed over instead of keeping to the shadows? I cross Quai des Orfèvres, to the sunny side of the street.

Robin Maugham
Conversations with Willie £1.25

Through the last years of his life, Somerset Maugham lived in the
south of France. Bestselling author, renowned playwright, close
friend of Churchill and Coward, he was wealthy, famous,
embittered, gloomy, malevolent. Through the sunset decades at
the Villa Mauresque, Maugham's nephew Robin recorded the
charm, charisma and sardonic wit of 'the most famous author
alive . . . and probably the saddest'.

Maurice Chatelain
Our Ancestors came from
Outer Space £1.25

Did human civilization begin with an extraterrestrial visit 65,000
years ago ? Fantastic, maybe, but Maurice Chatelain, a designer
who worked on the Apollo project at NASA, produces a wealth of
scientific evidence to support his astounding theory : that all
mankind's knowledge was bequeathed suddenly by space
visitors ; that the travellers possessed dazzling knowledge of
mathematics, astronomy . . . even nuclear physics ; that these
ancient astronauts may be the secret behind Atlantis, and may be
watching us still . . .